Barbara Werbn

National
Geographic
Society

Field Guide to
the Birds of
North America

Second
Edition

5 EDINBURGH DR
PBG FL 33418
627 - 8960

National
Geographic
Society

Second
Edition

Field Guide to the

Birds
of North America

Published by
The National
Geographic Society

Gilbert M. Grosvenor
President and
Chairman of the Board

Michela A. English
Senior
Vice President

William R. Gray
Vice President
and Director,
Book Division

Prepared by
National Geographic
Book Service

Charles O. Hyman
Director

Ross S. Bennett
Associate Director

Consultants
for this book

Jon L. Dunn
Eirik A. T. Blom
Chief Consultants

Dr. George E. Watson
General Consultant

Dr. John P. O'Neill
Consultant on Songbirds

Staff for this book

Shirley L. Scott
Editor

Lise M. Swinson
Associate Editor

Mary B. Dickinson
Catherine Herbert Howell
Assistant Editors

David M. Seager
Art Director

Thomas B. Allen
Wayne Barrett
Seymour L. Fishbein
Philip Kopper
Edward Lanouette
David F. Robinson
Robert D. Selim
Jonathan B. Tourtellot
Writers

Paul A. Dunn
Martha B. Hays
Feroline B. Higginson
Diane S. Marton
Maura J. Pollin
Penelope A. Timbers
L. Madison Washburn
Jayne Wise
Researchers

Charlotte J. Golin
Design Assistant

Georgina L. McCormack
Teresita Cóquia Sison
Editorial Assistants

Karen F. Edwards
Traffic Manager

Richard S. Wain
Production Manager

Leslie A. Adams
Andrea Crosman
Production

John T. Dunn
Quality Control Director

David V. Evans
Engraving and Printing

John D. Garst, Jr.
Virginia L. Baza
Peter J. Balch
Joseph F. Ochlak
Publications Art

Teresa S. Purvis
Index

Contributions by
Caroline Hottenstein
Robert M. Poole
Deborah Robertson
Margaret Sedeen

First Edition (1983) 295,000 copies
Second printing (1985) 30,000 copies
Second Edition (1987) 50,000 copies
Second printing (1988) 75,000 copies
Third printing (1989) 50,000 copies
Fourth printing (1991) 50,000 copies
Fifth printing (1992) 100,000 copies
Sixth printing (1994) 100,000 copies

Library of Congress
CIP data page 463

Contents

Introduction

More than 800 species of birds breed in North America, or visit the continent regularly, or drop in occasionally. This is a daunting number for a beginning birdwatcher who is merely trying to identify a newcomer at the feeder. But no one has seen all these birds. Many species are found only in certain regions or specialized habitats, and some are extremely rare in North America.

Birdwatching—nowadays more frequently called birding—is enjoyed by millions of people. The challenge lies not only in finding birds but also in accurately identifying each bird seen, and this requires both preparation and experience.

Some birders want only to become better acquainted with the neighborhood birds. Others try to see as many species as possible. For every level of interest, the first place to use a field guide is at home. Leaf through it often to become familiar with the wonderful variety of birds that inhabit or visit our continent.

Species

Completely updated in a second edition, this guide includes all species known to breed in North America—defined for this book as the land extending northward from the northern border of Mexico, plus adjacent islands and seas within about two hundred miles of the coast. Also included are species that breed in Mexico or Central America or on other continents but are seen in North America when they spend the winter here or pass through on regular migration routes.

And we include species that are seen in North America only when they wander off course or are blown in by storms. Our standard requires that they have been seen at least three times in the past five years or five times in this century. A few species that do not yet meet this standard are nevertheless included because of a strong likelihood that they will be seen again, especially if knowledgeable watchers are looking for them.

We have also included *exotic* species, birds from other continents that have been introduced into North America as game-, park-, or cage birds and are now seen in the wild. A number of these species have established breeding populations here; a few, such as the European Starling, are abundant in the wild.

The sequence in this guide follows generally that of the American Ornithologists' Union (A.O.U.) Checklist (6th Edition, 1983 and Supplement of July 1985), which places species in the sequence of their presumed natural relationships. We departed from the A.O.U. sequence where it seemed more useful for field reference to group together the species that share similar life-styles or look somewhat alike.

The A.O.U. Check-list is the standard for species classification and scientific and common names. Many names have been changed in recent A.O.U. decisions. Some birds once classified as separate species are now regarded as different forms of a single species. (In this book, "form" is synonymous with "subspecies.") Some former subspecies are now designated as separate species. Such changes are incorporated in this field guide and cross-referenced under the old names. The entry for the Slate-colored Junco, for example, refers you to its new name, Dark-eyed Junco.

Families

Ornithologists organize the species into family groups that share certain structural characteristics. Some families have more than a hundred members; others have only one. Family resemblance is often helpful in identifying birds in the field. Members of the family Picidae (page 264), for example, are quickly recognizable as woodpeckers, narrowing the identification problem down from 800 possibilities to 22.

Read the brief family descriptions provided at the beginning of each group in this field guide for information applicable to all members of the family. You will also find within some family sections a description of distinctive smaller groups such as the sapsuckers (page 268), four species that share some unique traits.

Scientific Names

Each kind of bird, or species, has a two-part Latin scientific name. The first part, always capitalized, indicates the genus, a group of closely related species. Nine members of the family Picidae are placed in the genus *Picoides*. The second part of the name, not capitalized, indicates the species. *Picoides pubescens* is the name of one specific kind of woodpecker (commonly known as the Downy Woodpecker). *Picoides tridactylus* (or *P. tridactylus*) is the Three-toed Woodpecker. No two species share the same two-part scientific name.

Species are sometimes further divided into subspecies, when populations in different geographical regions show recognizable differences. Each subspecies bears a third Latin name. *Picoides tridactylus bacatus* (*P.t. bacatus*) identifies the dark-backed form of the Three-toed Woodpecker that inhabits eastern North America. *P.t. dorsalis* is the paler backed form found in the Rockies. Latin names are used in this book for the subspecies that cannot easily be described by color or range. We have endeavored to illustrate or describe the extremes of variations that look confusingly different from other forms of the same species.

Plumages

How much easier identification would be if every bird of each species always looked the same! But it is not enough for us to know what a bird's plumage—its overall feathering—looks like in only one season or sex or at one age. Most species undergo a complete molt in late summer or early fall, replacing all their feathers. This plumage is usually held through the fall and winter. Often the molt occurs before the birds migrate, and thus we see the birds in this plumage even if they spend the winter outside North America. In late winter or early spring, the birds undergo a partial molt to the plumage we see in spring and summer. Fall and winter plumage may vary considerably from spring and summer plumage, and a bird in the process of molting can confound even expert birders.

In many species the male and female look quite different, and the young birds are unlike either parent. And we must also keep in mind that some species of the same genus occasionally breed with other species, producing *hybrid* offspring that look partly like one parent, partly like the other. Subspecies also interbreed, producing *intergrade* populations.

Some species have two or more *color phases,* occurring regionally or within the same population. Female Spruce Grouse, for example, can be reddish or gray.

Where adult males and females are similar, we show only one. When male (♂) and female (♀) look different, we usually show both. If spring and fall, or breeding and nonbreeding, plumages differ only slightly, or if only one of these plumages is usually seen in North America, we show only one figure. Juvenile and immature birds are illustrated when they hold a different-looking plumage after they are old enough to be seen away from their more easily recognizable parents.

Plumage Sequence

Some nestlings wear fluffy *down*. The first coat of true feathers, acquired before the bird leaves the nest, is called the *juvenile* plumage. In many species, juvenile plumage is replaced in late summer or early fall by a *first-fall* or *first-winter* plumage that more closely resembles the adult. First-fall and any subsequent plumages that do not resemble the adult are termed *immature* plumages and may continue in a series that includes *first-spring* (when the bird is almost a year old), *first-summer,* and so on, until *adult* plumage is attained. When birds, such as the Bald Eagle, take more than one and a half years to reach adult plumage, we have labeled the interim plumages as *subadult* or with the specific year or season shown.

Some species wear colorful plumage in the breeding season and molt to duller colors for fall and winter. In some songbirds, the bright plumage of spring appears with the gradual wearing away of dull tips on the feathers of their winter plumage, with very little actual molting involved. By late summer, feathers become worn and faded; fresh fall plumage can be brighter than the colors of August.

In some species, breeding plumage looks much like winter plumage. Some changes are evident only during the brief period of courtship. In herons, for example, the colors of bill, lores, legs, and feet may change or deepen. When these colors are at their height, the birds are said to be in *high* breeding plumage.

Most ducks, after mating, molt into an *eclipse* plumage in which males acquire a female-like plumage and females show little change, although some are paler and duller. Eclipse plumage is generally held only for a few weeks, when another molt begins. All the flight feathers are lost simultaneously during eclipse; the ducks are unable to fly until new feathers grow in.

Field Marks

More often than not, there are good clues to a bird's identity in every plumage. These *field marks* are what birders must look for—marks such as the extent of streaking on a bird's sides, the color of its head in contrast to its back, and the shape of the bill. A field mark can be as obvious as the Killdeer's double breast bands (page 107) or as subtle as the difference in head shape between Greater and Lesser Scaups (page 81). Some field marks are plainly visible only in good light or from a certain angle or when the bird is in flight. Not every bird seen can be identified, even by experts.

It is important to become familiar with the terms commonly used in describing the parts of a bird. You will find these terms illustrated on pages 10-11.

The most distinctive field marks for each species in each plumage are usually listed first in our text descriptions, for quick reference. But few birds will hold still long enough for you to study your field guide. Instead you must study the bird, noting its overall size, shape, and colors and such details as eye ring, bill shape, and wing bars. After the bird has flown you can turn to your field guide or jot down notes for later review.

Parts of a Bird

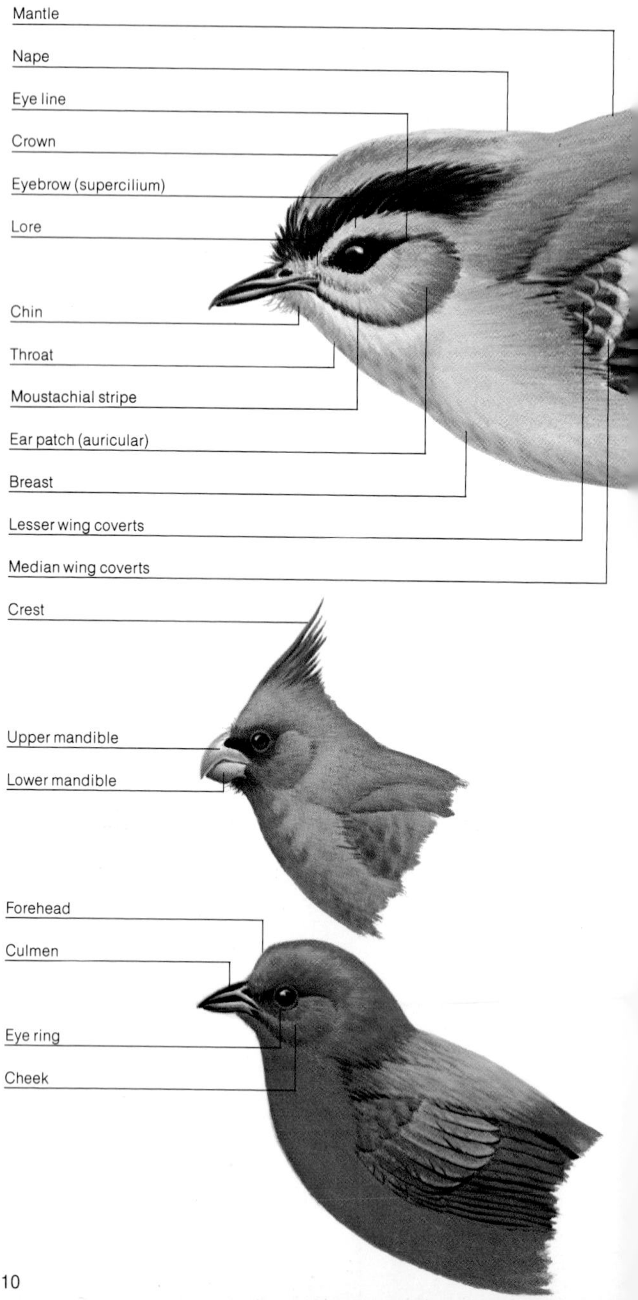

Mantle

Nape

Eye line

Crown

Eyebrow (supercilium)

Lore

Chin

Throat

Moustachial stripe

Ear patch (auricular)

Breast

Lesser wing coverts

Median wing coverts

Crest

Upper mandible

Lower mandible

Forehead

Culmen

Eye ring

Cheek

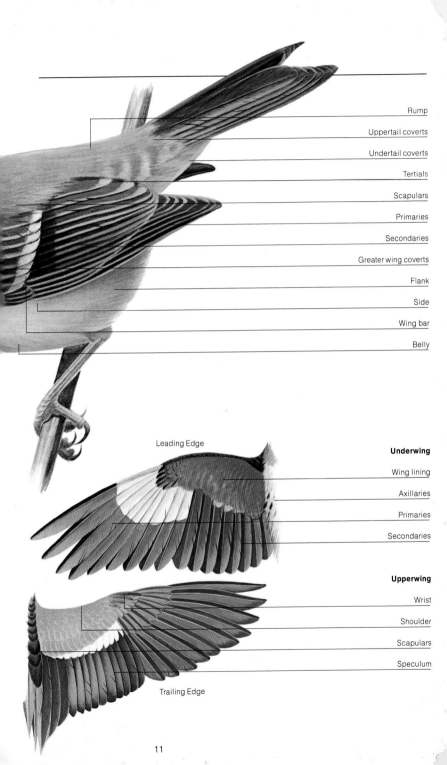

Rump

Uppertail coverts

Undertail coverts

Tertials

Scapulars

Primaries

Secondaries

Greater wing coverts

Flank

Side

Wing bar

Belly

Leading Edge

Underwing

Wing lining

Axillaries

Primaries

Secondaries

Upperwing

Wrist

Shoulder

Scapulars

Speculum

Trailing Edge

Successful birding requires that you recall and recognize quickly what field marks identify which species, and this ability comes with experience. Study more closely the familiar birds that you can identify without difficulty. What is distinctive about them? Get help from more experienced birders by joining the outings sponsored by local clubs and nature centers.

Measurements

If you are searching for a kinglet, it helps to know that the bird is only about four inches long. Relative size is also important. In mixed flocks, Greater and Lesser Yellowlegs are readily distinguished from each other by size alone.

The figures in this book, compiled from standard sources, represent measurements of museum study skins. The difficulty of accurately measuring a living and lively bird justifies the use of skin measurements at least as a general guide. Average length (L) from tip of bill to tip of tail is given for each species. If males and females differ markedly in size, average length for each sex is given. Where size varies greatly within a species (chiefly among the raptors), a range of smallest to largest is provided. And for large birds that you will most often see in flight, we indicate the average wingspan (W), measured from wing tip to wing tip.

Voice

A bird's songs and calls not only reveal its presence but also, in many cases, its identity. Some species—particularly nocturnal or secretive birds such as owls, nightjars, and rails—are more often heard than seen. A few species, such as some of the flycatchers, are most reliably identified by voice even when they are seen well.

Songs are sung primarily to attract a mate and claim a territory and thus are usually heard only in breeding season. Year-round we can hear the brief, simple calls used to maintain contact and express alarm, but calls are often more difficult to recognize than songs.

Distinctive songs and calls are described in our text. Transcription into words, such as *cheerily cheer-up cheerio* for the American Robin's song, helps to express tone and pattern. You may find it best to transcribe sounds into your own words as you hear them; one birder's *chip* is another's *tsip* or *chik* or even *peek*.

Behavior

Behavioral traits also provide clues. Is the bird's flight direct or undulating? Does it beat its wings rapidly or slowly? Does it forage on the ground or in the treetops? Is the bird shy or bold? Some species of warblers walk rather than hop. Turkey Vultures often soar with their wings held slightly raised; Black Vultures soar on level wings. Black-and-white Warblers climb up and down and around tree trunks; the similar Blackpoll Warbler does not. Such distinctive behavior is not only useful for identification but fascinating to watch.

Abundance and Habitat

Abundance must be considered in relation to habitat. A species that is *common* in one part of its range is sure to be only *fairly common* or even *uncommon* in other parts of that range. The House Sparrow is plainly *abundant* on city sidewalks and suburban lawns but *rare* in forests and deserts. The Cooper's Hawk is uncommon throughout its widespread range.

Seasons of the year, of course, also affect numbers. The Semipalmated Sandpiper is abundant on its northern breeding grounds; during migration it is common inland and on the east coast but rare in the west; in winter it is found in North America only in south Florida.

All of these terms refer to sightings of birds that occur every year. Birders call *casual* the species that turn up irregularly in small numbers in areas outside their normal range. Casual occurrences are not unexpected but neither are they annual. A *vagrant* has strayed off its usual migration route. A *visitor* is making a stopover during migration or has wandered out of its usual range. Vagrants and visitors are both unexpected.

Accidental refers to species that have been seen only a few times in an area that is far out of their normal range. They may never be seen there again. Almost any species can show up unexpectedly almost anywhere, but birders must be doubly cautious in the identification of such surprises.

Habitat information included in the text will help you find a particular species within its range. Some species are highly *local*, found only in a very specialized habitat. Bank Swallows, for example, are common in summer, but only near the steep sandy or gravelly banks they require for nesting.

Range Maps

Maps are provided for all species except those with very limited ranges, which instead are described in the text, and those species that do not ordinarily breed or winter in North America. Range boundaries are drawn where the species ceases to be regularly seen. Almost every species is rare at the edges of its range. The sample map on page 15 explains the colors and symbols used.

Range information is based on actual sightings and therefore depends upon the number of knowledgeable and active birders in each area. There is much to learn about bird distribution in every part of North America. One of the pleasures of birding is the discovery of expanding ranges. Breeding-bird surveys and atlas projects undertaken by federal and state governments and by birding clubs make a vital contribution to the general fund of information about each species.

Our maps were compiled by Eirik A. T. Blom especially for this guide and reflect his interpretation of the best information currently available. Data were obtained from published sources and from consultation with birders and ornithologists across the continent. Extensive help was provided in particular by Danny Bystrak, Jon L. Dunn, Kim Eckert, Kenn Kaufman, Hugh E. Kingery, Paul Lehman, Dr. John P. O'Neill, Dennis Paulson, Dr. J. V. Remsen, Robert F. Ringler, Chandler S. Robbins, Dr. William B. Robertson, Dr. John Trochet, Peter Vickery, and Dr. George E. Watson.

Remember that our maps are general guides for the entire continent. Specific, up-to-the-minute information for a particular area should be obtained from local checklists, books, and birders.

Birds are not, of course, bound by maps. Ranges continually expand and contract, making any map a tool rather than a rule. The Northern Cardinal, for instance, is steadily expanding its range in the northeast.

Irruptive species, such as the Snowy Owl, move southward in some years in large or small numbers and for great or small distances. These irregular movements are generally but not specifically predictable; certainly they cannot be precisely mapped.

In some species, birds leave the nesting grounds in late summer and move northward. These *postbreeding wanderers,* principally young birds, will migrate southward with the winter.

Range maps of *pelagic* species, birds that spend most of their time over the open sea, are of course somewhat conjectural, because seabird observers are few.

Birding

Time spent at home with your field guide will be repaid when you go out into meadows and woodlands, deserts and mountains, looking for birds. But much is also learned only from experience. When you have seen the Northern Harrier many times, for instance, its distinctive flight pattern signals its identity for you long before you can see its facial disk or white rump.

Experienced birders know how to move quietly and to stand patiently still. They know that a sudden riot of scolding songbirds may mean that an owl is roosting

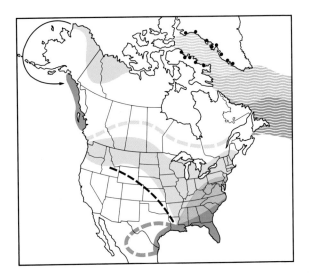

Range Map Symbols

 Breeding range, generally in spring and summer.

 Summer seabird range. *(Includes winter range of Southern Hemisphere species)*

 Year-round range.

 Year-round seabird range.

Winter range. *(If no winter or year-round range is shown, winters outside North America)*

 Winter seabird range.

 Extent of post-breeding dispersal in summer.

 Species migrates chiefly east of this line.

Extent of irregular or irruptive range in some winters.

 Direction of migration route.

 Breeding colonies.

nearby; that a flock of familiar Ring-billed Gulls should be studied closely to determine whether one or two other gull species might also be present.

The rule of quietness has an exception: If you make squeaking or "pishing" noises or imitate an owl's call, an inquisitive bird may come to investigate.

A rule that has no exceptions: Take care not to disturb either the birds or their habitats. Take particular care not to frighten parent birds away from nests.

The bird life of our continent has, on the whole, declined with the advance of human population and technology. Many local and national organizations, such as the National Audubon Society and The Nature Conservancy, work tirelessly toward the preservation of habitat and the protection of individual species. These and other such organizations welcome your support and active participation.

Binoculars

Expert birders sometimes leave their field guides at home. But no birder would leave behind the binoculars, essential equipment even for backyard birding.

Try several kinds before deciding what to buy. The best choice for beginning birders, and relatively inexpensive, is 7 x 35 binoculars with coated lenses and central focusing. The "7" indicates the power of magnification; a bird will appear seven times closer. The "35" is the lens size in millimeters. A ratio of 1 to 5 between magnification power and lens size is generally considered ideal for light-gathering capability; that is, the lens is large enough in relation to the magnification power to admit sufficient light for distinguishing colors in poor light conditions.

Central focusing is a convenient feature when speed is important. Coated lenses reduce glare and the halo effect common in uncoated lenses. Be sure to protect the coating with a special cleaning kit.

Using binoculars efficiently takes practice. Try them first on a stationary object to learn to locate and focus on it quickly. Then practice with any moving object—car, airplane, a bird in your backyard. You will soon form the important habit of keeping your eyes on the bird while raising the binoculars.

Telescopes

If you spend much time watching shorebirds or waterfowl, a telescope is particularly useful. Scopes are made in a variety of styles. You will need to decide whether you want one with a fixed eyepiece or a zoom lens and, if it is important to you, whether the scope is adaptable for photography. You will need a tripod; be sure that it has a center brace and that it can be raised high enough for you to use the scope comfortably. In places where a tripod isn't practical, or when you want to follow a moving bird, a shoulder mount (often called a gunstock mount) will help steady the scope.

You may also find useful a mount that clamps onto a car windowsill. Cars, where permitted, make fine bird-watching blinds; birds will often allow a car to approach them more closely than people on foot. You can sit comfortably in your car, put the scope on the window mount, and get excellent views.

Checklists

Most birders make lists of the birds they see. Some keep several lists, ranging from birds seen in a certain area to all birds ever seen—a *life list*. In addition to being a source of pride, such lists are a source of great pleasure, enabling you to look back and remember the first time you saw a bluebird or an eagle.

The index in this guide includes a check-off box beside the common-name entry for each species; you can use this for your life list. Better still, keep a notebook in which to record not only the name of the bird you see but also the date and place and notes about field marks, behavior, voice. Such information, reviewed over the years, will help you remember when and where to expect each species and how to identify it.

The Illustrations

Sixteen artists participated in the arduous task of painting the 220 plates in this guide. We are grateful for their meticulous and patient work. You will find a list of these artists on page 464.

It would have been impossible to produce this field guide without the use of extensive collections of study skins available in major museums. Such collections are the only way to confirm details of plumage variation and subtle field marks.

The following museums generously lent study skins from their collections: the National Museum of Natural History, Smithsonian Institution, Washington, D. C.; the Museum of Natural Science, Louisiana State University, Baton Rouge; the Museum of Vertebrate Zoology, University of California at Berkeley; the Denver Museum of Natural History, Colorado; the Museum of Natural History, Santa Barbara, California; and the Natural History Museum, San Diego, California.

We were also assisted by photographs provided by our consultants and by Stephen Bailey, Jen and Des Bartlett, Robert F. Ringler, Richard A. Rowlett, Lawrence Sansone III, Claudia P. Wilds, and others.

Loons (Family Gaviidae)

All five members of this family occur in North America. In all species, juvenile plumage is held through the first summer; they resemble winter adults but have more white on their upperparts.

Common Loon *Gavia immer* L 32″ (81 cm)
Large, thick-billed loon. Bill is black in breeding season. In winter plumage, bill is grayer; crown and nape darker than back; dark nape borders white throat in an irregular line, but note the white indentation at mid-neck. Many adults have a pale area encircling the eye. Forehead is steep, crown peaked at front; culmen is rounded, making bill look straight. Holds head level. In flight, large head and feet help distinguish Common from Arctic, Pacific, and Red-throated Loons. A few Commons are almost as small as Arctics and Pacifics. Fairly common; nests on large lakes. Migrates overland as well as coastally. Winters mainly on coastal waters, rarely inland. Loud yodeling calls are heard chiefly on breeding grounds.

Yellow-billed Loon *Gavia adamsii* L 34″ (86 cm)
Breeding adult has straw yellow bill; culmen is straight, giving bill a very slightly uptilted look. Bill is duskier or paler in winter and immature plumages but still shows yellowish tinge; note also pale face and distinct dark mark behind eye. Bill is usually longer than in Common Loon; back is browner; crown is peaked at front and rear, giving a subtle double-bump effect. Tends to hold head slightly uptilted. Breeds on tundra lakes and rivers. Replaces Common Loon in the high Arctic. Calls are similar to Common. Migrates coastally; very rare inland; rare south of Canada.

Pacific Loon *Gavia pacifica* L 26″ (66 cm)
In all plumages, may be indistinguishable from Arctic Loon; the two were formerly considered to be one species. Bill slim and straight; head smoothly rounded and held level. Breeding adult's head and nape are pale gray; throat's iridescent purple patch can appear black or even green. Winter bird's crown and nape are paler than back, unlike Common Loon; black cap extends to eye; neck is three-toned: front white, rear gray, bordered by a darker line. Most winter birds have a thin "chin strap" of brown spots. In flight, resembles Common Loon but head and feet are smaller. A coastal migrant; casual inland throughout the west. Very rare on east coast, but sightings there may be of Arctic Loons.

Arctic Loon *Gavia arctica* L 28″ (73 cm)
(Not shown.) Old World species, often indistinguishable from Pacific Loon. Siberian form, *G.a. viridugularis,* which breeds in western Alaska, has a dark green throat patch in breeding plumage. European form, *arctica,* probably accidental on our east coast, has a purple throat, like Pacific Loon.

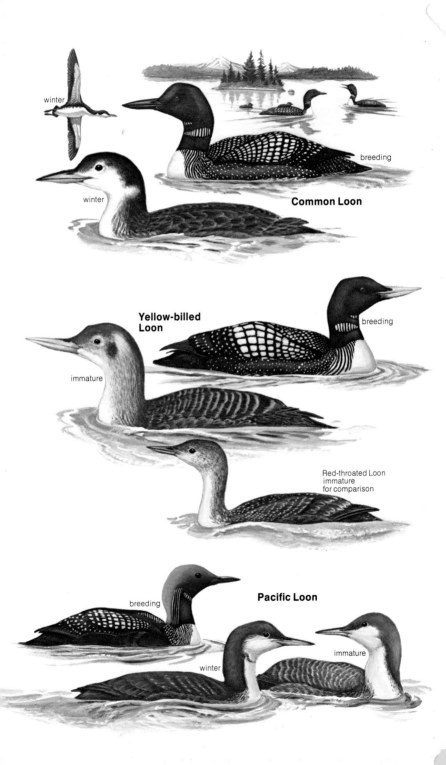

winter

winter

Common Loon

breeding

Yellow-billed Loon

breeding

immature

Red-throated Loon
immature
for comparison

breeding

Pacific Loon

winter

immature

Red-throated Loon *Gavia stellata* L 25" (64 cm)

Thin bill, slightly upturned; head smooth and rounded; tends to hold head tilted slightly up. In breeding plumage, has gray face and sides of neck; dark red patch on foreneck; brownish-black back. Winter bird has extensive, sharply defined white on face and extensive white spotting on back. Immature's face is gray-flecked but head is still paler than back and paler than in other winter loons (preceding page). In flight, shows smaller head and feet than does Common Loon; wingbeat is quicker. Migrates coastally; also overland in the east. Casual in the interior during winter.

Grebes (Family Podicipedidae)

A worldwide family; seven species occur in North America. Lobed toes make them strong swimmers. Grebes are rarely seen on land or in flight.

Clark's Grebe *Aechmophorus clarkii* L 25" (64 cm)

Resembles Western Grebe but bill is yellow-orange; black cap does not usually extend to eye; back and flanks are paler. In flight, Clark's white wing stripe is more extensive than in Western. Call is a single loud *kreek* note. Limits of range in both species are poorly known; Clark's occupies same general area and habitat as Western Grebe but much less common in northern and eastern part of range. Formerly considered one species with Western.

Western Grebe *Aechmophorus occidentalis* L 25" (64 cm)

Large grebe, strikingly black-and-white, with a swanlike neck and long, thin bill. Resembles Clark's Grebe but bill is yellow-green; black cap extends to include eyes; back and flanks are darker. In flight, Western's white wing stripe is less extensive than in Clark's. Call is a loud two-note *kreek-kreek*. Gregarious; nests in reeds along broad freshwater lakes. Winters on seacoasts and sheltered bays and large inland bodies of water. Occupies same general range and habitat as Clark's but predominates in northern and eastern part of range. Rare during migration and winter to the east coast. Formerly considered one species with Clark's Grebe; hybrids are occasionally seen.

Red-necked Grebe *Podiceps grisegena* L 20" (51 cm)

Large grebe with heavy, tapered, yellowish bill almost as long as the head. Breeding adult's whitish throat and cheeks contrast with reddish foreneck. In winter plumage, throat is dusky, white of chin extends onto rear of face in a crescent. First-winter bird has rounder head, paler eye; lacks strong facial crescent. Juvenile has striped head. In flight, Red-necked Grebe shows a white leading and trailing edge on inner wing; thick neck is often held slouched down. Generally solitary. Breeds on shallow lakes; winters mostly along coasts. Casual in winter along Gulf coast and inland.

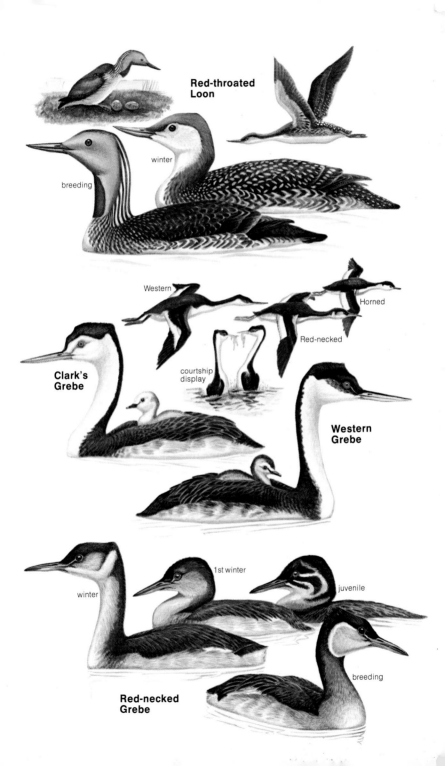

Red-throated Loon

breeding

winter

Western

Horned

Red-necked

courtship display

Clark's Grebe

Western Grebe

winter

1st winter

juvenile

breeding

Red-necked Grebe

Horned Grebe *Podiceps auritus* L 13¹/₂" *(34 cm)*

Breeding adult has chestnut foreneck, golden "horns." In winter plumage, white cheeks and throat contrast sharply with dark crown and nape; a few birds show some duskiness on the lower foreneck. Black on nape narrows to a thin stripe. All birds show a pale spot in front of eye. In flight (preceding page), white secondaries show as patch on trailing edge of wing; note also the inconspicuous white patch at shoulder. Bill is short and straight, thicker than Eared Grebe's. Crown is flat-. ter than in Eared Grebe. Smaller size and shorter, dark bill most readily separate winter Horned from Red-necked Grebe. Breeds on sheltered freshwater lakes and ponds. Winters mostly on salt water; a few winter inland.

Eared Grebe *Podiceps nigricollis* L 12¹/₂" *(32 cm)*

Breeding adult has blackish neck, golden "ears" fanning out behind eye. In winter plumage, throat is variably dusky; cheek dark; whitish on chin extends up as a crescent behind eye; compare with Horned Grebe. Note also the Eared Grebe's longer, thinner bill, usually with lower mandible angled upward; thinner neck; more peaked crown. Lacks pale spot in front of eye. Generally rides higher in the water than Horned Grebe, exposing fluffy white undertail coverts. In flight, white secondaries show as white patch on trailing edge of wing. Usually nests in large colonies on freshwater lakes. Winters inland and along coast. Rare but regular in Gulf coast states; casual along the Atlantic coast south of New York.

Pied-billed Grebe *Podilymbus podiceps* L 13¹/₂" *(34 cm)*

Breeding adult is brown overall, with black ring around stout, whitish bill; black chin and throat; pale belly. Winter birds lose bill ring; chin is white, throat tinged with pale rufous. Juveniles resemble winter adult but throat is much redder, eye ring absent, head and neck streaked with brown and white. First-winter birds lack streaking; throat is duller. A short-necked, big-headed, stocky grebe. In flight, shows almost no white on wing. Nests around marshy ponds and sloughs; sometimes hides from intruders by sinking until only its head shows. Common but not gregarious. Winters on fresh or salt water.

Least Grebe *Tachybaptus dominicus* L 9³/₄" *(25 cm)*

A small, short-necked grebe with golden yellow eyes, a slim, dark bill, and purplish-gray face and foreneck. Breeding adult has blackish crown, hindneck, throat, and back. Winter birds have white throat, paler bill, less black on crown. In flight, shows large white wing patch. Uncommon and local; sometimes stays hidden in thick vegetation near shores of ponds, sloughs, ditches. May nest at any time of year on any quiet inland water. Casual straggler to extreme southern Arizona and upper Texas coast.

Horned Grebe

breeding

winter

Eared Grebe

winter

breeding

Pied-billed Grebe

breeding

winter

Least Grebe

breeding

winter

Albatrosses (Family Diomedeidae)

Gliding on extremely long and narrow wings, these largest of seabirds spend most of their lives at sea, alighting on the water when becalmed or to feed on squid, fish, and refuse. Rarely do they come close enough to be seen from the shore. Most species nest in large colonies on remote oceanic islands.

Short-tailed Albatross *Diomedea albatrus*
L 36" (91 cm) W 83" (211 cm)   Formerly common, now extremely rare off the west coast. Large size, massive pink bill, and pale feet distinctive in all plumages. Adult is mostly white, with golden wash on head. First-year bird is dark brown; gradual molt to adult plumage produces a patchy coloration easily confused with some older Black-footed Albatrosses or with Black-foot-Laysan hybrids (not shown). Short-tailed subadult always has some white above. The entire world population of Short-taileds numbers only about 250 but is increasing. Breeds only on the Japanese island of Torishima.

Black-footed Albatross *Diomedea nigripes*
L 32" (81 cm) W 71" (180 cm)   Mostly dark in all plumages. White area around bill and on undertail coverts is more extensive on old birds, absent or barely visible on immatures. A few older birds have pale bellies. Smaller dark bill and lack of white on mantle distinguishes them from subadult Short-tailed Albatross. Seen year-round off west coast; common in summer. Often follows ships, feeding on garbage.

Laysan Albatross *Diomedea immutabilis*
L 32" (81 cm) W 82" (208 cm)   Back and upper wings dark except for white flash in primaries. Underwing is white, with irregular black margins. Rare but regular off the west coast; casual inland in spring in southeastern California; more numerous off Alaska. Blackfoot-Laysan hybrid (not shown) resembles the larger subadult Short-tailed Albatross but lacks white on back; bill is smaller.

Yellow-nosed Albatross *Diomedea chlororhynchos*
L 32" (81 cm) W 80" (203 cm)   Accidental off the Atlantic and Gulf coasts. Often confused with the Black-browed Albatross, but Yellow-nosed is slimmer and longer necked; bill is dark; predominantly white underwing has a narrow dark border. Yellow ridge on top of adult's bill is visible only at close range.

Black-browed Albatross *Diomedea melanophris*
L 35" (89 cm) W 88" (224 cm)   Accidental off New England and the Maritimes in summer. May be confused with Yellow-nosed Albatross. Black-browed is chunkier; adult's bill is pale and underwing has a much broader dark margin on leading edge. Immature has dark bill and dusky collar; underwing is almost entirely dark.

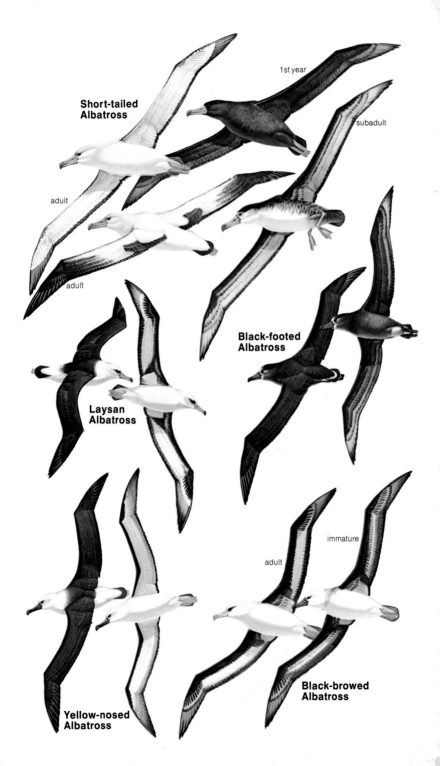

Short-tailed Albatross

1st year

subadult

adult

adult

Black-footed Albatross

Laysan Albatross

Yellow-nosed Albatross

adult

immature

Black-browed Albatross

Shearwaters, Petrels (Family Procellariidae)

These gull-size seabirds have longer wings than gulls; bills are topped with large nostril tubes. Rapid wingbeats alternating with stiff-winged glides present a distinctive flight pattern as these birds skim the waves in search of food. Highly pelagic; most species are rarely seen from shore.

Northern Fulmar *Fulmarus glacialis*
L 19" (48 cm) W 42" (107 cm) In most phases, color is nearly uniform, without strong contrast between upperparts and underparts. Light phases predominate in the Atlantic, dark phases in the Pacific. Intermediates of all shades are also seen; all appear uniform in color. Distinguished from gulls by nostril tube and stiff-winged glides; from shearwaters by thick, yellow bill and stockier head and neck. Common and increasing, Northern Fulmars gather in large flocks near fishing boats. Abundant in the Bering Strait in summer. In the Atlantic, winter north to limits of open water.

Flesh-footed Shearwater *Puffinus carneipes*
L 19¹/₂" (50 cm) W 43" (109 cm) Entirely dark above and below except for paler flight feathers, pale base of bill, pale legs. Compare especially with Sooty Shearwater, which has whitish wing linings, all-dark bill, and usually darker legs. Breeds on islands off Australia and New Zealand. Winters (our summer) in North Pacific; rare but regular off west coast. Formerly called Pale-footed Shearwater.

Sooty Shearwater *Puffinus griseus*
L 19" (48 cm) W 43" (109 cm) Whitish underwing coverts contrast with overall dark plumage; bill entirely dark. Otherwise resembles Flesh-footed Shearwater, but has a faster wingbeat, shorter glides. Almost identical to the smaller Short-tailed Shearwater. Fairly common off east coast. Abundant off west coast; often seen from shore. Dark shearwaters seen off Oregon and California in summer are invariably Sooties rather than Short-taileds.

Short-tailed Shearwater *Puffinus tenuirostris*
L 14" (36 cm) W 38" (97 cm) Usually dark overall, but often has pale wing linings; bill entirely dark. Almost identical to Sooty Shearwater. Note Short-tailed's smaller size, shorter bill, steeper forehead, and, usually, the more uniform color of wing linings and flight feathers. Birds with pale underwings also show pale throat contrasting with darker cheeks. Breeds off Australia. Winters (our summer) in North Pacific. Seen along west coast from British Columbia to California during southward migration in fall and winter. Some nonbreeding birds remain off California during our winter. Formerly called Slender-billed Shearwater.

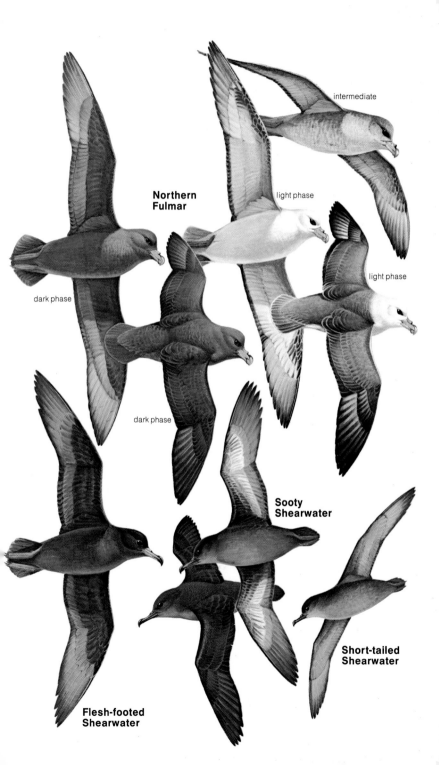

intermediate

**Northern
Fulmar**

light phase

dark phase

light phase

dark phase

**Sooty
Shearwater**

**Short-tailed
Shearwater**

**Flesh-footed
Shearwater**

Cory's Shearwater *Calonectris diomedea*

L 18" (46 cm) W 46" (117 cm) Grayish-brown upperparts merge into white underparts without sharp contrast; bill is yellowish. Similar Greater Shearwater has dark cap, dark bill. Flight of Cory's Shearwater is more leisurely and buoyant than that of other shearwaters, with slower, less frequent wingbeats. Breeds in eastern Atlantic and in the Mediterranean. Seen off east coast primarily in summer and fall. Generally uncommon in the Gulf of Mexico.

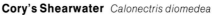

Greater Shearwater *Puffinus gravis*

L 19" (48 cm) W 44" (112 cm) Dark brown cap contrasts with grayish-brown upperparts and white cheeks. Rump usually shows a narrow, white, U-shaped band. Bill is dark; underparts white with indistinct dusky patch on belly. Compare especially with Cory's Shearwater. Some Greater Shearwaters have a white nape, may be confused with Black-capped Petrel, but lack white forehead and wide black bar on underwing (see also page 33). Breeds in South Atlantic. Fairly common off east coast during migration, chiefly in spring.

Manx Shearwater *Puffinus puffinus*

L 13¹/₂" (34 cm) W 33" (84 cm) Blackish above, white below, with gleaming white wing linings. White undertail coverts extend to end of short tail. Breeds on islands from Azores to Iceland; one colony nests in Newfoundland. Winters off eastern South America. Fairly common off northern Atlantic coast from June to October; less common farther south. Rare in winter from Maryland south. The Black-vented Shearwater (next page) of the Pacific was formerly considered a form of this species.

Audubon's Shearwater *Puffinus lherminieri*

L 12" (31 cm) W 27" (69 cm) Dark brown above, white below, with long tail, dark undertail coverts; undersides of primaries dark. Breeds on Caribbean islands. Common off southern Atlantic coast, chiefly from May to December; rare to casual wanderer as far north as New York.

Little Shearwater *Puffinus assimilis*

L 11" (28 cm) W 25" (64 cm) Accidental off the Atlantic coast in summer and fall. Resembles Manx Shearwater but is smaller, blacker above, with more white on face. Wings are very short; undersides of primaries pale. Flies with fast, whirring wingbeats, seldom gliding. Breeds on islands in eastern Atlantic.

Cory's
Shearwater

Black-capped Petrel
for comparison

Greater
Shearwater

Manx
Shearwater

Audubon's
Shearwater

Little
Shearwater

Pink-footed Shearwater *Puffinus creatopus*

L 19" (48 cm) W 43" (109 cm) Uniformly blackish-brown above; white wing linings and underparts are variably mottled; pink bill and feet distinctive at close range. Flies with slower wing-beats and more soaring than Sooty Shearwater (page 26). Breeds on islands off Chile; winters (our summer) in the northern Pacific, generally far offshore. Common from late spring through fall; rare throughout rest of year.

Streaked Shearwater *Calonectris leucomelas*

L 19" (48 cm) W 48" (122 cm) Asian species, casual off California in the fall. Pale, finely streaked head looks white at a distance; compare with light-phase Northern Fulmar (page 26). Pale fringes give upperparts a scaly look. Bill is mostly pink. Note also the white axillaries and dark underwing primary coverts.

Buller's Shearwater *Puffinus bulleri*

L 16" (41 cm) W 40" (102 cm) Gleaming white below, including wing linings. Gray above, with a darker cap and a long, dark, wedge-shaped tail. Dark bar across leading edge of upperwing extends across back, forming a distinct M. Flight is graceful and buoyant, with long periods of soaring. Breeds on islands off New Zealand. Irregular off west coast during southward migration. Most common from Washington to central California; rarer north and south along west coast. Formerly called New Zealand Shearwater.

Black-vented Shearwater *Puffinus opisthomelas*

L 14" (36 cm) W 34" (86 cm) Dark brown above, white below, with dark undertail coverts. Variable dusky mottling on sides of breast, often extending across entire breast. Seen off California from August to May; often visible from shore. Nests chiefly on islands off Baja peninsula. Formerly considered a subspecies of Manx Shearwater (preceding page) of the Atlantic. The Manx-type shearwaters, with white undertail coverts, reported several times off California may be the Hawaiian form of **Townsend's Shearwater** (not shown), *Puffinus auricularis newelli,* or stray Manx Shearwaters from the Atlantic.

Pink-footed Shearwater

Northern Fulmar
light phase
for comparison

Streaked Shearwater

Buller's Shearwater

Black-vented Shearwater

Gadfly Petrels

Fluttery wingbeats and high, erratic soaring named these fast-flying petrels. Unlike shearwaters, petrels hold their wings slightly forward from the shoulder and bent sharply back at the wrist. Rarely alight on water, but feed in flight, snapping up food from the surface. All species have short, stout, dark bills.

Black-capped Petrel *Pterodroma hasitata*
L 16" (41 cm) W 37" (94 cm) White forehead; white collar; white U-shaped band on rump. White wing lining, with variable dark diagonal bar on leading edge. Wing shape and white forehead distinguish Black-capped Petrel from Greater Shearwater (page 28); look also for flight pattern of rapid wingbeats that lift the Blackcap high above water, followed by a long, descending glide with wings bowed down. A few Blackcaps have only a little white on rump and nape; darkest birds cannot be distinguished from **Bermuda Petrel** (not shown), *P. cahow,* whose occurrence in southeastern waters is speculative. Blackcaps breed on Caribbean islands, especially Hispaniola. Fairly common along edge of Gulf Stream to North Carolina from spring to late fall. Accidental inland after hurricanes.

Mottled Petrel *Pterodroma inexpectata*
L 14" (36 cm) W 32" (81 cm) Gray belly contrasts with mostly white breast and throat. Underwing mostly white, with broad diagonal black bar on leading edge. In fresh plumage, back is lightly mottled with white. Flight rapid, bounding. Breeds on islands off New Zealand. Seen regularly well off southern Alaska during summer; casual elsewhere off Pacific coast. Formerly called Scaled Petrel.

Cook's Petrel *Pterodroma cookii*
L 13" (33 cm) W 30" (76 cm) Rare but regular off west coast. Upperparts uniformly gray, without contrasting dark cap of Stejneger's Petrel. Dark bar on upperwing extends across back, forming a distinct M. Wing linings almost entirely white. Flight of this and Stejneger's Petrel is rapid and erratic, with fluttery wingbeats and bounding, swooping arcs. Breeds on islands off New Zealand.

Stejneger's Petrel *Pterodroma longirostris*
L 11$\frac{1}{2}$" (29 cm) W 28" (71 cm) Accidental off coast of California; probably occurs more frequently very far offshore. Almost identical to Cook's Petrel but dark cap contrasts with gray upperparts. Breeds on islands off Chile.

Solander's Petrel *Pterodroma solandri*
L 16" (41 cm) W 37" (94 cm) (Not shown) Casual well off the west coast. Gray-brown overall, with conspicuous white patch on underwing at base of primaries; pale area around entire base of bill. Breeds on islands off Australia.

dark-naped

**Black-capped
Petrel**

**Mottled
Petrel**

**Cook's
Petrel**

**Stejneger's
Petrel**

Storm-Petrels (Family Hydrobatidae)

Sprightly fliers, these small seabirds hover close to the water, pattering or hopping across the waves to pluck up small fish and plankton. Some species follow ships. Identification is often difficult. Flight patterns may help to distinguish the various species, but flight can vary deceptively depending on weather.

Band-rumped Storm-Petrel *Oceanodroma castro*
L 9" (23 cm) Casual well off Gulf coast; rare off Atlantic. Deep wing strokes are followed by stiff-winged glides, like the flight of a shearwater but unlike the swooping, erratic flight of Leach's Storm-Petrel or the fluttery, skimming flight of Wilson's. White band crosses rump but is not as bold and broad on undertail coverts as in Wilson's. Tail squarish or slightly forked. Band-rumped is larger than Wilson's; stouter and darker than Leach's. Breeds on tropical islands. Formerly called Harcourt's Petrel.

Wilson's Storm-Petrel *Oceanites oceanicus*
L 7¹/₄" (18 cm) Skims across the waves with shallow, fluttery wingbeats like a swallow. Wings short and rounded; in flight, feet trail behind tip of squarish or rounded tail. Often hovers to feed, pattering its feet on the water. Bold white U-shaped rump band extends onto undertail coverts; white on lower flanks is conspicuous even on sitting bird. Brownish-black overall with pale wing patch. Smaller than Leach's and Band-rumped. Yellow webbing between toes is visible at close range. Common off Atlantic coast from May to September; uncommon off Gulf coast; very rare to central California coast from August to October, annual in Monterey Bay. On the west coast, compare Wedge-rumped Storm-Petrel (next page).

Leach's Storm-Petrel *Oceanodroma leucorhoa*
L 8" (20 cm) Distinctive erratic flight like that of a bat or butterfly, with deep strokes of long, pointed wings. Very rarely patters its feet like Wilson's; wings are narrower and more sharply angled. In close view, look for dusky line dividing white rump band. No white is visible on flanks of sitting bird. Blackish-brown overall, with pale wing stripes and forked tail. Amount of white on rump varies; a few birds seen off southern California have brown rumps. Fairly common off Pacific coast; uncommon south of breeding range along Atlantic coast.

White-faced Storm-Petrel *Pelagodroma marina*
L 7¹/₂" (19 cm) Very rare off the Atlantic coast from North Carolina to Massachusetts. Flies low, with stiff, shallow wingbeats and short glides. Sometimes swings from side to side like a forward-moving pendulum. Distinctive white underparts, wing linings, and face. Dark eye stripe, crown, and upperparts; paler rump.

Band-rumped Storm-Petrel

Wilson's Storm-Petrel

Leach's Storm-Petrel

White-faced Storm-Petrel

Leach's west coast

| Wilson's | Band-rumped | northern | intermediate | southern | Wedge-rumped |

Black Storm-Petrel *Oceanodroma melania* L 9″ (23 cm)

Deep, languid wing strokes, graceful flight. Largest of the all-dark storm-petrels. Blackish-brown overall with pale bar on upper surface of wing. Tail forked and fairly long. Slow, deep wingbeats and larger size distinguish Black from brown-rumped variation of Leach's Storm-Petrel (preceding page). Breeds from May to December on an islet off Santa Barbara Island. Common off southern California coast to Monterey from late summer through fall.

Ashy Storm-Petrel *Oceanodroma homochroa*

L 8″ (20 cm) Fluttery wingbeats, but flight fairly direct; not as swallowlike as Wilson's Storm-Petrel (preceding page). Gray-brown overall, darkest on crown, leading edge of wings, and upper surface of flight feathers. Pale mottling on underwing coverts may be visible at close range. Viewed from the side, Ashy appears long-tailed. Distinguished from Black Storm-Petrel by rapid, shallow wingbeats and overall paler, grayer appearance. Fairly common most of the year; rare in winter. Breeds on islands off central and southern California.

Fork-tailed Storm-Petrel *Oceanodroma furcata*

L 8½″ (22 cm) Wingbeats shallow, rapid, often followed by glides. Looks fairly long-tailed in flight. Occasionally makes shallow dives for food. Distinctively bluish-gray above, pearl gray below; undertail coverts and flanks sometimes white. Note also dark gray forehead and eye patch, dark wing linings. Now rare off California coast; progressively more abundant farther north.

Least Storm-Petrel *Oceanodroma microsoma*

L 5¾″ (15 cm) Small storm-petrel, the size of a sparrow. Swift, indirect flight, low over the water, with deep wingbeats like the much larger Black Storm-Petrel. Blackish-brown above; slightly paler below. Short-tailed; appears almost tailless in flight. Irregularly fairly common to abundant off the coast of southern California in late summer and fall.

Wedge-rumped Storm-Petrel *Oceanodroma tethys*

L 6½″ (17 cm) Casual off the California coast from August to January. Distinctive bold white wedge-shaped patch on tail gives the appearance of a white tail with dark corners. Compare with the rounded rump band and white flanks of Wilson's Storm-Petrel (preceding page). Almost as small as Least Storm-Petrel, with similar deep wingbeats. Breeds on the Galapagos Islands and on islands off Peru. Formerly called Galapagos Petrel.

Black
Storm-Petrel

Ashy
Storm-Petrel

Fork-tailed
Storm-Petrel

Least
Storm-Petrel

Wedge-rumped
Storm-Petrel

Frigatebirds (Family Fregatidae)

These large, dark seabirds have the longest wingspan, in proportion to weight, of all birds. Seafarers named these aerial predators for a swift warship.

Magnificent Frigatebird *Fregata magnificens*
L 40" (102 cm) W 90" (229 cm) Long, forked tail; long, narrow wings. Male is glossy black; orange throat pouch becomes bright red when inflated in courtship display. Female is blackish-brown, with white at center of underparts. Young birds show varying amount of white on head and underparts; require four to six years to reach adult plumage. Frigatebirds skim the sea, snatching up food from surface; also harass other birds in flight, forcing them to disgorge food. Generally seen along coast, but also accidental inland, especially after storms. Rare but regular in summer at Salton Sea. Breed on Marquesas Key off south Florida; casual north along both coasts.

Tropicbirds (Family Phaethontidae)

Long central tail feathers identify adults. These seabirds are usually seen far out at sea, diving for fish or resting on the waves, streamers held high.

White-tailed Tropicbird *Phaethon lepturus*
L 30" (76 cm) W 37" (94 cm) Tropical species, annual in spring on the Dry Tortugas, rare but regular in summer along Gulf and Atlantic coasts to North Carolina; most sightings are well offshore in the Gulf Stream. Smaller and slimmer than Red-billed Tropicbird; wings show distinctive black stripes; primaries show less black than in Red-billed. Bill usually yellow or orange; occasionally red. Immature lacks tail streamers; upperparts are boldly barred.

Red-billed Tropicbird *Phaethon aethereus*
L 40" (102 cm) W 44" (112 cm) Tropical species, rare well off southern California shore; very rare off Atlantic coast to North Carolina. Adult has red bill, black primaries, barring on back and wings, white tail streamers. Immature has black collar; lacks streamers; tail is tipped with black; barring on upperparts is finer than in other young tropicbirds; bill color varies from yellow to reddish.

Red-tailed Tropicbird *Phaethon rubricauda*
L 37" (94 cm) W 44" (112 cm) South Pacific species, accidental off California coast. Flight feathers mostly white. Adult has red bill; red tail streamers, narrower than in other tropicbirds. Juvenile lacks streamers; tail is all-white; upperparts barred; bill black, gradually changing to yellow and then red. Note also lack of black collar on nape.

Magnificent Frigatebird

juvenile

♂

♂

♀

White-tailed Tropicbird

immature

adult

Red-billed Tropicbird

immature

adult

Red-tailed Tropicbird

juvenile

adult

Pelicans (Family Pelecanidae)

These large and heavy water birds have massive bills and huge throat pouches used as dip nets to catch fish. In flight, pelicans hold their heads drawn back.

American White Pelican *Pelecanus erythrorhynchos*
L 62" (158 cm) W 108" (274 cm) White, with black primaries and outer secondaries. Breeding adult has pale yellow crest; bill is bright orange, usually with a fibrous plate on upper mandible. Plate is shed after eggs are laid; crown and nape become grayish. Juvenile is dusky overall. Immature is mostly white but wing coverts are mottled, head and neck grayish. White Pelicans do not dive for food but dip their bills into the water while swimming. Usually found in flocks. Nonbreeding birds are seen in summer throughout area enclosed by dashed line on map. Breeding birds may fly 150 miles from the nest to feed. In the fall, vagrants may appear almost anywhere, increasingly in the northeast.

Brown Pelican *Pelecanus occidentalis*
L 48" (122 cm) W 84" (213 cm) Nonbreeding adult has white head and neck, often washed with yellow; grayish-brown body; blackish belly. In breeding bird, hindneck is dark chestnut; yellow patch appears at base of foreneck. Molt during incubation and chick-feeding produces creamy head and foreneck. Juvenile is grayish-brown above, tipped with pale buff; underparts whitish. First-year bird is browner; acquires adult plumage by third year. Dives from the air after prey, capturing fish in its pouch. Rare inland. Wanderers are seen at any time of year, but chiefly in summer, to limit of dashed line on map. East coast populations are expanding northward.

Gannets and Boobies (Family Sulidae)

High-diving seabirds noted for their sudden, headlong plunges after prey. All have long, narrow wings, tapered tail, and a tapered bill. Species vary in the color of facial skin, bill, and feet. All are gregarious, nesting in colonies on small islands. The rest of the year, gannets roost at sea, boobies primarily on land.

Northern Gannet *Morus bassanus*
L 37" (94 cm) W 72" (183 cm) Large, white seabird with long, black-tipped wings, pointed white tail. Juvenile is dark gray above, with pale speckling; grayish below. First-year birds are whiter below; distinguished from juvenile and immature Masked Booby (next page) by dark bill and by lack of white patch on upper back. Full adult plumage is acquired in third year. Common; breeds in large colonies on rocky cliffs; winters at sea. Often seen from shore during migration and winter.

immature

nonbreeding

chick-feeding adult

breeding

American White Pelican

nonbreeding

1st year

chick-feeding adult

Brown Pelican

juvenile

nonbreeding

breeding

juvenile

adult

Northern Gannet

adult

1st year

2nd year

Brown Booby *Sula leucogaster* L 30" (76 cm) W 57" (145 cm)

Dark brown, with sharply contrasting white underparts and wing linings. Western form male has whitish head and neck. Bill and feet yellow to gray-green. Juvenile is also dark, but underparts and wing linings are pale brown, bill dark grayish-blue. Gradually acquires adult plumage over more than two years. The Brown Booby is casual at the Salton Sea, and along the Colorado River Valley, mostly in late summer. Fairly common in the Gulf of Mexico, but rarely seen from mainland shore. Accidental along Atlantic coast to New Jersey. Often follows ships. Also fishes close to land, may roost in trees or on buoys and oil rigs.

Red-footed Booby *Sula sula* L 28" (71 cm) W 60" (152 cm)

Tropical species; casual on Florida's Dry Tortugas; accidental on the Gulf and California coasts. Bright red feet adorn adults of both phases; one phase is brown with a white tail, the other white with black primaries and secondaries and a black patch on the underside of the outer wing. All birds have bright pink bare facial skin at base of bill. Young birds are pale brown, with yellowish feet; adult plumage is gradually acquired over two or three years. Smallest of the boobies, the Redfoot flies with grace and speed. May follow a ship for days, sometimes perching in the rigging.

Masked Booby *Sula dactylatra* L 32" (81 cm) W 62" (158 cm)

Adult readily distinguished from Northern Gannet (preceding page) by yellow bill and extensive black facial skin, black tail, black secondaries. Immature has yellowish bill; upperparts brown, with white on wing coverts, white patch on upper back, and often a white collar; underparts white; underwing largely white. Gradually acquires adult plumage over two years; rump stays brown longest. The Masked Booby hunts from high in the air, bill pointing straight down. Feeds mainly on flying fish. Rests on sandy atolls. Rarely seen from mainland, but fairly common in the Gulf of Mexico in summer; casual offshore to North Carolina. Formerly called Blue-faced Booby.

Blue-footed Booby *Sula nebouxii*

L 32" (81 cm) W 62" (158 cm)   Feet bright blue in adults, darker in young birds; bill dark bluish-gray; white nape patch and white on rump are also distinctive. Adults have streaked pale heads. Juveniles have brown head and neck; gradually acquire adult plumage in about three years. Blue-footed Boobies tend to fish in clear, shallow waters close to shore, working in small flocks. Closest breeding grounds are arid islands in the Gulf of California. Irregular wanderer in late summer and fall to inland waters of the southwest, particularly the Salton Sea, occasionally to the Pacific coast.

Brown Booby

western

eastern

eastern

western

Red-footed Booby

white-tailed dark phase

white-tailed dark phase

white phase

Masked Booby

immature

adult

Blue-footed Booby

♂

♀

immature

adult

immatures

Northern Gannet

Masked Booby

Blue-footed Booby

Brown Booby

Red-footed Booby

Anhingas (Family Anhingidae)

Long and slim neck helps to distinguish anhingas from cormorants. Anhingas often swim submerged to the neck. Sharply pointed bill is used to spear fish.

Anhinga *Anhinga anhinga* L 35" (89 cm) W 45" (114 cm)
Black above, with green gloss; silvery white spots and streaks on wings and upper back. During breeding season, male acquires pale, wispy plumes on upper neck; bill and bare facial skin become brightly colored. Female has buffy neck and breast. Immatures resemble adult female but are browner overall. Anhingas prefer freshwater habitats; often seen perched on branches or stumps with wings spread to dry. In flight, their profile looks headless. Slow, regular wingbeats alternate with high soaring on flat wings. Rare wanderer well north of breeding range.

Cormorants (Family Phalacrocoracidae)

Dark birds with set-back legs; long, hooked bill; and colorful bare facial skin and throat pouch. Dive from the surface for fish. Like the Anhinga, soar high on flat wings and may swim submerged to the neck.

Olivaceous Cormorant *Phalacrocorax olivaceus*
L 26" (66 cm) W 40" (102 cm) A small, long-tailed cormorant with pale-bordered yellow-brown or dull yellow throat pouch that tapers to a sharp point behind bill. In breeding plumage, adult acquires short white plumes on sides of neck; border around throat pouch becomes pure white. Distinguished from Double-crested Cormorant by smaller size, longer tail, and smaller, angled throat pouch (see also next page). Olivaceous immatures are browner than adults, particularly on underparts. Fairly common; found at marshy ponds or shallow inlets near perching stumps and snags. Regular in the southwest; casual to southeast California. Formerly called Neotropic Cormorant.

Great Cormorant *Phalacrocorax carbo*
L 36" (91 cm) W 63" (160 cm) A large, short-tailed cormorant with small yellow throat pouch broadly bordered with white feathering. In breeding plumage, adult shows white flank patches and wispy white plumes on head. Smaller Double-crested Cormorant has orange throat pouch; lacks flank patches; note also Great Cormorant's thicker neck and larger head. First-year birds are brown above; white belly contrasts with streaked brown neck, breast, and flanks. During second year, immatures resemble nonbreeding adults more closely but have a brown tinge above; compare with young Double-crested which has a slimmer bill and, often, a darker belly (see also next page). Generally rare in winter south of Chesapeake Bay but seen with increasing frequency as far south as Florida.

44

breeding ♂

Anhinga

♀

Great
2nd year

Double-crested
2nd year

Olivaceous
immature

breeding

immature

nonbreeding

2nd year

Double-crested
eastern
for comparison

**Olivaceous
Cormorant**

**Great
Cormorant**

1st year

breeding

Double-crested Cormorant *Phalacrocorax auritus*

L 32" (81 cm) W 52" (132 cm) Large, rounded throat pouch is orange year-round. Breeding adult has double crest of two tufts curving back from behind eyes. Tufts are largely white in western birds, dark and less conspicuous in eastern birds (preceding page). First-year birds are brown above, variably pale below, but usually palest on upper breast and neck. Among west coast cormorants, Double-crested's kinked neck is distinctive in flight. Common and widespread; found on rocky coasts, beaches, inland lakes and rivers. Breeding populations in the interior are local and irregular but increasing.

Brandt's Cormorant *Phalacrocorax penicillatus*

L 35" (89 cm) W 48" (122 cm) A band of pale buffy feathers bordering the throat pouch identifies all ages. Throat pouch becomes bright blue in breeding plumage; head, neck, and scapulars acquire fine, white plumes. First-year birds are dark brown above, slightly paler below. In all ages, appears more uniformly dark above than Double-crested; wings and tail are proportionately shorter. Head and bill are larger than in Pelagic Cormorant. Common and gregarious; often fishes in large flocks; flies in long lines between feeding and roosting grounds.

Pelagic Cormorant *Phalacrocorax pelagicus*

L 26" (66 cm) W 39" (99 cm) Dark and glossy overall; bill dark. Smaller and slenderer than other western cormorants. Breeding adult has tufts on crown and nape; fine white plumes on sides of neck; white patches on flanks. Distinguished from Red-faced Cormorant by darker and less extensive red facial skin and lack of yellow in bill. First-year bird is uniformly dark brown; closely resembles young Red-faced; note dark bill and smaller size. Pelagics are distinguished in flight from Brandt's by smaller head, very slender neck, and smaller overall size. Less gregarious than other species; breed in smaller colonies. Feed near cliffs and rocky shores, in tidal rips and surf.

Red-faced Cormorant *Phalacrocorax urile*

L 31" (79 cm) W 46" (117 cm) Partly yellow bill distinguishes all ages from the very similar Pelagic Cormorant. In adult, dull brown wings contrast with glossy upperparts. Throat pouch is bluish; dull red facial skin becomes brighter in breeding season. First-year bird is uniformly dark brown. More gregarious than Pelagics, Red-faced Cormorants nest in colonies on the ledges of steep coastal cliffs and on rocky sea islands, alongside gulls, murres, and auklets.

1st year

breeding

western

**Double-crested
Cormorant**

Double-crested

Pelagic

Brandt's

**Brandt's
Cormorant**

nonbreeding

nonbreeding

**Pelagic
Cormorant**

breeding

1st year

1st year

breeding

1st year

**Red-faced
Cormorant**

breeding

Herons (Family Ardeidae)

Wading birds; most have long legs, neck, and bill for stalking food in shallow water. Graceful crests and plumes adorn some species in breeding season.

Least Bittern *Ixobrychus exilis* L 13″ (33 cm) W 17″ (43 cm)
Buffy inner wing patches identify this small, rather secretive heron as it flushes briefly from dense marsh cover. When alarmed, may freeze with bill pointing up. In male back and crown are black; in female they are browner. Juvenile resembles female but has more prominent streaking on back and breast. Rare dark phase (not shown) of eastern populations is russet where typical plumage is pale. Least Bittern's calls include a series of harsh *kok* notes, heard chiefly in breeding season; similar to call of Black-billed Cuckoo. Fairly common. May breed sporadically beyond mapped range in west.

American Bittern *Botaurus lentiginosus*
L 28″ (71 cm) W 42″ (107 cm) Rich brown upperparts are set off by black neck streaks. Contrasting dark flight feathers are conspicuous in flight; note also that wings are somewhat pointed, not rounded as in night-herons. Juvenile lacks neck patches. Distinctive spring song, *oonk-a-lunk*, most often heard at dusk in dense marsh reeds. When alarmed, freezes with bill pointing up, or flushes with rapid wingbeats and nasal *haink* calls. Fairly common; casual breeder south of range. Casual in winter into southern part of breeding range.

Black-crowned Night-Heron *Nycticorax nycticorax*
L 25″ (64 cm) W 44″ (112 cm) Stocky heron with short neck and legs. Adult has black crown and back; white hindneck plumes are longest in breeding season. Juvenile distinguished from juvenile Yellow-crowned Night-Heron by browner upperparts with bolder white spotting; thicker neck; paler, less contrasting face; longer, thinner bill with mostly pale lower mandible. In flight, legs barely extend beyond tail. Full adult plumage is not acquired until third year. Calls include a low, harsh *woc*, more guttural than in Yellowcrown. Nocturnal feeder. Typically roosts in trees. Fairly common but local.

Yellow-crowned Night-Heron *Nyctanassa violacea*
L 24″ (61 cm) W 42″ (107 cm) Adult has buffy-white crown, black face with white cheek; acquires head plumes in breeding season. Juvenile distinguished from young Black-crowned Night-Heron by grayer upperparts with less conspicuous white spotting; thinner neck; stouter, mostly dark bill (pale only at base of lower mandible); and, in flight, by legs extending well beyond tail and by contrastingly darker flight feathers and trailing edge on wings. Full adult plumage is acquired in third year. Calls include a short *woc*, higher and less harsh than call of Blackcrown. Fairly common; roosts in trees in wet woods, swamps, low coastal shrubs. Casual in California.

Least Bittern
♂
♀
juvenile

American Bittern
juvenile

Black-crowned Night-Heron
2nd spring
breeding
1st spring
juvenile
juvenile
breeding

Yellow-crowned Night-Heron
juvenile
breeding
breeding

Green-backed Heron *Butorides striatus*

L 18" (46 cm) W 26" (66 cm) Small, chunky heron with short legs. Back and sides of adult's neck are deep chestnut; green on upperparts is mixed with blue-gray; center of throat and neck white. Greenish-black crown feathers, sometimes raised to form shaggy crest. Legs are usually dull yellow but in male turn bright orange in high breeding plumage. Immature is browner above; white throat and underparts heavily streaked with brown. Generally solitary; found in a variety of habitats, but prefers streams, ponds, marshes with woodland cover; often perches in trees. Common call is a loud, sharp *kyowk*. When alarmed, raises crest and flicks tail. Generally common, but rare in some parts of western range; a few winter north of resident limit. Formerly known as Green Heron.

Tricolored Heron *Egretta tricolor*

L 26" (66 cm) W 36" (91 cm) White belly and foreneck contrast with mainly dark blue upperparts; bill long and slender. Immature has chestnut hindneck and wing coverts. Common inhabitant of salt marshes and mangrove swamps of the east and Gulf coasts. Rare inland, but has bred in North Dakota and Kansas. Rare but regular on southern California coast; casual in the Southwest. Formerly known as Louisiana Heron.

Little Blue Heron *Egretta caerulea*

L 24" (61 cm) W 40" (102 cm) Slate blue overall. During most of year, plumage, head and neck are dark purple, legs and feet dull green. In high breeding plumage, head and neck become reddish-purple, legs and feet black. Immature is easily confused with immature Snowy Egret (next page); note Little Blue Heron's dull yellow legs and feet; thicker, two-toned bill with gray base and dark tip; grayish lores; and, in close view, the narrow, dusky primary tips. During first spring, immature's white plumage begins gradual molt to adult plumage. Little Blue Herons are slow, methodical feeders in freshwater ponds, lakes, and marshes and coastal saltwater wetlands. Common. Large numbers disperse widely after breeding season. Regular as far as northern California coast.

Reddish Egret *Egretta rufescens*

L 30" (76 cm) W 46" (117 cm) While feeding, this heron "dances," dashing about with wings spread in a canopy. Breeding adult has shaggy plumes on rufous head, neck. Bill is pink with black tip; legs cobalt blue. Nonbreeding plumage varies, but in general is duller, plumes shorter. Immature is gray with some pale cinnamon on head, neck, inner wing; bill is dark. Compare with adult Little Blue Heron. White-phase adult resembles immature Little Blue Heron or Snowy Egret (next page), but note pink-and-black bill, shaggy plumes, dark legs. Some dark-phase birds have considerable white on wings, resemble molting immature Little Blue Heron. Uncommon; inhabits shallow, open salt pans. Wanders along Gulf coast in postbreeding dispersal; rare in southern California.

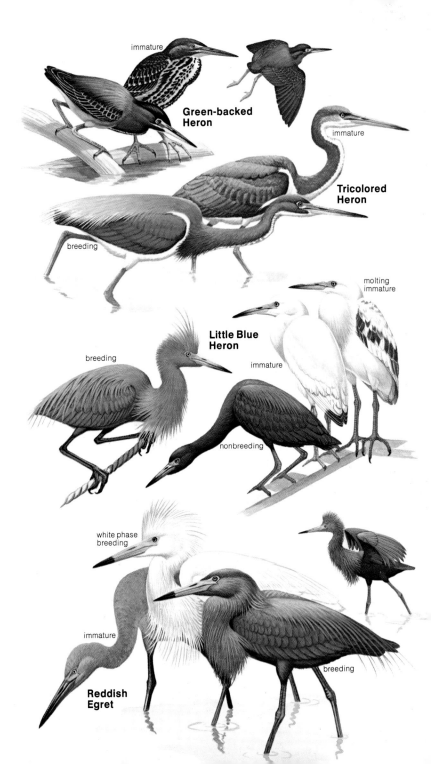

immature

Green-backed Heron

immature

Tricolored Heron

breeding

molting immature

Little Blue Heron

breeding

immature

nonbreeding

white phase breeding

immature

breeding

Reddish Egret

Cattle Egret *Bubulcus ibis* L 20" (51 cm) W 36" (91 cm)
Small, stocky white heron with large, rounded head. Breeding adult is adorned by orange-buff plumes on crown, back, and foreneck. At height of breeding season, bill is red-orange, lores purplish, legs dusky-red. Nonbreeding adult has shorter, whitish plumes, yellow bill, yellowish legs. Juvenile lacks plumes; bill is black; begins to acquire yellow bill in late summer. Immature lacks plumes but otherwise resembles nonbreeding adult. Often seen among livestock in pastures and fields, feeding on insects stirred up by hooves or tractors; also picks insects off animals' backs. In flight, resembles Snowy Egret but is smaller; bill and legs shorter; wingbeats faster. An Old World species, the Cattle Egret spread to South America, became established in Florida in the early 1950s, reached California by the mid-1960s, and continues to expand throughout North America. In summer and fall, postbreeding wanderers reach far north of mapped breeding range.

Snowy Egret *Egretta thula* L 24" (61 cm) W 41" (104 cm)
Snow white heron with slender black bill, yellow eyes, black legs, and bright yellow feet. Graceful plumes on head, neck, and back, where they curve upward, are striking in breeding adult. In high breeding plumage, lores turn red, feet orange. In nonbreeding plumage, bill, leg, and eye colors are duller, plumes shorter. Immature lacks plumes and sometimes shows a bit of bluish-gray at base of black bill. Back of leg is yellow-green, but remainder is dark and feet are yellow as in adult. Can be confused with immature Little Blue Heron (see also preceding page); note young Snowy Egret's slimmer, mostly black bill; yellow lores; predominantly dark legs; and white wing tips. Snowy Egrets move briskly in the water, stirring up prey with their feet, stabbing repeatedly to catch it. Common in marshes, ponds, mangrove swamps; occasionally found in dry fields. In summer, postbreeding wanderers reach far north of mapped breeding range. This species was once hunted extensively for its plumes. Now protected, populations have recovered; range is expanding.

Great Egret *Casmerodius albus* L 39" (99 cm) W 51" (130 cm)
Large white heron with heavy yellow bill, blackish legs and feet. In breeding plumage, long plumes trail from back, extending beyond tail. In immature and nonbreeding adult, bill and leg colors are duller, plumes absent. Distinguished from most other white herons by large size; from white form of the larger Great Blue Heron by black legs and feet. Common in marshes, mangrove swamps, mud flats. Partial to open habitats for feeding; stalks prey slowly, methodically. Population was greatly reduced by plume hunters at the turn of the century; now mostly recovered and is still expanding in some parts of range. Occasionally breeds far north of usual range. Postbreeding wanderers reach far north of range. Formerly called Common Egret and American Egret.

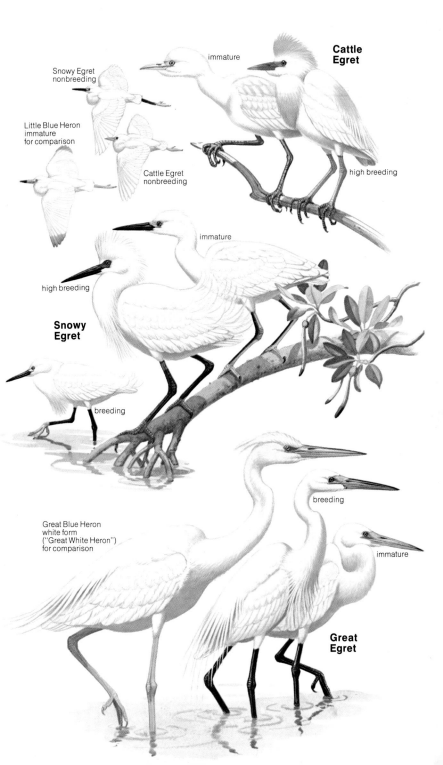

Cattle Egret

immature

Snowy Egret
nonbreeding

Little Blue Heron
immature
for comparison

Cattle Egret
nonbreeding

high breeding

immature

high breeding

Snowy Egret

breeding

breeding

immature

Great Blue Heron
white form
("Great White Heron")
for comparison

Great Egret

Great Blue Heron *Ardea herodias*

L 46" (117 cm) W 72" (183 cm) Large, gray-blue heron; black stripe extends above eye; white foreneck is streaked with black. Breeding adult has yellowish bill and ornate plumes on head, neck, and back. Nonbreeding adult lacks plumes; bill is yellower. Juvenile has black crown, no plumes. All-white form found in southern Florida was formerly considered a separate species, "Great White Heron" (preceding page). In the "Wurdemann's Heron" phase found chiefly on the Florida Keys, head is all-white. The Great Blue Heron is common but breeds sporadically across large parts of range. A few birds winter far north into breeding range.

Storks (Family Ciconiidae)

Large, long-legged birds that walk sedately and fly with slow, deliberate beats of their long, broad wings, soaring and circling like hawks over open wetlands.

Wood Stork *Mycteria americana*

L 40" (102 cm) W 61" (155 cm) Black flight feathers and tail contrast with white body. Adult has bald, blackish-gray head; thick, dusky, downcurved bill. Immature's head is feathered and grayish-brown; bill is yellow. Wood Storks inhabit wet meadows, swamps, ponds, coastal shallows. A few wander beyond normal range in postbreeding dispersal; accidental as far north as Maine and British Columbia.

Jabiru *Jabiru mycteria* *L 52" (132 cm) W 90" (229 cm)*

Huge stork of Central and South America, accidental straggler in south Texas. Distinguished from Wood Stork by larger size; large bill, slightly upturned; and all-white wings and tail. Immature is patchy brown-gray; head is blackish-brown. Usually seen with flocks of Wood Storks.

Flamingos (Family Phoenicopteridae)

Large waders with big, bent bills, used to strain food from the waters of shallow lakes, lagoons.

Greater Flamingo *Phoenicopterus ruber*

L 46" (117 cm) W 60" (152 cm) Caribbean species, rare vagrant to south Florida. Note pink legs, black flight feathers, tricolored bill. Immature is grayer, with pink wash below; paler bill. Most sightings in Florida and elsewhere are escaped zoo birds, which are sometimes duller pink than wild birds. Other similar escapes include a European subspecies with pink-and-black bill; the **Chilean Flamingo** *(P. chilensis),* which has grayish legs with pink joints; and the **Lesser Flamingo** *(Phoeniconaias minor),* with dark red bill and blotchy red wing coverts and axillaries.

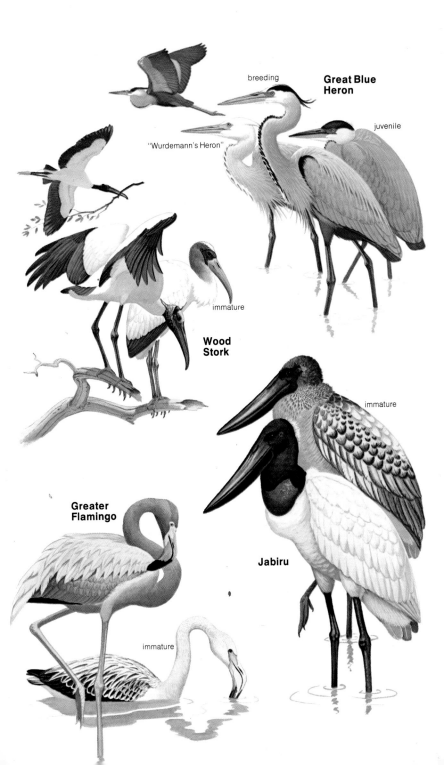

Great Blue Heron

breeding

juvenile

"Wurdemann's Heron"

Wood Stork

immature

immature

Greater Flamingo

immature

Jabiru

immature

Ibises, Spoonbills (Family Threskiornithidae)

Gregarious, heron-like birds, these long-legged waders feed with long, specialized bills: slender and curved downward in ibises, wide and spatulate in spoonbills.

Glossy Ibis *Plegadis falcinellus* L 23" (58 cm) W 36" (91 cm)
Breeding adult's chestnut plumage is glossed with green or purple; looks all-dark at a distance. Distinguished from White-faced Ibis by brownish-olive bill, brown eye, gray-green legs with red joints, and lack of distinct white border to bare facial skin. Pale blue edge to gray facial skin does not extend behind eye or under chin; turns cobalt blue at height of breeding season. Winter adult closely resembles winter White-faced; look for gray facial skin and pale blue line from eye to bill. First-fall bird closely resembles immature White-faced Ibis but by late winter acquires the gray face and pale blue line of the winter adult. Adult breeding plumage is acquired in second spring. Glossy Ibises inhabit freshwater and saltwater marshes. Fairly common but local. Range is expanding north along the east coast. Rare inland wanderer.

White-faced Ibis *Plegadis chihi* L 23" (58 cm) W 36" (91 cm)
Breeding adult distinguished from Glossy Ibis by reddish bill, red eye, all-red legs, and white, feathered border around red facial skin; border extends behind eye and under chin. Winter adult plumage is like Glossy, but lacks pale blue line from eye to bill; facial skin is pale pink. Immature closely resembles immature Glossy Ibis until late winter; look for reddish eye. Fairly common; prefers freshwater marshes but also frequents brackish areas.

White Ibis *Eudocimus albus* L 25" (64 cm) W 38" (97 cm)
Adult's white plumage and pink facial skin are distinctive. In breeding adult, facial skin, bill, and legs turn scarlet. Dark tips of primaries visible only in flight. Immatures have white underparts and wing linings, pinkish bill; gradually molt into adult plumage, attained by second fall. Locally abundant in coastal salt marshes, swamps, mangroves. Closely related **Scarlet Ibis** *(Eudocimus ruber)*, a South American species introduced or escaped in Florida, hybridizes with White Ibis; offspring are various shades of pink or scarlet.

Roseate Spoonbill *Ajaia ajaja* L 32" (81 cm) W 50" (127 cm)
Adult has pink body with red highlights; long, spatulate bill; unfeathered greenish head. The head may become buffy during courtship. First-fall bird has white feathering on head; body is mostly pale pink. Spoonbills feed in shallow waters, swinging their bills from side to side. Fairly common locally along the Gulf coast; accidental north to Virginia. Strays from Mexico are seen irregularly in western Arizona and southeastern California.

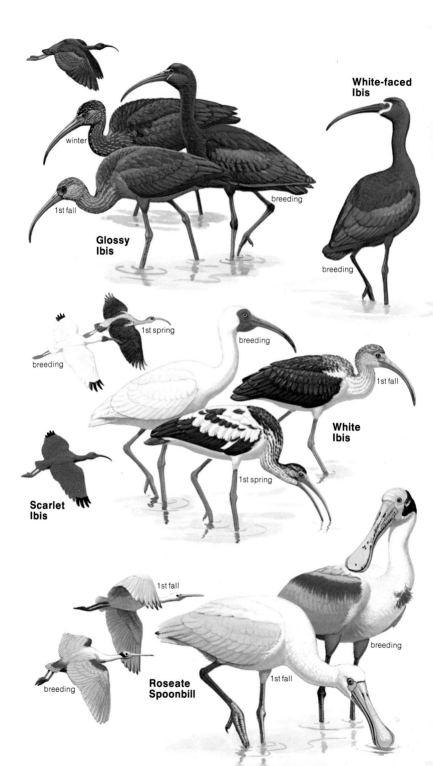

White-faced Ibis

winter

1st fall

Glossy Ibis

breeding

breeding

White-faced Ibis

breeding

1st spring

breeding

breeding

1st fall

White Ibis

Scarlet Ibis

1st spring

1st fall

1st fall

breeding

Roseate Spoonbill

breeding

Cranes (Family Gruidae)

Tall, stately birds with long necks and legs and fairly long, heavy bills. Tertials droop over the rump in a "bustle" that distinguishes cranes from herons. Cranes fly with their necks and legs fully extended. Courtship rites include a frenzied, leaping dance.

Sandhill Crane *Grus canadensis*
L 41" (104 cm) W 73" (185 cm) Adult is gray overall, with dull red skin on the crown and lores; whitish chin, cheek, and upper throat; and blackish primaries. Immatures lack red patch; head and neck vary from pale to tawny; gray body is irregularly mottled with brownish-red. Full adult plumage is reached after two and a half years. Similar Great Blue Heron (page 54) lacks bustle. Preening with muddy bills, cranes may stain the feathers of upper back, lower neck, and breast with ferrous solution contained in the mud. Locally common; breeds on tundra and in marshes and grasslands. In winter, regularly feeds in dry fields, returning to water at night. Resident along parts of the Gulf coast; other populations highly migratory. Casual during fall and winter on east coast from Massachusetts south. Migrating flocks fly at great heights, sometimes too high to be seen from the ground. Common call is a trumpeting, rattling *gar-oo-oo,* audible for more than a mile.

Common Crane *Grus grus* *L 44" (112 cm) W 75" (191 cm)*
Eurasian species, accidental vagrant to the Great Plains, western Canada, and Alaska, almost always with migrating flocks of Sandhill Cranes. Adult distinguished from Sandhill Crane by blackish head and neck marked by broad white stripe. Immature bird resembles immature Sandhill; may show trace of white head stripe in spring. In flight, in all ages, black primaries and secondaries show as a broad black trailing edge on gray wings.

Whooping Crane *Grus americana*
L 52" (132 cm) W 87" (221 cm) Endangered. Sparse wild population breeds in freshwater marshes of Wood Buffalo National Park, Alberta, winters in Aransas National Wildlife Refuge on Gulf coast of Texas. A small population has been introduced in southeast Idaho; winters principally in New Mexico. Adult is white overall, with red facial skin; black primaries show in flight. Immature bird is whitish, with pale reddish-brown head and neck and scattered reddish-brown feathers over the rest of its body; begins to acquire adult plumage after first summer. Call is a shrill, trumpeting *ker-loo ker-lee-loo.* Breeding birds currently number about a hundred. Intensive management and protection programs seem to be slowly succeeding.

immature

Sandhill Crane

stained

immature

Common Crane

immature

Whooping Crane

Swans, Geese, Ducks (Family Anatidae)

Worldwide family: aquatic, web-footed, gregarious birds, ranging from small ducks to large swans. Most feed on water; geese and swans also graze on land.

Tundra Swan *Cygnus columbianus* L 52" (132 cm)

In adult, black facial skin tapers to a point in front of eye and cuts straight across forehead; many birds have a yellow spot in front of eye. Head is rounded, bill slightly concave. In Eurasian form, "Bewick's Swan," seen casually on the west coast, facial skin and base of bill are yellow, but usually only above the nostril; compare with Whooper Swan. Immature Tundras molt earlier than immature Trumpeters and Whoopers; appear much whiter by late winter. Immature "Bewick's" has whitish bill patch. When relaxed, the Tundra Swan tends to hold its neck straight up from breast. Call is a noisy, high-pitched whooping or yodeling. Nests in tundra or sheltered marshes; winters in flocks on shallow ponds, lakes, estuaries. Uncommon and local in winter throughout interior U.S. The North American subspecies was formerly called Whistling Swan.

Trumpeter Swan *Cygnus buccinator* L 60" (152 cm)

Adult's black facial skin tapers to a broad point at the eye, dips down in a V on forehead. Forehead slopes evenly to straight bill. Immatures retain gray-brown plumage through first spring. At rest, Trumpeters tend to hold neck kinked back at base. Most common call is a sonorous single or double honk. Locally fairly common in its few remaining breeding areas and being reintroduced in some former breeding areas.

Whooper Swan *Cygnus cygnus* L 60" (152 cm)

Eurasian species closely related to Trumpeter Swan. Regular winter visitor to outer and central Aleutians. Large yellow patch on lores and bill usually extends in a point to the nostrils; compare with "Bewick's Swan." Forehead slopes evenly to straight bill. When relaxed, tends to hold its neck kinked back. Common call is a bugle-like double note. Immature retains dusky plumage through first winter; by first fall, bill attains whitish patches in same shape as adult's bill patch. Whooper Swans are found on shallow freshwater ponds and lakes and in sheltered brackish and salt water.

Mute Swan *Cygnus olor* L 60" (152 cm)

Prominent black knob at base of orange bill. Juvenile plumage may be white or brownish; bill gray with black base. Darker juvenile begins to molt to white plumage by midwinter; bill becomes pinkish. Mute Swan usually holds its long neck in an S-curve, with bill pointed down. Often swims with wings arched over back. Gives a variety of hisses and snorts, but generally silent. An Old World species, introduced in U.S. Commonly seen in parks. Wild populations on the east coast are growing; most others are not yet fully self-sustaining.

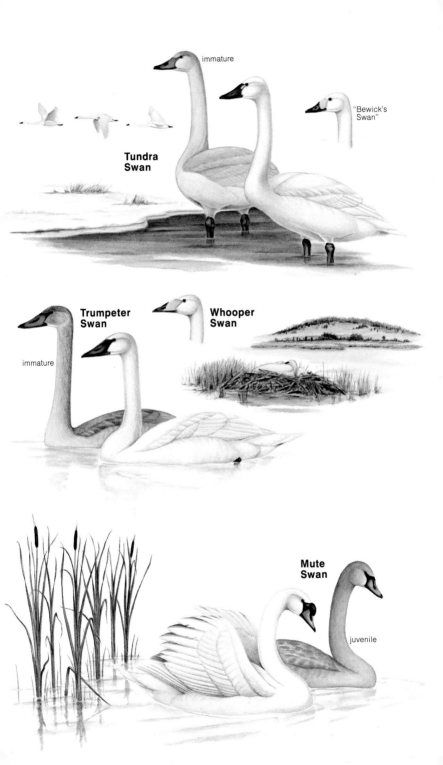

immature

"Bewick's
Swan"

**Tundra
Swan**

**Trumpeter
Swan**

**Whooper
Swan**

immature

**Mute
Swan**

juvenile

Greater White-fronted Goose *Anser albifrons*

L 28" (71 cm) Named for the distinctive white band at base of bill. Medium-size, grayish-brown goose, with irregular black barring on underparts; orange feet and legs. Bill pink (orange in Greenland form) with whitish tip. In flight, note grayish-blue wash on wing coverts and white U-shaped rump band. Most young birds acquire white front and bill tip during first winter; acquire black belly markings by second fall; distinguished from similar Bean Goose by bill color; from Pink-footed Goose by bill and leg color; compare also with immature blue-phase Snow Goose (next page). Color and size vary in adults: small, pale, arctic tundra birds have heavy barring; taiga breeding birds are larger, darker, with less barring; Greenland's intermediate-size tundra form is grayer, with the heaviest barring and distinctive orange bill. Whitefronts prefer to breed and feed near fresh water. Seen in migration and winter west of the Mississippi Valley in wetlands, grassy fields, grainfields. Flocks may number in the thousands. V-formations resemble Canada Geese, but flight is more agile, call a laughing *kah-lah-aluck.* Casual and increasing winter visitor, including Greenland form, on east coast from Quebec to Georgia; occasional winter visitor outside mapped range in all western states and north into southern Canada. Breeding distribution in Canada may be more extensive than shown. Occasionally hybridizes with Canada Goose.

Bean Goose *Anser fabalis* *L 31" (79 cm)*

Eurasian species; rare spring migrant on western and central Aleutians, casual in western Alaska. Grayish-brown goose with plain underparts, orange legs and feet; darker head and neck noticeable in flight. Similar to plain-bellied immature White-fronted Goose; best distinguished by different bill color: black with yellow, orange, or pink midsection, usually without white area at base. In flight, Bean Goose lacks strong contrast between wing coverts and flight feathers. Of the two Siberian forms shown here, *A.f. serrirostris* is seen more often; *middendorffii* has a longer, narrower bill and a longer, thinner neck. Generally silent; call is a low, reedy *ung-unk.*

Pink-footed Goose *Anser brachyrhynchus* *L 26" (66 cm)*

East coast vagrant from breeding grounds in eastern Greenland. Several records between Long Island and Newfoundland; some sightings may be of birds escaped from captivity. Distinguished from plain-bellied immature White-fronted Goose by pink legs and dark base and tip to pinkish bill; bill is also stubbier, neck shorter than Whitefront. In flight, Pinkfoot shows an extensive area of bluish-gray on mantle and all wing coverts that turns brownish with wear; darker head and neck contrast with grayish body. Considered by some authorities to be a small Bean Goose subspecies.

Greater White-fronted Goose

1st winter

taiga

tundra

Greenland

Bean Goose

middendorffii

serrirostris

Pink-footed Goose

Snow Goose *Chen caerulescens* L 28" (71 cm)

Two color phases. All adults distinguished from smaller Ross' Goose by larger, pinkish bill with black "grinning patch," longer neck, flatter head. In flight, less agile than Ross', with slower wingbeat; rusty stains often visible on face in summer. White phase has black primaries; immature is grayish above, with dark bill. Blue phase formerly considered a separate species, Blue Goose. Adult has mostly white head and neck, brown back, variable amount of white on underparts. Primaries and secondaries are black, wing coverts bluish-gray. Immature has dark head and neck; distinguished from White-fronted Goose (preceding page) by dark legs and bill and lack of white on face. Intermediates between white and blue phases have mainly white underparts and whitish wing coverts. Immatures of both phases resemble adults by first spring. Abundant. Breeds on high Arctic tundra; seen in winter in grasslands, grainfields, coastal wetlands. Occasionally hybridizes with Ross' Goose. A larger form, the "Greater Snow Goose," (not shown) breeds around Baffin Bay, winters only along mid-Atlantic coast; blue phase almost unknown. Smaller form, the "Lesser Snow Goose" (different phases shown here), winters casually throughout the interior U. S. and in southern Canada. Blue phase is abundant on the Gulf coast; extremely rare in winter on the west coast; uncommon but increasing in the east.

Ross' Goose *Chen rossii* L 23" (58 cm)

Stubby, triangular bill lacks Snow's "grinning patch" and shows warty bluish or greenish base at close range; neck shorter, head rounder. In flight, more agile than larger Snow Goose, with faster wingbeat; white head generally lacks rusty stains. Ross' has two color phases. White phase has black primaries; immature may have grayish wash on head, back, and flanks, but far less than immature white-phase Snow Goose. Extremely rare blue phase is darker than blue-phase Snow Goose; face and belly are white. Ross' Goose nests typically on lake islands on high Arctic tundra; occasionally hybridizes with Snow Goose. Seen during migration and winter in grasslands, grainfields. Casual winter visitor to much of west outside mapped range. Very rare visitor to mid-Atlantic states; always seen with Snow Geese.

Emperor Goose *Chen canagica* L 26" (66 cm)

Fairly stocky, small goose with short, thick neck. Head and back of neck white; chin and throat black; face often stained rusty in summer. Bill pinkish or purplish; lower mandible is sometimes black. Black-and-white edging to silvery gray plumage creates a scaled effect below; upperparts appear barred. Juvenile has dark head and bill. During first fall, immature acquires white flecking on head; resembles adult by first winter. Emperor Goose breeds in tidewater marsh and tundra; winters on seashores, reefs. Casual south on Pacific coast to central California and inland to northeastern California.

Snow Goose

blue phase

blue phase variant

white phase immature

blue phase immature

white phase

Ross' Goose

white phase immature

white phase

blue phase

Emperor Goose

immature

Canada Goose *Branta canadensis*

L 25"-45" (64 cm-114 cm) Our most common and familiar goose. Black head and neck marked with distinctive white "chin strap" stretching from ear to ear. In flight, shows large, dark wings, white undertail coverts, white U-shaped rump band. Subspecies vary geographically in breast color, in general paler in eastern populations, darker in western; ranging from pale *B.c. canadensis* of the eastern seaboard to dark *occidentalis* of southern Alaska. Size decreases northward, with the smallest forms breeding on the high Arctic coastal tundra: pale-breasted *hutchinsii* in central and western Canada, and *minima,* smallest of all, in western Alaska. Endangered Aleutian subspecies, *leucopareia,* is distinguished from *minima* by slightly larger size, paler breast, and often a broad white neck ring; *minima* may show a very narrow ring. Canada Geese breed in open or forested areas near water. Flocks usually migrate in V-formation, stopping to feed in wetlands, grasslands, or cultivated fields. Call is a deep, musical *honk-a-lonk* in larger forms, a rapid, high cackle in smaller ones. Breeding programs have produced expanding populations south of mapped range and along Atlantic and Pacific coasts.

Brant *Branta bernicla* *L 25" (64 cm)*

A small, dark, stocky sea goose with black head, neck, and breast and whitish patch on either side of neck. Extensive white uppertail coverts almost conceal black tail. White undertail coverts conspicuous in flight. Wings comparatively long and pointed, wingbeat rapid. Immature birds show bold white edging to wing coverts and secondaries, and fainter neck patches than adults. Juveniles are brownish; usually lack neck patches entirely. In eastern subspecies, *B.b. hrota,* pale belly contrasts with black chest, and neck patches do not meet in front. Western *nigricans,* formerly the Black Brant, has dark belly, and neck patches meet in front. Primarily a sea goose; rare inland, but a few eastern birds are sighted during migrations through the Great Lakes region. Flocks fly low in ragged formation; feed on aquatic plants of shallow bays and estuaries. Call, a low, hoarse *cronk.* Locally common; both forms casual during migration and winter on opposite coasts; eastern *hrota* casual south of their mapped range. Regular at Salton Sea in spring and summer.

Barnacle Goose *Branta leucopsis* *L 27" (69 cm)*

Breeds in northeastern Greenland, accidental vagrant in Maritime Provinces. Distinctive head pattern: white or creamy face with black streak extending from bill to eye; rest of head, neck, and breast black. Bluish-gray upperparts, barred with black, and white U-shaped rump band. Silver gray wing linings show in flight. More of a land goose than the Brant, feeding in fields near the ocean. Fairly common in captivity. East coast sightings south of the Maritime Provinces and those in the interior are probably escaped birds.

Canada Goose

canadensis

occidentalis

leucopareia

minima

hutchinsii

hrota

Brant

nigricans

hrota immature

Barnacle Goose

Dabbling Ducks

The familiar "puddle ducks" of freshwater shallows and, chiefly in winter, salt marshes. Seldom diving, dabblers feed by tipping tail-up to reach aquatic plants, seeds, and snails. They require no running start to take off but spring directly into flight. In most species, a distinguishing swatch of bright color, the speculum, marks the trailing edge of the secondaries. Many species are known to hybridize.

Mallard *Anas platyrhynchos* L 23" (58 cm)
Male readily identified by metallic green head and neck, yellow bill, narrow white collar, chestnut breast. Black central tail feathers curl up. Both sexes have white tail, white underwings, bright blue speculum with both sides bordered in white (see page 93). Female's mottled plumage resembles other *Anas* species; look for orange bill marked with black. Juvenile and eclipse male resemble female but bill is dull olive. Abundant and widespread. Mallards in Mexico, formerly considered a separate species, Mexican Duck, are darker, lack distinctive male plumage; intergrades occur in southwestern U.S.

Mottled Duck *Anas fulvigula* L 22" (56 cm)
Both sexes resemble American Black Duck but body is paler, throat unstreaked; speculum green. Differs from female Mallard by darker plumage; greener speculum, bordered in black; and absence of white in tail or black on bill. Common year-round in coastal marshes. Begins pairing in January or February, much earlier than the migratory American Black Ducks and Mallards. Some authorities consider the Mottled Duck to be a subspecies of the Mallard.

American Black Duck *Anas rubripes* L 23" (58 cm)
Blackish-brown, paler on face and foreneck. In flight (page 92), white wing linings contrast more sharply with otherwise dark plumage than in similar female Mallard. Violet speculum is bordered in black, may show a thin white trailing edge. Male's bill is yellow; female's dull green, may be flecked with black. Nesting pairs favor woodland lakes and streams, freshwater or tidal marshes. Small introduced populations are now established in British Columbia and Washington. In many parts of range, especially deforested areas, Mallards are replacing American Black Ducks; Mallard-Black Duck hybrids are increasingly common.

Spot-billed Duck *Anas poecilorhyncha* L 22" (56 cm)
Asian species, casual vagrant on Aleutians and Kodiak Island. Dark bill's pale tip, visible at a great distance, sets this species apart from similar American Black Duck and female Mallard. The subspecies that has reached North America lacks the red spots at base of bill for which this duck is named.

eclipse ♂

Mallard

juvenile

♀

♂

Mottled Duck

"Mexican"-Mallard Intergrade

American Black-Mallard Hybrid

♂

American Black Duck

Spot-billed Duck

Gadwall *Anas strepera* L 20" (51 cm)

Male is mostly gray, with white belly, black tail coverts, pale chestnut on wings. Female's mottled brown plumage resembles female Mallard (preceding page), but belly is white, forehead steeper; upper mandible is gray with orange sides. Both sexes have white inner secondaries that show as small patch on swimming bird and identify the species in flight (page 93). Fairly common in the west, less common in the east. Widespread breeding range appears to be expanding eastward.

Falcated Teal *Anas falcata* L 19" (48 cm)

Asian species, rare visitor to the western Aleutians. Named for male's long, falcated—sickle-shaped—tertials that overhang tail. Both sexes are chunky, with large head. Female's all-dark bill distinguishes her from female wigeons (next page) and Gadwall. In flight (page 93), both sexes show a broad, dark speculum bordered in white. Birds sighted on U. S. west coast may be escapes from captivity rather than true vagrants.

Green-winged Teal *Anas crecca* L 14¹⁄₂" (37 cm)

Our smallest dabbler. Male's chestnut head has dark green ear patch outlined in white. Female distinguished from other female teals (see also page 74) by smaller bill and by largely white undertail coverts that contrast with mottled flanks. A fast-flying, agile duck. In flight (page 92), shows green speculum bordered in buff on leading edge, white on trailing edge. In the subspecies seen in most of North America, *A.c. carolinensis*, male has vertical white bar on side. Larger *nimia*, resident on Aleutians and probably on Pribilofs, lacks vertical bar but has white stripe along scapulars. Eurasian form, *crecca*, resembles *nimia* in pattern, *carolinensis* in size; rare visitor in Alaska and on east and west coasts. Eurasian *crecca* and *nimia* were formerly considered a separate species, Common Teal.

Baikal Teal *Anas formosa* L 17" (43 cm)

Asian species, a casual vagrant in Alaska and in west coast states. Accidental elsewhere; birds seen may be escapes from captivity rather than true vagrants. Adult male's intricately patterned head is distinctive. Long, drooping dark gray scapulars are edged in rufous and white. Gray sides are set off front and rear by vertical white bars. Female similar to female Green-winged Teal; note white spot outlined in dark brown at base of bill; second white area below eye. On a few females, face has bridle marking. In flight (page 92), Baikal Teal's underwing shows less extensive white than in Green-winged Teal. Green speculum has a bold cinnamon buff inner border.

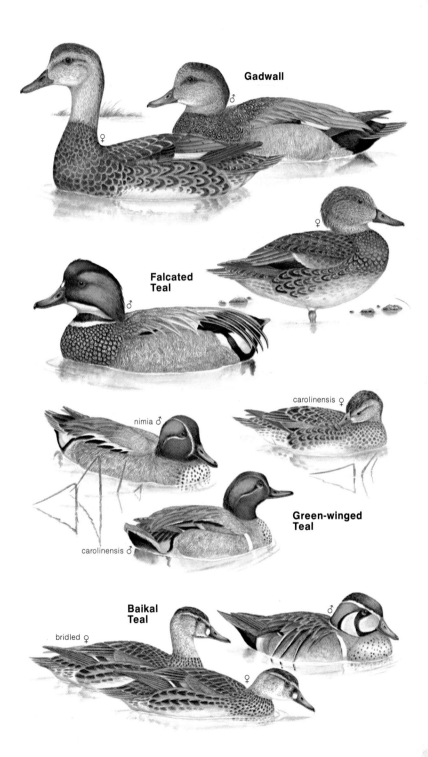

Gadwall

♀

♂

Falcated Teal

♀

♂

nimia ♂

carolinensis ♀

carolinensis ♂

Green-winged Teal

Baikal Teal

bridled ♀

♂

♀

American Wigeon *Anas americana* L 19″ (48 cm)
Male's white forehead and cap are conspicuous in mixed flocks foraging in fields, marshes, and shallow waters. In flight (page 92), identified by white axillaries and large white patches on upperwing. Female lacks white on head, closely resembles gray-phase female Eurasian Wigeon; white axillaries are the best distinguishing field mark. Wing patches are grayish on adult female and immatures. Common. A recently established breeder on the east coast; casual during winter north to the Aleutians and the Great Lakes.

Eurasian Wigeon *Anas penelope* L 20″ (51 cm)
Dark head and pale sides make males conspicuous in flocks of American Wigeons. Adult male has reddish-brown head and neck with creamy forehead and cap. Many fall males retain some brown eclipse feathers but show distinctive reddish head. Immature male begins to acquire adult head and breast color but retains some brown juvenile plumage. In flight (page 92), Eurasian Wigeon's large white upperwing patches are like American Wigeon, but axillaries are grayish, not white. Gray-phase female closely resembles female American Wigeon; look for gray axillaries. Rufous phase has reddish head. The Eurasian Wigeon is a regular winter visitor along both coasts, more common in the west; casual inland. Regular migrant and winter visitor on western and central Aleutians.

Northern Pintail *Anas acuta* ♂ L 26″ (66 cm) ♀ L 20″ (51 cm)
Male's chocolate brown head tops long, slender white neck, the white extending in a thin line onto head. Black central tail feathers extend far beyond rest of long, wedge-shaped tail. Female is mottled brown, paler on head and neck; bill uniformly grayish. In both sexes, flight profile (page 92) shows long neck; slender body; long, pointed wings; dark speculum bordered in white on trailing edge. In flight, female's mottled brown wing linings contrast with white belly; tail long and wedge-shaped but lacks male's extended feathers. An abundant and widespread duck, common in marshes and open areas with ponds, lakes; in winter often feeds in grainfields. Much more common in west than in east. Casual in winter north to the Aleutians and the Great Lakes.

White-cheeked Pintail *Anas bahamensis* L 17″ (43 cm)
Casual vagrant from the West Indies to southern Florida; accidental elsewhere along the Gulf coast. White cheeks and throat contrast with dark forehead and cap; blue bill has red spot near base. Long, pointed tail is buffy; tawny or reddish underparts are heavily spotted. Female is paler than male; tail slightly shorter. In flight, both sexes reveal green speculum broadly bordered on each side with buff. Sightings of this species other than in Florida and along Gulf coast are probably birds escaped from captivity.

American Wigeon

♂

eclipse ♂

♀

rufous phase ♀

gray phase ♀

♂

Eurasian Wigeon

immature ♂

♀

♂

Northern Pintail

♂

White-cheeked Pintail

Northern Shoveler *Anas clypeata* L 19" (48 cm)

Large, spatulate bill, longer than head, identifies both sexes. Male distinguished by green head, white breast, brown sides. Most immature males have a white crescent on each side of face, like Blue-winged Teal. Female's grayish bill is tinged with orange on cutting edges and lower mandible. In flight (page 93), both sexes show blue forewing patch. Common in the west; increasing in the east. Found in marshes and on ponds, bays.

Blue-winged Teal *Anas discors* L 15½" (39 cm)

Lead gray head with white crescent on each side identifies male. Female distinguished from female Green-winged Teal (page 70) by larger bill, more heavily spotted undertail coverts, yellowish legs. In comparison with female Cinnamon Teal, look for Bluewing's grayer plumage, bolder facial markings, and smaller bill. Male in eclipse plumage resembles female. In flight (page 93), in both sexes, wing patterns match those of Cinnamon Teal. Blue-winged Teal is fairly common in marshes and on ponds and lakes in open country. Uncommon on the west coast.

Garganey *Anas querquedula* L 15½" (39 cm)

Old World species, regular migrant on western Aleutians; very rare elsewhere along west and east coasts; accidental in midwest. Male's bold white eyebrows separate dark crown, red-brown face. In flight (page 93), shows gray-blue forewing and green speculum bordered fore and aft with white. Wing pattern is retained when male acquires female-like eclipse plumage, held well into fall. Female has strong facial pattern: dark crown, pale eyebrow, dark eye line, white lore spot bordered by a second dark line; note also dark bill and legs, dark undertail coverts. Larger and paler overall than female Green-winged Teal (page 70). Female in flight (page 93) shows gray-brown forewing, dark green speculum bordered in white. Note also pale gray inner webs of primaries, visible from above.

Cinnamon Teal *Anas cyanoptera* L 16" (41 cm)

Cinnamon head, neck, and underparts identify male. Female closely resembles female Blue-winged Teal but plumage is a richer brown, lore spot and eye line less distinct, bill longer and more spatulate. Compare also with Green-winged Teal (page 70). Young birds and males in eclipse resemble female. Males more than eight weeks old have red-orange eyes; Blue-winged Teal's eyes are dark. Wing pattern (page 93) is almost identical to Blue-winged Teal. Common in marshes, ponds, lakes. Casual east of mapped range; some sightings may be escaped birds. Cinnamon Teal is known to interbreed with Blue-winged Teal.

Northern Shoveler

immature ♂

♀

♂

Blue-winged Teal

♀

♂

Garganey

♀

♂

fall ♂

Cinnamon Teal

♂

♀

Stiff-tailed Ducks

Long, stiff tail feathers serve as a rudder. When alarmed, these ducks tend to dive rather than fly. In both species, male's bill is blue in breeding season.

Ruddy Duck *Oxyura jamaicensis* *L 15" (38 cm)*
Chunky, thick-necked duck with large head, broad bill, long tail, often cocked up. Male's white cheeks are conspicuous both in breeding plumage, generally held April to August, and in dull winter plumage. In female, single dark line crosses cheek. Young resemble female through first winter. Common; nests in dense vegetation of freshwater marshes, lakes, ponds. During migration and winter, found on large lakes, shallow bays, salt marshes. Shown in flight on page 92.

Masked Duck *Oxyura dominica* *L 13¹⁄₂" (34 cm)*
Tropical species, rare visitor to southern Texas and along Gulf coast to Florida. Accidental along Atlantic coast to Pennsylvania. Male's black face on reddish-brown head is distinctive. In female, winter male, and juvenile, two dark stripes cross face. Secretive; found on small, densely vegetated ponds. Unlike Ruddy Duck, Masked Duck launches vertically into flight without a running start. In all plumages, white wing patches are conspicuous in flight (page 93).

Whistling-Ducks

Named for their whistling calls, these gooselike ducks have long legs, long necks. Wingbeats are slower than ducks, faster than geese. Formerly called Tree Ducks.

Fulvous Whistling-Duck *Dendrocygna bicolor*
L 20" (51 cm) Overall a rich tawny color; back darker, edged with tawny. Dark stripe along hindneck is continuous in female, usually broken in male. Bill and legs dark. Whitish rump band conspicuous in flight. Distinctive call, a loud, squealing *pe-chee*. Forages in rice fields, marshes, shallow waters; sometimes dives to feed. More active at night than day. Irregular wanderer in any season north to dashed line on map; casual farther north. Declining in the west. Formerly called Fulvous Tree Duck, this species seldom perches in trees.

Black-bellied Whistling-Duck
Dendrocygna autumnalis *L 21" (53 cm)* Gray face with white eye ring, red bill. Legs red or pink; belly, rump, and tail black. Lacks the whitish rump band of Fulvous Whistling-Duck. White wing patch shows as broad white stripe in flight. Juvenile is paler, with gray bill. Call is a high-pitched, four-note whistle. Inhabits woodland streams, ponds, marshes; nests in trees. Casual west to southeastern California, east to Louisiana. Formerly called Black-bellied Tree Duck.

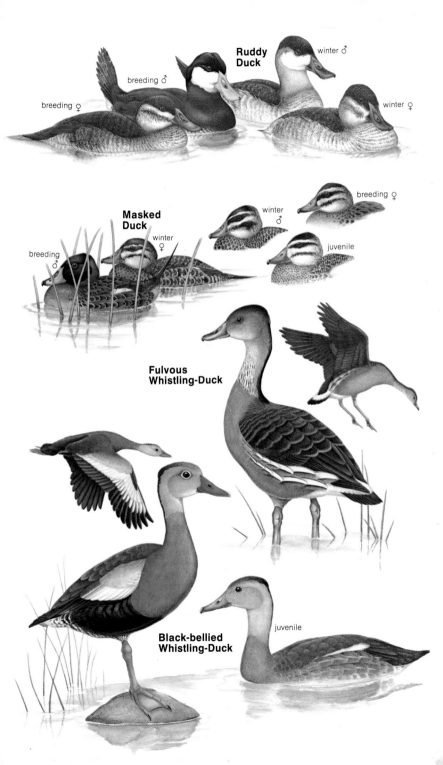

Ruddy Duck

breeding ♀

breeding ♂

winter ♂

winter ♀

Masked Duck

breeding ♂

winter ♀

winter ♂

breeding ♀

juvenile

Fulvous Whistling-Duck

Black-bellied Whistling-Duck

juvenile

Perching Ducks

These woodland ducks, equipped with sharp claws, sometimes perch on snags, stumps, or branches. Nests are made in tree cavities or nest boxes.

Wood Duck *Aix sponsa* L 18½" (47 cm)

Male's glossy, colorful plumage and sleek crest are distinctive. Head pattern and bill colors are retained in drab eclipse plumage. Female identified by short crest and large, white, teardrop-shaped eye patch; compare with female Mandarin Duck (page 90). Juvenile resembles female but is spotted below. In all plumages, flight profile (page 92) is distinctive: large head with bill angled downward; long, squared-off tail. Female's squealing flight call is also distinctive: a loud, rising *oo-eek*. Fairly common in open woodlands near ponds or rivers. Casual during winter throughout most of breeding range, especially in mild winters.

Pochards

Diving ducks, with legs set far back and far apart—which makes walking awkward. Heavy bodies require a running start on water for take-off.

Canvasback *Aythya valisineria* L 21" (53 cm)

Forehead slopes to long, black bill. Male's head and neck are chestnut, back and sides whitish. Female and eclipse male have pale brown head and neck, pale brownish-gray back and sides. In flight (page 94), whitish belly contrasts with dark breast, dark undertail coverts. Wings lack the contrasting pale stripe of Common Pochard and Redhead. Locally common on open lakes, marshes; feeds in large flocks. Migrating flocks fly in irregular V's or in lines.

Common Pochard *Aythya ferina* L 18" (46 cm)

Eurasian species, rare migrant to Pribilofs and to western and central Aleutians. Resembles Canvasback in plumage and head shape. Bill similar to Redhead's but dark at base and tip, gray in center. In flight (page 94), wings show gray stripe along trailing edge.

Redhead *Aythya americana* L 19" (48 cm)

Rounded head and shorter, tricolored bill separate this species from Canvasback. Bill is mostly pale blue or slate, with narrow white ring bordering black tip. Male's back and sides are smoky gray. Female and eclipse male are brown, with darker crown, pale patch bordering black bill tip; compare female scaups (next page). Redheads in flight (page 94) show gray stripe on trailing edge of wings. Locally common in marshes, ponds, lakes. May be expanding breeding range eastward.

Wood Duck

juvenile ♂

♂

♀

Canvasback

♀

♂

Common Pochard

♂

♀

Redhead

♀

♂

Ring-necked Duck *Aythya collaris* L 17" *(43 cm)*

Peaked head; bold white ring near tip of bill. Male has second white ring at base of bill; white crescent separates black breast from gray sides. Cinnamon collar is very hard to see in the field. Female has dark crown, white eye ring; may have a pale line extending back from eye; face is mottled with white. In flight (page 94), all plumages show a gray stripe on secondaries. Fairly common in freshwater marshes and on woodland ponds, small lakes; during winter, found also in southern coastal marshes. Range is variable; may breed south or winter north of mapped range. Rare but regular breeder in Alaska.

Tufted Duck *Aythya fuligula* L 17" *(43 cm)*

Old World species; regular visitor to western Alaska. Rare winter visitor along east coast as far south as Maryland, and on west coast to southern California. Head is rounded; crest distinct in male, smaller in female and immatures; may be absent in eclipse male. Gleaming white sides further distinguish male from male Ring-necked Duck. First-winter male has gray sides but lacks the white crescents conspicuous in male Ring-neck. Female is blackish-brown above; lacks white eye ring and white bill ring of female Ringneck. Some females have a small white area at base of bill. In flight (page 94), all plumages show a broad white stripe on secondaries and extending onto primaries. Found on ponds, rivers, bays, often with Ringnecks and Scaups.

Greater Scaup *Aythya marila* L 18" *(46 cm)*

Larger size and smoothly rounded head help distinguish this species from Lesser Scaup. In close view, note Greater Scaup's slightly larger bill with wider black tip. In good light, male's head may show a green gloss. In both species, female has bold white patch at base of bill. Some female Greater Scaups, especially in spring and summer, have a paler head with a distinct whitish ear patch. In flight (page 94), Greater Scaup shows a bold white stripe on secondaries and well out onto primaries, unlike Lesser Scaup. Locally common; found on large, open lakes, bays. Breeds irregularly as far south as Michigan and Nova Scotia. Migrates and winters in small or large flocks, often with Lesser Scaups. Rare but regular winter visitor throughout the Gulf states.

Lesser Scaup *Aythya affinis* L 16½" *(42 cm)*

Smaller size and peaked crown distinctive from Greater Scaup. In close view, note Lesser Scaup's slightly smaller bill with smaller black tip. In good light, male's head may show a purple gloss, sometimes mixed with green. Female is brown overall, with bold white patch at base of bill. In some females, especially in spring and summer, head is paler, with whitish ear patch less distinct than in female Greater Scaup. In flight (page 94), Lesser Scaup shows bold white stripe on secondaries only. Common; breeds in marshes, small lakes, ponds. In winter, found in large flocks on sheltered bays, inlets, lakes.

Ring-necked Duck

♂ ♀

1st winter ♂

Tufted Duck

♂ ♀

Greater Scaup

1st winter ♂ ♂ ♀

Lesser Scaup

♂ ♀

Eiders

Large, bulky diving ducks with dense down feathers that help insulate them from the cold northern seas. Females pluck their own down to line nests.

Common Eider *Somateria mollissima* L 24" (61 cm)

Female distinguished from female King Eider by larger size, sloping forehead, and evenly barred sides and scapulars. Feathering extends along sides of bill to or beyond nostril, with minimal feathering on top of bill. Females range in overall color from rust to gray. Eastern *S.m. dresseri* is reddish-brown. Western *v-nigra* is duller brown; eclipse plumage paler. Male's head pattern is distinctive. Most western and a few eastern males show a thin black V on throat; *v-nigra* male has orange-yellow bill. Eclipse and first-winter males resemble female, except that first-winter has white on breast; full adult plumage is attained by fourth winter. In flight (page 94), adult male shows white back with black tail, black primaries and secondaries. Locally abundant on shallow bays, rocky shores; casual on the Great Lakes. Winters casually on the east coast as far south as Virginia.

King Eider *Somateria spectabilis* L 22" (56 cm)

Female distinguished from female Common Eider by smaller size, more rounded head, and crescent or V-shaped markings on sides and scapulars. Feathering extends only slightly along sides of bill but extensively down the top, making bill look stubby. Male's head pattern is distinctive. In flight (page 95), shows black back, black wings with white patches. First-winter male has brown head, pinkish or buffy bill, buffy eye line; lacks white wing patches. Full adult plumage is attained by fourth winter. A common species on tundra and coastal waters in northern part of range; very rare on the Great Lakes. Winters casually on west coast and on east coast to Virginia.

Spectacled Eider *Somateria fischeri* L 21" (53 cm)

Male has green head with white, black-bordered eye patches and orange bill. In flight (page 95), black breast distinguishes adult male from other eiders. Drab female has less distinct spectacle pattern; bill is gray-blue; feathering extends far down upper mandible. Uncommon; found on coastal tundra, usually near lakes and ponds. Winter range poorly known.

Steller's Eider *Polysticta stelleri* L 17" (43 cm)

Greenish head tufts, black eye patch, chin, and collar identify male. Female is dark cinnamon brown with distinct pale eye ring, unfeathered dark bill. In flight (page 95), adults, immature males, and some immature females show blue speculum bordered fore and aft in white. Found along rocky coasts; nests on inland grassy areas or tundra. Winters casually south to northern California coast.

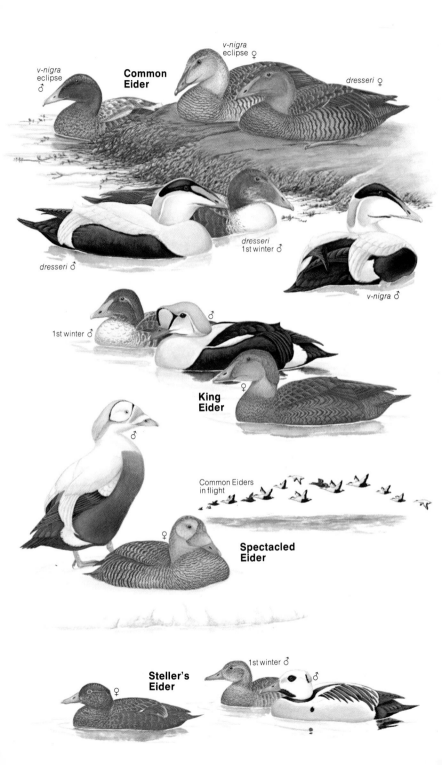

v-nigra
eclipse
♂

**Common
Eider**

v-nigra
eclipse ♀

dresseri ♀

dresseri ♂

dresseri
1st winter ♂

v-nigra ♂

1st winter ♂

♂

**King
Eider**

♀

♂

Common Eiders
in flight

**Spectacled
Eider**

♀

**Steller's
Eider**

1st winter ♂

♀

♂

Sea Ducks

Stocky, short-necked diving ducks. Most species breed in the far north and migrate in large, compact flocks to and from their coastal wintering grounds.

Black Scoter *Melanitta nigra* L 19" (48 cm)
Male is black overall, with orange-yellow knob at base of dark bill. Female's dark crown and nape contrast with pale face and throat; feathering does not extend onto bill. In both sexes, forehead is strongly rounded; feet and legs are dark. In flight (page 95), blackish wing linings contrast with paler flight feathers. Immatures resemble females but are whitish below; immature male has yellow at base of bill. Fairly common; nests along tundra and woodland rivers, lakes, ponds. Casual inland migrant. Winters on coastal waters.

White-winged Scoter *Melanitta fusca* L 21" (53 cm)
White secondaries, conspicuous in flight (page 94), may show as a small white patch on swimming bird. Forehead slightly rounded. Feathering extends almost to nostrils on top and sides of bill. Female and immatures lack contrasting dark crown and paler face of other scoters; white facial patches are distinct on immatures, often indistinct on adult female. Immatures are whitish below. Adult male has black knob at base of colorful bill; white crescent-shaped patch below white eye. Fairly common on inland lakes and rivers in breeding season, coastal areas in winter. Uncommon inland migrant. Small numbers winter on the Great Lakes each year.

Surf Scoter *Melanitta perspicillata* L 20" (51 cm)
Male's black plumage sets off colorful bill, white eye, white patch on forehead and nape. In all birds, note that forehead is sloping, not rounded. Female is brown, with dark crown; usually has two white patches on each side of face; feathering extends down top of bill only, unlike White-winged Scoter. Adult female and first-winter male may have whitish nape patch. All immatures are whitish below, usually have white face patches. In flight (page 94), more uniform color of underwings helps distinguish Surf from Black Scoter; note also orangish legs and feet. Common; nests on tundra and in wooded areas near water. Casual inland migrant. Winters on coastal waters.

Harlequin Duck *Histrionicus histrionicus* L 16½" (42 cm)
A small duck, with steep forehead, rounded head, stubby bill. Male's colorful plumage appears dark at a distance. Female has three white spots on each side of head; belly is pale. Juveniles resemble adult female; young male begins to acquire some adult plumage by late fall. Locally common along rocky coasts; moves inland along swift streams for nesting. Flight is rapid, low. Compare female in flight (page 95) with female Bufflehead. Male's call is a high-pitched nasal squeaking.

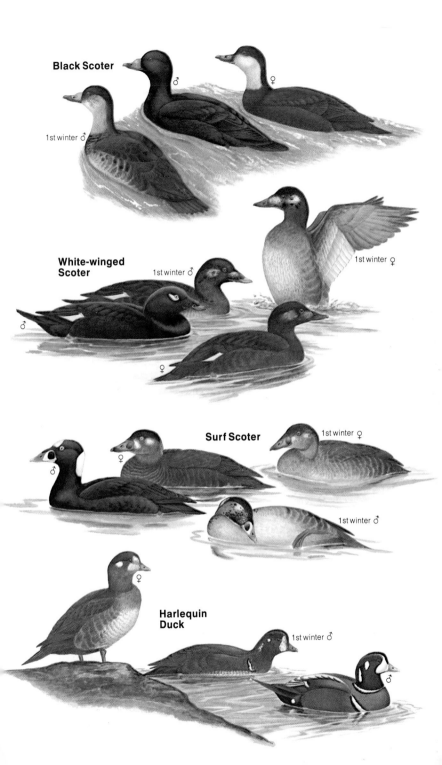

Black Scoter

1st winter ♂

♂

♀

White-winged Scoter

1st winter ♂

1st winter ♀

♂

♀

Surf Scoter

1st winter ♀

♂

♀

1st winter ♂

Harlequin Duck

♀

1st winter ♂

♂

Oldsquaw *Clangula hyemalis* ♂ *L 22" (56 cm)* ♀ *16" (41 cm)*
Male's long tail is conspicuous in flight, may be submerged in swimming bird. Male in winter and spring is largely white; breast and back dark brown, scapulars pearl gray; stubby bill shows pink band. In partial eclipse plumage, acquired in late spring, male becomes mostly dark, with pale facial patch, bi-colored scapulars. Molt into full eclipse plumage continues until early fall. Female lacks long tail; bill is dark; plumage whiter overall in winter, darker in summer. First-fall birds (see page 95) are even darker. Common, active, and noisy, Old-squaws are identifiable at some distance by their swift, careening flight and loud, yodeling, three-part calls. Both sexes show uniformly dark underwings.

Barrow's Goldeneye *Bucephala islandica* *L 18" (46 cm)*
Male has white crescent on each side of face; white patches on scapulars show on swimming bird as a row of spots; dark color of back extends forward in a bar partially separating white breast from white sides. Female and male in eclipse plumage closely resemble the Common Goldeneye. Puffy, oval-shaped head, steep forehead, and stubby triangular bill help identify Barrow's. Adult female's head is slightly darker than female Common; bill mostly yellow, except in eastern birds and young females, which may have only a yellow band near tip of bill. In all plumages, white wing patches visible in flight (page 95) differ subtly between the two species. Both summer on open lakes and small ponds, often near woodlands where nest holes are available; winter in sheltered coastal areas, inland lakes and rivers. Barrow's is much less common.

Common Goldeneye *Bucephala clangula* *L 18¹/₂" (47 cm)*
Male has round white spot on each side of face; scapulars are mostly white. Female and eclipse male closely resemble Barrow's Goldeneye. Head of Common Goldeneye is more triangular; forehead more rounded; bill longer. Female's head is slightly paler than female Barrow's; bill generally all-dark or with yellow near tip only; rarely all-yellow. In all plumages, white wing patches visible in flight (page 95) differ subtly between the two species. Both species summer on open lakes, often near woodlands where nest holes are available; winter in sheltered coastal areas, inland lakes and rivers.

Bufflehead *Bucephala albeola* *L 13¹/₂" (34 cm)*
A small duck with a large, puffy head, steep forehead, short bill. Male is glossy black above, white below, with large white patch on head. Female is duller, with small, elongated white patch on each side of head. Young male and male in eclipse re-semble female. In flight (page 95), males show white patch across entire wing; female has white patch only on inner sec-ondaries. Fairly common, Buffleheads nest in woodlands near small lakes, ponds. During migration and winter, found also on sheltered bays, rivers, lakes.

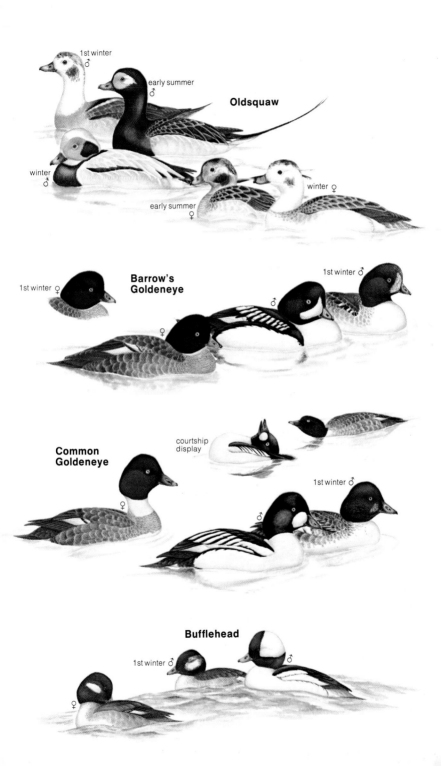

1st winter ♂

early summer ♂

Oldsquaw

winter ♂

early summer ♀

winter ♀

1st winter ♀

**Barrow's
Goldeneye**

1st winter ♂

♀

♂

**Common
Goldeneye**

courtship
display

♀

1st winter ♂

♂

Bufflehead

1st winter ♂

♂

♀

Mergansers

Long, thin, serrated bills help these divers catch fish, crustaceans, and aquatic insects. Mergansers in flight show pointed wings and a distinctive profile: head looks like a bump between long neck and bill.

Common Merganser *Mergus merganser* L 25" (64 cm)

Large duck with long, slim neck and thin, hooked, red bill. White breast and sides and lack of crest distinguish male from Red-breasted Merganser. Female's bright chestnut, crested head and neck contrast sharply with white chin, white breast. Adult male in flight (page 94) shows white patch on upper surface of entire inner wing, partially crossed by a single black bar. Eclipse male resembles female but retains wing pattern. Female has white inner secondaries, partially crossed by black bar. As in all species on this page, young male resembles adult female; begins molt to adult plumage in first spring. Common Mergansers nest in crevices in woodlands near lakes and rivers; in winter, sometimes also found on brackish water.

Red-breasted Merganser *Mergus serrator* L 23" (58 cm)

Shaggy double crest, white collar, and streaked breast distinguish male from male Common Merganser. Female's head and neck are paler than in female Common; chin and foreneck are white. Adult male in flight (page 94) shows white patch on upper surface of entire inner wing, partially crossed by two black bars. Eclipse male resembles female but retains male wing pattern. Female's white inner secondaries are crossed by a single black bar. Red-breasted Mergansers nest in woodlands near lakes and rivers or in sheltered coastal areas. Much more likely to be found on brackish or salt water in winter than is Common Merganser. Smaller size helps distinguish Red-breasteds in mixed flocks.

Hooded Merganser *Lophodytes cucullatus* L 18" (46 cm)

Puffy, rounded crest; thin bill. Male's bill is dark; white head patches are fan-shaped and conspicuous when crest is raised. Compare with male Bufflehead (preceding page). Female brownish overall; upper mandible dark, lower mandible yellowish. In flight (page 95) both sexes show black-and-white inner secondaries. Crest is flattened in flight; male's head patch shows only as a white line. Uncommon. In breeding season, found on woodland ponds, rivers, sheltered backwaters; less often on large lakes. Winters chiefly on fresh water.

Smew *Mergellus albellus* L 16" (41 cm)

Eurasian species, rare visitor on Aleutians; accidental elsewhere on the west and east coasts and the Great Lakes. Bill is dark and relatively short. In female, white throat and lower face contrast sharply with reddish head and nape. Adult male is white with black markings; black-and-white wings are conspicuous in flight (page 95).

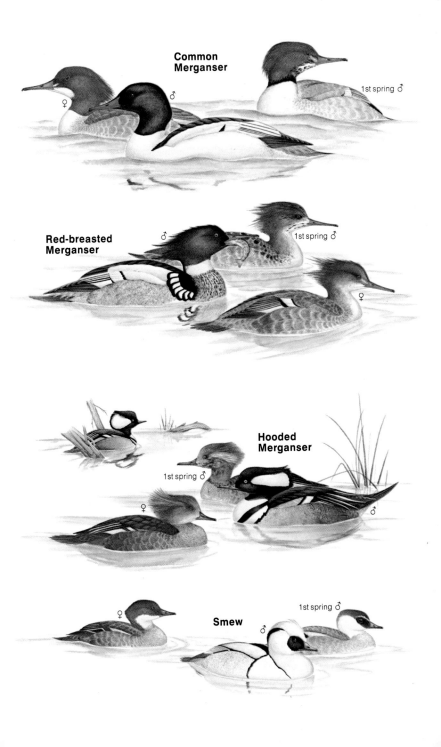

Common Merganser

♀

♂

1st spring ♂

Red-breasted Merganser

♂

1st spring ♂

♀

Hooded Merganser

1st spring ♂

♀

♂

♀

Smew

1st spring ♂

♂

Exotic Waterfowl

Many waterfowl species are brought into North America from other continents for zoos, farms, parks, and private collections. These birds occasionally escape from captivity. The species shown here are among those most often seen; none has become established in the wild.

Black Swan *Cygnus atratus* L 60" (152 cm)
The dark beauty of this Australian species makes it a popular addition to parks, zoos, and estates, primarily on the east coast. Also popular is the South American **Black-necked Swan,** *C. melancoryphus,* with a white body, black head and neck.

Red-breasted Goose *Branta ruficollis* L 22" (56 cm)
Popular in private collections, chiefly on the east and west coasts. Breeds in northwestern Siberia.

Greylag Goose *Anser anser* L 34" (86 cm)
Eurasian species, progenitor of most domestic geese. May be confused with immature Greater White-fronted Goose or Bean Goose (page 62).

Bar-headed Goose *Anser indicus* L 30" (76 cm)
Asian species, fairly common in zoos and private waterfowl collections across the continent.

Muscovy Duck *Cairina moschata* L 28" (71 cm)
This common domestic duck varies from glossy purplish to black-and-white to all-white. Recent sightings along the lower Rio Grande are believed to be wild birds from Mexico.

Chinese Goose *Anser cygnoides* L 45" (114 cm)
Asian species, domesticated in many variations. Wild form is slimmer, has long, swanlike bill lacking knob at base. Also called Swan Goose.

Domestic Goose *Anser "domesticus"* L 22-45" (56-114 cm)
Common on farms. Individuals sometimes desert the barnyard to join a flock of wild geese or ducks.

Northern Shelduck *Tadorna tadorna* L 25" (64 cm)
Eurasian species, common in North American zoos and private collections. Female is smaller, lacks knob on bill. Also called Shelduck or Common Shelduck.

Ruddy Shelduck *Tadorna ferruginea* L 26" (66 cm)
Afro-Eurasian species, common in zoos and private collections. Compare with Fulvous Whistling-Duck (page 76).

Mandarin Duck *Aix galericulata* L 18" (46 cm)
Asian species, common in zoos and private collections. Female closely resembles female Wood Duck (page 78).

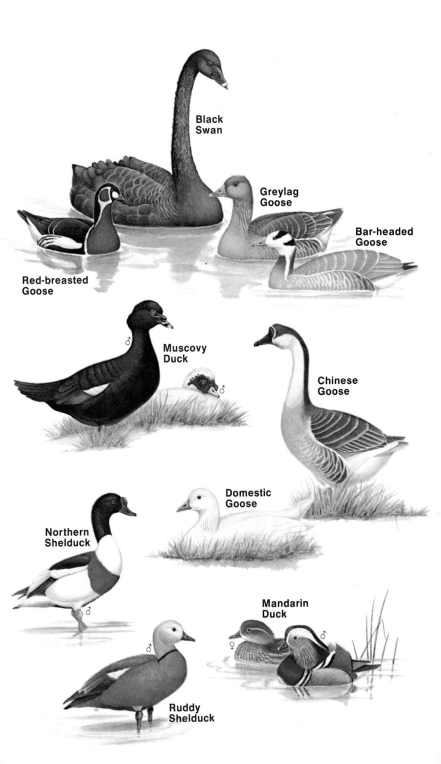

Black Swan

Greylag Goose

Bar-headed Goose

Red-breasted Goose

Muscovy Duck ♂ ♂

Chinese Goose

Domestic Goose

Northern Shelduck ♂

Mandarin Duck ♀ ♂

Ruddy Shelduck ♂

Ducks in Flight

Northern Pintail ♂

American Black Duck ♂

♀

Eurasian Wigeon ♂

American Wigeon ♂

♀

gray phase ♀

Baikal Teal ♂

♀

Wood Duck ♂

♀

carolinensis ♂

Green-winged Teal

Ruddy Duck ♂

♀

carolinensis ♀

Mallard

Gadwall ♂ ♀

Northern Shoveler ♂ ♀

Falcated Teal ♂ ♀

Cinnamon Teal ♂

Blue-winged Teal ♂ ♀

Garganey ♂ ♀ immature ♂

Masked Duck ♂ ♀

Ducks in Flight

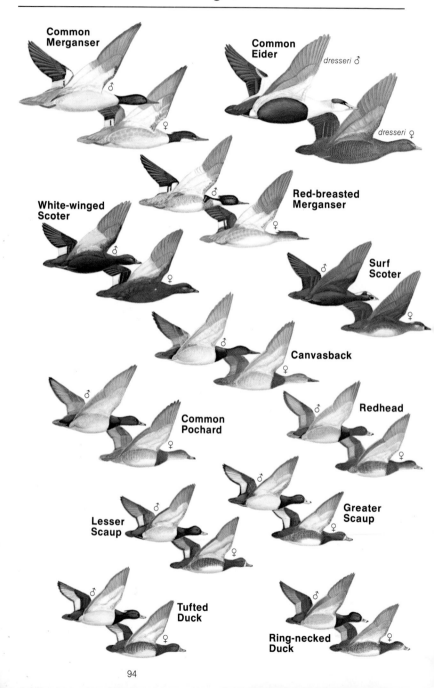

Common Merganser ♂

Common Eider ♀

dresseri ♂

dresseri ♀

Red-breasted Merganser ♂ ♀

White-winged Scoter ♂ ♀

Surf Scoter ♂ ♀

Canvasback ♂ ♀

Common Pochard ♂ ♀

Redhead ♂ ♀

Lesser Scaup ♂ ♀

Greater Scaup ♂ ♀

Tufted Duck ♂ ♀

Ring-necked Duck ♂ ♀

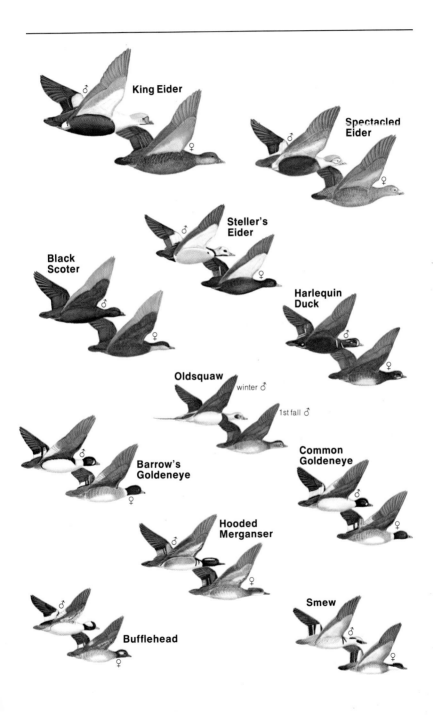

King Eider ♂ ♀

Spectacled Eider ♂ ♀

Steller's Eider ♂ ♀

Black Scoter ♂ ♀

Harlequin Duck ♂ ♀

Oldsquaw winter ♂ 1st fall ♂

Barrow's Goldeneye ♂ ♀

Common Goldeneye ♂ ♀

Hooded Merganser ♂ ♀

Bufflehead ♂ ♀

Smew ♂ ♀

Limpkin (Family Aramidae)

Large, long-necked wading bird, named for its unusual limping gait. Once nearly extirpated by hunters, this bird is again common in southern swamps, marshes.

Limpkin *Aramus guarauna* L 26" (66 cm)

Chocolate brown overall, densely streaked with white above. Long bill, slightly downcurved. Long legs and large, webless feet are dull grayish-green. Juvenile is paler than adult. Locally common in swamps and wetlands, where it wades or swims in search of snails, frogs, insects. Call, heard chiefly at night, is a wailing *krr-oww*. Accidental north to Maryland.

Rails, Gallinules, Coots (Family Rallidae)

Marsh birds with short tails and short, rounded wings. Most species are local and secretive. Some, especially the rails, are identified chiefly by call and habitat.

King Rail *Rallus elegans* L 15" (38 cm)

Large freshwater rail with long, slightly downcurved bill. Much larger than similar Virginia Rail (next page). Adult distinguished from Clapper Rail by tawny edges on black-centered back feathers, tawny wing coverts. Head slate, with brown or grayish cheeks, buffy eyebrow; underparts cinnamon; flanks strongly barred black-and-white. Juvenile is darker above, paler below. Common in freshwater and brackish swamps and marshes but hard to see. Most often heard at dusk and dawn. Some birds winter in coastal marshes with Clapper Rails. Hybridizes with Clapper Rail in narrow zone of overlap; some authorities consider them to be one species. Some calls of the two are identical. Usually distinctive King Rail call is a series of fewer than ten *kek kek kek* notes, fairly evenly spaced.

Clapper Rail *Rallus longirostris* L 14¹/₂" (37 cm)

Much larger than Virginia Rail (next page). Usually duller than King Rail. Plumage variable but always has grayish edges on brown-centered back feathers, olive wing coverts. East coast forms such as *R.l. crepitans* are buffy below; cheeks are gray; flanks less strongly barred than in King Rail. Gulf coast forms such as *scottii* are brighter cinnamon below. West coast forms such as *levipes* and the inland *yumanensis* are brighter below than east coast birds; cheeks brownish-gray. A common rail of coastal salt marshes; also found along lower Colorado River and at Salton Sea. Distinctive call is a series of ten or more dry *kek kek kek* notes, accelerating and then slowing. More often heard than seen, Clappers call chiefly at dusk and dawn.

Limpkin

juvenile

**King
Rail**

crepitans

yumanensis

scottii

levipes

**Clapper
Rail**

Virginia Rail *Rallus limicola* L 9½" (24 cm)

Similar to King Rail (preceding page) but smaller; cheeks grayer; wings richer chestnut; legs and bill often redder. Juvenile is blackish-brown above, mottled black or gray below. Common but secretive; found in freshwater and brackish marshes and wetlands; also in coastal salt marshes. Some calls resemble those of King and Clapper Rails. Distinctive call is a series of *kid kid kidick kidick* phrases, heard chiefly in breeding season. Also gives a descending series of *oink* notes.

Sora *Porzana carolina* L 8¾" (22 cm)

Short, thick bill, yellow or greenish-yellow. Breeding adult is coarsely streaked above. Face and center of throat and breast are black. In winter plumage, black throat is somewhat obscured by gray edgings. Juvenile lacks black on face and throat; underparts are paler. Compare with Yellow Rail; juvenile Sora is not as black above; upperparts are streaked, not barred, with white. Common in freshwater and brackish marshes, rice fields, grainfields. Also found in saltwater marshes during migration and winter. Calls include a plaintive *ker-wee*, heard chiefly in breeding season, and a descending whinny. Common winter call is a descending *wee-er*.

Yellow Rail *Coturnicops noveboracensis* L 7¼" (18 cm)

A small, dark rail, deep tawny-yellow above with wide dark stripes crossed by white bars. In flight, shows a large white patch on trailing edges of wings. Bill is comparatively short and thick; color varies from yellowish to greenish-gray. Juvenile is darker than adult. Uncommon and local; extremely secretive. Breeds in grassy marshes, boggy swales, damp fields; not found in deepwater marshes or swamps. Winters in fresh, brackish, or salt marshes, rice fields, dry fields. Distinctive call, heard chiefly in breeding season, is a four- or five-note *tick-tick, tick-tick-tick,* given in alternate twos or twos and threes, like the sound made by tapping two pebbles together.

Black Rail *Laterallus jamaicensis* L 6" (15 cm)

A very small, extremely secretive rail. Blackish above, with white speckling; chestnut nape. Bill short and black. Underparts grayish-black, with narrow white barring on flanks. Uncommon and local; inhabits marshes, swamps, wet meadows. Distinctive call, heard chiefly in breeding season, is a repeated *kik-kee-do* or *kik-kee-derr*. Most vocal in the middle of the night, unlike other rails.

Corn Crake *Crex crex* L 10½" (27 cm)

European species, formerly a very rare vagrant along the east coast in fall but not seen in recent years. European populations are seriously declining. A rail of damp, grassy fields, croplands; not found in marshes. Dull buffy-yellow overall, with short, thick, brownish bill; distinctive large chestnut wing patch.

Virginia Rail

juvenile

Sora

winter ♀

juvenile

breeding ♂

juvenile

Yellow Rail

Black Rail

Corn Crake

Purple Gallinule *Porphyrula martinica* L 13″ (33 cm)

Bright purplish-blue head, neck, and underparts, with pale blue forehead shield, red-and-yellow bill. Back is brownish-green, legs and feet yellow. Juvenile is buffy-brown overall, with brownish-olive back, greenish wings; forehead dark brown, bill mostly dark olive, legs and feet dull olive. Molts into winter plumage after fall migration but may retain traces of juvenile plumage into first spring. In all ages, all-white under-tail coverts are conspicuous. Fairly common in overgrown swamps, lagoons, marshes. Highly migratory; winters from southern Florida to Argentina. Wanderers are seen in all seasons far north of mapped range; frequently breeds north of area shown, occasionally far north.

Common Moorhen *Gallinula chloropus* L 14″ (36 cm)

Black head and neck, with red forehead shield, red bill with yellow tip. Back brownish-olive; underparts slate; white streaking on flanks shows as a thin white line. Outer undertail coverts white, inner ones black. Legs and feet yellow. Juvenile is paler, browner; throat whitish; bill and legs dusky. Distinguished at all ages from Purple Gallinule and coots by white line along side. Winter adult has brownish facial shield and usually a brownish bill with dusky-yellow tip. Common in freshwater marshes, ponds, placid rivers; uncommon in brackish marshes. Formerly called Common Gallinule.

American Coot *Fulica americana* L 15½″ (39 cm)

Blackish head and neck, with small reddish-brown forehead shield, whitish bill with dark band near tip. Body slate; outer feathers of undertail coverts are white, inner ones black. Leg color ranges from greenish-gray in young birds to yellow or orangish in adults. Toes are lobed, unlike gallinules. Juvenile is paler, with whitish feather tips, especially below. In flight, white trailing edge on most of wing is distinctive. Common to abundant. Nests in freshwater marshes, wetlands, or near lakes or ponds; winters in both fresh and salt water, usually in large flocks. Often dives to feed.

Caribbean Coot *Fulica caribaea* L 15½″ (39 cm)

Possible vagrant to southern Florida, chiefly in Miami area; many records are uncertain. Resembles American Coot but forehead shield is broader and white, sometimes tinged with yellow. A few American Coots, however, also have extensively white facial shields. Identification requires extreme caution. The Caribbean Coot is considered by some authorities to be a subspecies or color phase of the American Coot.

Eurasian Coot *Fulica atra* L 15¾″ (40 cm)

Accidental straggler to Newfoundland, Labrador, and the Pribilofs. Slightly darker than the American Coot; undertail coverts all-black. Forehead shield and bill entirely white.

juvenile

Purple Gallinule

Common Moorhen

winter

juvenile

breeding

American Coot

juvenile

Caribbean Coot

Eurasian Coot

Jacanas (Family Jacanidae)

Extremely long toes and claws allow these tropical birds to walk on lily pads and other floating plants.

Northern Jacana *Jacana spinosa* L 9¹/₂″ (24 cm)
Mexican and Central American species, accidental visitor to ponds and marshes in southern Texas, southeast Arizona. Often raises its wings, revealing yellow flight feathers.

Oystercatchers (Family Haematopodidae)

These chunky shorebirds have laterally flattened, heavy bills that can reach into mollusks and pry the shells open; also probe sand for worms and crabs.

Black Oystercatcher *Haematopus bachmani*
L 17¹/₂″ (45 cm) Resident on rocky shores and islands along the Pacific coast from the Aleutians to Baja California. Large red-orange bill, all-dark body, pinkish legs. Immatures are browner; outer half of bill is dusky during first year.

American Oystercatcher *Haematopus palliatus*
L 18¹/₂″ (47 cm) Large red-orange bill. Black head and dark brown back; white wing and tail patches, white underparts. Juvenile is scaly-looking above; dark tip on bill is kept through first year. Oystercatchers feed in small, noisy flocks on coastal beaches and mud flats. Range is expanding northward in the east. Casual in southern California.

Stilts and Avocets (Family Recurvirostridae)

Sleek and graceful waders with long, slender bills and spindly legs. Two species inhabit North America.

American Avocet *Recurvirostra americana* L 18″ (46 cm)
Black and white above, white below; head and neck rusty in breeding plumage, gray in winter. Juveniles have cinnamon wash on head and neck. Fairly common on shallow ponds, marshes, lakeshores. Avocets feed by sweeping their bills from side to side through the water. Male's bill is longer, straighter, than female's. Common call is a loud *wheet*.

Black-necked Stilt *Himantopus mexicanus* L 14″ (36 cm)
Male's glossy black back and bill contrast sharply with white underparts, long red or pink legs. Female is browner above. Juvenile is brown above, with buffy edgings. The Stilt breeds and winters in a wide variety of wet habitats. Rare breeder on the east coast; widespread but very local in the interior. Common call is a loud *kek kek kek*.

Black Oystercatcher

Northern Jacana

immature

American Oystercatcher

juvenile

American Avocet

juvenile

breeding ♀

winter ♂

Black-necked Stilt

juvenile

♂

Plovers (Family Charadriidae)

These compact birds dart across the ground, stop suddenly, then sprint off again. Shape and behavior identify plovers in general; species are more difficult. All juveniles resemble adults but backs look scaly.

Snowy Plover Charadrius alexandrinus L 6¹/₄" (16 cm)
Pale above, very pale in Gulf coast birds; thin dark bill; dark or grayish legs; partial breast band; dark ear patch. Females and juveniles resemble Piping Plover; note thinner bill, darker legs. Inhabits barren sandy beaches and flats. Uncommon and declining. Uncommon resident on west coast of Florida. Calls include a low *krut* and a soft, whistled *ku-wheet*.

Piping Plover Charadrius melodus L 7¹/₄" (18 cm)
Very pale above; orange legs; white rump conspicuous in flight (page 138). In breeding plumage, shows dark narrow breast band, sometimes incomplete, especially in females. In winter, bill is all-dark. Distinguished from Snowy Plover by thicker bill, paler back; legs are brighter than in Semipalmated Plover. Distinctive call, a clear *peep-lo*. Found on sandy beaches, lakeshores, dunes. Uncommon; rare and declining breeder in the midwest; casual winter visitor in California.

Wilson's Plover Charadrius wilsonia L 7³/₄" (20 cm)
Long, very heavy, black bill; broad neck band is black in male, brown in female; legs grayish-pink. Juvenile resembles adult female but note scaly-looking upperparts. Breeding male may have cinnamon buff ear patch. Fairly common but declining on barrier islands, sandy beaches, mud flats. Casual to New England and California. Call is a sharp, whistled *whit*.

Semipalmated Plover Charadrius semipalmatus
L 7¹/₄" (18 cm) Dark back distinguishes this species from Piping and Snowy Plovers; bill much smaller than in Wilson's Plover. (All shown in flight on page 138.) At very close range, Semipalmated shows partial webbing between toes. Breeding adult male often lacks white above eye. Juvenile has darker legs than adults. Common on beaches, lakeshores, tidal flats; seen throughout the continent in migration. Distinctive call is a whistled, upslurred *chu-weet*.

Common Ringed Plover Charadrius hiaticula
L 7¹/₂" (19 cm) Almost identical to Semipalmated Plover; best distinguished by call, a soft, fluted *pooee*. Breast band is usually broader in center than Semipalmated's, sometimes extends farther up toward throat. White eyebrow is usually more distinct, especially in breeding male. Webbing between toes is less extensive, bill is slightly longer. Regular but rare spring migrant on western Alaska islands; occasionally breeds on St. Lawrence Island.

Snowy Plover

Gulf coast ♂

♀

♂

juvenile

Piping Plover

winter

breeding ♂

breeding ♂

breeding ♀

Wilson's Plover

juvenile

♂

♀

winter

breeding ♂

juvenile

Semipalmated Plover

breeding ♀

breeding ♂

breeding ♀

Common Ringed Plover

Killdeer *Charadrius vociferus* L 10^1/$_2$" (27 cm)

Double breast bands are distinctive, as is this plover's loud, piercing call: *kill-dee* or *dee-dee-dee*. Bright reddish-orange rump is visible in flight (page 138). Downy juvenile has only one breast band. Common in meadows, farm fields, airfields, lawns; also on shores and riverbanks. Nests on open ground, usually on gravel. Like many birds, will feign a broken wing or leg to lead intruders away from the nest. Generally seen singly or in pairs; in winter, may form loose flocks. In mild winters a few birds are seen north into summer range. Vagrant north of breeding range in summer.

Mongolian Plover *Charadrius mongolus* L 7^1/$_2$" (19 cm)

Asian species, rare migrant on Aleutians and off western Alaska; casual along west coast. Casual in summer in western and northwestern Alaska, where it has bred. Bright rusty-red breast; black-and-white facial pattern. Females are duller. Juvenile has broad buffy wash across breast; upperparts edged with buff. Winter birds lack reddish tones; underparts are white except for broad grayish patches on sides of breast.

Eurasian Dotterel *Charadrius morinellus* L 8^1/$_4$" (21 cm)

Eurasian species; uncommon, sporadic breeder in northwestern Alaska; accidental along west coast. Narrow whitish band on lower breast is somewhat obscured in young and winter birds. Bold white eyebrow extends around entire head. Unlike other plovers, females are brighter than males. Juvenile is edged with cinnamon buff above; underparts are extensively buff. A chunky bird; generally unwary and easily overlooked.

Mountain Plover *Charadrius montanus* L 9" (23 cm)

In breeding plumage, unbanded white underparts separate this plover from all other brown-backed plovers. Buffy tinge on breast is more extensive in winter plumage; may be confused with winter Lesser Golden-Plover (next page), but has paler, unspotted upperparts, paler legs. In flight, Mountain Plover shows white underwings; Lesser Golden-Plover's are grayish. Calls heard on breeding grounds include low, drawn-out whistles and harsh notes. In migration and winter, gives a harsh *krrr* note. Common in dry upland prairies and plains, semidesert. In winter usually found on bare dirt fields. Gregarious, especially during migration and winter. Large flocks, sometimes more than a hundred birds, may form.

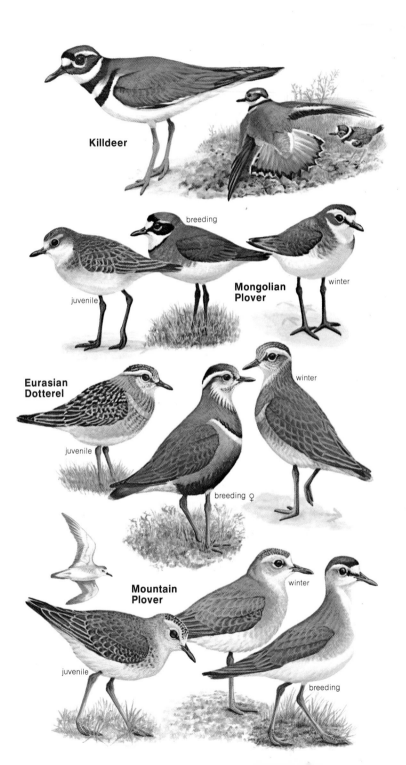

Killdeer

breeding

Mongolian Plover

juvenile

winter

Eurasian Dotterel

juvenile

winter

breeding ♀

Mountain Plover

winter

juvenile

breeding

Black-bellied Plover *Pluvialis squatarola* L 11¹/₂" (29 cm)
In black-and-white breeding plumage, white stripe extends across forehead, crown, and nape and down sides of breast; undertail coverts white. Winter and juvenile birds distinguished from Lesser Golden-Plover by larger size, larger bill, grayer plumage, but note that juvenile is gold-speckled above. Distinguished in flight in all plumages by white uppertail coverts, barred white tail, black axillaries, bold white wing stripe (see also page 138). Nests on arctic tundra. Winters on sandy beaches and in fields and marshes. Usually seen singly or in small flocks. Typical call is a drawn-out, mournful, three-note whistle, the second note lower pitched.

Lesser Golden-Plover *Pluvialis dominica* L 10¹/₂" (27 cm)
Smaller than Black-bellied Plover, with proportionately smaller bill. In flight (see also page 138), distinguished by uniformly dark upperparts and uniformly grayish underwing and axillaries. Breeding adult is speckled above with gold and white. In the widespread subspecies, *P.d. dominica,* white stripe extends from forehead to sides of neck and breast, where it bulges into patches. In *fulva,* whose breeding range overlaps with *dominica* in western Alaska, the white stripe is narrower and extends onto flanks, as in breeding adult Greater Golden-Plover. Juvenile and winter *dominicas* are darker above than Black-bellied Plover; *fulvas* are on average much brighter above. Fall migration is mostly over the Atlantic for *dominica* and the Pacific for *fulva. Dominica* winters in South America, *fulva* on Pacific islands and southern Asia, with small numbers remaining locally along our Pacific coast. Spring migration (*dominica*) crosses mid-continent; seen in large flocks in fields, less often on tidal flats. Call is a loud, whistled *chu-leet,* the second note higher in pitch. Some authorities consider the two forms to be separate species. Formerly called American Golden Plover.

Greater Golden-Plover *Pluvialis apricaria*
L 11¹/₂" (29 cm) Eurasian species, seen regularly in Greenland, casually in spring in Newfoundland. Distinguished from *dominica* subspecies of Lesser Golden-Plover by brighter upperparts, larger size, proportionately larger bill, and, in flight, by pale underwing with white axillaries. In breeding plumage, white stripe usually extends continuously from forehead to flanks. Calls are mournful single- and double-note whistles. Most sightings are of birds in patchy spring plumage.

Northern Lapwing *Vanellus vanellus* L 12¹/₂" (32 cm)
Eurasian species, accidental in late fall on northeast coast of North America. All sightings have been immature birds. First-winter plumage is dark and green-glossed above, white below, with black breast; wispy but prominent crest. Wings broad and rounded, with white tips, white wing linings. Flight call is a whistled *pee-wit.*

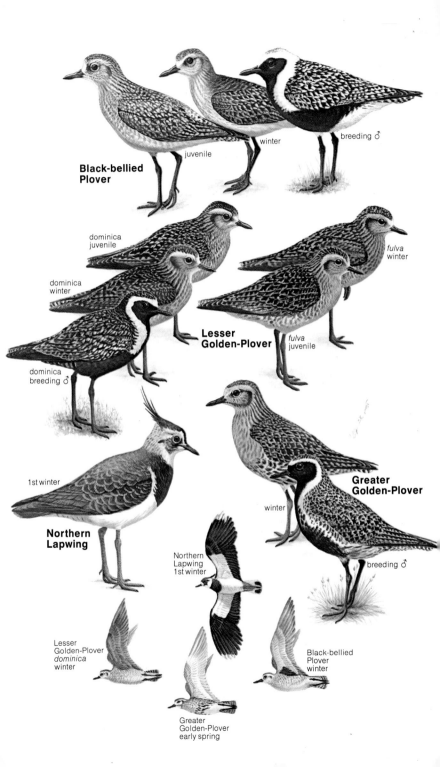

Black-bellied Plover

juvenile

winter

breeding ♂

Lesser Golden-Plover

dominica juvenile

dominica winter

fulva winter

dominica breeding ♂

fulva juvenile

Northern Lapwing

1st winter

Greater Golden-Plover

winter

breeding ♂

Northern Lapwing 1st winter

Lesser Golden-Plover *dominica* winter

Greater Golden-Plover early spring

Black-bellied Plover winter

Sandpipers (Family Scolopacidae)

Rising in unison, wheeling, settling back on the sand, flocks of shorebirds are a joy to watch—and hard to identify. Most species have at least three distinct plumages. In most species, adults migrate earlier in fall than juveniles. The molt to winter plumage usually begins as the birds near or reach their winter grounds.

Marbled Godwit *Limosa fedoa* L 18" (46 cm)
Long bicolored bill, usually upcurved, sets all godwits apart from other large shorebirds. The tawny-brown Marbled Godwit is mottled with black above, barred below. Barring is much less extensive on winter birds and juveniles. In all birds, bill and legs are longer than in Bar-tailed Godwit. In flight (page 136), cinnamon wing linings and cinnamon on primaries are distinctive. Nests in grassy meadows, near lakes and ponds. Common on west coast in winter, fairly common on Gulf coast; rare but regular in the east.

Bar-tailed Godwit *Limosa lapponica* L 16" (41 cm)
Long bicolored bill, slightly upcurved. Breeding male is reddish-brown below; lacks heavy barring of Black-tailed Godwit. Female is larger and much paler than male. In winter plumage, resembles Marbled Godwit but lacks cinnamon tones. Note also shorter bill, shorter legs. Black-and-white barred tail distinctive but hard to see. Juvenile resembles winter adult but is buffier overall. Two subspecies of this Eurasian godwit occur in North America. *L.l. baueri,* shown opposite, breeds in Alaska, appears casually in migration along Pacific coast; rump is heavily mottled, wing linings brown with white barring. European *lapponica*, very rare migrant along Atlantic coast, has a whiter rump, white wing linings, and brown-barred axillaries. Both forms are shown in flight on page 136.

Black-tailed Godwit *Limosa limosa* L 16½" (42 cm)
Eurasian species, rare but regular spring migrant on western Aleutians; casual along Atlantic coast. Long bicolored bill is straight or only slightly upcurved. Tail is mostly black, uppertail coverts white. In breeding plumage, shows chestnut head and neck and heavily barred sides and flanks. Winter birds are gray above, whitish below. In all plumages, white wing linings and broad wing stripe are conspicuous in flight (page 136).

Hudsonian Godwit *Limosa haemastica* L 15½" (39 cm)
Long bicolored bill, slightly upcurved. Tail is black, uppertail coverts white. Breeding male is dark chestnut below, finely barred. Female is larger and much duller. Juvenile's buff feather edges give upperparts a scaled look. Winter adult resembles Black-tailed Godwit. Dark wing linings and narrower white wing stripe are distinctive in flight (page 136). Breeding range not fully known. Migrates through Great Plains in spring, primarily off the east coast in fall.

Marbled Godwit
breeding
winter

Bar-tailed Godwit
breeding ♂
winter
juvenile

Black-tailed Godwit
winter
breeding

Hudsonian Godwit
winter
breeding ♂
juvenile

Eskimo Curlew *Numenius borealis* *L 14" (36 cm)*

Nests on arctic tundra; winters in South America. Most sightings in this century have been along the Texas coast during spring migration. This species is almost extinct; identification must be made with great care. Resembles Whimbrel but is much smaller; upperparts darker; bill thinner and less curved; crown less strongly patterned; wing linings pale cinnamon. Calls are soft twittering whistles.

Bristle-thighed Curlew *Numenius tahitiensis*

L 17" (43 cm) Rusty-orange rump and tail distinguish this species from the Whimbrel. Stiff feathers on thighs and flanks are very hard to see in the field. Typical call is a loud, whistled *chu-a-whit*. Only known breeding area is in western Alaska. Migrates directly across Pacific to and from its winter grounds on Pacific islands. Shown in flight on page 136.

Whimbrel *Numenius phaeopus* *L 17½" (45 cm)*

Boldly striped crown; dark eye line; long, downcurved bill. Typical call is a series of hollow whistles on one pitch. Fairly common; nests on open tundra; winters on beaches, mud flats, wet fields. In flight (page 136), the North American subspecies, *N. p. hudsonicus,* shows dark rump and underwings. European *phaeopus,* rare vagrant to east coast, has white rump and underwings. Asian *variegatus,* regular migrant off western Alaska, shows whitish, variably streaked rump and underwings.

Long-billed Curlew *Numenius americanus* *L 23" (58 cm)*

Cinnamon brown above, buff below, with very long, strongly downcurved bill. Lacks dark head stripes of Whimbrel. Juveniles have shorter bill. Cinnamon buff wing linings, visible in flight (page 136) are distinctive in all plumages. Typical call is a loud, musical, ascending *cur-lee*. Fairly common; nests in both wet and dry uplands; in migration and winter, found on coastal and lake beaches, salt marshes, and grainfields. Rare on east coast from Virginia south in fall and winter.

Far Eastern Curlew *Numenius madagascariensis*

L 17" (43 cm) Asian species, casual in spring and early summer on the Aleutians and Pribilofs. Brown overall, with heavy streaking below; bill long and strongly downcurved. Wing linings (see page 136) are white with dark barring; note also that rump is same color as back.

Eurasian Curlew *Numenius arquata* *L 22" (56 cm)*

Shown in flight on page 136. Eurasian species, accidental on the east coast in fall and winter. Brown overall, heavily streaked below; bill long, strongly downcurved. Distinguished from Long-billed Curlew by white rump, white wing linings; from European subspecies of Whimbrel (*N. p. phaeopus*) by larger size, longer bill, and lack of dark stripes on head.

Eskimo Curlew

Bristle-thighed Curlew

Whimbrel

hudsonicus juvenile

hudsonicus

juvenile

Long-billed Curlew

Far Eastern Curlew

Willet *Catoptrophorus semipalmatus* L 15" (38 cm)
Large and plump; heavily mottled above and below; underparts grayish-brown, belly white. Bill is heavier and shorter
than Greater Yellowlegs; legs are gray. Winter bird is uniformly pale gray above, whitish below. In flight (page 137), Willets
show a striking black-and-white wing pattern. Nest in wet
fields, marshes, lakeshores; winter on coastal beaches and at
Salton Sea, often in small flocks. Fairly common; conspicuous
and noisy; typical territorial call sounds like *pill-will-willet*.

Greater Yellowlegs *Tringa melanoleuca* L 14" (36 cm)
Legs yellow to orange; rarely red-orange. Larger than Lesser
Yellowlegs; bill longer, stouter, often slightly upturned, and
usually faintly two-toned, black with grayer base. In breeding
plumage, throat and breast are heavily streaked; sides and
usually the belly are spotted and barred. In flight (page 137),
shows pale spotting on inner primaries, absent on Lesser Yellowlegs. Greater's call is a loud, slightly descending series of
three or more *tew* notes. Fairly common; nests on tundra, winters on coastal mud flats and marshes, inland lakeshores, in
small, noisy flocks. Winter birds are best distinguished from
Lesser by overall size, bill size and color, and voice.

Lesser Yellowlegs *Tringa flavipes* L 10¹/₂" (27 cm)
Legs yellow to rarely orange. Smaller than Greater Yellowlegs;
bill shorter, thinner, straight, and uniformly dark. In breeding
plumage, breast is finely streaked; sides and flanks show fine,
short bars. In flight (page 137), shows all-dark primaries.
Lesser Yellowlegs' call is higher, shorter than Greater Yellowlegs, usually one to three *tew* notes. Both species give a similar
alarm call, a series of five to twenty loud *tew* notes. Common in
the east and midwest; uncommon in the far west. Nests on
sheltered tundra or in open woodlands. Winters chiefly in
South America; a few remain in the U.S. Winter birds are best
distinguished from Greater Yellowlegs by overall size, bill size
and color, and voice.

Common Greenshank *Tringa nebularia* L 13¹/₂" (34 cm)
Eurasian species, regular migrant through the Aleutians
and Pribilofs. Similar to Greater Yellowlegs but less heavily
streaked; legs are greenish. In flight (page 137), wings look
uniformly dark; white wedge extends up to middle of back.
Typical flight call is a loud *tew-tew-tew*, all on one pitch.

Spotted Redshank *Tringa erythropus* L 12¹/₂" (32 cm)
Eurasian species, rare spring and fall visitor to Aleutians and
Pribilofs; casual on both coasts during migration and winter.
Long bill droops at tip; base of lower mandible red. Breeding
adult is black overall with white spots above; legs very dark
red. Juvenile and winter adult paler, with orange or red-orange
legs. In flight (page 137), shows white wedge extending up to
middle of back; wing linings are white. Call, a loud rising *chu-
weet*, similar to call of Semipalmated Plover.

114

Willet

breeding

winter

juvenile

breeding

winter

Greater Yellowlegs

juvenile

breeding

winter

Lesser Yellowlegs

juvenile

juvenile

Spotted Redshank

juvenile

breeding

Common Greenshank

breeding

winter

Solitary Sandpiper *Tringa solitaria* L 8¹/₂" (22 cm)
Dark brown above, heavily spotted with buffy-white. White below; lower throat, breast, and sides streaked with blackish-brown. Bolder white eye ring and shorter, olive legs distinguish Solitary Sandpiper from Lesser Yellowlegs (preceding page). In flight (page 137), shows dark central tail feathers, white outer feathers barred with black. Underwing is dark. Fairly common at shallow backwaters, pools, small estuaries, even rain puddles. Often keeps wings raised briefly after alighting; on the ground, often bobs its tail. Generally seen singly or in small flocks. Calls include a shrill *peet-weet*, higher pitched than calls of Spotted Sandpiper.

Spotted Sandpiper *Actitis macularia* L 7¹/₂" (19 cm)
Striking in breeding plumage, with barred upperparts, spotted underparts. Juvenile and winter birds lack spotting below, resemble Common Sandpiper. Note Spotted's shorter tail; in flight, shows shorter white wing stripe, shorter white trailing edge. In juvenile and first-winter birds, barred wing coverts contrast with back. Note also that tertials have a black bar on tip; barring, if any, on edge of tertials extends no farther than halfway along each feather. Both species fly with stiff, rapid, fluttering wingbeats. On the ground, both nod and teeter constantly. The Spotted Sandpiper is common and widespread, found at sheltered streams, ponds, lakes, or marshes. Generally seen singly; may form small flocks in migration. Most winter in Central and South America. Casual in winter to southern edge of breeding range. Calls include a shrill *peet-weet* and, in flight, a series of *weet* notes, lower pitched than the calls of Solitary Sandpiper.

Common Sandpiper *Actitis hypoleucos* L 8" (20 cm)
Eurasian species, rare but regular migrant, usually in spring, on the outer Aleutians, Pribilofs, St. Lawrence Island. Breeding adult is brown above with dark barring and streaking; white below; upper breast finely streaked. Juvenile and winter birds resemble Spotted Sandpiper. Note Common Sandpiper's longer tail; in juvenile, barring on edge of tertials extends along the entire feather. In flight, shows longer white wing stripe and longer white trailing edge. Call in flight is a shrill, piping *twee-wee-wee*.

Terek Sandpiper *Xenus cinereus* L 9" (23 cm)
Eurasian species, rare migrant on outer Aleutians; casual on Pribilofs, St. Lawrence, and southern Alaska coast. Note long, upturned bill, short orange-yellow legs. In breeding adult, dark-centered scapulars form two dark lines on back. In flight, shows distinctive wing pattern: dark leading edge, grayer median coverts, dark greater coverts, white-tipped secondaries. Flight call is a series of shrill whistled notes, usually in threes.

Solitary Sandpiper

breeding

juvenile

1st winter

juvenile

juvenile

Spotted Sandpiper

breeding

breeding

juvenile

Common Sandpiper

juvenile

breeding

Terek Sandpiper

breeding

juvenile

juvenile

Wandering Tattler *Heteroscelus incanus L 11" (28 cm)*
Uniformly dark gray above; white eyebrow flecked with gray;
bill is dark, legs dull yellow. In breeding plumage, underparts
are heavily barred. Juvenile and winter birds have only a dark
gray wash over breast and sides; juvenile has pale spots above.
Closely resembles Gray-tailed Tattler; best distinguished by
voice. Wandering Tattler's call is a rapid series of clear, hollow
whistles, all on one pitch. Breeds chiefly on gravelly stream
banks. Winters on rocky coasts. Often teeters and bobs as it
feeds. Generally seen singly or in small groups. Casual inland
during migration.

Gray-tailed Tattler *Heteroscelus brevipes L 10" (25 cm)*
Asian species, regular spring and fall migrant on outer Aleutians, Pribilofs, St. Lawrence Island; casual visitor to northern
Alaska mainland. Closely resembles Wandering Tattler; upperparts are slightly paler; barring on underparts finer and less
extensive; whitish eyebrows are more distinct and meet on
forehead. Best distinction is voice. Gray-tailed Tattler's common call is a loud, ascending *too-weet*, similar to call of Lesser
Golden-Plover. Formerly called Polynesian Tattler.

Green Sandpiper *Tringa ochropus L 8 ³/₄" (22 cm)*
Eurasian species, casual in spring on outer Aleutians and St.
Lawrence Island. Resembles Solitary Sandpiper (preceding
page) in plumage, behavior, and calls. Note white rump and
uppertail coverts, with less extensively barred tail; lacks solid-
ly dark central tail feathers of Solitary Sandpiper; wing linings
are darker. Similar Wood Sandpiper has more spotting above,
more barring on tail, and paler wing linings.

Wood Sandpiper *Tringa glareola L 8" (20 cm)*
Eurasian species, fairly common spring migrant and occasional breeder on the outer Aleutians; rare but regular on the Pribilofs and St. Lawrence Island. Dark upperparts are heavily
spotted with buff; prominent whitish eyebrow. In flight (page
137), distinguished from Green Sandpiper by paler wing linings, smaller white rump patch, and more densely barred tail.
Note also the shorter bill. Common call is a loud, sharp whistling of three or more notes, similar to the call of the Long-
billed Dowitcher.

Wandering Tattler

breeding

winter

juvenile

Gray-tailed Tattler

breeding

juvenile

juvenile

breeding

Solitary Sandpiper

Green Sandpiper

Green Sandpiper

breeding

juvenile

Wood Sandpiper

breeding

Phalaropes

These elegant shorebirds have partially lobed feet and dense, soft plumage. Feeding on the water, phalaropes often spin like tops, stirring up larvae, crustaceans, and insects. Females, larger and more brightly colored than the males, do the courting; males incubate the eggs and care for the chicks.

Wilson's Phalarope *Phalaropus tricolor* L 9¹/₄" (24 cm)
Long, thin bill; bold blackish stripe on face and neck. In winter plumage, upperparts are gray, underparts white; note also lack of distinct dark ear patch. Briefly held juvenile plumage resembles winter adult but back is browner and mottled, breast buffy. In flight (page 137), white uppertail coverts, whitish tail, and absence of white wing stripe distinguish juvenile and winter birds from other phalaropes (page 139). Common to abundant, Wilson's is primarily an inland phalarope, nesting on the grassy borders of shallow lakes, marshes, reservoirs. Feeds as often on land as on water. Calls include a hoarse *wurk* and other low, croaking notes. Range is expanding in eastern Canada. Uncommon migrant on east coast.

Red-necked Phalarope *Phalaropus lobatus*
L 7³/₄" (20 cm) Chestnut on front and sides of neck distinctive in breeding female, less prominent in male. Both have dark back with bright buff stripes along sides. Bill is shorter and thicker than in Wilson's Phalarope, thinner than in Red Phalarope. Winter birds are blue-gray above with whitish stripes; underparts and front of crown white; dark patch extends back from eye. In flight (page 139), shows white wing stripe, whitish stripes on back, dark central tail coverts. Juvenile resembles winter adult but is blacker above, with bright buff stripes. Red-necked Phalaropes breed on arctic and subarctic tundra and winter chiefly at sea in the Southern Hemisphere. Common inland in the west and off the west coast during migration; rare in the midwest and east; uncommon off the east coast. Call, a high, sharp *kit,* often given in a series. Formerly known as Northern Phalarope.

Red Phalarope *Phalaropus fulicaria* L 8¹/₂" (22 cm)
Bill shorter and much thicker than in other phalaropes; yellow with black tip in breeding adult, usually all-dark in juvenile and winter adult. Female in breeding plumage has black crown, white face, chestnut red underparts. Male is duller. Juvenile resembles male but is much paler below; juveniles molting to winter plumage resemble Red-necked Phalaropes. Winter bird is uniformly pale gray above. In flight (page 139), shows a bold white wing stripe and dark central tail coverts. Breeds on arctic shores, islands; winters at sea. Irregularly common off west coast during fall migration; rare inland. Generally uncommon off east coast in spring and fall. Call is higher and sharper than Red-necked's.

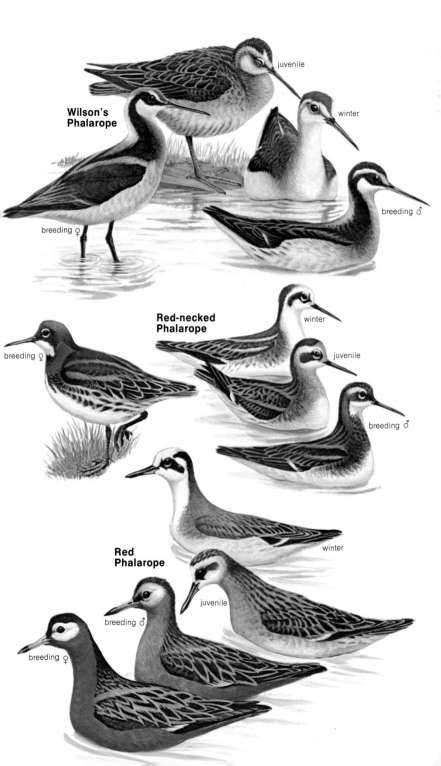

Wilson's Phalarope

juvenile

winter

breeding ♂

breeding ♀

Red-necked Phalarope

breeding ♀

winter

juvenile

breeding ♂

Red Phalarope

winter

breeding ♂

juvenile

breeding ♀

Dowitchers

Medium-size, chunky, dark shorebirds with long, straight bills and distinct pale eyebrows. Feeding in mud or shallow water, they probe with a rapid jabbing motion. Dowitchers in flight (see also page 137) show a white wedge from barred tail to middle of back. Distinguishing the two species is easiest with juveniles, difficult with breeding adults, and usually impossible in winter except by voice.

Short-billed Dowitcher *Limnodromus griseus*

L 11" (28 cm) Call is a mellow *tu tu tu*, repeated in a rapid series as an alarm call. In flight, tail generally looks paler than in Long-billed Dowitcher. Breeding plumage varies among the three subspecies: *L.g. griseus* (which breeds in northeast Canada), *hendersoni* (central and western Canada), and *caurinus* (Alaska). Unlike Longbill, most Shortbills show some white on the belly, especially *griseus*, which also has a heavily spotted breast and may have densely barred flanks. In *hendersoni*, which may be entirely reddish below, foreneck is much less heavily spotted than in Long-billed Dowitcher; sides have less or no barring; upperparts are brighter. *Caurinus* is variable but generally similar to *griseus*. In all forms, juvenile is brighter above, redder below than juvenile Longbill; tertials and greater wing coverts have broad reddish-buff edges and conspicuous internal bars, loops, or stripes. Winter birds are brownish-gray above, white below, with gray breast; at close range note fine dark speckling on and below the breast on many birds. Common in migration along the Atlantic coast (*griseus*), from the eastern plains to Atlantic coast from New Jersey south (*hendersoni*), and along the Pacific coast (*caurinus*). Over much of North America, fall migration begins earlier than Long-billed Dowitcher, generally in late June or early July. Juveniles migrate later than adults and are most common in August and September.

Long-billed Dowitcher *Limnodromus scolopaceus*

L 11¹⁄₂" (29 cm) Call is a sharp, high-pitched *keek,* given singly or in a rapid series. Bill on most birds is no longer than on Short-billed Dowitcher. In flight, tail generally looks darker than in Shortbill. Breeding adult is entirely reddish below; foreneck heavily spotted; sides usually barred. Bold white scapular tips in April and May help separate this species from Shortbills in the east. Juvenile is darker above, grayer below than Shortbill; tertials and greater wing coverts are plain, with thin gray or red edges, red tips; some birds show two pale spots near the tips. In winter birds, breast is unspotted and more extensively dark than on most Shortbills. Common in migration in western half of continent; less common in the east in fall, rare in spring. Fall migration generally begins later than Shortbill, in mid-July (west) or late July (east). Juveniles migrate later than adults; generally rare before September.

122

juvenile

winter

winter

griseus breeding

caurinus breeding

hendersoni breeding

Short-billed Dowitcher

winter

juvenile

breeding

Long-billed Dowitcher

breeding

Stilt Sandpiper *Calidris himantopus* L 8¹/₂" (22 cm)
Breeding adult has striped crown, chestnut patch on sides of head; slender, slightly downcurved bill, drooped at the tip in most birds; and heavily barred underparts. Compare with dowitchers (preceding page) and yellowlegs (page 114). Winter adult grayer above, whiter below, with distinct eyebrow. Juvenile is like winter adult but has streaked crown, more sharply patterned upperparts, and bolder eyebrow; early juvenile shows some chestnut on sides of face and buffy wash on breast. Juvenile and winter adult resemble Curlew Sandpiper (page 128), but note usually straighter bill, yellow-green legs, and, in flight (page 137), lack of prominent wing stripe, slightly different tail pattern. Often seen with dowitchers; feeding styles are similar. Breeds on tundra. Rare in spring on east coast; common in fall. Rare but regular migrant on west coast, especially in fall. Small numbers often winter at the Salton Sea. Call is a low, hoarse *querp.*

Common Snipe *Gallinago gallinago* L 10¹/₂" (27 cm)
Stocky, with short legs, long bill. Boldly patterned above and below, with white belly; distinctive striped head and rusty tail; wings pointed. Fairly secretive in breeding season, usually seen only when flushed. Takeoff is explosive; flight rapid and zigzagging, accompanied by a distinctive harsh *skipe* call. Fairly common. On breeding grounds in marshes and bogs, often sings from high perches a series of loud *wheet-wheet* notes. During erratic, swooping display flight, vibrating tail feathers make an eerie fluttering sound. Casual in winter in southern part of breeding range. Formerly called Wilson's Snipe. The Old World form, regular off western Alaska in migration, has a broad white trailing edge on its wings, visible in flight.

American Woodcock *Scolopax minor* L 11" (28 cm)
Very chunky, short-necked and short-legged, with long bill, barred crown, large eyes set high in large head. Wings are rounded. Nocturnal and secretive; seldom seen until flushed. Flies up abruptly, wings making a twittering sound. Common call is a nasal *peent,* heard mostly in spring but also at other times of year, especially on warm winter nights at dusk and dawn. In elaborate flight display, male circles high in the night sky giving a constant twittering, then plummets to earth in a series of zigzags, wings whistling. Woodcocks are fairly common but local; nest in moist woodlands and thickets. During mild winters, a few birds are found in the breeding range.

juvenile

Stilt Sandpiper

winter

molting fall

breeding

Common Snipe

American Woodcock

Ruddy Turnstone *Arenaria interpres* L 9¹/₂″ (24 cm)

Striking black-and-white head and bib, black-and-chestnut back, and orange legs mark this stout bird in breeding plumage. Female is duller than male. Bib pattern and orange leg color are retained in winter plumage. Juvenile resembles winter adult but back has a scaly appearance. Distinctive call, a low-pitched, guttural rattle. Nests on coastal tundra. Turnstones use their slender bills to flip aside shells and pebbles in search of food. In flight, complex pattern on back and wings identifies both turnstone species.

Black Turnstone *Arenaria melanocephala* L 9¹/₄″ (24 cm)

Black head, breast, and back in breeding plumage are marked by white eyebrow and lore spot, white spotting on sides of neck and breast. Legs dark reddish-brown in all plumages. Juvenile and winter adult are slate gray, lack lore spot and mottling. Calls include a guttural rattle, higher than call of Ruddy Turnstone. Breeds in coastal Alaska. Winters on rocky coasts.

Surfbird *Aphriza virgata* L 10″ (25 cm)

Base of short, stout bill is yellow; legs yellowish-green. Breeding adult's head and underparts are heavily streaked and spotted with dusky-black; upperparts edged with white and chestnut; scapulars mostly rufous. Winter adult has a solid dark gray head and breast. Juvenile's head and breast are flecked with white; back appears scaly. In flight, all plumages show a conspicuous black band at end of white tail and rump. Nests on mountain tundra; winters along rocky beaches and reefs. Casual in spring on Texas coast.

Rock Sandpiper *Calidris ptilocnemis* L 9″ (23 cm)

Black patch on lower breast in breeding plumage; compare with belly patch of Dunlin (next page). Crown and back are black, edged with chestnut. Breeding birds on the Pribilofs have paler chestnut above, less black below. Long, slender bill, slightly downcurved; base is greenish-yellow. Legs greenish-yellow. Winter bird is not safely distinguishable from Purple Sandpiper except by range; distinguished from Surfbird by longer bill, smaller size, and more patterned upperparts and breast. In flight (page 139), shows white wing stripe and all-dark tail. Nests on tundra; winters on rocky shores, often with Black Turnstones and Surfbirds. Migrates late in fall.

Purple Sandpiper *Calidris maritima* L 9″ (23 cm)

Breeding adult has tawny-buff crown, streaked with black; back is edged with white and tawny-buff; breast and flanks spotted with blackish-brown. Long, slender bill, slightly downcurved; base is orange-yellow. Legs orange-yellow. In flight (page 139) and in winter, adult resembles Rock Sandpiper. Migrates late in fall. Casual migrant in the Great Plains; rare at Great Lakes. Winters on rocky shores, jetties, often with Ruddy Turnstones and Sanderlings.

juvenile

Ruddy Turnstone

winter

breeding ♂

Black Turnstone

winter

breeding

winter

winter

juvenile

Surfbird

breeding

Rock Sandpiper

winter

juvenile

Pribilofs breeding

breeding

juvenile

winter

breeding

Purple Sandpiper

Red Knot *Calidris canutus* L 10¹/₂" (27 cm)
Chunky and short-legged. Breeding adult is dappled brown, black, and chestnut above, with buffy-chestnut face and breast. In winter, back is pale gray; underparts white. Distinguished from dowitchers (page 122) by shorter bill, paler crown, and, in flight (page 137), by whitish rump finely barred with gray. Juveniles similar to winter adults but have buffy wash on breast, scaly-looking upperparts. Feeds along sandy beaches and on mud flats, often with dowitchers.

Great Knot *Calidris tenuirostris* L 11" (28 cm)
Asian species, casual spring migrant in western Alaska. Larger than Red Knot, with longer bill and less rufous on back, none on head and breast. Compare also with Surfbird and Rock Sandpiper (preceding page). In breeding plumage, shows black breast and bold black flank pattern. Juvenile has buffy wash and distinct spotting below; dark back feathers are edged with rust. Resembles Red Knot in flight but wing bar is much less bold.

Dunlin *Calidris alpina* L 8¹/₂" (22 cm)
Distinctive breeding plumage: reddish back; whitish, finely streaked underparts with conspicuous black belly patch. Rock Sandpiper (preceding page) has similar patch, but on chest. Note sturdy bill, curved at tip. Short-necked; appears hunchbacked. In flight (page 139), shows dark center on rump. In winter plumage, the upperparts are grayish-brown; breast is washed with gray-brown; belly is white. Juveniles are rusty above, spotted below. Distinctive call, a harsh, reedy *kree*.

Sanderling *Calidris alba* L 8" (20 cm)
Palest sandpiper of winter: pale gray above; white below. Bill and legs black. Prominent white wing stripe shows in flight (page 139). In breeding plumage (not acquired until May), head, mantle, and breast are rusty. Feeds on sandy beaches, sprinting just out of surf's reach to snatch up mollusks and crustaceans exposed by the retreating waves. Juveniles are similar to winter adults, but with more black and buff on the upperparts. Call is a sharp *kip*, often given in a series.

Curlew Sandpiper *Calidris ferruginea* L 8¹/₂" (22 cm)
Eurasian species, casual migrant throughout North America, rare on Atlantic coast. Long, downcurved bill has whitish area at base. In breeding plumage, rich chestnut underparts and mottled chestnut back are distinctive. Female is paler than male. Many sightings are of birds in patchy spring plumage or molting to winter plumage, showing grayer upperparts and partly white underparts. Juvenile appears scaly above; in fresh plumage, shows rich buff wash across breast. White rump is conspicuous in flight (page 137). Compare also with Stilt Sandpiper (page 124). Call is a soft, rippling *chirrup*. Very rare breeder in northern Alaska.

winter

Red Knot

juvenile

breeding

breeding

juvenile

Great Knot

winter

breeding

juvenile

Dunlin

juvenile   winter

breeding

Sanderling

molting fall adult

winter

juvenile

breeding

Curlew Sandpiper

Semipalmated Sandpiper *Calidris pusilla* L 6¼" (16 cm)
Black legs; tubular-looking, straight bill, of variable length.
Easily confused with Western Sandpiper. In breeding birds,
note that Semipalmated lacks spotting on flanks and shows
only a tinge of rufous on crown, ear patch, and scapulars. Juveniles are distinguished by stronger eyebrow, darker crown,
and more uniform upperparts. Winter plumage of these two
species is almost identical (see also page 139), but Semipalmated is plumper; bill shape is different; face shows slightly
more contrast; center of breast never shows the faint streaks
visible on some winter Westerns. Call is a short *churk*. Abundant. A common migrant in eastern half of continent. Rare migrant in the west; very rare in winter in south Florida.

Western Sandpiper *Calidris mauri* L 6½" (17 cm)
Black legs; tapered bill, of variable length; tip is usually slightly drooped. Easily confused with Semipalmated Sandpiper. In
breeding plumage, Western has spotting along sides, rufous at
base of scapulars, and a bright rufous wash on crown and ear
patch. Juvenile is distinguished from juvenile Semipalmated
by less prominent eyebrow, paler crown, and brighter rufous
edges on back. Winter plumage is almost identical to Semipalmated (see also page 139). Common in wet habitats. Call is a
high, raspy *jeet*.

Least Sandpiper *Calidris minutilla* L 6" (15 cm)
Note small size and short, thin bill, slightly downcurved. Always darker above than Western and Semipalmated Sandpipers. Winter plumage (see also page 139) has a prominent
brown breast band. Juvenile has a strong buffy wash across
breast. Legs are yellowish, but appear dark in poor light or
when smeared with mud. Common in wet habitats. Call note is
a shrill, high *kreee*, unlike the dry rattle of the similar Temminck's Stint (next page).

White-rumped Sandpiper *Calidris fuscicollis*
L 7½" (19 cm) Long wings extend beyond tail in standing bird.
Similar to Baird's Sandpiper but grayer overall and usually has
an entirely white rump. In breeding plumage, streaking extends to flanks. Juvenile (see also page 139) shows rusty edges
on crown and back. In winter birds, head and neck are dark
gray, giving a hooded look. Call note, a high-pitched, insectlike
jeet. Fairly common; feeds in marshes and on mud flats.

Baird's Sandpiper *Calidris bairdii* L 7½" (19 cm)
Long wings extend past tail in standing bird. Buff-brown
above and across breast. Pale edgings on juvenile's back give a
scaly appearance (see also page 139). Distinguished from
Least Sandpiper by larger size, longer and straighter bill. Call
is a low, raspy *kreeep*. Fairly common; found on upper beaches
and inland on lakeshores, wet fields. Migration is through center of continent. Uncommon migrant, usually juveniles, on
both coasts in fall.

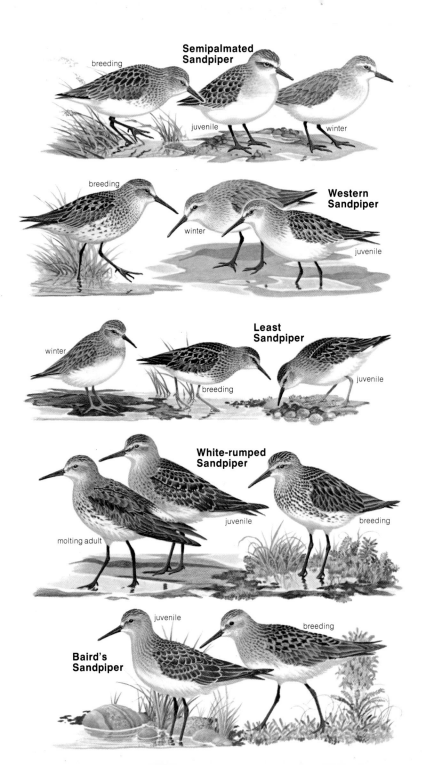

Semipalmated Sandpiper

breeding

juvenile

winter

Western Sandpiper

breeding

winter

juvenile

Least Sandpiper

winter

breeding

juvenile

White-rumped Sandpiper

juvenile

molting adult

breeding

Baird's Sandpiper

juvenile

breeding

Long-toed Stint *Calidris subminuta* L 6" (15 cm)

Asian species, casual in spring on St. Lawrence Island and the Pribilofs; can be fairly common on the outer Aleutians. Distinguished in all plumages from Least Sandpiper (preceding page) by dark forehead and bolder eyebrow, broadening behind eye; breeding adult lacks distinct dark necklace. Note also bolder pale line on sides of back.

Little Stint *Calidris minuta* L 6" (15 cm)

Eurasian species, casual on east coast; very rare off western Alaska islands in spring and fall. Breeding birds are brightly fringed with rufous above; throat and underparts white, with bright buff wash and bold spotting on sides of breast. Redder above than Western and Semipalmated Sandpipers (preceding page); compare also with Rufous-necked Stint. Juvenile distinguished from juvenile Rufous-necked by extensively black-centered, buff-fringed wing coverts and tertials.

Temminck's Stint *Calidris temminckii* L 6¹/₄" (16 cm)

Eurasian species, rare spring and fall migrant on Pribilofs, Aleutians, and St. Lawrence Island. White outer tail feathers distinctive in all plumages. Breeding adult resembles the larger Baird's Sandpiper (preceding page), but legs are dull yellow or greenish-yellow. In juvenile, feathers of upperparts have dark subterminal edges, buffy fringe. Call is a repeated, rapid dry rattle, unlike Least Sandpiper's shrill call.

Rufous-necked Stint *Calidris ruficollis* L 6¹/₄" (16 cm)

Asian species, casual migrant on both coasts; regular migrant on western Alaska coast and islands. Breeding range in Alaska is conjectural. Rufous on throat and upper breast may be pale and indistinct; look for necklace of dark streaks on white lower breast. Juveniles distinguished from juvenile Little Stint by plainer gray wing coverts and tertials.

Spoonbill Sandpiper *Eurynorhynchus pygmeus*

L 6" (15 cm) Asian species, accidental migrant in Alaska and coastal British Columbia. In breeding plumage, may be mistaken for Rufous-necked Stint. Bill is longer; bill shape is distinctive but requires a close view. Juvenile has darker cheek patch than juvenile Rufous-necked.

Broad-billed Sandpiper *Limicola falcinellus*

L 7" (18 cm) Eurasian species, accidental fall migrant on the Aleutians. All sightings so far have been of juveniles. Plump body, short legs, and long bill form a distinctive profile. Upper mandible droops at tip. Note also the unusual forked eyebrow. In all plumages, head pattern and long bill suggest Common Snipe (page 124).

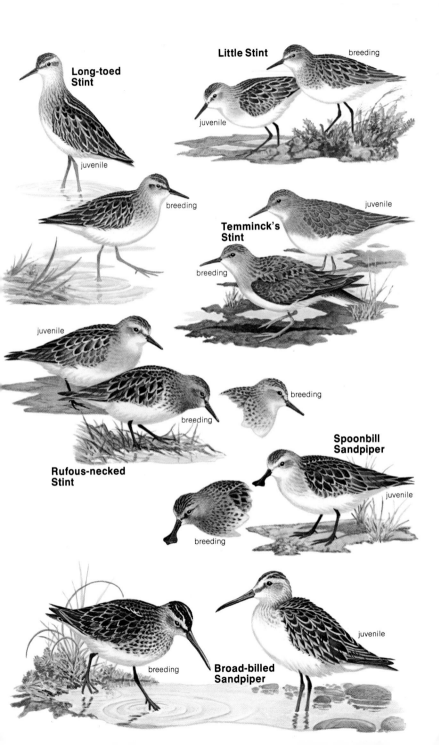

Long-toed Stint

juvenile

breeding

Little Stint

juvenile

breeding

Temminck's Stint

juvenile

breeding

juvenile

breeding

breeding

Rufous-necked Stint

Spoonbill Sandpiper

juvenile

breeding

breeding

Broad-billed Sandpiper

juvenile

Sharp-tailed Sandpiper *Calidris acuminata*

L 8¹/₂" (22 cm) A Siberian breeder, casual spring and fairly common fall migrant in western Alaska; rare but regular in fall migration along entire Pacific coast. Casual in fall across rest of continent. Most sightings are juveniles, distinguished from juvenile Pectoral Sandpiper by white eyebrow that broadens behind the eye; bright buffy breast lightly streaked on upper breast and sides; streaked undertail coverts; and brighter rufous cap and edging on upperparts (see also page 139). Adult in breeding plumage is similar to juvenile, but more spotted below. Call is a mellow, two-note whistle.

Pectoral Sandpiper *Calidris melanotos* *L 8³/₄" (22 cm)*

Prominent streaking on breast, darker in male, contrasts sharply with clear white belly. Male is much larger than female. Juvenile has buffy wash on streaked breast. Compare especially with juvenile Sharp-tailed Sandpiper (see also page 139). Often feeds in wet meadows, marshes, pond edges. More common in east and interior than on west coast, where it occurs mainly in fall. Call is a rich, low *churk*.

Ruff *Philomachus pugnax* ♂ *L 12" (31 cm)* ♀ *L 10" (25 cm)*

Old World species, casual migrant throughout North America; rare along coasts; annual in winter in California; has bred in Alaska. Breeding males acquire dramatic ruffs in colors that range from black to rufous to white. Female lacks ruff, is smaller, and has a variable amount of black below. Both sexes have a plump body, small head, and white underwings. Leg color may be yellow, orange, or red. Juvenile is buffy below, has prominently fringed feathers above. In flight (page 139), the U-shaped white band on rump is distinctive in all plumages.

Upland Sandpiper *Bartramia longicauda* *L 12" (31 cm)*

Small head, with large, dark, prominent eyes; long, thin neck, long tail, long wings. Legs yellow. Prefers upland fields, where often only its head and neck are visible above the grass. Also perches on posts and stumps. In flight (page 137), blackish primaries contrast strikingly with mottled brown upperparts. Fairly common except in eastern range, where declining. Casual on west coast and the southwest in migration. Call is a rolling *pulip pulip*. Formerly called Upland Plover.

Buff-breasted Sandpiper *Tryngites subruficollis*

L 8¹/₄" (21 cm) Face, throat, and breast are buff, much paler on the belly and undertail coverts. In flight, in all plumages, shows pure white underwings. In mixed flocks of shorebirds, its longer, thinner neck, small head, and longer legs are distinctive. Prefers shortgrass fields, wet rice fields. Migrates through the interior of the continent. In fall, rare on the west coast, uncommon in the east; most sightings on coasts are of juveniles (see also page 137).

juvenile

Pectoral Sandpiper

breeding ♂

breeding ♀

juvenile

breeding

Sharp-tailed Sandpiper

juvenile ♂

winter ♂

breeding ♂♂

breeding ♀

Ruff

breeding ♂

Upland Sandpiper

juvenile

juvenile

Buff-breasted Sandpiper

Shorebirds in Flight

Marbled Godwit
winter

Bar-tailed Godwit
baueri winter

Hudsonian Godwit
winter

Bar-tailed Godwit
lapponica winter

Black-tailed Godwit
winter

Far Eastern Curlew

Eurasian Curlew
juvenile

Long-billed Curlew

phaeopus juvenile

variegatus

hudsonicus

Whimbrel

Bristle-thighed Curlew

Eskimo Curlew

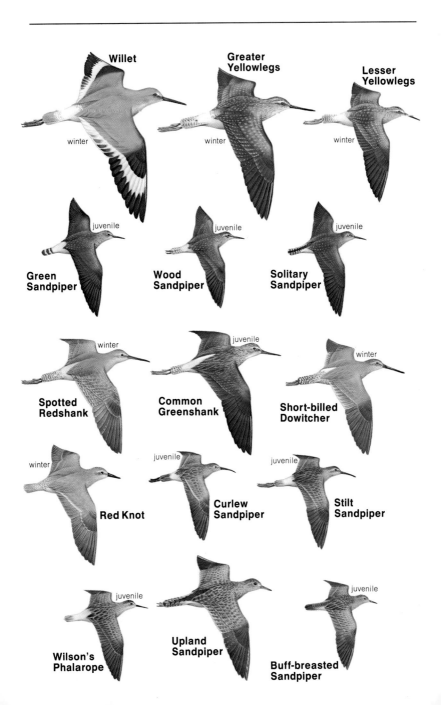

Willet

winter

Greater Yellowlegs

winter

Lesser Yellowlegs

winter

juvenile

Green Sandpiper

Wood Sandpiper

juvenile

Solitary Sandpiper

juvenile

Spotted Redshank

winter

Common Greenshank

juvenile

Short-billed Dowitcher

winter

Red Knot

winter

Curlew Sandpiper

juvenile

Stilt Sandpiper

juvenile

Wilson's Phalarope

juvenile

Upland Sandpiper

Buff-breasted Sandpiper

juvenile

Shorebirds in Flight

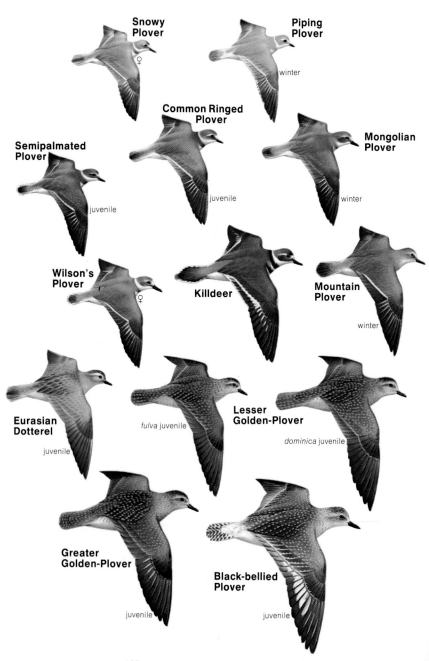

Snowy Plover ♀

Piping Plover winter

Common Ringed Plover juvenile

Mongolian Plover winter

Semipalmated Plover juvenile

Wilson's Plover ♀

Killdeer

Mountain Plover winter

Eurasian Dotterel juvenile

fulva juvenile

Lesser Golden-Plover

dominica juvenile

Greater Golden-Plover juvenile

Black-bellied Plover juvenile

Rock Sandpiper
winter

Purple Sandpiper
winter

Dunlin
winter

Sanderling
winter

Red Phalarope
winter

Red-necked Phalarope
winter

Western Sandpiper
winter

Semipalmated Sandpiper
winter

Least Sandpiper
winter

Temminck's Stint
juvenile

Baird's Sandpiper
juvenile

White-rumped Sandpiper
juvenile

Pectoral Sandpiper
juvenile

Sharp-tailed Sandpiper
juvenile

Ruff
juvenile ♀

Skuas, Jaegers, Gulls, Terns (Family Laridae)

Large seabirds with strong wings, powerful flight. Some species are highly pelagic, spending most of their time over the open sea. Others are seen in coastal waters, and some frequent inland waters.

Great Skua *Catharacta skua* L 23" (58 cm) W 55" (140 cm)

Large, heavy, and barrel-chested; wings broader and more rounded than jaegers (next page); tail shorter, broader. Both skua species show a distinctly hunchbacked appearance in flight and a large, conspicuous white bar at base of primaries; bill is heavier than in jaegers. Great Skua is distinguished from South Polar Skua by overall reddish or ginger brown color and heavy streaking on back, wing coverts, and much of underparts; sometimes shows dark brown cap. Immature shows less streaking, especially on underparts. Uncommon; breeds in Iceland and northern Europe; winters in North Atlantic. Seen well offshore from November to April; very rare in summer off Atlantic coast. Strong, powerful fliers, skuas pursue gulls and other seabirds and rob them of their prey.

South Polar Skua *Catharacta maccormicki*

L 21" (53 cm) W 52" (132 cm) Large, heavy, and barrel-chested; wings broader and more rounded than jaegers (next page); tail shorter, broader. Like Great Skua, shows a distinctly hunchbacked appearance in flight, a bold white bar at base of primaries, and a heavier bill than in jaegers. In all ages, South Polar Skua shows a uniform back and wing color and lacks the reddish tones and streaking seen on upperparts of Great Skua. In light-phase birds, contrastingly pale nape is distinctive. Dark phase is uniformly blackish-brown across mantle, with golden hackles on nape; distinguished from subadult Pomarine Jaeger by larger size, broader and more rounded wings, more distinct white wing bar. Light phase has grayish head, nape, and underparts. Immatures of both color phases are darker than light-phase adults, ranging from dark brown to dark gray. In the field, birds under two years of age are generally indistinguishable from juveniles; birds over two years old are generally indistinguishable from full adults. The South Polar Skua breeds in the Antarctic; winters (our summer) in North Atlantic and North Pacific, usually from May to early November. Most numerous in spring and fall off west coast, in spring off east coast; casual off south coast of Alaska; accidental in Gulf of Mexico. Generally stays well offshore; seen casually from shore in the west. Difficulty of identification makes range information somewhat speculative for both skua species.

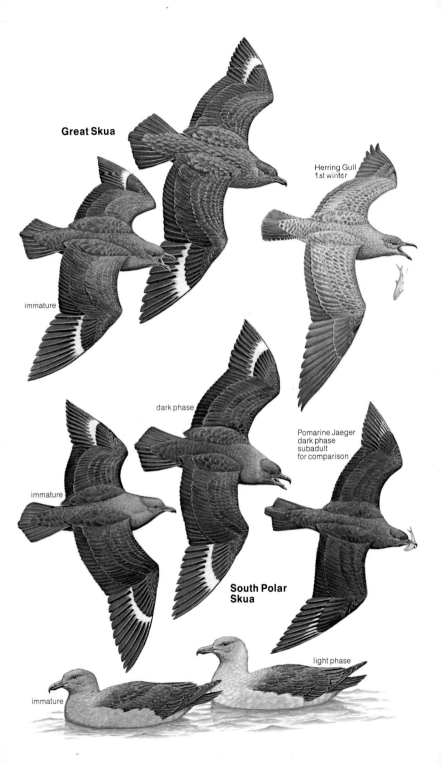

Great Skua

immature

Herring Gull
1st winter

dark phase

immature

Pomarine Jaeger
dark phase
subadult
for comparison

**South Polar
Skua**

immature

light phase

Jaegers

Predatory seabirds with long, pointed, angled wings. Adult plumage and long central tail feathers take three or four years to develop. Complex and variable plumages make identification extremely difficult. Most molts occur after the fall migration.

Pomarine Jaeger *Stercorarius pomarinus*
L 21" (53 cm) W 48" (122 cm) Adult's tail streamers, twisted at ends, form dark blobs when seen from side; length is variable. Body bulkier, bill larger, than Parasitic Jaeger; compare also with South Polar Skua (preceding page). Wingbeats are deep and regular, slower than Parasitic. In light-phase bird, breast band is usually heavier than on other jaegers, especially in adult female. Most birds show a distinctive second pale underwing patch at base of primary coverts. Juvenile plumage varies: light phase (rare), or barred (shown), or dark phase; tail streamers are barely visible. Barred phase has more prominent barring below than Parasitic. In all ages, white at base of primaries on upperwing is more extensive than in other jaegers. Breeds on low, swampy tundra; winters at sea; seen rarely from east coast, more commonly from west. Uncommon off east coast during fall migration; casual inland.

Parasitic Jaeger *Stercorarius parasiticus*
L 19" (48 cm) W 42" (107 cm) Smaller, more slender than Pomarine Jaeger; wing stroke faster. Tail streamers are pointed; white on wing less prominent than in Pomarine. Juvenile varies from light to dark, much like Pomarine. In all ages, note less white on upperwings, and pointed tail streamers. On light-phase juvenile, barring below is comparatively muted. Rufous-brown tint is unlike Long-tailed juvenile. Immature loses barring gradually with age. Fairly common; breeds on low tundra, stony areas. Uncommon on east coast during fall migration; fairly common on west coast; very rare inland.

Long-tailed Jaeger *Stercorarius longicaudus*
L 22" (56 cm) W 40" (102 cm) Most lightly built jaeger, with proportionally long tail in all ages. Adult has very long, pointed tail streamers. Flight is more graceful, ternlike. In all plumages, note distinctive contrast between grayish mantle and darker flight feathers. Adult lacks white patch on underwings; juvenile does have white there but is grayer overall than Parasitic Jaeger; light-phase juvenile has pale belly and stronger barring on tail coverts. Some juveniles have a very pale head and nape. In all ages, white at base of primaries on upperwing is less extensive than in Parasitic. Juvenile tail streamers are more rounded than in Parasitic; in older immatures they become pointed. Common in dry, upland-tundra breeding area; migration routes far offshore; migrating birds uncommon off west coast, rare in fall off east coast, and very rare inland and off Gulf coast.

Pomarine Jaeger

dark phase breeding

light phase breeding

light phase subadult

barred phase juvenile

Parasitic Jaeger

light phase breeding

dark phase breeding

light phase juvenile

dark phase juvenile

light phase subadult

Long-tailed Jaeger

light phase juvenile

dark phase juvenile

breeding

subadult

Gulls

A large, widespread group; often called seagulls, but many species nest inland. Gulls take two, three, or four years to reach their first full breeding plumage.

Many are highly variable and hard to identify in immature plumage. Most species have a complete molt in late summer and a partial molt in spring.

Heermann's Gull *Larus heermanni*

L 19" (48 cm) W 51" (130 cm) Three-to-four-year gull. Adult distinctive with white head, streaked gray-brown in winter; red bill; dark gray body; black tail with white terminal band; white trailing edge on wings. Second-winter bird is browner, bill two-toned, tail band buff. First-winter bird has dark brown body, lacks contrasting tail tip and trailing edge on wing. Wings are fairly long, flight buoyant. Common postbreeding visitor along the west coast; very rare at Salton Sea.

Franklin's Gull *Larus pipixcan* L 14¹⁄₂" (37 cm) W 36" (91 cm)

Three-year gull. Breeding adult has black hood, white underparts variably tinged with pink, slate gray wings with white bar and black-and-white tips on primaries. Distinguished from Laughing Gull by white bar and large white tips on primaries; pale gray central tail feathers; and broader white eye crescents. All winter birds have a dark half-hood, more extensive than in any winter Laughing Gull. Second-summer Franklin's has partial or no bar on primaries. First-summer bird like winter adult but lacks white primary bar; bill and legs black. First-winter bird resembles first-winter Laughing; note white outer tail feathers, half-hood, broader eye crescents, white underparts, and, in flight (page 160), pale inner primaries. Juvenile is like first-winter bird but back is brown. At all ages, distinguished from Laughing Gull by smaller size, smaller bill with less prominent hook, rounder forehead, less extensive dark on underside of primaries, shorter legs and wings, giving a stocky look when standing, and by more graceful flight. Rare migrant along both coasts; very rare in winter along Gulf coast and in southern California.

Laughing Gull *Larus atricilla* L 16¹⁄₂" (42 cm) W 40" (102 cm)

Three-year gull. Adult in breeding plumage has black hood, white underparts, slate gray wings with black outer primaries. In winter, shows gray wash on nape; compare with the half-hood of Franklin's Gull. Second-summer bird has partial hood, some spotting on tip of tail. Second-winter bird (see also page 160) is similar to second-summer but has gray wash on sides of breast, lacks hood. First-winter bird has extensively gray sides, complete tail band, gray wash on nape, slate gray back, dark brown wings; compare with first-winter Franklin's Gull. Juvenile is like first-winter bird but brown on head and body. Common along coasts; very rare inland except at Salton Sea, where it is fairly common.

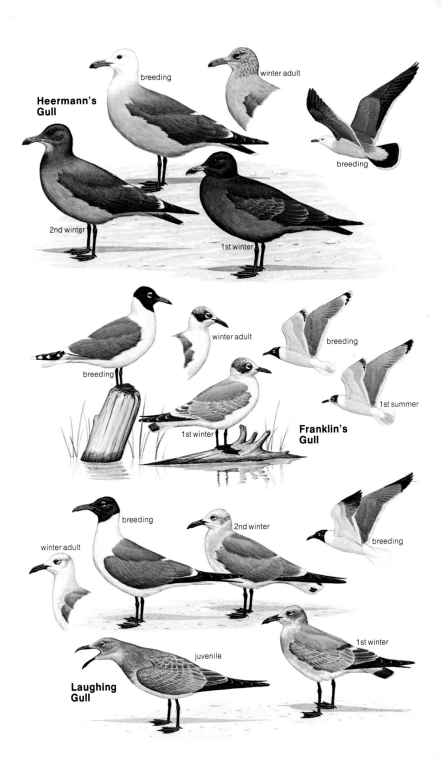

Heermann's Gull

breeding

winter adult

breeding

2nd winter

1st winter

Franklin's Gull

breeding

winter adult

breeding

1st winter

1st summer

Laughing Gull

winter adult

breeding

2nd winter

breeding

juvenile

1st winter

Bonaparte's Gull *Larus philadelphia*

L 13¹/₂″ (34 cm) W 33″ (84 cm) Two-year gull. Breeding adult has slate black hood, black bill, gray mantle with black wing tips that are pale on underside; white underparts, red legs. In winter, head is white with dark smudge behind eye. In flight, shows white wedge on wing. First-summer bird has partial hood; wings and tail are like first-winter. First-winter bird has a dark brown carpal bar on leading edge of wing, dark band on secondaries, black tail band (see also page 160); compare with first-winter Black-legged Kittiwake (pages 158, 160). Flight is buoyant, wingbeats rapid. Querulous, chattering call distinctive. Uncommon inland migrant, common on the Great Lakes.

Common Black-headed Gull *Larus ridibundus*

L 16″ (41 cm) W 40″ (102 cm) Two-year gull. Breeding adult has dark brown hood; red bill and legs; mantle slightly paler gray than Bonaparte's Gull; black wing tips; white underparts. Winter adult has dark spot behind eye. First-summer bird has incomplete hood; wings and tail like first-winter. In flight, shows white wedge on wing; compare with Bonaparte's. Juvenile and first-winter birds have two-toned bill, pale legs, dark tail band, dark brown carpal bar (see also page 160). Distinguished from Bonaparte's by size, bill color, darker underside of primaries. Colonizer from Europe, casual breeder in eastern Canada. Uncommon in winter on east coast and as migrant off western Alaska, rare elsewhere in North America.

Little Gull *Larus minutus* *L 11″ (28 cm) W 24″ (61 cm)*

Three-year gull. Breeding adult has black hood, black bill, pale gray mantle, white wing tips, white underparts, red legs. Winter adult has dusky cap, dark spot behind eye. Wings uniformly pale gray above, dark gray to black below, with white trailing edge. Second-winter bird is like adult but underwing pattern is incomplete; shows some black in primaries (page 160). First-summer has partial hood, some brown in primaries and coverts, partial tail band. First-winter is like Bonaparte's but primaries blackish above, lack white wedge; wings show strong blackish W; crown shows more black. In all plumages, note short, rounded wings. Old World species, now breeding around Great Lakes and at Churchill, Manitoba. Uncommon winter visitor and migrant on east coast, rare elsewhere in U.S.

Ross' Gull *Rhodostethia rosea* *L 13¹/₂″ (34 cm) W 33″ (84 cm)*

Old World arctic species, recently found breeding in northern Canada and Greenland. Common fall migrant along northern coast of Alaska; presumably winters at sea. Accidental south to northern U. S. Two-year gull. Adults variably pale pink to bright pink below; upperwing pale gray; underwing pale to dark gray. Black collar in summer; collar partial or absent in winter. First-winter bird has black at tip of tail, dark spot behind eye; in flight, shows W pattern like Little Gull. In all plumages, note long, pointed wings; long, wedge-shaped tail; and broad, white trailing edge to wings.

Bonaparte's Gull

breeding

winter adult

1st winter

winter adult

Common Black-headed Gull

breeding

1st summer

winter adult

1st winter

winter adult

Little Gull

breeding

1st winter

breeding

winter adult

Ross' Gull

winter adult

1st winter

breeding

Ring-billed Gull *Larus delawarensis*

L 17½" (45 cm) W 48" (122 cm) Three-year gull. Typical of three-year gulls, acquires a new and different plumage in each of the first three falls; summer plumage varies only slightly from winter. Adult has pale gray mantle; white head and underparts; yellow bill with black subterminal ring; pale eyes; yellowish legs; black primaries tipped with two white spots. Head streaked with brown in winter. Second-winter birds are like winter adult but bill has broader band, black of primaries is more extensive, tail usually has some blackish terminal spots. First-winter bird has gray back, brown wings with dark blackish-brown primaries, brown-streaked head and nape; underparts mostly white, with brown spots and scalloping on breast and throat; tail has medium-wide brown band and extensive mottling above band; uppertail and undertail coverts are lightly barred; secondary coverts medium gray; wing linings mostly white, with some barring (page 160). Distinguished from first-winter Mew Gull by white underparts spotted on breast and throat, tail pattern, darker primaries, heavier bill, paler back. Juvenile is like first-winter but back is brown, spotting below more extensive, bill has more black. On east coast, compare with European form of Mew Gull. Abundant and widespread; winters uncommonly outside mapped range.

Mew Gull *Larus canus* L 16" (41 cm) W 43" (109 cm)

Three-year gull. Adult has white head, heavily washed with brown in winter; dark gray mantle; primaries tipped with black and white; thin, unmarked yellow bill; large dark eye. Second-winter bird is like adult but bill is two-toned, blackish on primaries more extensive; first primary has large white spot; spotty tail band (page 160). First-winter birds are heavily washed with brown below, almost solid brown on belly; spotted with white on breast. The head and nape are washed with soft brown; mantle dark gray; primaries light brown with pale edges. The tail is almost entirely brown, with heavily barred uppertail and undertail coverts; wing lining evenly pale brown (page 160). Juvenile is like first-winter, but dark brown on the back and head, darker below. The Siberian form (not shown) recorded in the Aleutians is most like American birds but male is almost as large as Ring-billed Gull. European form resembles American birds in second-winter and adult plumage but is more like Ring-billed Gull in first-winter; note the mostly white tail with dark subterminal band, unbarred white uppertail and undertail coverts, darker gray back, pale brown secondary coverts, white wing linings mottled with brown. Winter adults sometimes have a faint dusky subterminal ring on the bill. All Mew Gulls are comparatively smaller than Ring-billed Gulls, with rounder heads, thinner bills, larger eyes. Adults in flight show much more white in primaries. Rare inland in winter; European and American forms casual on east coast in winter.

Ring-billed Gull

winter adult

breeding

2nd winter

juvenile

1st winter

breeding

Mew Gull

breeding

winter adult

breeding

2nd winter

European 1st winter

juvenile

1st winter

Herring Gull *Larus argentatus* *L 25" (64 cm) W 58" (147 cm)*
Highly variable four-year gull. Adult has pale gray mantle; white head, streaked with brown in winter; white underparts; primaries black toward the tips; legs and feet pink; bill yellow with red spot. Third-winter plumage is like winter adult but with black smudge on bill, some brown on body and wing coverts. Second-winter bird has gray back, brown wings, pale eye, two-toned bill; gray back (usually acquired in late winter) is distinctly paler than Lesser Black-backed and Western Gulls (pages 154, 156), slightly paler than California Gull. First-winter birds are brown overall, with dark brownish-black primaries and tail band, dark eye, dark bill, usually with some pale at base by midwinter; some can have bill like first-winter California Gull; usually distinguished by more extensively dark bill, paler face and throat, and, in flight (page 161), by pale area at base of primaries and single dark bar on secondaries. Distinguished from first-winter Western Gull by smaller bill, paler and more mottled body plumage, and in flight by paler wings and lack of contrast between back and rump. Distinguished from first-winter Lesser Black-backed Gull by generally darker, less contrasting body plumage, usually darker belly, and in flight by pale primary and secondary coverts and less contrasting rump pattern. A very few Herring Gulls in all ages can show yellowish legs. Abundant and spreading.

California Gull *Larus californicus*
L 21" (53 cm) W 54" (137 cm) Four-year gull, less variable than larger species. Adult has dark gray mantle, slightly darker than Herring Gull, paler than Lesser Black-backed Gull (page 154); white head, heavily streaked with brown in winter; dark eye; yellow bill with black and red spots, the black spot often greatly reduced in breeding season; gray-green or greenish-yellow legs. In flight, shows dusky trailing edge on underwing. Bill is smaller, head rounder than in Herring Gull. Third-winter plumage is like adult but bill is more extensively smudged with black; wings show some brown; tail has some brown spotting. Second-winter bird has gray back, brown wings, grayish legs, two-toned bill. First-winter bird is brown overall with veiled gray on back, unlike other large gulls; usually palest on throat, breast, and upper belly; legs pinkish; bill two-toned, the colors sharply defined. In flight (page 161), first-winter birds show double dark bar along trailing edge of wing; primaries and primary coverts more extensively dark; uppertail coverts more heavily barred than Herring Gull. Distinctly smaller than Western Gull (page 156), with thinner bill. Common throughout most of range; casual on the east coast and Gulf coast in winter. First-winter birds should be compared carefully with first- and second-winter Herring and Lesser Black-backed Gulls.

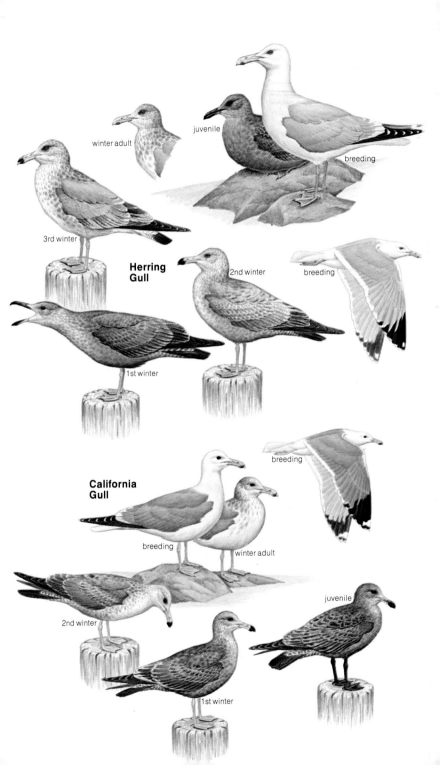

winter adult

juvenile

breeding

3rd winter

**Herring
Gull**

2nd winter

breeding

1st winter

breeding

**California
Gull**

breeding

winter adult

breeding

2nd winter

juvenile

1st winter

Glaucous Gull *Larus hyperboreus*

L 27" (69 cm) W 60" (152 cm) Heavy-bodied four-year gull. In all ages, note translucent tips of white primaries. Adult has pale gray wings and mantle, yellow eye, yellow bill with red spot. Head is streaked with brown in winter. Third-winter plumage like adult but has dark smudge on bill and some buff on body. Late second-winter bird has gray back and pale eye. First-winter birds may be buffy or almost all-white; bill is bicolored. Distinguished from Iceland Gull by size; heavier, longer bill; flatter crown; slightly paler mantle of adults; proportionately shorter wings, barely extending beyond tail. At all ages, distinguished from Glaucous-winged Gull (pages 156, 161) by translucent primaries; in first-winter plumage, by two-toned bill. Rare in winter south to Gulf states and southern California. Birds from Alaska are slightly smaller and adults are slightly darker mantled than birds from eastern Canada. Occasionally hybridizes with Herring Gull.

Iceland Gull *Larus glaucoides* *L 22" (56 cm) W 54" (137 cm)*

Highly variable four-year gull. Adult has translucent white tips on primaries, usually marked with gray above; gray mantle, yellow bill with red spot, white head, streaked with brown in winter. Most adults have yellow eye; a few have brown. Late second-winter birds have pale eye, gray back, two-toned bill. First-winter birds are buffy to mostly white; black bill is short, thin, and pointed; eye dark; wing tips white or irregularly washed with brown. Distinguished from first-winter Thayer's Gull by translucent primaries, usually paler body plumage, and speckled tail (see also page 161). Distinguished from Glaucous Gull by smaller size, rounder head, all-dark bill; proportionately longer wings, extending well beyond tail at rest. Casual south to Gulf states, rare on Great Lakes.

Thayer's Gull *Larus thayeri* *L 23" (58 cm) W 55" (140 cm)*

Variable four-year gull. In most adults, eye is dark brown, mantle slightly darker than Iceland or Herring Gull (preceding page); bill yellow with dark red spot; legs darker pink than similar species. Primaries pale gray below, with thin, dark trailing edge; irregularly dark gray above. A few adults have yellow eye flecked with brown. Second-winter bird has gray mantle, contrasting gray-brown tail band, dark eye. First-winter birds variable but primaries always uniformly pale below, darker than mantle above. Distinguished from Herring Gull by more evenly colored plumage, shorter, stubbier bill, and lack of contrasting dark secondaries (pages 150, 161). Distinguished from Iceland Gull by generally darker plumage, primaries darker above than mantle, and usually by unspeckled tail. Compare with Glaucous-winged Gull (page 156), which is larger, with larger bill, less noticeable speckling in subadult plumage, and wing tips the same color as mantle. Rare winter visitor in the east and throughout the interior, but identification is difficult. Formerly a subspecies of Herring Gull; considered by some a form of Iceland Gull.

Glaucous Gull

breeding

2nd winter

winter adult

winter adult

1st winter

1st winter

Iceland Gull

1st winter

winter adult

breeding

winter adult

1st winter

2nd winter

Thayer's Gull

winter adult

winter adult

2nd winter

breeding

1st winter

1st winter

Slaty-backed Gull *Larus schistisagus*

L 25" (64 cm) W 58" (147 cm) Northern coastal species of Asia. Uncommon summer and rare fall visitor to the Aleutians and western Alaska, rare on north and south coasts. A heavy, four-year gull only seen at sea and along the coasts. Adult has very dark gray back and wings, blackish outer primaries separated by a whitish bar. Underside of primaries gray, not black. Note broad white trailing edge to wings. Legs bright pink; eyes yellow. Third-summer bird is like adult but note brown primaries. Second-summer has dark back, very pale wings. First-summer (page 161) is quite pale and has dark bill, dark eyes. Eastern Siberian form of Herring Gull (not shown), widespread in western Alaska, has slightly paler upperparts, lacks broad white trailing edge; underside of primaries darker.

Lesser Black-backed Gull *Larus fuscus*

L 21" (53 cm) W 54" (137 cm) European species; casual to uncommon but increasing on Atlantic coast; casual inland, accidental to west coast. A four-year gull. Adult has white head, streaked with brown in winter; white underparts; yellow legs. Third-winter bird has dark smudge on bill; yellow or, rarely, pink legs; some brown in wings. Second-winter plumage resembles second-winter Herring Gull (page 150) but note dark gray of back; legs are sometimes yellow. First-winter bird is very much like first-winter Herring Gull but head and belly are usually paler, upperparts more contrastingly dark and light. Bill is always entirely black. Identified in flight (page 161) by the darker primary and secondary coverts, more extensively dark primaries and white outer tail feathers; paler rump contrasts with back. Much smaller than Great Black-backed Gull. Smaller on average than Herring Gull, with smaller bill, but note substantial range of overlap; also note longer wings, usually extending well beyond tail at rest. Scandinavian subspecies (not shown), reported from the northeast, has back as dark as in Great Black-backed Gull.

Great Black-backed Gull *Larus marinus*

L 30" (76 cm) W 65" (165 cm) Four-year gull. In all ages, huge size and massive bill are distinctive. Adult has white head, virtually unstreaked in winter; black upperparts; white underparts; pale eye; pink legs. In flight, note outer primary's white tip and white spot on second primary. Third-winter bird is like adult but shows some dark on bill, some brown in wings, sometimes dark in tail. Second-summer bird has pale eye, black back; wings and tail are like first-winter. Second-winter is like first-winter but base of bill is paler, secondary coverts more evenly brown. First-winter bird resembles Herring Gull (page 150) but head and body are much paler, back and wings have the checkered look of young Lesser Black-backed Gull; in flight (page 161), shows almost white rump, more diffuse tail band. Uncommon on Great Lakes, casual inland throughout the east, rare on Gulf coast to Texas. Breeding range is expanding southward on the Atlantic coast.

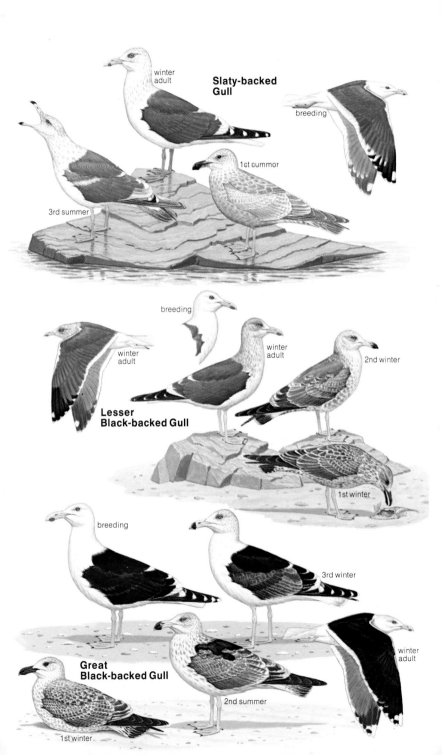

Slaty-backed Gull

winter adult

breeding

3rd summer

1st summer

Lesser Black-backed Gull

breeding

winter adult

winter adult

2nd winter

1st winter

Great Black-backed Gull

breeding

3rd winter

winter adult

1st winter

2nd summer

Yellow-footed Gull *Larus livens*

L 27" (69 cm) W 60" (152 cm) Breeds in the Gulf of California. Increasingly common as a postbreeding visitor to the Salton Sea. Three-year gull, formerly considered a subspecies of Western Gull. Adult is like Western but has yellow legs and feet; note also massive yellow bill with red spot; very dark gray wings with black-tipped primaries; yellow eyes. Second-winter bird is like adult but tail looks entirely black, bill two-toned. In first-winter plumage (shown in flight on page 161), head and body are mostly white, back and wings brown, eyes dark, bill mostly dark, legs pinkish. Juvenile resembles first-winter Western Gull but white belly contrasts sharply with streaked breast; upperparts are more boldly patterned; rump whiter.

Western Gull *Larus occidentalis*

L 25" (64 cm) W 58" (147 cm) Variable four-year gull. Adults north of Monterey have paler backs and darker eyes than southern birds. All adults have white head, dark gray back, pink legs, very large bill. In winter, head is moderately streaked with brown in northern birds, faintly streaked in southern. Third-winter plumage resembles second-winter Yellow-footed Gull but tail is mostly white. Second-winter bird has a dark gray back, yellow eyes, two-toned bill, dark brown wings. First-winter bird is one of the darkest young gulls; bill is black; in flight (page 161), distinguished from young Herring Gull by contrast of dark back with paler rump. Note also the often sootier underparts and head, heavier bill. Juvenile is like first-winter but darker. Western Gulls hybridize extensively with Glaucous-winged Gulls in the northwest; hybrids are seen all along the west coast in winter; two ages are shown here. These are easily confused with Thayer's Gull (page 152); note large bill, pattern of wing tips. Western Gulls are casual inland.

Glaucous-winged Gull *Larus glaucescens*

L 26" (66 cm) W 58" (147 cm) Variable four-year gull. Adult has white head, moderately streaked with brown in winter. Body is white, mantle pale gray; primaries are the same color as remainder of wing above, paler below. Eyes dark; large bill is yellow with red spot; legs pink. Third-winter bird is like adult but has some buff on body, bill is smudged black; some have a partial tail band. In second-winter plumage, back is gray, rest of body and wings are pale buff to white with little mottling; tail evenly gray; bill mostly dark. First-winter bird (shown in flight on page 161) is uniformly pale gray-brown to whitish with subtle mottling or contrast; primaries are the same color as the mantle, and not translucent. Young Glaucous Gull (pages 152, 161) has sharply two-toned bill, translucent primaries. Young Thayer's Gull (page 152) is smaller, with smaller bill, more speckled body plumage, and contrastingly darker primaries. Glaucous-winged Gull hybridizes extensively with Western Gull; with Herring Gull in south-central Alaska. Hybrids are extremely variable. Glaucous-winged Gull is rare inland.

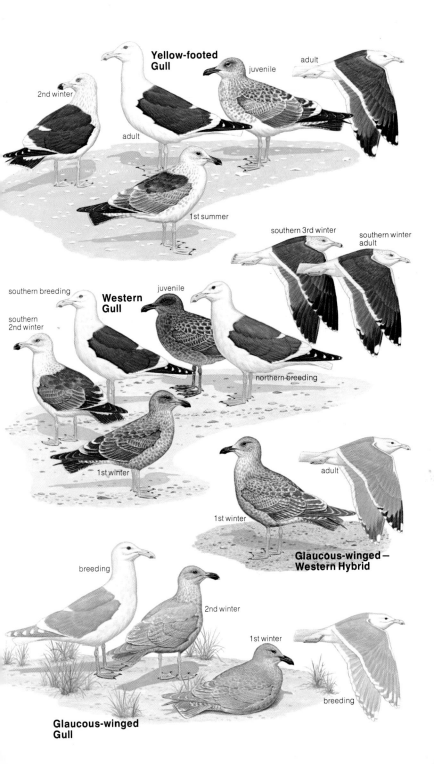

Yellow-footed Gull

2nd winter

adult

juvenile

adult

1st summer

southern 3rd winter

southern winter adult

southern breeding

Western Gull

southern 2nd winter

juvenile

northern breeding

1st winter

1st winter

adult

Glaucous-winged– Western Hybrid

breeding

2nd winter

1st winter

breeding

Glaucous-winged Gull

Black-legged Kittiwake   *Rissa tridactyla*

L 17" (43 cm) W 36" (91 cm)   Highly pelagic three-year gull. Adult has white head, nape smudged with gray in winter; dark eye; unmarked yellow bill; white body; gray mantle, darkest on back and inner wings; inner primaries pale; wing tips inky black. Legs black. Second-year Blackleg like adult but with more black on outermost primary. First-winter bird has dark half-collar; black bill, usually pale at base; black spot behind eye; dark tail band; and in flight (page 160), dark W across the wings. Distinguished from young Bonaparte's Gull (page 146) by half-collar, paler secondaries, slightly forked tail, larger size; from young Sabine's Gull by half-collar, dark carpal bar. A very few young birds have pinkish legs. Nests in large cliff colonies; winters at sea. Seen uncommonly from shore on the west coast, commonly in some years; rarely on the east coast.

Red-legged Kittiwake   *Rissa brevirostris*

L 15" (38 cm) W 33" (84 cm)   Highly pelagic two-year gull. Adult distinguished from Black-legged Kittiwake by coral red legs; shorter, thicker bill; darker mantle; wings are not paler on inner primaries as in Blackleg; broader white trailing edge on wings; dusky underside of primaries. In first year, wing pattern resembles Sabine's Gull (page 160), but Red-legged Kittiwake is the only gull to have an all-white tail in first winter; similar to young Blackleg but lacks W pattern on wings. Breeds in cliff colonies, usually close to Black-legged Kittiwakes. Very rare away from breeding grounds, even in winter.

Sabine's Gull   *Xema sabini*   *L 13¹/₂" (34 cm) W 33" (84 cm)*

Two-year gull with striking black-gray-and-white wing pattern in all ages. Breeding adult has dark gray hood with thin black ring at bottom; black bill with yellow tip; forked tail. First-summer bird is like adult but hood is incomplete; may have spots on tail. In juvenile plumage (see also page 160), wing pattern is like adult but muted; crown and nape are soft gray-brown; bill shows little or no yellow; tail has dark band. Sabine's Gull winters at sea in the Southern Hemisphere; many adults migrate out of North America before acquiring white head and dark nape of winter plumage. Juveniles depart before acquiring first-winter plumage. Common migrant off west coast, uncommon along shore; very rare migrant, mostly juveniles, on east coast and in interior.

Ivory Gull   *Pagophila eburnea*   *L 17" (43 cm) W 37" (94 cm)*

Two-year arctic gull, ghostly pale. Adults in all plumages are strikingly white with a yellow-tipped bill, black eyes, black legs. Immature birds have a variable amount of speckling on the body, heaviest around the face; show tail band and spots on tips of primaries. A short-necked, stocky gull with long wings. Winters primarily in arctic seas; casual along the Atlantic coast to New York and inland to the Great Lakes; uncommon in northern and western Alaska.

Black-legged Kittiwake

breeding

winter adult

1st winter

Red-legged Kittiwake

breeding

breeding

1st summer

1st winter

breeding

breeding

1st summer

Sabine's Gull

juvenile

adult

Ivory Gull

1st winter

adult

Gulls in Flight

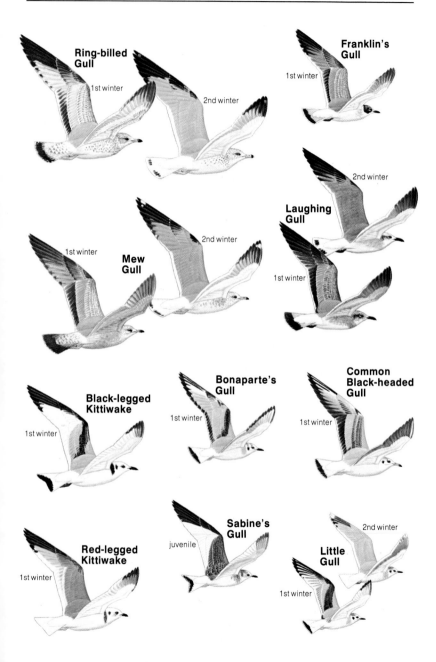

Ring-billed Gull — 1st winter — 2nd winter

Franklin's Gull — 1st winter

Laughing Gull — 2nd winter — 1st winter

Mew Gull — 1st winter — 2nd winter

Black-legged Kittiwake — 1st winter

Bonaparte's Gull — 1st winter

Common Black-headed Gull — 1st winter

Red-legged Kittiwake — 1st winter

Sabine's Gull — juvenile

Little Gull — 2nd winter — 1st winter

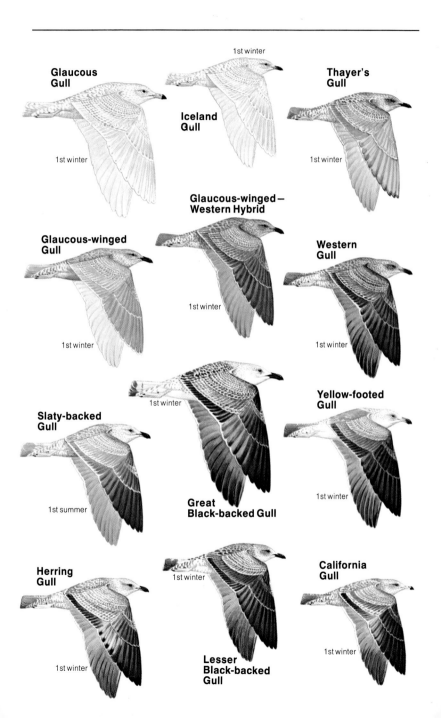

Glaucous
Gull

1st winter

1st winter

Iceland
Gull

Thayer's
Gull

1st winter

Glaucous-winged—
Western Hybrid

Glaucous-winged
Gull

1st winter

Western
Gull

1st winter

1st winter

Slaty-backed
Gull

1st winter

Yellow-footed
Gull

1st summer

Great
Black-backed Gull

1st winter

Herring
Gull

1st winter

1st winter

California
Gull

Lesser
Black-backed
Gull

1st winter

Terns

Distinguished from gulls by pointed wings and bill and by feeding technique. Most terns plunge-dive into the water after prey. Most species have a forked tail.

Common Tern *Sterna hirundo* L 14¹/₂" (37 cm) W 30" (76 cm)
Medium gray above, with black cap and nape; paler below. Bill red, usually black-tipped. Slightly stockier than the Arctic Tern, with flatter crown, longer neck and bill. In flight, usually displays a dark wedge, variably shaped, near tip of upperwing. Note also that head projects farther than in Arctic Tern. Common Tern's shorter tail gives it a chunkier look. Early juvenile is brownish above, white below, with mostly dark bill. Juvenile's forehead is white, crown and nape blackish; compare with juvenile Forster's Tern (next page). All immature and winter plumages have a dark shoulder bar. Full adult breeding plumage is acquired by third spring. Siberian subspecies, *S.h. longipennis*, seen regularly on islands of western Alaska, is darker overall; bill and legs black. Common Terns nest in large colonies. Common throughout breeding range; very rare in winter along the Gulf coast and in southern California. Fairly common to common migrant on Pacific coast from Washington south. Calls are similar to Arctic Tern; distinctive in Common Tern is a low, piercing, drawn-out *kee-ar-r-r-r*.

Arctic Tern *Sterna paradisaea* L 15¹/₂" (39 cm) W 31" (79 cm)
Medium gray above, with black cap and nape; paler below. Bill deep red. Slightly slimmer than the Common Tern, with rounder head, shorter neck and bill. In flight, upperwing appears uniformly gray, lacking dark wedge of Common Tern; underwing shows very narrow black line on trailing edge of primaries; all flight feathers appear translucent. Note also that tail is longer and head does not project as far as in Common Tern. Juvenile largely lacks brownish wash of early juvenile Common; shoulder bar less distinct; secondaries whitish. Forehead is white, crown and nape blackish; compare juvenile Forster's Tern (next page). Full adult breeding plumage is acquired by third spring. Arctic Terns migrate well offshore; casual inland during migration, especially in late spring. Calls include a raspy *tr-tee-ar,* higher than Common Tern's call.

Aleutian Tern *Sterna aleutica* L 13¹/₂" (34 cm) W 29" (74 cm)
Dark gray above and below, with white forehead, black cap, black bill, black legs. In flight, distinguished from Common and Arctic Terns by shorter tail and by white forehead and dark, white-edged bar on secondaries, most visible from below. Juvenile is buff and brown above; legs and lower mandible reddish. Aleutian Terns nest in loose colonies, sometimes with Arctic Terns. Migration routes and winter range unknown. Call is a squeaky *twee-ee-ee,* unlike any other tern.

Common Tern

breeding

1st summer

juvenile

2nd summer

longipennis breeding

breeding

1st fall

Arctic Tern

breeding

1st fall

1st summer

breeding

juvenile

Aleutian Tern

breeding

juvenile

Roseate Tern *Sterna dougallii* L 15¹/₂" (39 cm) W 29" (74 cm)
Breeding adult is white below with slight, variable pinkish cast visible in good light; pale gray above with black cap and nape. Much paler overall than Common and Arctic Terns (preceding page). Lacks dark trailing edge on underside of outer wing. Bill black; in breeding season has variable amount of red at base. Wings shorter than in Common and Arctic Terns; flies with rapid wingbeats. Deeply forked all-white tail extends well beyond wings in standing bird. Legs and feet bright red-orange. Juvenile's brownish cap extends over forehead; mantle looks coarsely scaled, lower back barred with black; bill and legs black. First-summer bird has white forehead; lacks dark secondaries of immature Common. Full adult plumage is attained by second spring. Uncommon and highly maritime, Roseate Terns usually come ashore only to nest. Casual migrant on Gulf coast. Call is a soft *chi-weep;* alarm signal a drawn-out *zra-ap,* like ripping cloth.

Forster's Tern *Sterna forsteri* L 14¹/₂" (37 cm) W 31" (79 cm)
Breeding adult is snow white below, pale gray above, with black cap and nape; mostly orange bill, orange legs and feet. Wingbeat much slower than in Roseate Tern. Legs and bill longer than in Common and Arctic Terns (preceding page). Long, deeply forked gray tail has white outer edges. In flight, shows pale upperwing area formed by silvery primaries; white rump contrasts with gray back, gray tail. Winter plumage resembles Common and Arctic Terns but is acquired by mid-August, much earlier than those species, which molt chiefly after migration out of U. S. Note also lack of dark shoulder bars; most have dark eye patches not joined at nape as in Common, but many have dark streaks on nape. Juvenile and first-winter bird have shorter tails than adults and more dark color in wings. Juvenile has ginger brown cap, dark eye patch; shoulder bar is faint or absent. Forster's Terns nest in widely scattered colonies in marshes. Calls include a hoarse *kyarr,* lower and shorter than in Common Tern.

Gull-billed Tern *Sterna nilotica* L 14" (36 cm) W 34" (86 cm)
Breeding adult is white below, pale gray above, with black crown and nape, stout black bill, black legs and feet. Stockier and paler than Common Tern (preceding page); wings broader; tail shorter and only moderately forked. Winter birds have white crown with fine, dark streaks. Juvenile has pale edgings on upperparts, bill is brownish. Fairly common but local; nests in salt marshes and on beaches; often seen hunting for insects over fields and marshes. Rare inland. In western U. S., found only at the Salton Sea. Adult call is a raspy, sharp *kay-wack;* call of juvenile is a faint, high-pitched *peep peep.*

Roseate Tern

juvenile

breeding

juvenile

1st summer

breeding

Forster's Tern

breeding

1st winter

juvenile

winter

Gull-billed Tern

juvenile

breeding

winter

Least Tern *Sterna antillarum* L 9″ (23 cm) W 20″ (51 cm)
Smallest North American tern. Breeding adult is gray above,
with black cap and nape, white forehead, orange-yellow bill
with dark tip; underparts are white; legs orange-yellow. In
flight, black wedge on outer primaries is conspicuous; note
also the short, deeply forked tail. Juvenile is pinkish-buff
above, with brownish U-shaped markings; crown is dusky;
wings show dark shoulder bar. By first fall, upperparts are
gray, crown whiter, but dark shoulder bar is retained. First-
summer birds are more like adults but have dark bill and legs,
shoulder bar, black line through eye, dusky primaries. Fairly
common and local on east and Gulf coasts; less common and
declining inland and on the west coast. Nests in colonies on
beaches, sandbars. Winters from Central America south. Calls
include high-pitched *kip* notes and a harsh *chir-ee-eep*. Flight
is rapid and buoyant. Formerly considered a form of an Old
World species, Little Tern *(S. albifrons)*.

Black Tern *Chlidonias niger* L 9³/₄″ (25 cm) W 24″ (61 cm)
Breeding adult is mostly black, with dark gray back, wings,
and tail, white undertail coverts. In flight, shows uniformly
pale gray underwing and fairly short tail, slightly forked. Bill is
black in all plumages. Juvenile and winter birds are white below, with dark gray mantle and tail; dark ear patch extends
from dark crown; flying birds show dark bar on side of breast.
Some juveniles show a contrastingly paler rump. Shoulder bar
on upper wing is much darker than in juvenile White-winged
Tern. First-summer birds can be almost all-white below or
patchy black-and-white; full breeding plumage is acquired in
second spring. Adults also appear patchy black-and-white as
they molt into winter plumage in late summer; these birds are
easily confused with the White-winged Tern. Black Terns are
common inland, nesting on lakeshores and in marshes; common on east coast during migration, uncommon on west coast.
Calls include a metallic *kik* and a slurred *k-seek*.

White-winged Tern *Chlidonias leucopterus*
L 9¹/₂″ (24 cm) W 23″ (58 cm) Eurasian species, casual vagrant to
east coast, accidental inland and on western Aleutians. Bill
and tail shorter than in Black Tern; tail less deeply notched. In
breeding plumage, red bill, white tail, whitish upperwing coverts, and black wing linings are distinctive; upperwing shows
black outer primaries. Molting birds are patchy black-and-
white but whitish tail and rump are distinctive. Winter adult
has white wing linings; lacks dark bar on sides of breast. Juvenile's brown back contrasts with grayish wing coverts and
whitish rump. Juveniles and winter adults have crown speckled with black rather than solid black; dark ear patch not usually connected to crown; bill is black. Formerly called
White-winged Black Tern.

Least Tern

breeding

breeding

juvenile

1st summer

Black Tern

breeding

winter

1st summer

breeding

juvenile

White-winged Tern

breeding

juvenile

winter

molting adult

Sandwich Tern   *Sterna sandvicensis*

L 15" (38 cm) W 34" (86 cm)   Long, slender, black bill, tipped with yellow. Breeding adult is pale gray above with black crown, short black crest. In flight, shows long, slender wings with some dark in the outer primaries. White tail is deeply forked, comparatively short. Legs and feet black. Adult in winter plumage, seen as early as July, has a white forehead, streaked crown, grayer tail. Juvenile's tail less deeply forked; bill often lacks yellow tip; in a few birds, bill is entirely yellow. By late summer, juvenile loses the dark V-shaped markings and spots on back and scapulars. Sandwich Terns nest on coastal beaches and islands. Calls include abrupt *gwit gwit* and *skee-rick* notes, similar to calls of the Elegant Tern. Casual spring visitor to southern California.

Elegant Tern   *Sterna elegans*   *L 17" (43 cm) W 34" (86 cm)*

Bill longer, thinner than in Royal Tern; color ranges from reddish-orange in adults to yellow in some juveniles. Elegant Tern is smaller and slimmer overall than Royal. In flight, note that underside of primaries is mostly pale; compare with Caspian Tern. Breeding adult Elegant Tern is pale gray above with black crown and nape, black crest; white below, often with pinkish tinge. Winter adult and juvenile have white forehead; black on crown extends forward around eye and over top of crown; compare with Royal Tern. Juvenile has variable dark mottling on upperparts, may have orange legs; some juveniles have less black on crown, resemble juvenile Royal Tern. Elegant Terns disperse northward after breeding season as far as northern California; accidentally to Canada. Sharp *kee-rick* call is similar to call of Sandwich Tern.

Royal Tern   *Sterna maxima*   *L 20" (51 cm) W 41" (104 cm)*

Orange-red bill, thinner than in Caspian Tern. In flight, shows underside of primaries mostly pale; tail is more deeply forked than in Caspian. Adult Royal Tern shows white crown most of year; black cap is acquired briefly early in breeding season. In nonbreeding plumage and juvenile, black on nape does not usually extend to encompass eye; compare Elegant Tern. Royal Terns nest in dense colonies. Regular but rare north of breeding range along Atlantic coast in late summer; fairly common in winter on southern California coast. Calls include a bleating *kee-rer* and a plover-like whistled *tourreee*.

Caspian Tern   *Sterna caspia*   *L 21" (53 cm) W 50" (127 cm)*

Large, stocky tern; bill orange to coral red, much thicker than in Royal Tern. In flight, shows dark underside of primaries; tail is less deeply forked than in Royal. Adult acquires black cap in breeding season; in nonbreeding plumage and immature, crown is dusky or streaked; never shows the fully white forehead of Royal Tern. Caspian Terns nest in small colonies along coasts and inland lakes, rivers, marshes. Adult's calls include low, harsh *kowk* and *ca-arr*. Immature has a distinctive call, a high-pitched, whistled *whee-you*.

Sandwich Tern

juvenile

winter

breeding

juvenile

Elegant Tern

winter

breeding

juvenile

Royal Tern

breeding

juvenile

winter

juvenile

Caspian Tern

winter

immature

breeding

Bridled Tern *Sterna anaethetus* L 15" (38 cm) W 30" (76 cm)
Common on nesting grounds in the Bahamas and West Indies; regular in summer in the Gulf of Mexico, well offshore, and in the Gulf Stream to North Carolina. Tropical storms may drive them as far north as New England. White collar between brownish-gray upperparts and black cap. Slimmer than Sooty Tern; wings more pointed; underwings and tail edges more extensively white; tail grayer. A close look shows that Bridled Tern's white forehead patch extends behind the eye; Sooty's stops at the eye. Juvenile has pale mottling above.

Sooty Tern *Sterna fuscata* L 16" (41 cm) W 32" (81 cm)
Large breeding colony located on the Dry Tortugas, Florida; also nests on islands off Texas and Louisiana. This large tern spends nearly all its time in the air over tropical seas. Tropical storms can carry it many miles inland and as far north as coastal New England and the Maritime Provinces. Blackish above, white below; white forehead. Lacks white collar of Bridled Tern. Tail is deeply forked and edged with white. Juvenile is sooty-brown overall, with whitish stippling on back; pale lower belly and undertail coverts; pale wing linings. Sooties do not dive; they feed on small fish and squid plucked from the water's surface. Nesting colonies are noisy day and night; typical call is a high, nasal *wacky-wack*.

Black Noddy *Anous minutus* L 13¹/₂" (34 cm) W 30" (76 cm)
Tropical species, rare in North America; a few are seen among Brown Noddies on the Dry Tortugas. In comparison, the Black Noddy is smaller, with shorter legs; bill is thinner and proportionately longer; white area on head is more sharply defined; overall color slightly blacker in fresh plumage.

Brown Noddy *Anous stolidus* L 15¹/₂" (39 cm) W 32" (81 cm)
Nests in a colony on the Dry Tortugas, Florida. Sometimes seen along Gulf coast to Texas after tropical storms; may be driven as far north as North Carolina. Overall dark gray-brown color is broken only by a whitish-gray cap; in immature this is only a small whitish line on the forehead. Unlike other terns, noddies have a long, wedge-shaped tail with only a small notch at tip. Feeding over open ocean, they snatch prey from the surface. Usually silent; rippling, crowlike *karrk* is heard mostly around the breeding colonies.

Black Skimmer *Rynchops niger* L 18" (46 cm) W 44" (112 cm)
No other bird but the skimmer has a lower mandible longer than the upper. A long-winged coastal bird, it furrows the shallows with its red, black-tipped bill, nodding to seize small fish with a sudden snap. At rest, its black back and crown, white face and underparts, red legs, and bill shape are distinctive. Female is distinctly smaller than the male. Juvenile is mottled dingy brown above. Winter adults are slightly duller above, with a white collar. A few hundred pairs nest in California around San Diego and a variable number at the Salton Sea.

Bridled Tern
adult
juvenile

Sooty Tern
juvenile
adult

Black Noddy

immature

Brown Noddy
adult

Black Skimmer
juvenile
breeding
winter

Auks and Puffins (Family Alcidae)

These black-and-white "penguins of the north" have set-back legs that give them an upright stance on land. In flight, wingbeats are rapid and shallow.

Razorbill Alca torda L 17″ (43 cm)

A chunky bird, big-headed and thick-necked; black above, white below. Pointed tail, heavy head, and massive, arching bill distinguish Razorbill from murres. Swimming birds often hold tail cocked up. A white band crosses the bill; in breeding plumage, another line runs from bill to eye. Immature lacks white line from eye; bill is smaller but still distinctively shaped. Nests on rocky cliffs. Winters in large numbers on the Grand Banks off Newfoundland. A few winter well offshore as far south as Maryland, coming closer to shore in stormy weather.

Common Murre Uria aalge L 17½″ (45 cm)

Large, with a long, slender, pointed bill. Upperparts dark sooty-gray, head brownish; underparts white. Some Atlantic birds have a "bridle"—a white eye ring and spur. In winter plumage, a dark stripe extends from eye across white cheek. Juvenile has shorter bill; generally distinguished from Thick-billed Murre by white facial stripe, paler upperparts, and thinner bill. Molting birds (early fall) are more difficult to identify. Abundant off west coast, common off east. Nests in dense colonies on rocky cliffs. Chicks accompany adults at sea and are sometimes mistaken for Xantus' Murrelets.

Thick-billed Murre Uria lomvia L 18″ (46 cm)

Stocky, with a thick, fairly short bill, arched at tip to form a blunt hook. Upperparts and throat of adult are darker than Common Murre; white of underparts usually rises to a sharp point on the foreneck. In Pacific birds, bill is slightly longer and thinner than in Atlantic birds. On both coasts, most birds show a more or less distinct white line on cutting edge of upper mandible. In immature and winter plumage, face and neck are more extensively dark than Common Murre. First-summer bird is browner above than adult and may retain much of winter plumage. Molting birds (early fall) are harder to identify. Nests in colonies on rocky cliffs. Common on breeding grounds. On east coast, much more numerous south of Canada than Common Murre. Casual on west coast to central California.

Dovekie Alle alle L 8¼″ (21 cm)

A plump little seabird with short neck, stubby bill. Breeding adult is black above, white below; black upper breast contrasts sharply with pure white underparts. In winter plumage, the throat, chin, and lower face are white, with white curving around behind eye. Abundant on breeding grounds. Winter chiefly in the North Atlantic; casual farther south. In some years, found at scattered inland locations after late fall storms.

Razorbill

winter

breeding

breeding

immature

Common Murre

bridled

breeding

juvenile

winter

breeding

Thick-billed Murre

Atlantic breeding

Pacific winter

Atlantic breeding

breeding

winter

Dovekie

breeding

Black Guillemot *Cepphus grylle* L 13″ *(33 cm)*

Long, black bill; fairly long, slender neck; swims with head held high. Breeding adult black overall, with large white patch on upperwing. Winter adult white; upperparts heavily mottled with black except on nape; wing patch less distinct. Juvenile is sooty above; sides and wing patches are mottled. First-summer birds are patchily black-and-white with mottled wing patches. Fairly common in the east; usually seen close to shore in breeding season. Uncommon in Alaska, where it overlaps with Pigeon Guillemot. In all plumages, white axillaries and wing linings distinguish Black from Pigeon Guillemot.

Pigeon Guillemot *Cepphus columba* L 13¹/₂″ *(34 cm)*

Long, black bill; fairly long, slender neck; swims with head held high. Breeding adult black overall, usually with white upperwing patch marked by black triangle. Winter adult is white with black-mottled upperparts; wing patch less distinct. Juvenile is dusky above; crown and nape darker; wing patch obscured by black edgings; breast and sides gray-mottled. Compare especially with juvenile Marbled Murrelet. First-winter Pigeon Guillemot resembles winter adult but is darker overall. Fairly common; usually seen close to shore in breeding season. In all seasons, dark or dusky axillaries and wing linings distinguish Pigeon from Black Guillemot.

Marbled Murrelet *Brachyramphus marmoratus*

L 9³/₄″ *(25 cm)* Dark bill, longer than bill of Kittlitz's Murrelet. Tail all-dark, but white on overlapping uppertail coverts may be mistaken for Kittlitz's white outer tail feathers. Breeding adult dark above, heavily mottled below. In winter plumage, white on scapulars distinguishes Marbled from other murrelets except Kittlitz's, which has a shorter bill and a nearly complete breast band; amount of white on face of Marbled is variable but always less than Kittlitz's. Juvenile resembles winter adult but is dusky-mottled below; by first winter, underparts are mostly white. Fairly common in breeding range; rare in southern California; casual inland throughout North America. Nests inland, usually in trees. Highly vocal; call is a series of loud, high *kree* notes. All murrelets have more pointed wings and faster flight than auklets.

Kittlitz's Murrelet *Brachyramphus brevirostris*

L 9¹/₂″ *(24 cm)* Dark bill, shorter than bill of Marbled Murrelet. Outer tail feathers white. Breeding adult's dark upperparts heavily patterned with buff, white, gray, tawny. Throat, breast, and flanks are mottled; belly white. In winter plumage note extensive white on face, making eye conspicuous; nearly complete breast band; and white edges on secondaries. Juvenile distinguished from Marbled by shorter bill, paler face, and white outer tail feathers. Fairly common but local.

Black Guillemot

winter

juvenile

winter

breeding

Pigeon Guillemot

winter

juvenile

breeding

winter

Marbled Murrelet

juvenile

winter

breeding

winter

breeding

Kittlitz's Murrelet

winter

breeding

breeding

juvenile

winter

Xantus' Murrelet *Synthliboramphus hypoleucus*

L 9¾" (25 cm) Slate black above, white below. Southern California form, *S.h. scrippsi,* has a partial white eye ring. The form that breeds on islands off Baja California, *hypoleucus,* has more white on face; seen rarely off southern and central California coast in fall. Both forms distinguished from Craveri's Murrelet by lack of partial collar; slightly shorter, stouter bill; lack of black under the bill; and white wing linings, visible when birds rise to flap wings before taking off. Usually seen a few miles offshore; nests in colonies on rocky islands, ledges, and sometimes in dense vegetation. Uncommon to fairly common; regular late-summer and fall postbreeding wanderer as far north as Washington. Call, a shrill whistle or series of whistles, is heard year-round.

Craveri's Murrelet *Synthliboramphus craveri*

L 10" (25 cm) Slate black above, white below. Distinguished from Xantus' Murrelet by variably dusky-gray wing linings; dark partial collar extending onto breast; slightly slimmer, longer bill; and black color of face extending under the bill. In good light, upperparts have a brownish tinge. Usually seen a few or many miles offshore. Breeds on rocky islands off Baja California. Regular late-summer and fall postbreeding visitor to coast of southern and central California. Call is a shrill whistle or series of whistles, heard year-round.

Ancient Murrelet *Synthliboramphus antiquus*

L 10" (25 cm) Black crown and nape contrast with gray back. White streaks on head and nape of breeding adult give it an "ancient" look. Note also black chin and throat, yellowish bill. Winter adult's bib is smaller and white-flecked, streaks on head less distinct. Immature lacks head streaks; throat is mostly white; distinguished from winter Marbled Murrelet (preceding page) by heavier, paler bill and by sharp contrast between head and back. In flight, the Ancient Murrelet holds its head higher than other murrelets; dark stripe on body at base of wing contrasts with white underparts, white wing linings. Uncommon to common; breeds primarily on the Aleutians and other Alaska islands; winters occasionally as far south as southern California. Casual inland throughout North America. Call, heard year-round, is a low, piping whistle.

Cassin's Auklet *Ptychoramphus aleuticus* L 9" (23 cm)

Small, plump, dark gray bird; wings more rounded than in murrelets; bill short and stout, with pale spot at base of lower mandible; pale eyes. Upperparts are dark gray, shading to paler gray below, with whitish belly. Prominent white crescents above and below eye. Juvenile is paler overall; throat whitish. Common; nests in colonies on islands and on isolated coastal cliffs and headlands. Highly pelagic; usually seen farther from shore than murrelets. Call, heard only on the breeding grounds, is a weak croaking.

176

**Xantus'
Murrelet**

hypoleucus

scrippsi

**Craveri's
Murrelet**

**Ancient
Murrelet**

immature

winter

breeding

**Cassin's
Auklet**

Parakeet Auklet *Cyclorrhynchus psittacula* L 10" (25 cm)
In breeding plumage, acquired by late January, broad up-turned bill is orange-red; white plume extends back from behind the eye; dark slate upperparts and throat contrast sharply with white underparts; sides are mottled gray. In winter plumage, bill becomes duskier; underparts, including throat, are entirely white. Compare especially with larger Rhinoceros Auklet (next page). Immature resembles winter adult. Fairly common on breeding grounds; nests in scattered pairs on rocky shores, sea cliffs. Found in pairs or small flocks in winter, generally on open ocean. Winters casually as far south as California. Silent except on breeding grounds, when call is a musical trill, rising in pitch. Like other auklets, wings are rounded and wingbeats are fluttery in comparison to those of murrelets.

Crested Auklet *Aethia cristatella* L 10½" (27 cm)
Sooty-black overall; prominent quail-like crest curves forward from forehead; narrow white plume trails from behind yellow eye. Breeding adult's bill is enlarged by bright orange plates. In winter, bill is smaller and browner; crest and plume reduced. Juvenile lacks crest and plume; bill much smaller. First-summer bird has a single plume back from eye, but bill is still small. Common and gregarious; often seen in large flocks that may include Parakeet and Least Auklets. Nests in crevices of sea cliffs, rocky shores. Winters throughout breeding range and east to Kodiak Island.

Whiskered Auklet *Aethia pygmaea* L 7¾" (20 cm)
Dark overall; three white plumes splay from each side of face; thin crest curls forward. In breeding plumage, bill is orange-red with white tip. In winter, bill is dusky, plumes and crest less conspicuous. Juvenile is paler below; bill smaller; lacks crest and plumes. First-summer bird may lack crest and show only traces of plumes; bill is still small. Fairly common but local; nests on central Aleutians and islands off Siberia.

Least Auklet *Aethia pusilla* L 6¼" (16 cm)
Small, chubby, and short-necked; dark above, with white-tipped scapulars and primaries; forehead and lores streaked with white bristly feathers. Stubby, knobbed bill is dark red, with pale tip. In breeding plumage, acquired by January, a streak of white plumes extends back from behind eye; underparts are variable, heavily mottled with gray or nearly all-white. In winter plumage, underparts are entirely white. Juvenile resembles winter adult. Abundant and gregarious, Least Auklets are found in immense flocks. Nest on boulder-strewn beaches and islands. Winter throughout the Aleutians; often seen far from shore.

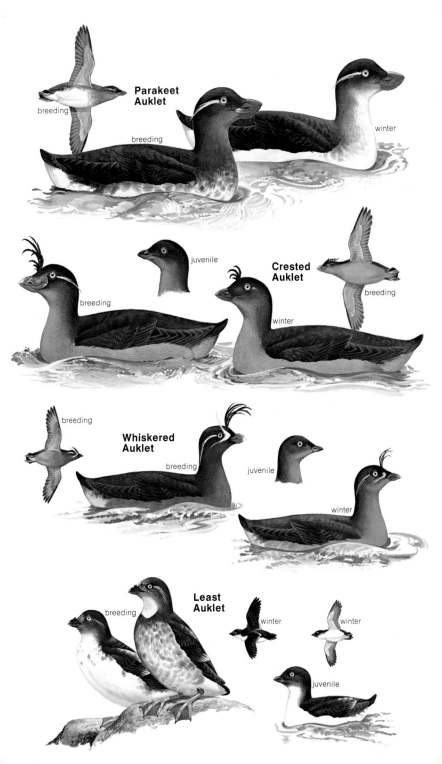

Parakeet Auklet
breeding
breeding
winter

Crested Auklet
breeding
juvenile
breeding
winter

Whiskered Auklet
breeding
breeding
juvenile
winter

Least Auklet
breeding
winter
winter
juvenile

Rhinoceros Auklet *Cerorhinca monocerata* L 15″ (38 cm)
A large, heavy-billed auklet with large head and short, thick neck. Blackish-brown above; paler on sides, neck, and throat. In flight, whitish on belly blends into dark breast; compare with extensively white underparts of similar Parakeet Auklet (preceding page). In breeding plumage, acquired by February, Rhinoceros Auklet has distinct white plumes and a pale yellow "horn" at base of orange bill. Winter adult lacks horn; plumes are less distinct, bill paler. Juvenile and immature lack horn and plumes; bill is dusky, eyes darker. Compare with much smaller Cassin's Auklet (page 176). Rhinoceros Auklets are common along most of the west coast in fall and winter; often seen in large numbers close inshore.

Atlantic Puffin *Fratercula arctica* L 12¹/₂″ (32 cm)
The only east coast puffin. Breeding adult identified by massive, brightly colored bill; white face and underparts contrast with dark upperparts. Winter adult has smaller, duller bill, dusky face. In juvenile and first-winter birds, face is even duskier, bill much paler and smaller. Full adult bill takes five years to develop. In flight, distinguished from murres and Razorbill (page 172) by red-orange legs, rounded wings, grayish wing linings, absence of white trailing edge on wing. Locally common in breeding season; winters at sea, casually south to Maryland. Formerly called Common Puffin.

Horned Puffin *Fratercula corniculata* L 15″ (38 cm)
A stocky North Pacific species with thick neck, large head, massive bill; underparts are white in all plumages. Breeding adult's face is white, bill brightly colored. Dark, fleshy "horn" extending up from eye is visible only at close range. Winter adult's bill is smaller, duller; face is dusky. Bill of juvenile and first-winter birds smaller and duskier than adult; full adult bill takes several years to develop. In flight, bright orange legs are conspicuous; wings are rounded; wing linings grayish; wings lack white trailing edge. Locally common; winters at sea and around breeding areas. Irregular straggler along the west coast to southern California, mainly in late spring.

Tufted Puffin *Fratercula cirrhata* L 15″ (38 cm)
Stocky, with thick neck, large head, massive bill. Underparts are dark in adults. Breeding adult's face is white, bill brightly colored; pale yellow head tufts droop over back of neck. Winter adult has smaller, duller bill; face is gray, tufts shorter or absent. Juvenile has smaller, dusky bill; dark eye; white or dark underparts. First-winter bird looks like juvenile until spring molt. As in other puffins, full adult bill and plumage take several years to develop. Red-orange feet are conspicuous in flight; wings are rounded; wing linings grayish; wings lack white trailing edge. Common in northern breeding range; less common in California. Winters far out at sea.

immature

winter

Rhinoceros Auklet

breeding

Atlantic Puffin

breeding

winter

juvenile

juvenile

Horned Puffin

winter

breeding

juvenile

juvenile

Tufted Puffin

winter

breeding

American Vultures (Family Cathartidae)

Small, unfeathered head and hooked bill aid these scavengers in consuming carrion. Their weak talons are ill suited for grasping live prey. Vultures do not build nests, but lay their eggs in a sheltered spot: cliff ledge or cave, hollow log, or abandoned building. Flocks often roost together at night.

Turkey Vulture *Cathartes aura* L 27" (69 cm) W 69" (175 cm)
Seen from below, contrastingly two-toned wings aid identification: flight feathers are silver gray; linings black. Wings are often held upward in a shallow V (called a dihedral). Rocks from side to side in flight, seldom flapping its wings. Long tail extends beyond legs and feet in flight. Adult has red head, white bill; immature's head and bill are dark. Feeds chiefly on carrion and refuse. Common in dry, open country, woodlands, farmlands. Range is expanding northward in the east. Often miscalled buzzard, the British name for certain buteos.

Black Vulture *Coragyps atratus* L 25" (64 cm) W 57" (145 cm)
In flight, shows large white patches at base of primaries. Tail is shorter than Turkey Vulture; wings shorter and broader; feet usually extend to edge of tail or beyond. Flight is heavy, with rapid flapping and short glides, usually with wings flat. Gregarious and aggressive. Less efficient at spotting carrion, Black Vultures may flock to Turkey Vultures' find and claim it. Occasionally prey on unprotected young birds and small mammals. Common in open country and around human settlements, where they scavenge in garbage dumps and at fishing wharves. Range is expanding in the northeast.

California Condor *Gymnogyps californianus*
L 47" (119 cm) W 108" (274 cm) Now probably extinct in the wild. Formerly found in arid foothills and mountains of southern and central California. Huge size distinctive. Adult has white wing linings, orange head; immature's wing linings are mottled, head dusky. Condors soar on flat wings, circling for altitude, then giving one deep wingbeat to soar off at great speed in search of large carrion—deer, cattle, sheep. Recent decline to near extinction resulted largely from pesticides, lead poisoning, and habitat destruction. Intensive rescue efforts continue; captive breeding program may eventually return birds to the wild.

Turkey Vulture

adult

immature

Black Vulture

California Condor

adult

immature

adult

adult

Kites, Hawks, Eagles (Family Accipitridae)

A large, worldwide family of diurnal birds of prey, equipped with hooked bills and strong talons. In most species, males are smaller than females.

Golden Eagle *Aquila chrysaetos*

L 30-40" (76-102 cm) W 80-88" (203-224 cm) Brown, with variable golden wash over back of head and neck; bill mostly horn-colored; tail faintly banded. Immatures, seen in flight from below, show well-defined white patches at base of primaries, white tail with distinct dark terminal band. Compare with first-year Bald Eagle's larger head, shorter tail, blotchier underwing pattern. Golden Eagle often soars with wings slightly uplifted. Inhabits mountainous or hilly terrain, hunting over open country for small mammals, snakes, birds, carrion. Nests on cliffs or in trees. Uncommon to rare in the east; fairly common in the west.

White-tailed Eagle *Haliaeetus albicilla*

L 26-35" (66-89 cm) W 72-94" (183-239 cm) Ranges over northern Eurasia and Greenland in diminishing numbers. Very rare visitor to outer Aleutians, where it has nested. Note short, wedge-shaped white tail. Plumage mottled; head may be very pale and appear white at a distance; undertail coverts are dark, unlike Bald Eagle. Immature's tail has variable dark mottling and tip and is less wedge-shaped.

Steller's Sea-Eagle *Haliaeetus pelagicus*

L 27-37" (69-94 cm) W 80-95" (203-241 cm) Nests in northeastern Asia; casual on Aleutians, Pribilofs, Kodiak Island. White shoulders show as white leading edge of wings in flight. Immense yellow-orange bill; white, wedge-shaped tail; white thighs. Immatures lack white on shoulder; end of tail is dark.

Bald Eagle *Haliaeetus leucocephalus*

L 31-37" (79-94 cm) W 70-90" (178-229 cm) Adults readily identified by white head and tail, huge yellow bill. First-year birds are mostly dark, may be confused with immature Golden Eagle; compare blotchy white on underwing and tail with Golden Eagle's more sharply defined pattern; note also Bald Eagle's proportionately larger head, shorter tail. Neck is shorter and tail longer than White-tailed Eagle; Steller's Sea-Eagle has longer, wedge-shaped tail. Flat-winged soar distinguishes young Bald Eagle from Turkey Vulture (preceding page). Bald Eagles require four or five years to reach full adult plumage. Common in Alaska, locally rare to uncommon in rest of range. Seen most often on seacoasts or near rivers and lakes. Feed mainly on fish. Nest in tall trees or on cliffs. Seriously diminished in number in the lower 48 states due to shooting, pesticides, and human encroachment; intense recovery programs appear to be increasing populations in the east.

immature

**Golden
Eagle**

adult

adult

immature

**White-tailed
Eagle**

adult

immature

**Steller's
Sea-Eagle**

adult

2nd year

1st year

Bald Eagle

adult

1st year

adult

Mississippi Kite *Ictinia mississippiensis*

L 14¹/₂″ *(37 cm)* W 35″ *(89 cm)* Long, pointed wings with first primary distinctly shorter; long, flared tail. Dark gray above, paler below, with pale gray head. White secondaries show in flight as white wing patch. Chestnut at base of primaries is often hard to see. Black tail readily distinguishes Mississippi from Black-shouldered Kite. Compare also with male Northern Harrier (next page). Unlike those species, Mississippi Kite never hovers. Juvenile is heavily streaked and spotted, with pale bands on tail. First-summer bird (page 206) resembles adult but wings and tail are like juvenile. At all ages, may be confused with Peregrine Falcon (page 204); compare wing and tail shapes. Gliding, banking, wheeling in the wind, Mississippis pursue flying insects. Also drop to the ground, feet-first, upon insects, mice, lizards, frogs. Gregarious, often nesting in loose colonies. Found in open woodlands and swamps, semiarid rangelands. Regular straggler, chiefly first-summer birds, far north and west of usual range. Winters in South America.

American Swallow-tailed Kite *Elanoides forficatus*

L 23″ *(58 cm)* W 48″ *(122 cm)* Seen in flight, deeply forked tail and sharply defined pattern of black and white are like no other large bird except the young Magnificent Frigatebird (page 38). Perched, the Swallowtail's coloring more closely resembles Black-shouldered and Mississippi Kites; again, look for long, forked tail. Young birds are similar to adults, but tail is shorter, primaries and tail tipped with white. Agile and graceful, Swallowtails snatch flying insects; also drop down upon snakes, lizards, young birds; do not hover. Often eat prey in flight; also drink in flight, skimming the water like swallows. Found in open woods, bottomlands, wetlands. Nest in the tops of tall trees. Somewhat social; several may hunt in the same territory. Strays are seen in spring and summer as far north as Ontario and Nova Scotia and as far west as Arizona. Most winter in South America.

Black-shouldered Kite *Elanus caeruleus*

L 16″ *(41 cm)* W 42″ *(107 cm)* Long, pointed wings; long tail. White underparts and mostly white tail distinguish adults from the similar Mississippi Kite. Compare also with male Northern Harrier (next page). Juvenile's underparts and head are lightly streaked with rufous. In all ages, black shoulders show in flight as black leading edge of inner wings from above, small black patches from below. Flight is graceful, buoyant. Hovers while hunting, unlike any other North American kite. Eats mainly rodents, insects. Populations have fluctuated strongly, are now on the increase, with range expanding rapidly. Fairly common in brushy grasslands, farmlands, even highway median strips. Formerly known as White-tailed Kite.

Mississippi Kite

juvenile

♂

♂

♀

American Swallow-tailed Kite

Black-shouldered Kite

juvenile

adult

Snail Kite *Rostrhamus sociabilis*

L 17" (43 cm) W 46" (117 cm) Male is slate black above and below, with white uppertail and undertail coverts, white tail with broad, dark band and paler terminal band; legs orange-red; eyes and facial skin reddish. Female is dark brown, with white on forehead and throat. Immature resembles adult female but has paler eyes and legs. Hunting flight is slow, with considerable flapping of wings, and with head down as the kite searches for apple snails, its chief and perhaps only food. A tropical species, uncommon and local resident in southern Florida. Formerly called Everglade Kite.

Hook-billed Kite *Chondrohierax uncinatus*

L 16" (41 cm) W 33" (84 cm) Tropical species, uncommon over most of its range. Rare resident in lower Rio Grande Valley. Plumage varies considerably. Look for large, heavy bill with long hook; banded tail. Males are generally gray overall, with barred underparts. Females are brown, with a reddish collar and reddish, barred underparts. Immatures have whitish underparts indistinctly barred with dark brown. In the black phase, not yet seen in U. S., adult is all-black except for a single white or grayish tail band and whitish tail tip; immatures are mostly brownish-black, with two or more grayish tail bands. In flight, the Hook-billed Kite's broad, rounded wings and long tail resemble Red-shouldered Hawk (page 192). Eats insects and small amphibians, but prefers snails of various kinds. A pile of broken snail shells beneath a tree may indicate a favorite perch or a nest site above.

Northern Harrier *Circus cyaneus*

L 17-23" (43-58 cm) W 38-48" (97-122 cm) White rump and owl-like facial disk distinctive in all ages and both sexes. Body slim; wings long and narrow with somewhat rounded tips. Adult male is grayish above, mostly white below, with black wing tips. Female is brown above, whitish below with heavy brown streaking on breast and flanks, lighter streaking and spotting on belly. Immatures resemble adult female but are cinnamon below and streaked only on the breast; wing linings are cinnamon, distinctly darker on inner half. Harriers generally perch low and fly close to the ground, wings upraised, as they search for mice, rats, frogs, and other prey. Fairly common in wetlands and open fields. Seldom soar high except during migration and in exuberant, acrobatic courtship display. Adult males migrate later in fall, earlier in spring, than females and immatures. Formerly called Marsh Hawk.

Snail Kite

♂

♀

immature

♂

black phase

black phase immature

molting immature

Hook-billed Kite

♂

♀

immature

immature

Northern Harrier

♀

♂

Accipiters

Comparatively long tails and short, rounded wings give these woodland hawks greater agility. The three species in North America are confusingly similar.

Sharp-shinned Hawk *Accipiter striatus*

L 10-14" (25-36 cm) W 20-28" (51-71 cm) Distinguished from Cooper's Hawk by shorter, squared tail, often appearing notched when folded, and by proportionately smaller head and neck. Adult lacks Cooper's strong contrast between crown and back. Immature is whitish below with bold, blurry, reddish streaking on breast and belly; narrow white tip on tail; undertail coverts entirely white; head less tawny than in other accipiters. In flight (see also page 207), again note smaller head and proportionately shorter tail and longer wings than in Cooper's Hawk. Fairly common over much of its range; found in mixed woodlands. Preys chiefly on small birds. Migrates singly or in small flocks.

Cooper's Hawk *Accipiter cooperii*

L 14-20" (36-51 cm) W 29-37" (74-94 cm) Distinguished from Sharp-shinned Hawk by longer, rounded tail, larger head, and, in adult, stronger contrast between back and crown. Tail is proportionately longer and wings shorter than in Northern Goshawk. Immature has whitish or buffy underparts with fine streaks on breast; streaking is reduced or absent on belly; white tip on tail is broader than on Sharpshin; undertail coverts entirely white. In flight (see also page 207), again note larger head and proportionately longer tail and shorter wings. Uncommon and may be declining. Inhabits broken woodlands or streamside groves, especially deciduous. Preys largely on songbirds, some small mammals. Often perches on telephone poles, unlike Sharpshins. Usually migrates singly or in groups of two or three.

Northern Goshawk *Accipiter gentilis*

L 21-26" (53-66 cm) W 40-46" (102-117 cm) Conspicuous eyebrow, flaring behind eye, separates adult's dark crown from blue-gray back. Underparts are white with dense gray barring; appear gray at a distance. Adult has conspicuous fluffy undertail coverts. Immature is brown above, buffy below, with dense, blurry streaking, heaviest on flanks; tail has wavy, dark bands bordered with white and a thin white tip; undertail coverts have dark streaks. In flight (see also page 207), note proportionately shorter tail, longer wings than Cooper's Hawk. Sometimes confused with Gyrfalcon (page 204) and Red-shouldered Hawk (next page). The Goshawk inhabits deep, conifer-dominated mixed woodlands; preys chiefly on birds and ducks; also on mammals as large as hares. Uncommon; winters irregularly south of mapped range in the east. Southward irruptions occur in some winters.

Sharp-shinned Hawk

immature

immature ♀

♂

Cooper's Hawk

immature

immature ♀

♂

Northern Goshawk

immature

immature ♀

♂

Buteos

High-soaring hawks, most with broad, banded tails and rounded wings. Buteos are among the easiest daytime birds of prey to spot, especially in migration.

Red-shouldered Hawk *Buteo lineatus*

L 19" (48 cm) W 40" (102 cm) Relatively long-winged and long-tailed. In flight, shows pale crescent at base of primaries and dark tail with narrow white bands (see also page 207). Reddish shoulders and white barring on wings visible from above; from below, note reddish wing linings and underparts. Flight is accipiter-like, with several quick wingbeats and a glide. Florida form is smaller and paler. Western forms are much darker red below; red shoulders less conspicuous. Fairly common in moist, mixed woodlands; often seen near streams. Preys on snakes, frogs, mice, crayfish, sometimes young birds. Call is an evenly spaced series of clear, high *kee-ah* or *kah* notes. Usually seen singly or in small flocks in migration.

Broad-winged Hawk *Buteo platypterus*

L 16" (41 cm) W 34" (86 cm) White underwings have dark borders; tail has broad black and white bands, with last white band broader than the others. Wings broad but more pointed than Red-shouldered Hawk's; wing linings buffy or white; tail shorter, broader. Wingbeats are slower than in Redshoulder. Immatures typically have black whisker streak, dark-bordered underwings, indistinct bands on tail; very similar to immature eastern Redshoulder but paler below; may have a pale area at base of primaries but lack the distinct pale crescent. Rare dark phase (page 207) breeds in western Canada. A woodland species, the Broadwing perches low waiting for prey: mice, frogs, insects, or snakes. Call, heard mainly on breeding grounds, is a thin, shrill, slightly descending whistle: *pee-teee*. Often migrates in very large flocks. Rare migrant in the west. Most winter in South America; a very few winter in extreme southern Florida and coastal California.

Gray Hawk *Buteo nitidus* *L 17" (43 cm) W 35" (89 cm)*

Tropical species; very local nester in southeastern Arizona. Casual in New Mexico, rare in Rio Grande Valley. Gray upperparts, gray-barred underparts and wing linings, and rounded wing tips distinguish it from Broad-winged Hawk (see also page 207). Flight is accipiter-like: several rapid, shallow wingbeats and a glide. Immature resembles immature Broadwing, but has a stronger face pattern and a white U-shaped rump band. Dark trailing edge on wings is smaller or absent. Inhabits deciduous growth along streams with nearby open land; swoops down from perch in foliage upon lizards, snakes, frogs.

adult

immature

eastern

adult

eastern

immature

Florida

Red-shouldered Hawk

immature

western

adult

Broad-winged Hawk

immature

adult

adult

Gray Hawk

immature

immature

adult

adult

immature

Red-tailed Hawk *Buteo jamaicensis*

L 22" (56 cm) W 50" (127 cm) Our most common buteo; wings
broad and fairly rounded; plumage extremely variable. Most
adult Redtails, especially in the east, show a belly band of dark
streaks on whitish underparts; dark bar on leading edge
of underwing, contrasting with paler wing linings (see also
page 208). Note reddish uppertail; paler red undertail; variable pale mottling on scapulars, contrasting with dark mantle
and often forming a V in perched birds. A Great Plains bird,
"Krider's Hawk," has paler upperparts, whitish tail with pale
reddish wash and, in flight, pale rectangular patches at base of
primaries on upperwing. Many southwestern Redtails lack
belly band and have uniformly light underparts. Dark phase of
western form has dark wing linings and underparts, obscuring
the bar on leading edge and belly band; tail is dark reddish
above. In "Harlan's Hawk," formerly considered a separate
species, the dark phase has dusky-white tail, diffuse blackish
terminal band; shows some white streaking on its dark breast;
may lack scapular mottling. "Harlan's Hawk" breeds in Alaska
and Canada, winters primarily in central U. S. Immatures of
all forms have gray-brown tails with many blackish bands; otherwise heavily brown-streaked and spotted below. Habitat
variable: woods with nearby open land; also plains, prairie
groves, desert. Preys on rodents. Distinctive call, a harsh, descending *keeeeer*.

Swainson's Hawk *Buteo swainsoni*

L 21" (53 cm) W 52" (132 cm) Distinguished from most other
buteos by long, narrow, pointed wings; plumage is extremely
variable. In light phase, whitish or buffy-white wing linings
contrast with darkly barred brown flight feathers (see also
page 208). Dark bib; underparts otherwise whitish to pale
buff. Swainson's Hawk lacks Redtail's pale mottling on scapulars; bill is smaller than Redtail's. Dark-phase bird is dark
brown with white undertail coverts; lacks sharp contrast between wing linings and flight feathers. Compare with first-
year White-tailed Hawk (next page). Intermediate colorations
between light and dark phases include a reddish plumage.
Light-phase and intermediate immatures have dark whisker
streak and conspicuous whitish eyebrows that meet on the
forehead; underparts are boldly streaked, with streaks running together to make brown patches on the sides of the
breast; show less contrast between wing linings and flight
feathers than adult birds (page 208). Swainson's Hawk soars
over open plains and prairie with uptilted wings in teetering,
vulture-like flight. Perches on posts, banks, or stones and usually pounces on prey, largely insects. Very rare fall visitor to
eastern U. S., usually in flocks of Broad-winged Hawks. Winters chiefly in South America, casually in southern Florida.

Red-tailed Hawk

adult

immature

"Harlan's Hawk"

"Krider's Hawk"

light phase

dark phase

light phase immature

Swainson's Hawk

dark phase

light phase

light phase

intermediate

Rough-legged Hawk *Buteo lagopus*

L 22" (56 cm) W 56" (142 cm) Long white tail with dark band or bands helps to identify this hawk in all plumages. Adult male has multibanded tail with a broad blackish subterminal band. Adult female's tail is brown toward tip with a thin black subterminal band. Immatures show a single broad brown tail band. Wings are long, fairly narrow. Seen in flight from above, white at base of tail is conspicuous; in immature, note also the small white patches at base of primaries on upperwings. From below, look for dark wrist patches, legs feathered to the toes. In the common light phase, pale head contrasts with darker back and dark belly band, especially in females and immatures. Dark phase is less common. A hawk of open country, the Roughleg often hovers while hunting. During breeding season gives a soft, plaintive courting whistle. Alarm call is a loud screech or squeal. Roughlegs migrate in loose flocks but are otherwise generally seen singly or in pairs.

Ferruginous Hawk *Buteo regalis*

L 23" (58 cm) W 53" (135 cm) Rust back and shoulders; paler head; white tail washed with pale rust. Wings are long, broad, and pointed. On upperwing surface, large, white, crescent-shaped patches make a bold flash. Seen from below, flight feathers lack barring; rusty leggings form a conspicuous V against whitish underparts. Dark phase (not shown) is rare; absence of dark tail bands distinguishes it from similar dark-phase Rough-legged Hawk. Immature Ferruginous Hawk almost or entirely lacks rusty leggings; resembles "Krider's Hawk" form of Red-tailed Hawk (preceding page), but wings are longer and more pointed. The Ferruginous Hawk inhabits dry, open country. Often hovers when hunting. Perches in trees, on poles, or on the ground. Harsh alarm calls, *kree-a* or *kaah* are heard chiefly in breeding season. Fairly common, but may be declining over much of range. Casual east to Wisconsin, Illinois, Arkansas, Louisiana, and Florida in migration and winter. Rare migrant in Minnesota; may breed there.

White-tailed Hawk *Buteo albicaudatus*

L 23" (58 cm) W 50" (127 cm) Wings fairly long and pointed; at rest, adult's wing tips project to or beyond end of short tail. Rusty shoulders highly visible against dark gray upperparts. Tail is whitish with single black band. Underparts and wing linings vary from snow white to lightly barred. First-year birds are brown above, heavily streaked below; shoulder feathering edged with rust; tail is longer than adult's and faintly barred. Compare especially with dark-phase Swainson's Hawk (preceding page). Whitetail's call is a repeated series of high-pitched, musical *kil-la* or *ke* notes. Rare to fairly common in open coastal grasslands and semiarid inland brush country.

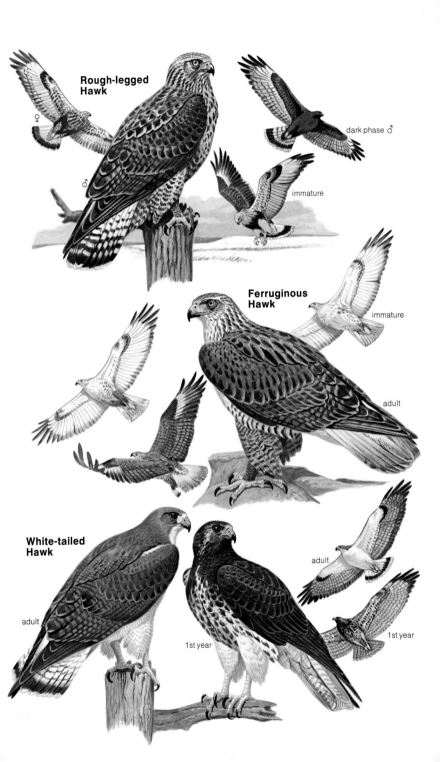

Rough-legged Hawk

♀

♂

dark phase ♂

immature

Ferruginous Hawk

immature

adult

White-tailed Hawk

adult

adult

1st year

1st year

Common Black-Hawk *Buteogallus anthracinus*

L 21" (53 cm) W 50" (127 cm) Wings broad and rounded; tail short, broad. Adult uniformly blackish, but tail has broad white band and narrow white tip. Legs and cere (fleshy area at base of bill) bright yellow. In flight, whitish patch at base of primaries is smaller and less distinct than on Black Vulture (page 182). Distinguished from Zone-tailed Hawk by broader wings; broader tail with different pattern; more extensive yellow under eye. Immature has a strong face pattern; underparts and wing linings are generally buffy. Calls include a series of high whistles and a harsh *ka-a-a-ah*. Rare, local, and declining; found along rivers and streams. Hunts from low perch, preying on crustaceans, frogs, fish, reptiles. Casual in summer north to Utah; very rare in southern Texas.

Harris' Hawk *Parabuteo unicinctus*

L 21" (53 cm) W 46" (117 cm) Chocolate brown overall, with conspicuous chestnut shoulder patches, leggings, and wing linings; white at base and tip of long tail; rounded wingtips. Immature is streaked with brown below; chestnut shoulders are less distinct. Inhabits semiarid woodland, brushland. Nests in mesquite, yucca, and saguaro. Generally silent away from nest. May straggle north and west of mapped range, but birds sighted there and elsewhere in the U. S. most likely have escaped from falconers.

Zone-tailed Hawk *Buteo albonotatus*

L 20" (51 cm) W 51" (130 cm) Slate black or dark gray overall, with barred flight feathers. Legs and cere bright yellow. Has much slimmer wings than Common Black-Hawk, and longer tail with several gray (above) or whitish (below) bands. Soars teetering on uptilted wings like Turkey Vulture; look for Zone-tailed Hawk's banded tail, yellow cere; larger, feathered head. Immature has narrowly banded grayish tail, some white flecking on breast. Uncommon; found in mesa and mountain country, often near watercourses; drops from low glide on rodents, lizards, fish, frogs, small birds. Call is an insistent squealing whistle. Rare in southern California.

Short-tailed Hawk *Buteo brachyurus*

L 15¹/₂" (39 cm) W 35" (89 cm) A small, chunky hawk, resident but uncommon in Florida south of the Panhandle; in winter, found south of Lake Okeechobee. Two color phases: All adults are black above, but underparts and wing linings are either all-black or all-white; tail dark-banded. Seen in flight from below, light-phase bird resembles light-phase Swainson's Hawk (page 194), but wings and tail are shorter and broader; lacks chest band. Immatures are either buff below with some dark streaks or dark with some buff mottling. Found in mixed woodland-grassland. Generally silent away from nest.

**Common
Black-Hawk**

adult

immature

**Harris'
Hawk**

adult

immature

Turkey Vulture
for comparison

immature   adult

adult

**Zone-tailed
Hawk**

adult

**Short-tailed
Hawk**

light phase

dark phase

light phase

Osprey *Pandion haliaetus*

L 22-25" (56-64 cm) W 58-72" (147-183 cm) Dark brown above, white below, with white head, prominent dark eye stripe. Males are usually all-white below; females have a necklace of dark streaking. Immature plumage is edged with pale buff above. In flight, the Osprey's long, narrow wings are bent back at the wrist, like a gull's; dark wrist patches are conspicuous. Wings are slightly arched in soaring. Ospreys nest near fresh or salt water; eat fish almost exclusively. Hovering over water, they dive toward prey, then plunge feetfirst to snatch it. Bulky nests are built in trees, on sheds, poles, docks; also on platforms specially constructed for Ospreys. Conservation programs and elimination of DDT in recent years have halted decline of species. Now fairly common in coastal range. Uncommon and local inland; seen chiefly during migration. Common call is a loud, whistled *kyew kyew kyew kyew kyew*.

Falcons and Caracara (Family Falconidae)

These powerful hunters are distinguished from hawks by their long wings, bent back at the wrist and, except in the Crested Caracara, narrow and pointed. Females are larger than the males.

Aplomado Falcon *Falco femoralis*

L 15-16½" (38-42 cm) W 40-48" (102-122 cm) Once fairly common in open grasslands and deserts from southern Texas to southern Arizona; now probably extirpated from U. S. and northern Mexico. In flight, long, pointed, and rather narrow wings and long, banded tail resemble young Mississippi Kite (page 186); often hovers. Note slate gray crown, boldly marked head. Pale eyebrows join at back of head. Dark patches on sides sometimes extend across breast; adults that were seen in our area usually had streaks on breast. Immature is cinnamon below, with a streaked breast.

Crested Caracara *Polyborus plancus*

L 23" (58 cm) W 50" (127 cm) Large head, long neck, long legs. Blackish-brown overall, with white throat and neck and red-orange bare facial skin. Immature is browner; upperparts are edged and spotted with buff; underparts streaked. Uncommon. Inhabits open brushlands; often seen on the ground in company with vultures. Feeds chiefly on carrion; also hunts insects and small animals. In flight, shows white patches at ends of rounded wings. Soars on flat wings. Call is a harsh cackle, for which the bird is named.

Osprey

♂

♀

immature ♀

immature ♀

Aplomado Falcon

♂

adult

immature

Crested Caracara

Eurasian Kestrel *Falco tinnunculus*

L 13¹/₂" (34 cm) W 29" (74 cm) Casual on the western Aleutians; accidental on the east coast (New Jersey) in fall. Resembles American Kestrel, but note larger size and single, not double, dark facial stripe. Adult male has russet wings, gray tail. In flight, distinguished by wedge-shaped tail and two-toned upperwing, with back and inner wing paler. Hovers as it hunts.

American Kestrel *Falco sparverius*

L 10¹/₂" (27 cm) W 23" (58 cm) Smallest and most common of our falcons. Identified by russet back and tail, double black stripes on white face. Seen in flight from below, often shows a distinctive row of translucent spots on trailing edge of wings. Male has blue-gray wing coverts; compare with Merlin and much larger Peregrine Falcon (next page). Found in open country and in cities, kestrels feed on insects, reptiles, and small mammals, hovering over prey before plunging. Also eat small birds, chiefly in winter. Often perch on telephone wires. Call is a shrill *killy killy killy*. Formerly called Sparrow Hawk.

Merlin *Falco columbarius* L 12" (31 cm) W 25" (64 cm)

Adult male is gray-blue above; female and immatures usually dark brown. Merlins lack the strong facial markings and russet upperparts of kestrels. Plumage varies geographically from the very dark form, *F.c. suckleyi*, of the Pacific northwest to the pale *richardsonii* of central Canada and the Great Plains. The widespread *columbarius* is intermediate in plumage. In flight (page 206), strongly barred tail distinguishes Merlin from the much larger Peregrine and Prairie Falcons. Underparts and underwing darker and head larger than in kestrels; does not hover. Nests in open woods or wooded prairies; otherwise found in a variety of habitats. Preys on birds, caught in flight, usually by a sudden burst of speed rather than by diving. Also eats large insects, small rodents. Uncommon; very local in southern portion of breeding range. Uncommon to rare throughout U. S. in winter. Many individuals in the Prairie Provinces do not migrate but concentrate in or near cities in winter. Formerly called Pigeon Hawk.

Eurasian Kestrel

♀

♂

American Kestrel

♀

immature ♂

♂

columbarius

♀

♂

Merlin

suckleyi

♂

♀

♂

richardsonii

Prairie Falcon *Falco mexicanus*

L 15^1/$_2$-19^1/$_2$" (39-50 cm) W 35-43" (89-109 cm) Pale brown above; creamy white and heavily spotted below. Crown is streaked; facial markings are narrower and plumage paler overall than Peregrine Falcon. Compare also with female Merlin (preceding page). In flight (see also page 206), all ages show distinctive dark axillaries and dark bar on wing lining. Immature is streaked below, rather than spotted. Prairie Falcons inhabit dry, open country, prairies. Prey chiefly on birds and small mammals. Uncommon to fairly common. Small numbers winter throughout the breeding range.

Peregrine Falcon *Falco peregrinus*

L 16-20" (41-51 cm) W 36-44" (91-112 cm) Crown and nape black; black wedge extends below eye, forming a distinctive helmet, absent in smaller Merlin (preceding page) and similar Prairie Falcon. Plumage varies from pale in the subspecies *F.p. tundrius* of the north to very dark in *pealei* on the northwest coast and Aleutians. Intermediate *anatum* form of the west once ranged the continent. Immature Peregrine is dark brownish above; underparts heavily streaked. Immature *tundrius* has an extensively pale forehead and thinner dark bar on sides of face. In flight, absence of contrasting axillaries and wing coverts distinguishes all Peregrines from Prairie Falcons. Peregrines inhabit open wetlands near cliffs; prey chiefly on ducks, shorebirds, seabirds. Occasionally seen in cities, on bridges and tall buildings. Rare and local in the west. Eastern breeding populations were extirpated in recent decades, due largely to pesticides. Peregrines have now been reintroduced in parts of their former range and are seen year-round. Most eastern sightings, however, are of migrating *tundrius* birds, usually along the coast in fall. Uncommon to rare in winter in U. S.

Gyrfalcon *Falco rusticolus*

L 20-25" (51-64 cm) W 50-64" (127-163 cm) Heavily built; wings are more broad-based than in Peregrine and Prairie Falcons; lacks dark helmet. Tail long; note that in perched bird, tail extends far beyond wingtips, unlike Peregrine and Prairie Falcons. Compare also with Goshawk (page 190). Plumages vary throughout the range from white to very dark. Tail may be barred or unbarred. Inhabits open tundra near rocky outcrops and cliffs. Preys chiefly on birds. Uncommon throughout its range; winters irregularly south to dashed line on map. Casual to accidental further south.

Prairie Falcon

Peregrine Falcon

immature
pealei
adult

adult
anatum

tundrius
immature

adult

immature

Gyrfalcon

gray phase
dark phase

white phase

Female Hawks in Flight

Black-shouldered Kite

Mississippi Kite

1st summer

Hook-billed Kite

Snail Kite

American Kestrel

Peregrine Falcon

anatum

Merlin

columbarius

Gyrfalcon

gray phase

Prairie Falcon

Sharp-shinned
Hawk

Cooper's
Hawk

Northern
Goshawk

Northern
Harrier

Gray
Hawk

Broad-winged
Hawk

Broad-winged
Hawk

Red-shouldered
Hawk

dark phase

eastern

Female Hawks in Flight

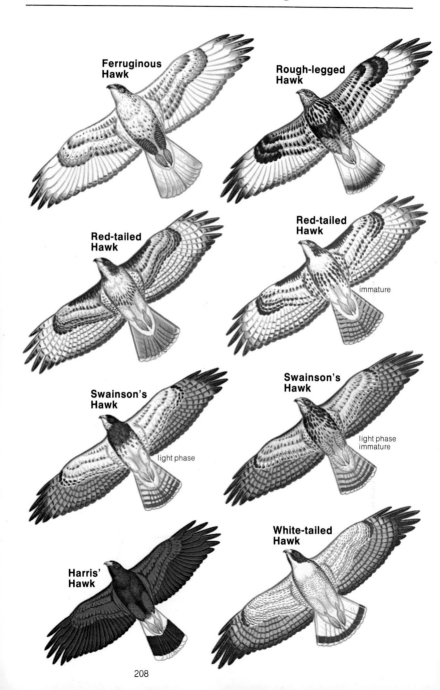

Ferruginous Hawk

Rough-legged Hawk

Red-tailed Hawk

Red-tailed Hawk

immature

Swainson's Hawk

light phase

Swainson's Hawk

light phase immature

Harris' Hawk

White-tailed Hawk

Crested Caracara

Osprey

Zone-tailed Hawk

immature

Bald Eagle

2nd year

Common Black-Hawk

Golden Eagle

Black Vulture

Turkey Vulture

Grouse, Ptarmigans (Family Phasianidae)

Ground-dwellers with feathered nostrils, short, strong bills, and short, rounded wings. Flight is brief but strong. Males perform elaborate courting displays. In some species, birds gather at the same strutting grounds, known as leks, every year.

Ruffed Grouse *Bonasa umbellus* L 17" (43 cm)
Small crest; black ruffs on sides of neck, usually inconspicuous; multibanded tail with a wide, dark band near tip; dark band is incomplete in female. The two color phases, red and gray, are most apparent in tail color. Fairly common in deciduous and mixed woodlands. Flushed birds burst into flight with a roar of wings. In spring, the male attracts females to his territory by raising ruffs and crest, fanning his tail, and beating his wings to make a hollow, accelerating drumming noise.

Spruce Grouse *Dendragapus canadensis* L 16" (41 cm)
Male has dark throat and breast, edged with white; red eye combs. Over most of range, both sexes have black tail with chestnut tip. Birds of the northern Rockies and Cascades, "Franklin's Grouse," have white spots on uppertail coverts; male's tail is all-dark. In all forms of Spruce Grouse, females have two color phases, red and gray; generally resemble female Blue Grouse but are smaller and have black barring and white spots below. Juveniles resemble red-phase female. Spruce Grouse inhabit open coniferous forests with dense undergrowth. Often seen along roadsides or perched in trees. Female's high-pitched call is thought to be territorial. In courtship strutting display, male spreads his tail, erects the red combs above eyes, and rapidly beats his wings; some males also give a series of low-pitched hoots. In territorial flight display, the male flutters upward on shallow wing strokes; "Franklin's Grouse" ends this performance by beating his wings together, making a clapping sound.

Blue Grouse *Dendragapus obscurus* L 20" (51 cm)
Male's sooty-gray plumage sets off yellow-orange comb above eye. On each side of neck, white-based feathers cover an inflatable bare patch, the yellow or reddish-purple neck sac. Females are mottled brown above, with plain gray belly. Both sexes have dark tail with gray band, except populations in the northern Rockies, which show no band. Coastal form, *D. o. fuliginosus*, also known as Sooty Grouse, is darker overall than interior birds. Blue Grouse inhabit open coniferous or mixed woodlands, brushy lowlands and mountain slopes, moving to higher altitudes in winter. Call is a series of hoots, higher pitched than those of Spruce Grouse. Courting males stand on a high spot and inflate their neck sacs to amplify their hooting. Display also involves fluttering above the ground or making short circular flights, then strutting with tail fanned, body tipped forward, head drawn in, wings dragging.

gray phase ♂

red phase ♂

Ruffed Grouse

red phase ♀

red phase ♀

gray phase ♀

Spruce Grouse

"Franklin's Grouse"

♂

♂

Blue Grouse

northern Rockies ♂

coastal ♂

southern Rockies ♀

Ptarmigans

Hardy northern birds with feathered legs and feet. Plumage is molted three times a year, matching seasonal changes in habitat. Birds are dark and mottled in summer, more finely mottled in early fall, and white in winter. Red eye combs can be concealed or inflated in courtship and aggression displays.

White-tailed Ptarmigan *Lagopus leucurus*

L 12¹/₂" (32 cm) Distinguished from other ptarmigans in all seasons by white tail. Winter bird is white except for dark bill and eyes and red eye combs. In summer, body is mottled blackish or brown with white belly, wings, and tail. Spring and fall molts give a patchy appearance. Locally common on rocky alpine slopes, high meadows. Calls include a henlike clucking and soft, low hoots. Small numbers have been introduced in the central High Sierra with apparent success.

Rock Ptarmigan *Lagopus mutus* *L 14" (36 cm)*

Mottled summer plumage is black, dark brown, or grayish-brown, male generally lacks the reddish tones of male Willow Ptarmigan. In winter plumage, male has a black line from bill through eye, lacking in male Willow. Acquires breeding plumage later in spring than does Willow. In both sexes, bill and overall size are slightly smaller than in Willow. Females are otherwise difficult to distinguish from Willows. Plumage is patchy white during spring and fall molts. Both species retain white wings and black tail year-round. The Rock Ptarmigan is common on high, rocky slopes and tundra. In breeding season, generally prefers higher and more barren habitat than does the Willow Ptarmigan. Calls include low growls and croaks and noisy cackles.

Willow Ptarmigan *Lagopus lagopus* *L 15" (38 cm)*

Mottled summer plumage of male is generally redder than in Rock Ptarmigan. White winter plumage lacks the black eye line of male Rock Ptarmigan. Bill and overall size are slightly larger in Willow Ptarmigan. Female is otherwise difficult to distinguish from Rock Ptarmigan. Both species retain white wings and black tail year-round. Plumage is patchy white during spring and fall molts. Willow Ptarmigan is common on tundra, especially in thickets of willow and alder. In breeding season, generally prefers wetter, brushier habitat than Rock Ptarmigan. Calls include low growls and croaks, noisy cackles. In courtship and territorial displays, male utters a raucous *go-back go-back go-backa go-backa go-backa*.

White-tailed Ptarmigan

winter

summer ♀

molting fall ♂

summer ♂

Rock Ptarmigan

winter ♂

winter ♀

summer ♀

summer ♂

fall ♂

Willow Ptarmigan

summer ♀

molting spring ♂

winter

summer ♂

summer ♂

Greater Prairie-Chicken *Tympanuchus cupido*
L 17" (43 cm) Heavily barred with dark brown, cinnamon, and pale buff above and below. Compare with Lesser Prairie-Chicken and Sharp-tailed Grouse. Short, rounded tail is all-dark in male, barred in female. Male has fleshy yellow-orange eye combs. Both sexes have elongated dark neck feathers, longer in males and erected during courtship to display inflated golden neck sacs. Courting males make a deep *oo-loo-woo* sound, known as "booming," like the sound made by blowing across the top of an empty bottle. Uncommon, local, and seriously declining. Found in areas of natural tallgrass prairie interspersed with cropland. A smaller, darker form, the endangered "Attwater's Prairie-Chicken," is found in small numbers in southeastern Texas.

Lesser Prairie-Chicken *Tympanuchus pallidicinctus*
L 16" (41cm) Resembles Greater Prairie-Chicken, but slightly smaller, paler, less heavily barred below. Male has yellow eye combs, blackish tail; female's tail is barred. Courting male displays dull orange-red neck sacs and erects dark neck tufts. Uncommon, local, and declining; found in sagebrush and shortgrass prairie country. Male's courtship "booming" is similar to Greater Prairie-Chicken, but notes are higher pitched.

Sharp-tailed Grouse *Tympanuchus phasianellus*
L 17" (43 cm) Very similar to prairie-chickens, but underparts are scaled and spotted, not barred; tail is mostly white and pointed; yellowish eye combs are less prominent. Compare also with female Ring-necked Pheasant (page 222). Birds are darkest in Alaska and northern Canada (standing figure), palest in the Plains (flying figure). Male's purplish neck sacs are inflated during courtship display. His courting notes include cackling and a single, low *coo-oo* call accompanied by the rattling of wing quills. Inhabits grasslands, sagebrush, woodland edges, and river canyons. Fairly common over most of range. Where ranges overlap, occasionally hybridizes with Greater Prairie-Chicken and Blue Grouse (page 210).

Sage Grouse *Centrocercus urophasianus* *L 28" (71 cm)*
Blackish belly, long pointed tail feathers, and very large size are distinctive. Male is larger than female and has yellow eye combs, black throat and bib, and large white ruff on breast. In flight, dark belly, absence of white outer tail feathers and much larger size distinguish this bird from Sharp-tailed Grouse. Courting male fans tail and rapidly inflates and deflates air sacs, emitting a loud, bubbling popping. Fairly common but local; found in sagebrush areas of foothills and plains.

Greater Prairie-Chicken ♀ ♂

Lesser Prairie-Chicken ♀ ♂

Sharp-tailed Grouse

Sage Grouse ♀ ♀ ♂

Northern Bobwhite *Colinus virginianus* L 9³/₄" (25 cm)
Mottled reddish-brown quail with short gray tail. Flanks are striped with reddish-brown. Throat and eye stripe are white in male, buffy in female. Juvenile is smaller and duller; compare with Japanese Quail. Common in brushlands and open woodlands, the Bobwhite feeds and roosts in coveys except during nesting season. Male's call is a rising, whistled *bob-white*, heard chiefly in spring and summer; whistled *hoy* call is heard year round. The Bobwhite population in the northwest is introduced. At northern edge of range, numbers are greatly reduced after harsh winters. The "Masked Bobwhite," an endangered subspecies, has been reintroduced from Mexico to its former range in southeastern Arizona but without success to date. Male has black throat and cinnamon underparts.

Japanese Quail *Coturnix japonica* L 7¹/₂" (19 cm)
Rarely seen in the wild; attempts to establish this Asian bird in the wild in North America have met with little success, but it is often raised on hunting preserves. Smaller than the Northern Bobwhite; appears almost tailless. Mottled brown above, buffy below, with pale eye stripes. Female is heavily streaked on breast. A secretive quail, more often heard than seen. Calls include a low *chuck-churrr*. Formerly considered a subspecies of Coturnix Quail.

Montezuma Quail *Cyrtonyx montezumae* L 8³/₄" (22 cm)
Plump, short-tailed, round-winged quail. Male has distinctive facial pattern and rounded pale brown crest on back of head. Back and wings mottled black, brown, and tan; breast dark chestnut; sides and flanks dark gray with white spots. Female is mottled pinkish-brown below with less distinct head markings. Juvenile is smaller, paler, with dark spotting on underparts. Uncommon, secretive, and local in grassy undergrowth of open juniper- or pine-oak woodlands on semiarid mountain slopes. Call heard in breeding season is a loud, quavering, descending whinny. Formerly called Harlequin Quail.

Scaled Quail *Callipepla squamata* L 10" (25 cm)
Grayish quail with conspicuous white-tipped crest. Bluish-gray breast and mantle feathers have dark edges, creating a shingled or scaly effect. Female's crest is buffy and smaller. Males in southernmost Texas tend to show a dark chestnut patch on belly. Juvenile resembles adult but is more mottled above, with less conspicuous scaling. Fairly common; found on barren mesas and plateaus, semidesert scrublands, and grasslands with mixed scrub. In fall, forms large coveys. During breeding season, both sexes give a location call when separated, a low, nasal *chip-churr*, accented on the second syllable. Introduced populations exist in Washington and Nevada.

Northern Bobwhite

♂

♀

"Masked Bobwhite"

juvenile

Japanese Quail

♀

♂

Montezuma Quail

♂

♀

juvenile

Scaled Quail

♂

♂

juvenile

Gambel's Quail *Callipepla gambelii* *L 11" (28 cm)*

Grayish above, with prominent teardrop-shaped plume or double plume. Chestnut sides and lack of scaling on underparts distinguish Gambel's from California Quail. Male has dark forehead, black throat, black patch on belly. Smaller juvenile is tan and gray with pale mottling and streaking. Shows less scaling and streaking than darker California juvenile; nape and throat are grayer. Common in desert scrublands and thickets, usually near permanent water source. Gregarious; in fall and winter, assembles in coveys of as many as 40 birds. Calls include varied grunts and cackles and a plaintive *qua-el;* loud, querulous *chi-ca-go-go* call is similar to California Quail but higher pitched and usually has four notes. Sometimes hybridizes with Scaled Quail (preceding page) and California Quail where range and habitat overlap. Introduced populations exist in Idaho and on California's San Clemente Island.

California Quail *Callipepla californica* *L 10" (25 cm)*

Gray and brown above, with prominent teardrop-shaped plume or double plume. Scaled underparts and brown sides distinguish California from Gambel's Quail. Body color varies from grayish, seen over most of range, to brown in coastal mountains of California; extremes are shown here in females. Male has pale forehead, black throat, and chestnut patch on belly. Juvenile is smaller; resembles Gambel's juvenile, but is darker, with traces of scaling on underparts. Common in open woodlands, brushy foothills, stream valleys, suburbs, usually near permanent water source. Gregarious; in fall and winter, assembles in coveys of up to 200 birds. Calls include varied grunts and cackles; loud, emphatic *chi-ca-go* call is similar to Gambel's Quail but lower pitched and usually has three notes rather than four. Most populations in northeastern portion of range and in Utah are probably introduced.

Mountain Quail *Oreortyx pictus* *L 11" (28 cm)*

Gray and brown above, with two long, thin head plumes that often appear to be one plume. Gray breast; chestnut sides boldly barred with white; chestnut throat outlined in white. Sexes alike, but female has shorter head plumes. Amount of brown and gray in upperparts varies in different forms of this species. Smaller juvenile has grayer underparts and longer head plumes than Gambel's or California Quail juveniles. Locally common in chapparal, brushy ravines, mountain slopes, at altitudes up to 10,000 feet. Nonmigratory but descends to lower altitudes in winter. Gregarious, forming coveys of as many as 20 birds in fall and winter. Male's mating call, a clear, descending *quee-ark,* can be heard up to a mile away. An enthusiastic imitation of this call may lure this somewhat secretive species into view.

Gambel's Quail

juvenile

Scaled-Gambel's Hybrid

♂

gray form ♀

brown form ♀

California Quail

♂

brown form juvenile

Mountain Quail

juvenile

brown form ♂

gray form ♀

Chukar *Alectoris chukar L 14" (36 cm)*
Old World species, introduced in North America as a game-bird. Gray-brown above; flanks boldly barred black and white; buffy face and throat outlined in black; breast gray; belly buff; outer tail feathers chestnut. Bill and legs are red. Lacks white eyebrow of similar Red-legged Partridge. Sexes are similar, but males are slightly larger and have small leg spurs. Juvenile is smaller and mottled; lacks bold black markings of adults. Chukars have become established in rocky, arid, mountainous areas of the west; game farm birds are released for hunting in the east. In fall and winter, Chukars feed in coveys of 5 to 40 birds. Calls include a series of rapid *chuck chuck chuck* notes and a shrill *whitoo* alarm note.

Black Francolin *Francolinus francolinus L 14" (36 cm)*
Old World species, established tenuously, if at all, in Louisiana and in southern Florida. Male's glossy black plumage is heavily marked with white and buff; white cheek patch; chestnut collar. Female is mottled brown overall, with paler chestnut patch on nape. A secretive bird, partial to dense vegetation, grassy fields, and croplands. Song of male is a loud, rhythmic *chik-cheek-cheek-keraykek*.

Red-legged Partridge *Alectoris rufa L 14" (36 cm)*
A European species, widely introduced to North America but has not yet become established. Browner above than similar Chukar, with conspicuous white eyebrow, whitish chin and throat, black bib with gray speckles; flanks are gray, barred with black, white, and chestnut. Legs and bill red. A bird of mountainous regions and open, arid lands in the west; feeds chiefly on seeds and leaves, and on roots and tubers it digs from the ground with its bill. Call is a harsh, staccato *chuck-chuck-chuck-chukuk*.

Gray Partridge *Perdix perdix L 12¹/₂" (32 cm)*
Widely introduced from Europe. Grayish-brown bird with rusty face and throat, paler in female. Male has dark chestnut patch on belly; patch is smaller or absent in females. Flanks are barred with reddish-brown; outer tail feathers rusty. Inhabits open farmlands, grassy fields. In fall, forms coveys of 12 to 15 birds. Calls include a hoarse *kee-ah*.

Himalayan Snowcock *Tetraogallus himalayensis*
L 28" (71 cm) Large Asian bird, apparently successfully established only in the Ruby Mountains of northeastern Nevada. Gray-brown overall, with tan streaking above. Whitish face and throat, outlined with chestnut stripes; undertail coverts white. Inhabits mountainous terrain. Clucks and cackles constantly as it feeds.

Chukar

♀

juvenile

Black
Francolin

♀

♂

Red-legged
Partridge

♂

Himalayan
Snowcock

♂

Gray
Partridge

♀

♂

Ring-necked Pheasant *Phasianus colchicus*

♂L 33" (84 cm) ♀L 21" (53 cm) Introduced from Asia, this large, flashy bird has a long, pointed tail and short, rounded wings. Male is iridescent bronze overall, mottled with brown, black, and green; head varies from dark, glossy green to purplish, with fleshy red eye patches and iridescent ear tufts. Often shows a broad white neck ring. Female is buffy overall, much smaller and duller than male. Distinguished from female Sharp-tailed Grouse (page 214) by larger size, longer tail, lack of barring below, and white in tail. Locally common; found in open country, farmlands, brushy areas, woodland edges. When flushed, rises almost vertically with a loud whirring of wings. Male's territorial call is a loud, penetrating *kok-cack*. Both sexes give hoarse, croaking alarm notes. White-winged forms (not shown) have been established in some parts of the west. The "Green Pheasant," a Japanese form once considered a separate species, has been introduced in tidewater Virginia and southern Delaware.

Wild Turkey *Meleagris gallopavo*

♂L 46" (117 cm) ♀L 37" (94 cm) Largest gamebird in North America; slightly smaller, more slender than the domesticated bird. Male has dark, iridescent body, flight feathers barred with white, red wattles, blackish breast tuft, spurred legs; bare-skinned head is blue and pink. Tail, uppertail coverts, and lower rump feathers are tipped with chestnut on eastern birds, buffy-white on western birds. Female and immature are smaller and duller than male, often lack breast tuft. Birds of the open forest, Wild Turkeys forage mostly on the ground for seeds, nuts, acorns, insects. At night they roost in trees. In spring a male's gobbling call may be heard a mile away. Re-stocked in much of former range; introduced in other areas; may become more widely established.

Chachalacas (Family Cracidae)

Tropical-forest birds with short, rounded wings and long tails. Generally secretive but highly vocal. One species of this family is found in North America.

Plain Chachalaca *Ortalis vetula* L 22" (56 cm)

Gray to brownish-olive above, with small head, slight crest; long, lustrous, dark green tail tipped with white. Patch of bare skin on throat, usually grayish, is pinkish-red in breeding male. Inhabits tall chaparral thickets along the Rio Grande; feeds in trees, chiefly on leaves and buds. Introduced to Georgia's Sapelo Island. Male's voice is a deep, ringing *cha-cha-lac;* female's voice higher pitched. The sound of a flock in full chorus is memorable.

Ring-necked Pheasant

♂

♀

♀

♂ ♀
"Green Pheasant"

eastern

♂

Wild Turkey

♀

western ♂

♂

Plain Chachalaca

Pigeons and Doves (Family Columbidae)

Familiar traits of the city pigeon—plump body and small, bobbing head—hold true for our other pigeons and doves. Usually the larger species are called pigeons and the smaller ones doves. All are strong, fast fliers. Juveniles have pale-tipped feathers, lack the neck markings of adults. Pigeons and doves feed chiefly on grain, other seeds, and fruit.

Band-tailed Pigeon *Columba fasciata* L 14¹/₂" (37 cm)
Purplish head and breast; dark-tipped yellow bill, yellow legs; broad gray tail band; narrow white band on nape, absent on juvenile. Flocks in flight resemble Rock Doves but are uniform, not varied, in plumage and lack contrasting white rump or black band at end of tail. Locally common in low-altitude coniferous forests in the northwest, oak or oak-conifer woodlands in the southwest; also increasingly common in suburban gardens, parks. Call is a low *whoo-whoo*. Rare in Alaska; usually absent from Central Valley of California. Accidental east to the Atlantic coast.

Red-billed Pigeon *Columba flavirostris* L 14¹/₂" (37 cm)
Dark overall, with a mainly red bill. Distinctive call heard in early spring and summer, a long, high-pitched *cooooo* followed by three loud *up-cup-a-coo*'s. Perches in tall trees above a brushy understory; forages for seeds, nuts, figs. Seldom comes to the ground except to drink. Uncommon and local in Texas; rare in winter.

White-crowned Pigeon *Columba leucocephala*
L 13¹/₂" (34 cm) A large, square-tailed pigeon of the Florida Everglades and Keys. Crown patch varies from shining white in adult males to grayish-white in most females and grayish-brown in juveniles. Otherwise this species looks all-black; the iridescent collar is visible only in good light. Flocks commute from nest colonies in coastal mangroves to feed inland on fruit. Most winter on Caribbean islands. Calls include a loud, deep *coo-cura-cooo* or *coo-croo*.

Rock Dove *Columba livia* L 12¹/₂" (32 cm)
The highly variable city pigeon; multicolored forms were developed over centuries of near domestication. The birds most closely resembling their wild ancestors have head and neck darker than back, black bars on inner wing, white rump, black band at end of tail. Flocks in flight show a variety of plumage patterns, unlike Band-tailed Pigeon. Introduced from Europe by early settlers, now widespread and common, particularly in urban settings. Nests and roosts chiefly on high window ledges, bridges, barns. Feeds during the day in parks and fields. Call is a soft *coo-cuk-cuk-cuk-coooo*.

Band-tailed Pigeon

Red-billed Pigeon

White-crowned Pigeon

♂

♀

Rock Dove

color variations

Mourning Dove *Zenaida macroura* L 12" (31 cm)
Trim-bodied with long tail tapering to a point. Black spots on
upperwing; pinkish wash on underparts. In flight, shows
white tips on outer tail feathers. Juvenile has heavy spotting
and scaled effect on wings. Call is a mournful *oowoo-woo-woo-
woo.* Our most abundant and widespread dove; inhabits farmyards, grassy meadows, cultivated fields, frequents backyard
feeders, suburbs, and towns. Wings produce a fluttering whistle as the bird takes flight. May breed as far north as southeastern Alaska. Casual stray to south coastal Alaska.

Zenaida Dove *Zenaida aurita* L 10" (25 cm)
West Indian species, accidental on the Florida Keys, where it
formerly bred, and on the southernmost Florida mainland.
Distinguished from Mourning Dove by white on trailing edge
of secondaries and by shorter, rounded, gray-tipped tail. Lacks
the white wing patches and white tail tips of White-winged
Dove. Feeds on open ground close to water, usually near mangroves. Call is similar to the Mourning Dove's but briefer and
faster. Generally shy and difficult to approach.

White-winged Dove *Zenaida asiatica* L 11½" (29 cm)
Large white wing patches and shorter, rounded tail distinguish this species from Mourning Dove. On sitting bird, wing
patch shows only as a thin white line. Compare especially with
Zenaida Dove. Feeds on grain, wild seeds, and cactus fruits
and blossoms. Nests singly or in large colonies in dense mesquite, mature citrus groves, riparian woodlands, and saguaro-
paloverde deserts; also found in desert towns. Drawn-out,
cooing call, *who-cooks-for-you,* has many variations. Casual in
fall and winter on east coast to the Maritime Provinces.

Ringed Turtle-Dove *Streptopelia risoria* L 11" (28 cm)
Popular cage bird. Escapes have bred in many U. S. cities, but
not firmly established anywhere. Plumage variable; some
Ringed Turtle-Doves are pure white; a few lack dark collar.
Very tame. Call is a soft, rolling *coo-hrrrooo.* The **Collared Dove**
(not shown), *S. decaocto,* an Old World species, has recently
been found breeding widely in southeastern Florida. Distinguished from Ringed Turtle-Dove by call, a loud *coo-coo-coo.*
Averages darker gray than Ringed Turtle-Dove with more
prominent white edges on black collar; slightly larger with a
slightly longer tail and larger head. Fairly skittish.

Spotted Dove *Streptopelia chinensis* L 12" (31 cm)
An Asian species introduced in Los Angeles in early 1900s;
now well established in southwestern California in suburban
parks and gardens. Named for spotted collar, distinct in adults,
obscured in young birds. Wings and long, white-tipped tail are
more rounded than in Mourning Dove; wings are unmarked.
Call, a harsh *oo-hoo-oo-hurrrrp.*

juvenile

**Mourning
Dove**

**Zenaida
Dove**

**White-winged
Dove**

**Ringed
Turtle-Dove**

**Spotted
Dove**

Common Ground-Dove *Columbina passerina*
L 6¹/₂" (17 cm) A stocky dove with scaled effect on head and breast; short tail, often raised. Bright chestnut primaries and wing linings visible in flight. Male has a slate gray crown, pinkish-gray underparts. Female is grayer, more uniformly colored. Call, a repeated soft, ascending *wah-up*. Forages on open ground in the east and brushy rangeland in the west. Sometimes breeds north of its usual Gulf coast range; casual as far north as New York and Oregon in fall and winter.

Ruddy Ground-Dove *Columbina talpacoti* L 6³/₄" (17 cm)
Widespread in Latin America; casual from southern Texas to southern California. Lacks scaling of Common Ground-Dove. Male has gray crown, rich chestnut upperparts. Female has a chestnut wash on wings and uppertail coverts. Both show black on underwing coverts.

Inca Dove *Columbina inca* L 8¹/₄" (21 cm)
Plumage conspicuously scalloped, especially on the belly. In flight, shows chestnut on wings like Common Ground-Dove, but note the Inca Dove's longer, white-edged tail. Found in cactus and mesquite country, usually near human habitations, often in parks and gardens. Casual wanderer north to Kansas and Oklahoma. Call, a double *cooo-coo*.

White-tipped Dove *Leptotila verreauxi* L 11¹/₂" (29 cm)
This large, plump dove has a whitish forehead and throat and dark back. In flight, white tips show plainly on fanned tail. Gleans the ground along the Rio Grande Valley, keeping close to woodlands with dense understory. Low-pitched call is like the sound produced by blowing across the top of a bottle. Formerly called White-fronted Dove.

Ruddy Quail-Dove *Geotrygon montana* L 9³/₄" (25 cm)
A chunky tropical dove; accidental on the Dry Tortugas and Florida Keys. Male's rich rufous upperparts and prominent buffy line under the eye are distinctive. Females are brown above and have a plainer facial pattern. In both sexes, underparts are cinnamon buff. Quail-doves are so named because they resemble quails and have a similar terrestrial life-style.

Key West Quail-Dove *Geotrygon chrysia* L 12" (31 cm)
West Indian species, now rare over most of its range; accidental on the Florida Keys and south Florida. Larger and proportionately longer tailed than Ruddy Quail-Dove, with a white line under the eye. Upperparts, primaries, and tail are chestnut, glossed with purple and green. Male is highly iridescent above; female is duller. Both are whitish below.

Common
Ground-Dove
♂ ♀
♂

Ruddy
Ground-Dove
♀ ♂
♂

Inca
Dove

White-tipped
Dove

Ruddy
Quail-Dove
♂ ♀

Key West
Quail-Dove
♂

Parrots (Family Psittacidae)

Most of the many parakeets and parrots seen in the wild in North America are escaped cage birds. We show here the species that have established small populations or are seen as vagrants from Mexico.

Budgerigar *Melopsittacus undulatus* L 7" (18 cm)
Commonly called "parakeet." Seen in the wild throughout most of continent. Populations seem to be established in suburbs near Miami and along southwestern Florida coast. Plumage highly variable. In the most common variety, upperparts are yellow, heavily barred with black; rump and underparts are green, iris white. White wing stripe conspicuous in flight. Male has blue cere, gray-blue legs. Female's cere is brown, legs pinkish. Immature is duller, with barred forehead, dark iris; black throat spots less distinct or absent. Budgies give a warbling call in flight or a muffled screech. Native to Australia.

Rose-ringed Parakeet *Psittacula krameri* L 16" (41 cm)
Small populations of this Asian and African species exist around Miami and Los Angeles. Note long, narrow tail. Adult male is bright green with reddish bill, black chin, pink collar, and blue wash on nape. Yellow wing linings conspicuous in flight. Adult female has shorter tail; lacks pink collar and black chin. Immature resembles adult female but has pink bill; male requires three years to attain full adult plumage. Call is a repeated screeching *kee-ak*.

Green Parakeet *Aratinga holochlora* L 13" (33 cm)
Mexican species, annual in extreme southern Texas, sometimes in small flocks. Escapes are also seen in southern Florida and elsewhere. A large parakeet, green overall, with a slender, pointed tail. Call is a loud, high-pitched screeching.

Monk Parakeet *Myiopsitta monachus* L 11¹/₂" (29 cm)
South American species, established in Florida. Escapes can be seen almost anywhere, but most birds are sighted in the east. Adult is green above with grayish face and throat. Breast is gray with whitish barring; note diffuse yellowish band across belly. Immatures show a green tinge on forehead. In flight, the Monk Parakeet appears dark below except for paler face and throat. Call is a loud, staccato shriek. Builds large, bulky stick nest in tree or atop telephone pole.

Canary-winged Parakeet *Brotogeris versicolurus*
L 8³/₄" (22 cm) South American species, fairly common in suburbs along southeastern Florida coast, less common around Los Angeles. Dull green overall with blue-green outer primaries. Remaining flight feathers are mostly white with yellow tinge. In flight, these white wing patches appear translucent. Call is a rapid series of shrill metallic notes.

Rose-ringed Parakeet

♂

♀

Budgerigar

♂

Green Parakeet

Monk Parakeet

Canary-winged Parakeet

Red-crowned Parrot *Amazona viridigenalis*

L 12¹⁄₂″ (32 cm) Mexican species, uncommon in southernmost Texas; may be visitors from Mexico or escaped cage birds. Escapes have established breeding populations in southeastern Florida and suburban Los Angeles. Adult male has red crown, forehead, wing patch. Female and young show less red on head. Call is a screaming *kree-o krak krak krak*.

Yellow-headed Parrot *Amazona oratrix* *L 14″ (36 cm)*

Mexican species, popular as a cage bird. Sightings in southernmost Texas are probably escapes. Introduced populations breed in suburbs of southeastern Florida and Los Angeles. Adult's green plumage sets off yellow head and thighs, red shoulder, red wing patch. Immature shows less yellow on head. Yellow-headed Parrots give a variety of raucous calls.

Thick-billed Parrot *Rhynchopsitta pachyrhyncha*

L 15″ (38 cm) Resident but increasingly rare in highland forests of Mexico. Formerly a rare and irregular visitor to mountains of southeastern Arizona, but no confirmed sightings since 1930s. Adult is green overall with red forehead, black bill, and red eyebrow; tail long and pointed. Bright yellow underwing patch shows in flight. Immatures lack red eyebrow; bill is light buff. Thickbills are known for loud screeching.

Trogons (Family Trogonidae)

These beautifully colored tropical birds have long, squared-off tails, small feet, and short, broad bills. Unlike parrots, trogons are usually solitary and quiet.

Elegant Trogon *Trogon elegans* *L 12¹⁄₂″ (32 cm)*

Yellow bill, white breast band; undertail delicately barred. Male is bronze green above, bright red below. At close range, look for copper highlights on uppertail. Female is brown above, with white, teardrop-shaped ear spot on gray-brown head. Juvenile resembles female, but wing coverts are spotted with pale buff, underparts barred. Call is a series of croaking *co-ah* notes. Found in streamside woodlands, chiefly at altitudes between 4,000 and 6,000 feet. Vagrants are seen in southwestern New Mexico and southern Texas. Formerly called Coppery-tailed Trogon.

Eared Trogon *Euptilotus neoxenus* *L 14″ (36 cm)*

Casual in late summer and fall in mountain streamside woodlands of southeastern Arizona. Larger than Elegant Trogon; bill is black or gray; lacks white breast band and barring on undertail. Calls include a loud upslurred squeal similar to a call of the Great-tailed Grackle but ending in a *chuck* note.

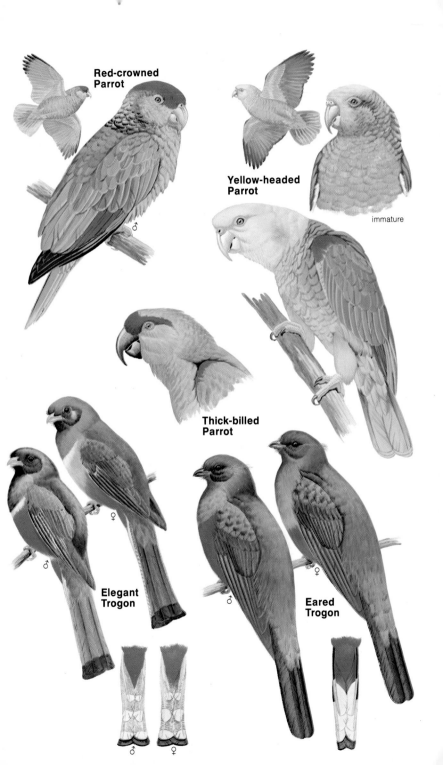

Red-crowned Parrot

Yellow-headed Parrot

immature

Thick-billed Parrot

Elegant Trogon

♂

♀

Eared Trogon

♂

♀

♂

♀

Cuckoos and Anis (Family Cuculidae)

A large family, widespread in the Old World. Only a few species are seen in North America. Most are slender and long-tailed; two toes point forward, two back.

Common Cuckoo *Cuculus canorus* L 13" (33 cm)
Old World species, very rare spring and summer visitor to central and western Aleutians and Pribilofs. Closely resembles Oriental Cuckoo. Adult male and adult gray-phase female are gray above, paler below, with whitish belly narrowly barred with gray. Barring is often slightly narrower and underparts paler than in Oriental Cuckoo. Hepatic-phase female is pale rusty-brown above, heavily barred with black on back and tail; rump is paler than hepatic-phase Oriental and either unmarked or only lightly spotted. In flight, both species resemble a small falcon. Male's song is the familiar *cuc-coo* for which the family is named but call has not been heard in North America.

Oriental Cuckoo *Cuculus saturatus* L 12½" (32 cm)
Eurasian species, accidental in summer in western Aleutians and Pribilofs. Adult male and adult gray-phase female are gray above, paler below, with pale belly barred in dark gray. Barring is often slightly broader and underparts buffier than in the Common Cuckoo. Hepatic-phase female is rusty-brown above, heavily barred on back, rump, and tail. The Oriental's song, a four-note *du-du-du-du*, has not been heard here.

Smooth-billed Ani *Crotophaga ani* L 14½" (37 cm)
Huge bill's upper mandible ridge rises above the crown and arches downward at base. Bill shape distinguishes both ani species from grackles (page 424). Black overall with iridescent bronze overtones. Long tail is often dipped and wagged. Found in brushy fields, scrublands; often feeds on insects stirred up by cattle. Both ani species are gregarious; several pairs usually share a nest and take turns incubating the eggs. Casual north along Atlantic coast to North Carolina and along Florida Gulf coast. Call, a whining, rising *quee-lick*.

Groove-billed Ani *Crotophaga sulcirostris* L 13½" (34 cm)
Bill smaller than in Smooth-billed Ani, does not extend above crown. Black overall with iridescent purple and green overtones; long tail, often dipped and wagged. Grooves in bill are visible only at very close range; absent in some adults and young birds. Common in summer in woodlands and farm fields; often seen feeding on insects stirred up by cattle. Casual north to Minnesota, west to California, and east to Virginia. Call is a liquid *tee-ho,* accented on the first syllable.

Common Cuckoo

hepatic phase ♀

gray phase ♂

Oriental Cuckoo

hepatic phase ♀

gray phase ♂

sunning

Smooth-billed Ani

Groove-billed Ani

Mangrove Cuckoo   *Coccyzus minor*   L 12" (31 cm)

Black mask and buffy underparts distinguish this species from other cuckoos. Upperparts grayish-brown; lacks rufous primaries of Yellow-billed Cuckoo. Black tail feathers are broadly tipped with white. In Florida subspecies, *C.m. maynardi*, paler throat and breast contrast with buffy flanks and belly. Underparts are entirely buffy in *C.m. continentalis*, an accidental vagrant along our Gulf coast from Mexico to northwest Florida. In all juveniles, mask is paler, tail pattern muted. Found chiefly in mangrove swamps. Like other cuckoos, perches quietly near center of tree. Call is a slow, guttural *gaw gaw gaw*.

Yellow-billed Cuckoo   *Coccyzus americanus*

L 12" (31 cm)   Grayish-brown above, white below; rufous primaries; lower mandible yellow. Undertail patterned in bold black and white. In juvenile plumage, held well into fall, tail has a much paler pattern and bill may show little or no yellow; may be confused with Black-billed Cuckoo. Common in open woods, orchards, and streamside willow and alder groves. Song sounds hollow and wooden, a rapid staccato *kuk-kuk-kuk* that usually slows and descends to a *kakakowlp-kowlp* ending. Once numerous but now a rare breeder in California. Rare vagrant to the Maritimes during fall migration.

Black-billed Cuckoo   *Coccyzus erythropthalmus*

L 12" (31 cm)   Grayish-brown above, pale grayish below. Bill is usually all-dark; may have a pale yellow spot on base of lower mandible. Lacks the rufous primaries of Yellow-billed Cuckoo. Note also reddish eye ring. Undertail patterned in gray with white tipping; compare juvenile Yellow-billed. Juvenile Black-billed has a buffy eye ring; undertail is paler; underparts may have buffy tinge, especially on undertail coverts; primaries may show a little rusty-brown. Uncommon to fairly common; found in woodlands and along streams. Song usually consists of monotonous *cu-cu-cu* or *cu-cu-cu-cu* phrases. Very rare breeder in north Texas, west Tennessee, west Idaho.

Greater Roadrunner   *Geococcyx californianus*

L 23" (58 cm)   A large ground-dwelling cuckoo streaked with brown and white. Speeds across the desert on long, strong legs. Note the long, heavy bill, conspicuous bushy crest, and long, white-edged tail. Short, rounded wings show a white crescent on the primaries. Common in scrub desert and mesquite groves; less common in chaparral. Eats insects, lizards, snakes, rodents, and small birds. Song is a dovelike cooing, descending in pitch.

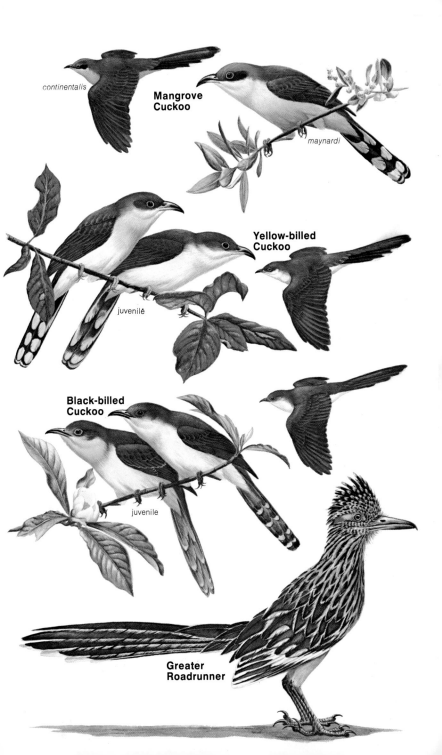

continentalis

Mangrove Cuckoo

maynardi

Yellow-billed Cuckoo

juvenile

Black-billed Cuckoo

juvenile

Greater Roadrunner

Owls (Families Tytonidae and Strigidae)

These distinctive birds of prey are divided by structural differences into two families, the Barn Owls (Tytonidae) and the Typical Owls (Strigidae). All have immobile eyes in large heads. Fluffy plumage makes their flight nearly soundless. Many species hunt at night and roost during the day. To find an owl, search the ground for regurgitated pellets of fur and bone below a nest or roost. Listen for flocks of small songbirds noisily mobbing a roosting owl.

Barn Owl *Tyto alba* L 16" (41 cm)

A pale owl with dark eyes in a heart-shaped face. Rusty-brown above; underparts vary from white to cinnamon. Darkest birds are always females, palest birds males. Compare with Snowy Owl (next page). The Barn Owl roosts and nests in dark cavities in city and farm buildings, cliffs, trees. Common in parts of western range, uncommon and declining in the east. Typical call is a raspy, hissing screech.

Short-eared Owl *Asio flammeus* L 15" (38 cm)

Tawny; boldly streaked on breast; belly paler, more lightly streaked. Ear tufts are barely visible. In flight, long wings show buffy patch above, black wrist mark below; these markings are usually more prominent than in Long-eared Owl. A bird of open country, marshes, tundra, weedy fields; nests on the ground. Hunts chiefly at dawn and dusk. Flight is wavering, wingbeats erratic. During the day it roosts on the ground or on open, low perches: short poles, muskrat houses, duck blinds. Fairly common. Somewhat gregarious in winter; groups may gather where prey is abundant. Typical call heard in breeding season is a raspy, high barking.

Long-eared Owl *Asio otus* L 15" (38 cm)

A slender owl with long, close-set ear tufts. Boldly streaked and barred on breast and belly. Wings generally have a less prominent buffy patch and smaller black wrist mark than Short-eared Owl; facial disk is rusty. Lives in thick woods; hunts at night over open fields, marshes. By day it roosts in a tree, close to the trunk. Uncommon. More gregarious in winter; flocks may roost together. Generally silent except in breeding season. Common call is one or more long *hooo*'s.

Great Horned Owl *Bubo virginianus* L 22" (56 cm)

Size, bulky shape, and white throat separate this owl from the Long-eared Owl; ear tufts distinguish it from other large species. Common; habitats vary from forest to city to open desert. Nests in trees, caves, or on the ground. Chiefly nocturnal. Takes prey as large as skunks, grouse. Call is a series of three to eight loud, deep hoots, the second and third hoots often short and rapid. A pale form inhabits forests at tundra's edge in central Canada; compare with Snowy Owl (next page).

Barn Owl

Short-eared Owl

Long-eared Owl

pale form

Great Horned Owl

Barred Owl *Strix varia* L 21" *(53 cm)*
A chunky owl with dark eyes, dark barring on upper breast, dark streaking below. Common in dense coniferous or mixed woods of river bottoms and swamps; also in upland woods. Chiefly nocturnal; daytime roost well hidden. Easily flushed; does not generally tolerate close approach. Distinctive call is a rhythmic series of loud hoots: *who-cooks-for-you, who-cooks-for-you-all;* also a drawn-out *hoo-ah,* sometimes preceded by an ascending agitated barking. Much more likely than other owls to be heard in daytime. Northwestern portion of range is expanding rapidly; now overlaps similar Spotted Owl. May be very rare breeder on southeastern coast of Alaska.

Great Gray Owl *Strix nebulosa* L 27" *(69 cm)*
Our largest owl. Heavily ringed facial disks make the yellow eyes look small. Lacks ear tufts. Inhabits boreal forests and wooded bogs in the far north, dense coniferous forests with meadows in the mountains farther south. Hunts over forest clearings and nearby open country, chiefly by night but also at dawn and dusk; hunts by day during summer in northern part of range. Call is a series of deep, resonant *whoo*'s. Generally uncommon; rare and irregular winter visitor to limit of dashed line on map.

Spotted Owl *Strix occidentalis* L 17½" *(45 cm)*
Large and dark-eyed, with white spotting on head, back, and underparts, rather than the barring and streaking of the similar Barred Owl. Inhabits thickly wooded canyons, humid forests. Strictly nocturnal. Main call is a series of three or four hesitant, doglike barks and cries. Uncommon; decreasing in number and range due to habitat destruction.

Snowy Owl *Nyctea scandiaca* L 23" *(58 cm)*
A large white owl, with rounded head, yellow eyes. Dark bars and spots are heavier on females, heaviest on young birds; old males may be pure white. An owl of open tundra; nests on the ground; preys chiefly on lemmings, hunting by day during the arctic summer, as well as at night. Retreats from northernmost part of range in winter; at least a few are seen annually to limit indicated by dashed line on map. In years when the lemming population plummets, Snowies may wander in winter as far south as northern Alabama, Oklahoma, and central California. These irruptives, usually heavily barred younger birds, are often highly visible, perched conspicuously on the ground or on low stumps, fence posts, and buildings.

Barred Owl

Great Gray Owl

Spotted Owl

Snowy Owl

immature

Eastern Screech-Owl *Otus asio* L 8¹/₂" (22 cm)

A small owl with yellow eyes and usually a pale bill. Ear tufts prominent if raised; when flattened, bird has a round-headed look. Underparts marked with bars and streaks; note heavy black streaks on upper breast. Red phase predominates in the south, gray in the north and in southernmost Texas. A very pale gray form, *O.a. maxwelliae,* is found in northwestern part of range. Eastern Screech-Owls are common in a wide variety of habitats: woodlots, forests, swamps, orchards, parks, suburban gardens. Nocturnal; best located and identified by voice. Two typical calls: a series of quavering whistles, descending in pitch; and a long single trill, all on one pitch. Formerly classified with Western Screech-Owl as one species; range separation is not yet fully known. Wanderers of both species are occasionally found at Big Bend National Park in Texas.

Western Screech-Owl *Otus kennicottii* L 8¹/₂" (22 cm)

A small owl with yellow eyes and usually a dark bill. Ear tufts prominent if raised; when flattened, bird has a round-headed look. Generally gray overall; some birds in the humid coastal northwest are brownish. Underparts are marked with blackish streaks and thinner bars. Nocturnal; best located and identified by voice. Two common calls: a series of short whistles accelerating in tempo; and a short trill followed immediately by a longer trill. Common in open woodlands, streamside groves, desert, suburban areas, and parks. Where range overlaps that of Whiskered Screech-Owl, the Western Screech-Owl is generally found at lower elevations. Formerly classified with Eastern Screech-Owl as one species; range separation is not yet fully known.

Whiskered Screech-Owl *Otus trichopsis* L 7¹/₄" (18 cm)

Small owl with yellow eyes, dark bill. Ear tufts fairly prominent if raised; when flattened, bird has a round-headed look. Closely resembles gray Western Screech-Owl but slightly smaller with smaller feet and usually coarser barring below. Identification must be based on voice. Two common calls: a series of short whistles on one pitch and at a fairly even tempo; and a series of very irregular hoots, like Morse code. Nocturnal. Inhabits dense oak and oak-conifer woodlands, primarily at elevations from 4,000 to 6,000 feet. Where range overlaps that of Western Screech-Owl, the Whiskered is usually found at higher elevations.

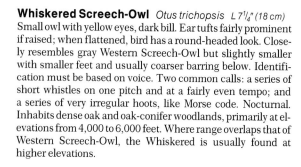

Eastern Screech-Owl

red phase

gray phase

gray phase juvenile

maxwelliae

northwest coast

Western Screech-Owl

Whiskered Screech-Owl

Flammulated Owl *Otus flammeolus L 6³/₄" (17 cm)*

Dark eyes; small ear tufts, often indistinct; variegated red and gray plumage. Birds in the northern part of the range are generally grayer; southern birds redder. Common in oak and pine woodlands, especially ponderosa. Sometimes nests in loose colonies. Strictly nocturnal; nests and roosts in tree cavities, usually old woodpecker holes. Best located at night by its call, a long series of single or sometimes paired hollow hoots. Highly migratory. Accidental east to Louisiana and Florida.

Elf Owl *Micrathene whitneyi L 5³/₄" (15 cm)*

Our smallest owl. Yellow eyes; very short tail. Lacks ear tufts. Common in desert lowlands and in canyons, especially in oaks and sycamores; fairly common in foothills. Generally scarce and declining in Texas and California. Strictly nocturnal; roosts and nests in cavities in saguaros and trees. Call is an irregular series of high *churp*'s and chattering notes. Rare in winter in southernmost Texas.

Ferruginous Pygmy-Owl *Glaucidium brasilianum*

L 6³/₄" (17 cm) Long tail, reddish with dark or dusky bars. Upperparts gray-brown; crown faintly streaked. Eyes yellow; black nape spots look like eyes on the back of the head. White underparts streaked with reddish-brown. Inhabits saguaro deserts and low, open woodlands in Arizona; Rio Grande Valley woodlands in Texas. Found at lower elevations than Northern Pygmy-Owl. Chiefly diurnal; most active at dawn and dusk. Roosts in crevices and cavities. Most common call is a rapid, repeated *took*. Unlike other North American owls, pygmy-owls fly with quick, unmuffled wingbeats.

Northern Pygmy-Owl *Glaucidium gnoma L 6³/₄" (17 cm)*

Long tail, dark brown with pale bars. Upperparts are either rusty-brown or gray-brown; crown spotted; underparts white with dark streaks. Eyes yellow; black nape spots look like eyes on the back of the head. Inhabits dense woodlands in foothills and mountains. Where the two species overlap, found at higher elevations than Ferruginous Pygmy-Owl. Chiefly diurnal; most active at dawn and dusk. Nests in cavities. Call is a mellow, whistled, *hoo* or *hoo hoo,* repeated in a well-spaced series. An aggressive predator, sometimes catching birds larger than itself, this owl is a favorite target for songbirds. Birders may locate the owl by watching for mobbing songbirds and, conversely, attract songbirds by imitating the owl's call.

Flammulated Owl

red phase

gray phase

Elf Owl

Ferruginous Pygmy-Owl

Northern Pygmy-Owl

gray phase

red phase

Northern Saw-whet Owl *Aegolius acadicus* *L 8″ (20 cm)*
Reddish-brown above; white below with reddish streaks; bill dark; facial disks reddish, without dark border. Juvenile strongly reddish above, tawny-rust below. Saw-whets inhabit dense coniferous or mixed forests, wooded swamps, tamarack bogs. Call, heard primarily in breeding season, is a monotonously repeated single-note whistle; also gives a raspy call like the sound of a saw being sharpened. Strictly nocturnal; roosts during day in or near nest hole in breeding season. In winter, preferred roost is in dense evergreens, usually close to end of branch. Large concentrations of regurgitated pellets and white "wash" build up below favored winter roosts. Once found, Saw-whets can be closely approached. Difficulty in locating this species obscures information about numbers and distribution. Very rarely reported over most of winter range.

Northern Hawk Owl *Surnia ulula* *L 16″ (41 cm)*
Long tail, falcon-like profile, and black-bordered facial disks identify this owl of the northern forests. Underparts are barred in brown. Flight is low and swift; sometimes hunts during daylight as well as at night. It is most often seen, however, perched high in a spruce tree. Usually can be closely approached. Call is a rapid, sharp *ki-ki-ki-ki*. Basically nonmigratory but retreats slightly in winter from northernmost part of range. Vagrants are only rarely seen south of mapped range.

Boreal Owl *Aegolius funereus* *L 10″ (25 cm)*
White underparts streaked with chocolate brown. Whitish facial disk has a distinct black border; bill is pale. Darker above than Saw-whet Owl. Juvenile is chocolate brown below. Boreal Owls inhabit dense northern forests and muskeg. Irruptive, usually in small numbers; otherwise seldom seen south of mapped range, but this may be due to difficulty of locating it. Recently discovered breeding at isolated locations high in the Rockies. Strictly nocturnal; roosts during daylight in dense cover, usually close to tree trunk. Call, heard only in breeding season, is a short, rapid series of hollow *hoo* notes.

Burrowing Owl *Athene cunicularia* *L 9¹/₂″ (24 cm)*
Long legs distinguish this ground dweller from all other small owls. Adult is boldly spotted and barred. Juvenile is buffy below. An owl of open country; at home on golf courses, road cuts, airports. Nests in single pairs or, more commonly, in small colonies. Nocturnal; flight is low and undulating; often hovers like a kestrel. Perches conspicuously during daylight at entrance to burrow nest or on low post. Calls include a soft *coo-coooo* and a chattering series of *chack* notes. Disturbed in its nest, the Burrowing Owl often gives an alarm call that effectively imitates the sound of a rattlesnake. Casual vagrant in spring and fall to east coast, north to Maine.

Northern Saw-whet Owl

juvenile

Northern Hawk Owl

Boreal Owl

juvenile

Burrowing Owl

juvenile

Nightjars (Family Caprimulgidae)

Wide mouths help these night-hunters snare flying insects. In daylight they roost on the ground or lengthwise along low branches, camouflaged by their muted, intricate plumage. Most species are best located and identified by their distinctive calls.

Chuck-will's-widow *Caprimulgus carolinensis*
L 12" (31 cm) Our largest nightjar. Mottled buff-brown overall; wings rounded; tail long and rounded. Loud whistling song sounds like *chuck-will's-widow;* first note is often inaudible. Larger and redder than Whip-poor-will; buff-brown throat and whitish necklace contrast with dark breast. Male's tail has less white than in male Whip-poor-will; tips of outer feathers are buff. Female's tail lacks white. Fairly common but local in oak-pine woodlands, live oak groves. Range is expanding in the east, replacing Whip-poor-will in some areas.

Whip-poor-will *Caprimulgus vociferus* L 9³/₄" (25 cm)
Mottled gray-brown overall; wings rounded; tail long, rounded. Song is a loud *whip-poor-will,* clear and mellow in eastern birds, with accent on first and last syllables; rough and burry in southwestern birds, with strongest accent on last syllable. Whip-poor-will is smaller and grayer than Chuck-will's-widow; dark throat contrasts with white or buffy necklace and pale underparts. Male's tail shows much more white than in male Chuck-will's-widow. Female's tail has contrasting pale tip on dark outer feathers. Fairly common but local in open coniferous and mixed woodlands in the east, wooded canyons in the southwest. Breeds locally in southern California.

Buff-collared Nightjar *Caprimulgus ridgwayi*
L 8³/₄" (22 cm) Rare, irregular and local in desert canyons of extreme southwestern New Mexico and southeastern Arizona. Usually roosts on the ground by day. Gray-brown plumage resembles Whip-poor-will, but note buff collar across nape. Song is an accelerating series of *cuk* notes ending with *cukacheea.* Also known as Ridgway's Whip-poor-will.

Common Poorwill *Phalaenoptilus nuttallii* L 7³/₄" (20 cm)
Our smallest nightjar, distinguished by short, rounded tail and short, rounded wings. Outer tail feathers are tipped with white, more boldly in males than in females. Song is a whistled *poor-will,* with a final *ip* note audible at close range. Plumage is variable; upperparts range from brownish-gray to pale gray. Broad white band crosses dark throat and breast. Fairly common in sagebrush and coniferous woodlands and on coastal chaparral slopes; often seen on roadsides. Roosts on the ground; flies up to catch an insect, then returns to the same or a nearby location. Known to hibernate in cold weather; may winter north into normal breeding range.

Chuck-will's-widow

Whip-poor-will

Buff-collared Nightjar

Common Poorwill

Pauraque *Nyctidromus albicollis* L 11" (28 cm)

In flight, long, rounded tail distinguishes Pauraque from nighthawks; note also shorter, rounder wings. Broad white bands on wings distinguish it from other nightjars (preceding page). White tail patches conspicuous on male, smaller and often buffy on female. In close view, note chestnut ear patch. Common in woodland clearings and scrub of Rio Grande Valley; winters in streamside thickets. Active chiefly at dawn and dusk. Flies close to the ground; often lands on roads and roadsides. Distinctive song, one or more low *pur* notes followed by a higher, descending *wheeer*.

Common Nighthawk *Chordeiles minor* L 9¹/₂" (24 cm)

Wings long and pointed; tail slightly forked. Bold white bar across primaries is slightly farther from wing tip than in Lesser Nighthawk. Nasal *peent* call distinguishes Common from both Lesser and Antillean Nighthawks. Subspecies range in overall color from dark brown in eastern birds to gray in the northern Great Plains form, *C.m. sennetti;* color variations are subtle in adults, distinct in juveniles. Pale spotting on wing coverts contrasts with darker back. Throat white in male, buffy in female; underparts whitish, with bold dusky bars. Female lacks white tail band, may be slightly buffy below. Juvenile shows little or no white on throat. Found in open woodlands, suburbs, towns, the Common Nighthawk is more active in daylight than other nightjars. Roosts on the ground and on branches, posts, roofs. As male swoops to the ground in courtship display, wings make a hollow booming sound. Common but slowly declining in parts of range.

Antillean Nighthawk *Chordeiles gundlachii*

L 8" (20 cm) Rare but regular in summer on Florida Keys; also seen on Dry Tortugas and southeast Florida mainland. Wings are long, pointed; tail slightly forked. Female and juveniles lack white tail band. Call, a variable katydid-like *pity-pit-pit,* best distinguishes Antillean from Common Nighthawk; note also the buffier underparts. Formerly considered a subspecies of Common Nighthawk.

Lesser Nighthawk *Chordeiles acutipennis* L 8¹/₂" (22 cm)

Resembles Common Nighthawk but wings are shorter and often more rounded; whitish bar across primaries is slightly closer to tip. Upperparts are paler and more uniformly mottled. Throat is white in males, usually buffy in females and juveniles. Underparts buffy, with faint barring. Male has white tail band. Female lacks tail band; wing bar is smaller, buffy. Juvenile's wing bar much smaller; often indistinct in juvenile female. Fairly common; found primarily in dry, open country, scrubland, desert. Active chiefly at dawn and dusk. Flies with a more fluttery wingbeat than Common Nighthawk. Often seen over ponds or perched on roadsides. Distinctive call, a rapid, tremulous trill. Casual in winter in southern California and on Texas coast, in spring and fall on Louisiana coast.

Pauraque

Common Nighthawk

sennetti juvenile

Antillean Nighthawk

Lesser Nighthawk

Swifts (Family Apodidae)

These fast-flying birds spend most of the day aloft, feeding on insects in midair.

Long, pointed wings bend closer to the body than those of the similar swallows.

Chimney Swift *Chaetura pelagica* L 5¼" (13 cm)
Small, cigar-shaped body with short, stubby tail. The only swift over most of its range, but compare with very similar Vaux's Swift. The Chimney Swift is larger, usually darker below; wings longer than Vaux's; has louder, chattering call and greater tendency to soar. Both species perform a rocking display: with wings upraised, bird rocks from side to side. Nests in chimneys, barns, hollow trees. Rare but regular in southern California. No winter records in the U. S.

Black Swift *Cypseloides niger* L 7¼" (18 cm)
Blackish overall; long, slightly forked tail, often fanned in flight. Uncommon. Nests in colonies on protected cliffs, beneath waterfalls; also on wet sea cliffs. Wingbeats are somewhat more leisurely than in other swifts; often soars. Winters mainly in Central America; rarely seen in migration.

Vaux's Swift *Chaetura vauxi* L 4¾" (12 cm)
Small, cigar-shaped body with short, stubby tail. Usually somewhat paler below and on rump than Chimney Swift; less inclined to soar. Call is softer, higher, more insectlike. Fairly common; found in woodlands near lakes and rivers. Nests in hollow trees, seldom in chimneys. Rare in winter in southern California, casual on Gulf coast from Louisiana to Florida.

Fork-tailed Swift *Apus pacificus* L 7¾" (20 cm)
Asian species, casual vagrant on western Aleutians and Pribilofs. White rump conspicuous in flight; tail's deep fork not always apparent. Formerly called White-rumped Swift.

White-collared Swift *Streptoprocne zonaris*
L 8½" (22 cm) Tropical species, accidental at scattered coastal locations in the United States. A large, black swift; note white collar, slightly forked tail. Soars with wings bent down.

White-throated Swift *Aeronautes saxatalis*
L 6½" (17 cm) Black above, black-and-white below, with long, forked tail. Distinguished from Violet-green Swallow (page 296) by longer, narrower wings, bicolored underparts. In poor light, may be mistaken for Black Swift; look for White-throated's smaller size, faster wingbeats. Common in mountains, rocky canyons, cliffs. Nests in cliff crevices.

White-throated Needletail *Hirundapus caudacutus*
L 8" (21 cm) (Not shown.) Large Asian swift, casual in spring on outer Aleutians. Dark overall, with pale patch on back, white throat and undertail coverts. Tail short, stubby.

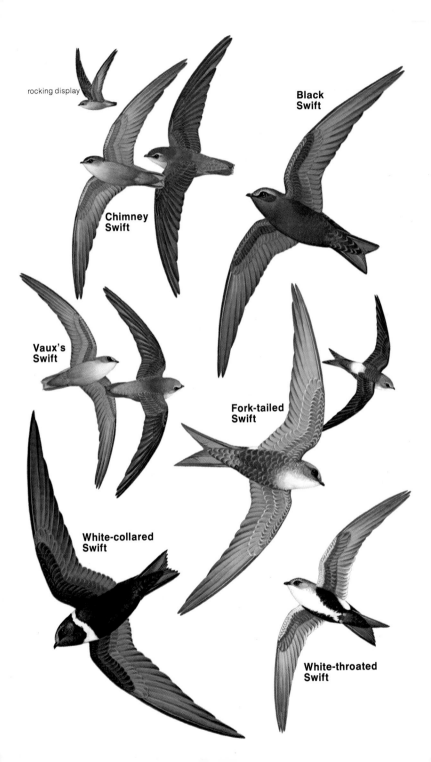

rocking display

Black
Swift

Chimney
Swift

Vaux's
Swift

Fork-tailed
Swift

White-collared
Swift

White-throated
Swift

Hummingbirds (Family Trochilidae)

Tiny, colorful birds that hover at flowers to sip nectar with needlelike bills. Often identified by twittery calls or the chattering "chase notes" given when driving intruders away. Males' iridescent throat feathers, called a gorget, look black in poor light.

Green Violet-ear *Colibri thalassinus* L 4³/₄" (12 cm)
Tropical species, casual in southern and central Texas, mainly in summer. Green overall; bill slightly downcurved. Male has blue-violet patches on face and breast. Female slightly duller; chest patch smaller or absent. Song is a repeated *tsip-tsup*.

Cuban Emerald *Chlorostilbon ricordii* L 4¹/₂" (11 cm)
West Indian species, accidental in south Florida in fall and winter. Note pinkish lower mandible, deeply forked tail. Male is green overall with white undertail coverts. Female is grayish below. Call is a metallic *tchiw-tchiw*.

Buff-bellied Hummingbird *Amazilia yucatanensis*
L 4¹/₄" (11 cm) Mexican species, fairly common in Rio Grande delta, especially around Brownsville, Texas. Very rare in winter along Gulf coast to Louisiana. Bronze green above, with chestnut tail. Bill pinkish-red with black tip. Throat and breast metallic green; belly buffy. Calls are shrill and squeaky.

Berylline Hummingbird *Amazilia beryllina* L 4¹/₄" (11 cm)
Rare summer visitor from Mexico to mountains of southeastern Arizona; occasionally breeds there. Green above and below, with chestnut wings, rump, and tail. Base of lower mandible red. Male's lower belly is chestnut, female's grayish.

Bahama Woodstar *Calliphlox evelynae* L 3³/₄" (10 cm)
Casual stray from Bahamas to southeastern Florida; sightings so far have been of adult females or immatures. Dull bronze green above, cinnamon below, with white breast. Male has a metallic purple-red gorget. Female is paler below; tail more rounded, outer feathers rufous at base, tipped with pale cinnamon. Immatures resemble adult females; young male gradually acquires purple throat. Call is a staccato *tit tit tit*.

Lucifer Hummingbird *Calothorax lucifer* L 3¹/₂" (9 cm)
Bronze green above; bill downcurved. Male is purple on throat and sides of neck; lacks purple crown of male Costa's Hummingbird (page 258); tail is deeply forked. In female, note pale, broadening streak behind eye; tail is rounded; outer tail feathers reddish at base, tipped with white; underparts are rich buff, often with whitish belly. Young male begins to show purple spotting on throat by late summer. Uncommon in Chisos Mountains of Texas; rare but annual in southeastern Arizona and extreme southwestern New Mexico in summer. Calls are shrill, squeaky *chip* notes.

**Green
Violet-ear**

♂

**Cuban
Emerald**

♂

♀

**Berylline
Hummingbird**

♀

♂

**Buff-bellied
Hummingbird**

♂

♂

immature ♂

**Bahama
Woodstar**

♀

♀

♀

immature ♂

♀

♂

**Lucifer
Hummingbird**

Broad-billed Hummingbird *Cynanthus latirostris*

L 4" (10 cm) Adult male is dark green above and below, with white undertail coverts, a glittering blue gorget, and mostly red bill. Broad, forked tail is blackish-blue. Adult female is duller above, gray below; often shows a narrow white eye stripe; tail is square-tipped. Juveniles resemble female; by late summer, male begins to show blue and green flecks on throat, green on sides; dark, forked tail helps distinguish it from White-eared Hummingbird. Common in desert canyons, low mountain woodlands. Chattering *je-dit* call is similar to Ruby-crowned Kinglet. Male's display call is a whining *zing*. Rare in southern California during fall and winter.

White-eared Hummingbird *Hylocharis leucotis*

L 3¾" (10 cm) Rare summer visitor from Mexico to southeastern Arizona mountains. Bill shorter than in Broad-billed Hummingbird; broad white stripe extends back from eye; black ear patch; square tail. Adult male has dark purple crown and chin, emerald green gorget; display call is a repeated, silvery *tink tink tink*. Chattering calls are loud and metallic.

Violet-crowned Hummingbird *Amazilia violiceps*

L 4½" (11 cm) Crown violet; underparts entirely white; upperparts bronze green; tail greenish. Long bill is mostly red. Uncommon in U. S. range. Favors streamside locations in low mesquite-sycamore or higher oak-sycamore canyons. Call is a loud chattering similar to Broad-billed Hummingbird. Male's song is a series of sibilant *ts* notes.

Blue-throated Hummingbird *Lampornis clemenciae*

L 5" (13 cm) Adult male's throat is blue, female's gray. Broad white eye stripe and faint white whisker stripe border dark ear patch. Tail has broad white tips on outer feathers; compare female Magnificent Hummingbird. Fairly common; found in mountain canyons, especially near streams. Casual north of mapped range. Male's call is a loud, very high, repeated *seep*.

Magnificent Hummingbird *Eugenes fulgens*

L 5¼" (13 cm) Adult male is green above, with purple crown; metallic green throat; breast and upper belly black and green; lower belly dull brown. Tail is dark green and deeply notched. Female is duller, lacks purple crown; squarish tail has small grayish-white tips on outer feathers; compare female Blue-throated Hummingbird. Fairly common in high mountain meadows, canyons. Casual north of mapped range. Call is a sharp *chip*. Formerly named Rivoli's Hummingbird.

Plain-capped Starthroat *Heliomaster constantii*

L 5" (13 cm) Casual stray in summer and fall from Mexico to arid foothills and deserts of southeastern Arizona. Broad white whisker stripe, white eye stripe, and white tufts on flanks are conspicuous. Throat shows variable amount of red; note also very long bill, white patch on rump. Call is a sharp *chip*.

Broad-billed Hummingbird

♀

immature ♂

♂

♂

White-eared Hummingbird

♀

♂

Blue-throated Hummingbird

♀

♂

Violet-crowned Hummingbird

♀

Magnificent Hummingbird

♂

Plain-capped Starthroat

Ruby-throated Hummingbird *Archilochus colubris*

L 3³/₄" (10 cm) The only hummingbird seen over most of the east. Metallic green above. Adult male has a brilliant red throat and black chin; underparts are whitish; sides and flanks dusky-green; tail forked. Female's throat is whitish; underparts grayish-white, with buffy wash on sides; tail is similar to female Black-chinned Hummingbird. Immatures resemble adult female but some immature males have a golden cast on upperparts, unlike Black-chinned Hummingbird. A few immature males begin to show red spotting on throat by early fall. As with all hummingbirds, adult males migrate much earlier than females and immatures. Rubythroats are fairly common in parts of range; found in gardens and woodland edges. Similar hummingbirds seen in the southeast in winter are more likely to be Black-chinned Hummingbirds, but females and immatures of these two species are almost indistinguishable. Rubythroat generally has a greener crown, shorter bill. Calls are almost identical.

Black-chinned Hummingbird *Archilochus alexandri*

L 3³/₄" (10 cm) Metallic green above. In good light, male shows violet band at lower border of black throat. Underparts are whitish; sides and flanks dusky-green. Female's throat can be all-white or show faint dusky or greenish streaks. Immatures resemble adult female; immature male may begin to show violet on lower throat in the fall. Common in lowlands and low mountains. Call is a soft *tchew;* chase note combines high squeals and *tchew* notes. A very few Blackchins winter in the southeast; may be mistaken for Ruby-throated Hummingbirds. Females and immatures of these species are almost indistinguishable; see Rubythroat description for details.

Costa's Hummingbird *Calypte costae* *L 3¹/₂" (9 cm)*

Male has deep violet crown and gorget extending far down sides of neck. Female is generally grayer above, whiter below, than female Black-chinned Hummingbird; note also tail differences. Best distinguished by voice. Call is a high, metallic *tink,* often given in a series. Male's call is a loud *zing.* Fairly common in desert washes, dry chaparral.

Anna's Hummingbird *Calypte anna* *L 4" (10 cm)*

Male's head and throat are deep rose red, the color extending a short distance onto sides of neck. Female's throat usually shows red flecks, often forming a patch of color. In both sexes, underparts are grayish, washed with a varying amount of green. Bill is proportionately short. Immatures resemble female; immature male usually shows some red on crown. Juveniles lack red on throat; compare with smaller female Black-chinned and Costa's Hummingbirds. Abundant in coastal lowlands, mountains; also in deserts, especially in winter. Common call note, a sharp *chick;* chase call is a rapid dry rattling. Male's song is a jumble of high squeaks and raspy notes.

immature ♂

Ruby-throated Hummingbird

♀

immature ♂

♂

♂

immature ♂

Black-chinned Hummingbird

immature ♂

♂

♀

Costa's Hummingbird

immature ♂

♀

juvenile

Anna's Hummingbird

Black-chinned ♀

Costa's ♀

Anna's ♀

♂

Calliope Hummingbird *Stellula calliope* *L 3¹/₄" (8 cm)*

Smallest North American bird; short tail, short bill. Male is green above, white below, with greenish flanks. Purple-red feathers on throat form streaks or V-shaped gorget. Female is green above; underparts tinged with pale cinnamon, especially on flanks; throat is spotted or lightly streaked, never shows central red spot often present on throat of adult female Allen's and Rufous Hummingbirds. Note also smaller size and shorter bill and tail. Juveniles resemble adult female. Immature male can show some red on throat by late summer. Common along streams in high meadows, canyons. Relatively silent; male's courtship call is a high *see-ree*.

Broad-tailed Hummingbird *Selasphorus platycercus*
L 4" (10 cm) Except during late-summer molt, adult male's wingbeats produce a loud, trilling whistle. Both sexes are metallic green above. Male has rose red throat, white underparts with green sides. Female has speckled throat, pale cinnamon wash on flanks; broad green tail shows rufous mostly on outer feathers. Common in the southern and central Rockies and the Great Basin mountains. Calls include a sharp *chip*, often given in a short series. Casual in fall and winter to Gulf coast.

Rufous Hummingbird *Selasphorus rufus* *L 3³/₄" (10 cm)*
Tail mainly rufous; pattern similar to Allen's Hummingbird, but feathers are broader. Adult male has reddish-brown back, sometimes with speckles or patches of green; crown is green, gorget iridescent orange-red. Adult female and immatures inseparable from Allen's; distinguished from female Calliope and Broad-tailed by more extensively rufous tail and sharper contrast of reddish sides, flanks, and undertail coverts with white breast and belly; in adult female, also by throat pattern. Juveniles resemble adult female; immature male may show reddish-brown back by winter before acquiring orange-red gorget. Common in forests, woodland edges, thickets; breeds in lowlands and mountains. Found mainly in mountains in fall, lowlands in spring. Rare in fall in the east, accidental in spring. Rare on Gulf coast in fall and winter. Wing whistle and calls are similar to Allen's Hummingbird.

Allen's Hummingbird *Selasphorus sasin* *L 3³/₄" (10 cm)*
Similar in all plumages to Rufous Hummingbird. Tail feathers are narrower. Adult male has a full iridescent orange-red gorget; distinguishable from Rufous by combination of all-green back and crown. Adult female and immatures inseparable from female Rufous. Allen's Hummingbird is common in brush and woodlands. Migrates earlier in fall and spring than Rufous Hummingbird. Casual vagrant on Gulf coast. Adult male's wingbeats produce a high, thin, trilling whistle. Calls include a sibilant *chup*, often given in a series; chase note, *zeee-chuppity-chup*. Wing whistle and calls are similar to Rufous Hummingbird.

Calliope Hummingbird

♀

♂

Broad-tailed Hummingbird

♂

♀

Rufous Hummingbird

immature ♂

♂

♀

green-flecked ♂

♂

Allen's Hummingbird

Calliope ♀   Allen's ♀   Rufous ♀   Broad-tailed ♀

Kingfishers (Family Alcedinidae)

Stocky and short-legged, with a large head, a large bill, and, in two species, a ragged crest. Look for kingfishers near woodland streams and ponds and in coastal areas. They hover over water or watch from low perches, then plunge headfirst to catch a fish. Heavy bill and strong feet also serve for digging long nest burrows in stream banks.

Belted Kingfisher *Ceryle alcyon* L 13" (33 cm)

The only kingfisher in most of North America. Both male and female have slate blue breast band. Female has rust belly band and flanks, may be confused with female Ringed Kingfisher; note white belly and undertail coverts and smaller size. Juvenile resembles adult but has rust spotting in breast band. Common and conspicuous along rivers and brooks, ponds and lakes, estuaries. Solitary except in nesting season. Call is a loud, dry rattle. Rare in winter north into summer range.

Ringed Kingfisher *Ceryle torquata* L 16" (41 cm)

Larger than Belted Kingfisher; generally frequents larger rivers and ponds, perches on higher branches. Male is rust below. Female has slate blue breast, narrow white band, rust belly and undertail coverts. Juveniles resemble adult female, but juvenile male's breast is largely rust. Calls include a harsh rattle, lower and slower than in Belted Kingfisher, and a slow series of *chack* notes, given chiefly in flight. Rufous underwing coverts distinctive in flight. Resident in lower Rio Grande Valley; casual elsewhere in southern Texas in fall and winter.

Green Kingfisher *Chloroceryle americana* L 8³⁄₄" (22 cm)

Smallest of our kingfishers; crest inconspicuous. Green above, with white collar; white below, with dark green spotting. Male has rust breast band; female has a band of green spots. Juvenile resembles adult female. Call is a faint but sharp *tick tick*. Often perches on low, sheltered branches. Flight is direct and very fast; white outer tail feathers conspicuous in flight. Fairly common resident of lower Rio Grande Valley; less common on Edwards Plateau. Casual wanderer along the Texas coast and to southeastern Arizona, mainly in fall and winter.

Belted
Kingfisher

Ringed
Kingfisher

♂

♀

Green
Kingfisher

♂

♀

Woodpeckers (Family Picidae)

Strong claws, short legs, and stiff tail feathers enable woodpeckers to climb tree trunks. Sharp bill is used to chisel out insect food and nest holes, and to drum a territorial signal to rivals.

Golden-fronted Woodpecker *Melanerpes aurifrons*

L 9³/₄" (25 cm) Black-and-white barred back, white rump, usually an all-black tail; golden orange nape, paler in females; yellow feathering above bill. Male has a small red cap. Yellow tinge on belly not easily seen. Juvenile has streaked breast, brownish crown. In flight, all plumages show white wing patches, white rump, black tail. Red-bellied and Gila Woodpeckers have barred tails. The Golden-fronted is fairly common in dry woodlands, pecan groves, mesquite brushlands. Calls, a rolling *churr-churr* and cackling *kek-kek,* are slightly louder and raspier than in Red-bellied Woodpecker.

Red-bellied Woodpecker *Melanerpes carolinus*

L 9¹/₄" (24 cm) Black-and-white barred back; white uppertail coverts; central tail feathers barred. Crown and nape red in males; females have red nape only. Small reddish patch or tinge on belly. Juvenile has streaked breast, dark gray crown. In all plumages, white wing patches and white uppertail coverts flash in flight. Similar Golden-fronted Woodpecker has black tail. Red-bellied Woodpeckers are common in open woodlands, suburbs, parks. May be extending breeding range northward. Withdraw in winter from higher elevations and northern edge of range. Call, a rolling *churr* or *chiv-chiv,* is slightly softer than that of Golden-fronted Woodpecker.

Gila Woodpecker *Melanerpes uropygialis* L 9¹/₄" (24 cm)

Black-and-white barred back and rump; central tail feathers barred. Male has a small red cap. In all plumages, white wing patches are visible in flight. A familiar and conspicuous inhabitant of towns, scrub desert, cactus country, streamside woods. Bores nest holes in giant saguaros as well as in cottonwood trees and mesquite. Calls, a rolling *churr* and a loud, sharp, high-pitched *yip,* often given in a series.

Northern Flicker *Colaptes auratus* L 12¹/₂" (32 cm)

Brown barred back; spotted underparts, with black crescent bib. White rump conspicuous in flight; lacks white wing patches. Females lack red or black moustachial stripe.. The three forms were once considered separate species: "Yellow-shafted Flicker" east of the Rockies; "Red-shafted" west of the Rockies; "Gilded Flicker" in the southwest. Intergrades of these three forms are regularly seen in the Great Plains and southwest. Large and active, Flickers are common in open woodlands and suburban areas; often feed on the ground. Calls include a loud, rapid *wik-wik-wik-wik* and *wick-er, wick-er, wick-er,* and a single, loud *klee-yer.*

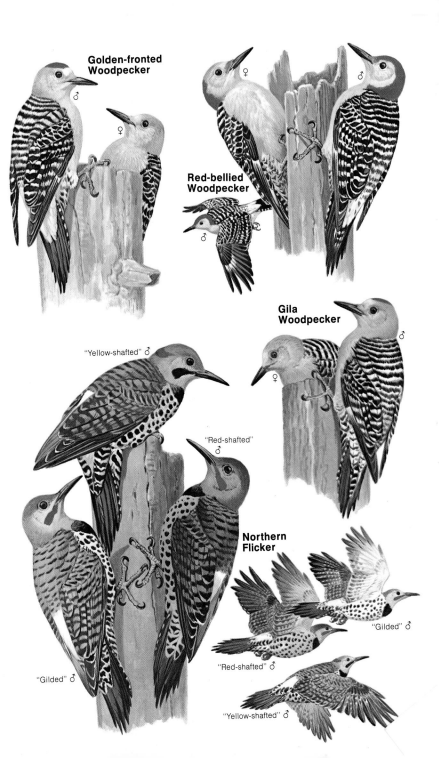

Golden-fronted Woodpecker

♂

♀

Red-bellied Woodpecker

♀

♂

♂

Gila Woodpecker

♀

♂

"Yellow-shafted" ♂

"Red-shafted" ♂

Northern Flicker

"Gilded" ♂

"Gilded" ♂

"Red-shafted" ♂

"Yellow-shafted" ♂

Red-headed Woodpecker

Melanerpes erythrocephalus L 9¹/₄" (24 cm) Entire head, neck, and throat are bright red in adults, contrasting with blue-black back and snowy white underparts. Juvenile is brownish; acquires red head during gradual winter molt. Look for distinctive white inner wing patches and white rump, highly visible in all ages in both perched and flying birds. Call is a loud *queark,* similar to Red-bellied Woodpecker (preceding page) but harsher and sharper. Inhabits open woods, farmlands, bottomlands, parks, backyards. Forages on tree trunks and on the ground for insects, berries, acorns; often seen flycatching. Bores nest holes in dead trees, fence posts, telephone poles, but uses any handy cavity to store acorns for the winter. Red-headed Woodpeckers have become rare in the northeast, due in part to habitat loss and competition with Starlings for nest holes. Somewhat more numerous in the rest of their range.

Acorn Woodpecker *Melanerpes formicivorus*

L 9" (23 cm) Black chin, yellowish throat, white cheeks and forehead, red cap. Female has smaller bill than male, less red on crown. In flight, white rump and small white patches on outer wings are conspicuous. Common in oak woods or pine forests where oak trees are abundant. Sociable; generally found in small, noisy colonies. Distinctive call, a raucous *ja-cob ja-cob.* Eats chiefly acorns and other nuts in winter, insects in summer. In the fall, this woodpecker is sometimes seen drilling small holes in a tree trunk and pounding an acorn into each hole for a winter food supply. Colonies use the same hole-riddled "granary tree" year after year.

White-headed Woodpecker *Picoides albolarvatus*

L 9¹/₄" (24 cm) Head and throat white. Male has a red patch on back of head. Body is black except for white wing patches. Juveniles have a variable patch of pale red on the crown. Nests in open coniferous mountain forests, especially in ponderosa and sugar pine; casual at lower altitudes in winter. Feeds primarily on seeds from ponderosa and sugar pine cones; also pries away loose bark in search of insects and larvae. Fairly common over most of range; rare and local in the north. Calls include a grating *pee-dink* or *pee-dee-dink.*

Lewis' Woodpecker *Melanerpes lewis L 10³/₄" (27 cm)*

Greenish-black head and back, with gray collar and breast; dark red face, pinkish belly. In flight, its darkness, large size, and slow, steady wingbeats give it a crow-like appearance. Juvenile lacks collar and red face; underparts may be only faintly pink. Common in open woodlands of interior foothills and valleys; less common on coast. Sometimes forms large flocks in fall and winter. Main food is insects, mostly caught in the air; also eats fruit, acorns, other nuts. Stores acorns, which it first shells, in tree bark crevices. Generally silent.

Red-headed
Woodpecker

juvenile

♀

♂

Acorn
Woodpecker

White-headed
Woodpecker

♂

♀

juvenile

Lewis'
Woodpecker

Sapsuckers

These woodpeckers drill evenly spaced rows of holes in trees, then visit these "wells" for sap and the insects it attracts.

All four species have a white rump, white wing patches, and at least some yellow on the belly. Calls include plaintive mews.

Williamson's Sapsucker *Sphyrapicus thyroideus*
L 9" (23 cm) Male has black back, white rump, large white wing patch; black head with narrow white stripes, bright red chin and throat. Breast is black, belly yellow, flanks barred with black and white. Female's head is brown; back, wings, and sides barred with dark brown and white; rump white; lacks white wing patch and red chin; breast has large dark patch; belly variably yellow. Juveniles resemble adults but are duller; attain adult plumage by first winter; juvenile male has white throat. Fairly common in dry, piney forests of the western mountains; moves south or to lower elevations in winter.

Red-breasted Sapsucker *Sphyrapicus ruber*
L 8¹/₂" (22 cm) Red head, nape, and breast; large white wing patch; white rump. Back is black, lightly spotted with yellow in northern subspecies, *S.r. ruber;* more heavily marked with white in southern *daggetti*. Belly is yellow in *ruber; daggetti* has paler belly, paler head with longer white moustachial stripe. In both forms, briefly held juvenile plumage is brownish, showing little or no red. Common in coniferous or mixed forests in coastal ranges, usually at lower elevations and in moister forests than Williamson's Sapsucker. Small numbers move south and to lower elevations in winter. Red-breasted occasionally hybridizes with Red-naped Sapsucker. Formerly considered a subspecies of Yellow-bellied Sapsucker.

Yellow-bellied Sapsucker *Sphyrapicus varius*
L 8¹/₂" (22 cm) Red forecrown on black-and-white head; chin and throat red in male, white in female. Back is blackish, with white rump, large white wing patch. Underparts yellowish, paler in female. Juvenile retains brownish plumage until first spring. Common in deciduous forests. Highly migratory; casual in the west during winter. Occasionally hybridizes with Red-naped Sapsucker. Range of overlap between these two species not fully known. Formerly classified with Red-naped and Red-breasted as one species.

Red-naped Sapsucker *Sphyrapicus nuchalis*
L 8¹/₂" (22 cm) Red forecrown, variable red patch on back of black-and-white head. Chin and throat red in male; female has white chin and variable amount of red on throat. Otherwise resembles Yellow-bellied Sapsucker. Juvenile is brownish overall; resembles adult by first fall. Common in deciduous forests. Formerly considered a subspecies of Yellow-bellied Sapsucker. Range of overlap between these two species not fully known.

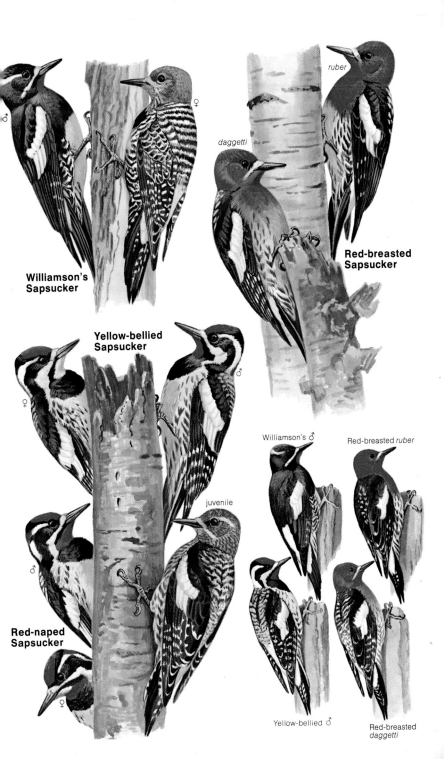

Williamson's Sapsucker ♂ ♀

Red-breasted Sapsucker *ruber* *daggetti*

Yellow-bellied Sapsucker ♂ ♀

Red-naped Sapsucker ♂ ♀ juvenile

Williamson's ♂   Red-breasted *ruber*

Yellow-bellied ♂   Red-breasted *daggetti*

Downy Woodpecker *Picoides pubescens* L 6³/₄" (17 cm)
White back generally identifies both this woodpecker and the similar Hairy Woodpecker. Downy is much smaller, with a smaller bill; outer tail feathers generally have faint dark bars or spots. Birds in the Pacific northwest have pale gray-brown back and underparts. Rocky Mountain birds have less white spotting on wings. Typical *pik* call and whinny are similar to those of the Hairy Woodpecker but slightly softer and higher pitched. Common; active, and somewhat unwary; often seen in suburbs, parklands, and orchards, as well as in forests. A familiar visitor to feeders.

Hairy Woodpecker *Picoides villosus* L 9¹/₄" (24 cm)
White back generally identifies both Hairy and the similar Downy Woodpecker. Hairy is much larger, with a larger bill; outer tail feathers are entirely white. Birds in the Pacific northwest have pale gray-brown back and underparts. Rocky Mountain birds have less white spotting on wings. Juveniles, particularly in the Maritime Provinces, have some barring on back and flanks; sides may be streaked. Juveniles on the Queen Charlotte Islands have heavily barred outer tail feathers. In young males, the forehead is spotted with white; crown streaked with red or orange. Hairy's calls include a loud, sharp *peek* and a slurred whinny. Fairly common; inhabits both open and dense forests.

Three-toed Woodpecker *Picoides tridactylus*
L 8³/₄" (22 cm) Black-and-white barring down center of back distinguishes most forms of Three-toed Woodpecker from similar Black-backed. Both have heavily barred sides. Male's yellow cap is usually more extensive in Three-toed but less solid. Density of barring on back is intermediate in northwestern form, *P. t. fasciatus*. In Rocky Mountain form, *dorsalis,* back is almost entirely white. Barring is very dense in eastern form, *bacatus;* thinner moustachial stripe helps distinguish it from Black-backed Woodpecker. Three-toed is found in coniferous forests, especially in burned-over areas. Call is a single *pik*. Less common than Black-backed in the east.

Black-backed Woodpecker *Picoides arcticus*
L 9¹/₂" (24 cm) Solid black back, heavily barred sides. Male has a solid yellow cap. Compare especially with eastern form of Three-toed Woodpecker, *P. t. bacatus,* which has a densely barred back. The Black-backed Woodpecker inhabits coniferous forests; often found in burned-over areas. Forages on dead conifers, flaking away large patches of loose bark rather than drilling into it, in search of larvae and insects. Call note is a single, sharp *pik,* similar to call of Three-toed. Casual south of mapped range in the east.

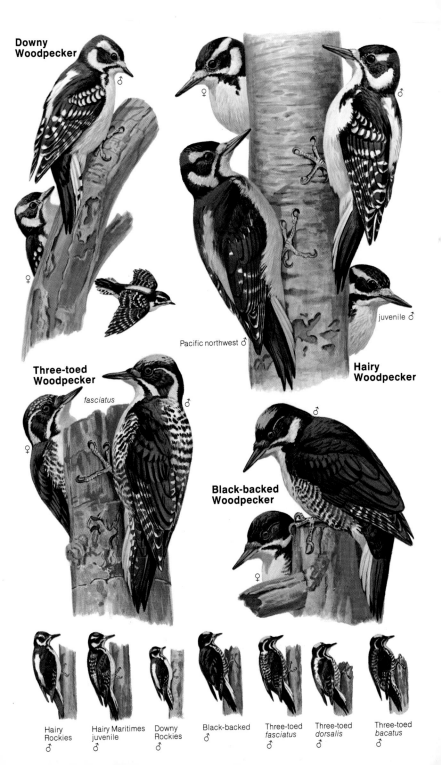

Downy Woodpecker

♂

♀

♀

Hairy Woodpecker

♂

Pacific northwest ♂

juvenile ♂

Three-toed Woodpecker

fasciatus

♂

♀

Black-backed Woodpecker

♂

♀

Hairy
Rockies
♂

Hairy Maritimes
juvenile
♂

Downy
Rockies
♂

Black-backed
♂

Three-toed
fasciatus
♂

Three-toed
dorsalis
♂

Three-toed
bacatus
♂

Ladder-backed Woodpecker *Picoides scalaris*

L 7¼" (18 cm) Black-and-white barred back, spotted sides; face and underparts slightly buffy or grayish; face marked with black lines. Male has red crown. In California, Ladderback may be confused with Nuttall's Woodpecker. Ladderback shows less black on face; white barring on back is more pronounced and extends to nape; white outer tail feathers are evenly barred rather than spotted. Call is a crisp *pik*, very similar to Downy Woodpecker's call and different from Nuttall's *prrrt;* also gives a descending whinny. May hybridize with Nuttall's where ranges overlap. Ladder-backed is common in dry brushlands, mesquite and cactus country; often seen in towns and rural areas. Feeds on beetle larvae from small trees; also eats cactus fruits, forages on the ground for insects.

Red-cockaded Woodpecker *Picoides borealis*

L 8½" (22 cm) Black-and-white barred back, black cap, and large white cheek patch identify this woodpecker more readily than the barely visible red tufts on the male's head. Similar Hairy and Downy Woodpeckers (preceding page) have solid white or gray-brown backs. Voices differ, too: Red-cockaded's raspy *sripp* and high-pitched *tsick* are much more nasal. Juvenile lacks red tufts but may show some red on crown. Inhabits open, mature pine or pine-oak woodlands. Bores nest hole only in a large living pine afflicted with heartwood disease, then drills small holes around the nest opening. Pine pitch oozing down the trunk from these holes may repel predators; also makes the tree a distinctive signpost. Populations have decreased with loss of habitat.

Nuttall's Woodpecker *Picoides nuttallii* *L 7½" (19 cm)*

Closely resembles the Ladder-backed Woodpecker. Nuttall's shows more black on face; white bars on back are narrower, with more extensive solid black just below the nape. White outer tail feathers are sparsely spotted rather than barred. Call is a low *prrrt,* much lower than the Ladderback's *pik;* also gives a high-pitched whinny. Nuttall's prefers less arid habitat than the Ladderback; usually seen in chaparral mixed with scrub oak and in wooded canyons, streamside trees. Forages on tree trunks, generally probing crevices and chipping away loose bark rather than drilling.

Strickland's Woodpecker *Picoides stricklandi*

L 7½" (19 cm) Solid brown back distinguishes this species from all other woodpeckers. Female lacks red patch on back of head. Compare with female sapsuckers (page 268), especially Williamson's, and with the Northern Flicker (page 264). Fairly common resident in foothills and mountains; generally found in oak or pine-oak forests or canyons. Call is a sharp *peek* similar to call of Hairy Woodpecker. Formerly called Arizona Woodpecker or Brown-backed Woodpecker.

Ladder-backed Woodpecker

Red-cockaded Woodpecker

Nuttall's Woodpecker

Strickland's Woodpecker

Ladder-backed
♂

Nuttall's
♂

Strickland's
♂

Red-cockaded
♂

Ivory-billed Woodpecker *Campephilus principalis*

L 19¹/₂" (50 cm) Probably extirpated in North America; a few may still be present in pine forests of eastern Cuba. Unconfirmed sightings in recent years in Georgia, Florida, Louisiana, and Texas may actually have been the smaller Pileated Woodpecker; last unequivocal sightings were in the 1950s. Note especially the Ivorybill's black chin and ivory bill and the extensive white wing patches visible in perched birds. Females have black rather than red crests. Compare also the black-and-white wing patterns of Ivorybills and Pileated Woodpeckers in flight. Distinctive call note is a loud, high-pitched, nasal *yank*. Our largest woodpecker, the Ivorybill requires large tracts of old-growth river forest; dead and dying trees supply nesting sites and food, the larvae of wood-boring beetles. Loss of habitat in U. S. and Cuba has brought this never-common species to the brink of extinction.

Pileated Woodpecker *Dryocopus pileatus*

L 16¹/₂" (42 cm) Perched bird is almost entirely black on back and wings, lacking the Ivorybill's large white wing patches. White chin and dark bill also distinguish Pileated Woodpecker, along with smaller size. Compare also the wing patterns of the two species in flight. Pileated is the largest woodpecker commonly seen in North America. Female's red cap is less extensive than in male. Juvenile plumage, held briefly, resembles adult but is duller and browner overall. Call is a loud, rising-and-falling *wuck-a-wuck-a-wuck-a,* similar to Flicker but higher and louder. Common in southeast; uncommon and local elsewhere. Prefers dense, mature forest, but also seems to be adapting well to human encroachment, becoming more common and more tolerant of disturbed habitats and second-growth woodlands, especially in the east. Generally shy; in woodlots and parklands as well as deep woods, listen for its slow, resounding hammering; look for the long rectangular or oval holes it excavates. Carpenter ants in fallen trees and stumps are its major food.

Ivory-billed Woodpecker

Pileated Woodpecker

Tyrant Flycatchers (Family Tyrannidae)

Perched upright on a branch, a typical flycatcher darts out and snaps up a flying insect. Drab colors predominate in this family. Most species have a large head, bristly "whiskers," and a broad-based, flat bill. Some species in worn and dull summer plumage may be distinguishable only by voice.

Eastern Kingbird *Tyrannus tyrannus* L 8¹/₂" (22 cm)
Black head, slate gray back; tail has a broad white terminal band. Underparts are white, with a pale gray wash across the breast. Orange-red crown patch is seldom visible. Juvenile is brownish-gray above, darker on breast. Eastern Kingbirds are common and conspicuous in woodland clearings, farms, orchards; often seen near water. Call is a harsh *dzeet* note, also given in a series.

Gray Kingbird *Tyrannus dominicensis* L 9" (23 cm)
Pale gray above, with blackish mask. Red crown patch seldom visible. Bill long and thick. Underparts mostly white, with pale yellowish wash on belly and undertail coverts. Forked tail with no white terminal band. Juvenile plumage, held well into fall, is browner above. Gray Kingbirds are common on the Florida Keys, local in mangroves on the mainland. Song is a buzzy *pecheer-ry,* accented on second syllable. Casual wanderer north along Atlantic coast to the Maritimes, inland to Michigan and Ontario, and along Gulf coast to southeastern Texas.

Loggerhead Kingbird *Tyrannus caudifasciatus*
L 9" (23 cm) West Indian species, casual in southernmost Florida. Blackish head; back washed with olive; bill long and thick; all wing coverts have distinct whitish edges; tail is tipped with buffy-white. Yellow crown patch is seldom visible. Underparts white, with pale yellowish wash on belly and undertail coverts. Distinguished from Gray Kingbird by head-and-back contrast; bill much larger than in Eastern Kingbird. Call is a rolling, chattering *teeerrp.*

Thick-billed Kingbird *Tyrannus crassirostris*
L 9¹/₂" (24 cm) Large kingbird with very large bill. Adult is dusky-brown above, with a slightly darker head and a seldom-seen yellow crown patch; whitish underparts washed with pale gray on breast, pale yellow on belly and undertail coverts. Yellow is brighter and more extensive in fresh fall adult and in first-fall birds, which have buffy edgings on wing coverts. Fall birds resemble Tropical Kingbird (next page), but have heavier bill and darker head. Thick-billed Kingbirds are common in the Guadalupe Canyon, uncommon elsewhere in southeastern Arizona. Casual during fall and winter in western Arizona and southern California. Perch high in sycamores of lowland streamsides. Common call is a loud, high *puareet.*

Eastern Kingbird

juvenile

Gray Kingbird

Loggerhead Kingbird

Thick-billed Kingbird

1st fall

summer

Western Kingbird *Tyrannus verticalis* L 8¾" *(22 cm)*

Black tail, with white edges on outer feathers. Bill much shorter than in Tropical and Couch's Kingbirds. Upperparts ashy gray, paler than in Cassin's Kingbird, tinged with olive on back; dark wings contrast with paler back. Throat and breast pale gray; belly bright lemon yellow. Orange-red crown patch is usually concealed. Juvenile has slightly more olive on back and buffy edges on wing coverts, brownish tinge on breast, paler yellow belly. Common in dry, open country; perches on fences, telephone lines. Regular straggler in fall and early winter along the east coast from the Maritime Provinces south; winters in small numbers in southern Florida. Common call is a sharp *whit*.

Cassin's Kingbird *Tyrannus vociferans* L 9" *(23 cm)*

Dark brown tail; narrow buffy tips and lack of white edges on outer tail feathers help distinguish this species from Western Kingbird. Bill is much shorter than in Tropical and Couch's Kingbirds. Upperparts darker gray than in Western, washed with olive on back; paler wings contrast with darker back. White chin contrasts with dark gray head and breast. Belly dull yellow. Orange-red crown patch is usually concealed. Juvenile is duller, slightly browner above, with bold buffy edges on wing coverts; paler below. Fairly common in varied habitats; generally prefers denser foliage than does Western Kingbird. Most common call, given year-round, is a short, loud *chi-bew*, accented on second syllable.

Tropical Kingbird *Tyrannus melancholicus* L 9¼" *(24 cm)*

Almost identical to Couch's Kingbird. Bill is thinner and longer; back slightly grayer, less green. Distinctive call is a very rapid, twittering *pip-pip-pip-pip*. Distinguished from Western and Cassin's Kingbirds by larger bill, darker ear patch, and slightly notched brown tail. Juvenile is duller overall, with buffy edges on wing coverts. Uncommon and local in southeastern Arizona; found in lowlands near water; often nests in cottonwoods. Rare but regular during fall and winter along the west coast to British Columbia.

Couch's Kingbird *Tyrannus couchii* L 9¼" *(24 cm)*

Almost identical to Tropical Kingbird. Bill is thicker; back slightly greener, less gray. Distinctive calls, a shrill, rolling *breeeer;* and a more common *kip,* given singly or in a series. Distinguished from Western and Cassin's Kingbirds by larger bill, darker ear patch, slightly notched brown tail. Juvenile is duller overall, with buffy edges on wing coverts. Fairly common in the lower Rio Grande Valley in summer; rare in winter. Found in groves and shrubs, generally close to water. Formerly classified as a subspecies of Tropical Kingbird.

Western
Kingbird

Cassin's
Kingbird

Tropical
Kingbird

Couch's
Kingbird

Western
Cassin's
Couch's
Tropical

Scissor-tailed Flycatcher *Tyrannus forficatus*

L 13" (33 cm) Adult has extremely long outer tail feathers, white with black tips; tail is often spread in flight. Male's tail is longer than female's. Upperparts are pearl gray, underparts whitish, with salmon pink sides, flanks, and undertail coverts. Salmon pink wing linings and reddish axillaries show in flight. Juvenile and immature are paler overall with a much shorter tail; distinguished in flight from Western Kingbird (preceding page) by buffy-pink wing linings, salmon axillaries, and black-tipped white outer tail feathers. Distinguished from immature Fork-tailed Flycatcher by absence of black cap. Common and conspicuous throughout most of breeding range; found in semi-open country. Winters primarily from central Mexico to Panama, but small numbers remain in southernmost Florida and the Keys. Casual winter visitor in southeastern Louisiana. Casual wanderer throughout much of North America. Calls include a harsh *kek* and a repeated *ka-leep.*

Fork-tailed Flycatcher *Tyrannus savana L 14¹⁄₂" (37 cm)*

Tropical species, casual vagrant along Atlantic coast; accidental inland to upper midwest and Texas. Extremely long black tail flutters in flight. Black cap, white underparts, and white wing linings distinguish Fork-tailed from Scissor-tailed Flycatcher. Many sightings are of immatures, which resemble adult but have a much shorter tail.

Sulphur-bellied Flycatcher *Myiodynastes luteiventris*

L 8¹⁄₂" (22 cm) Boldly streaked above and below. Upperparts often show an olive tinge; rump and tail rusty-red; underparts pale yellow. Fairly common in deciduous or mixed woodlands of mountain canyons, generally at elevations between 5,000 and 6,000 feet. Inconspicuous; frequently perches high in the canopy. Loud call sounds like the squeaking of a rubber duck, *kip-kip-kip squellya-squellya.* Song is a soft *tre-le-re-re.* Casual along the Gulf coast and in southern California. The similar **Variegated Flycatcher** (not shown), *Empidonomus varius,* a South American species accidental in the east, is smaller, with a much smaller bill; shows less streaking below and no streaking above.

Great Kiskadee *Pitangus sulphuratus L 9³⁄₄" (25 cm)*

Distinctive striped black-and-white head; yellow crown patch is often concealed. Underparts bright lemon yellow; upperparts brown, with reddish-brown wings and tail. Fairly common; found chiefly in wet woodlands or near watercourses. In addition to fly-catching, dives for fish like a kingfisher, but does not totally submerge. Calls include a loud, slow, deliberate *kis-ka-dee* and an incessant, raucous chattering. Casual vagrant in southeastern Arizona and along Gulf coast to Louisiana. Formerly known as Kiskadee Flycatcher.

juvenile

juvenile

♂

Scissor-tailed Flycatcher

♂

Sulphur-bellied Flycatcher

Fork-tailed Flycatcher

Great Kiskadee

Great Crested Flycatcher *Myiarchus crinitus*

L 8" (20 cm) Dark olive above, with bushy crest. Gray throat and breast contrast with olive on sides of lower breast and bright lemon yellow belly and undertail coverts. Seen from below, dusky tail feathers show entirely reddish inner webs. Common in a wide variety of open woods; feeds high in the canopy. Distinctive call, a loud whistled *wheep*. Also gives a rolling *prrrr-eet*. Casual on the west coast during fall migration.

Brown-crested Flycatcher *Myiarchus tyrannulus*

L 8³/₄" (22 cm) Brownish-olive above, with bushy brown crest; bill is longer, thicker, and broader than bill of Ash-throated Flycatcher. Throat and breast pale gray; belly and undertail coverts yellow, slightly paler than in Great Crested Flycatcher. Seen from below, dusky tail feathers show reddish only on outer two-thirds of the inner webs. Fairly common in saguaro desert, river groves, lower altitudes of mountain woodlands. Song is a clear musical whistle, a rolling *whit-will-do*. Call, a sharp *whit*. Formerly known as Weid's Crested Flycatcher.

Ash-throated Flycatcher *Myiarchus cinerascens*

L 8¹/₂" (22 cm) Grayish-brown above, with bushy crest; bill shorter and thinner than bill of Brown-crested Flycatcher. Throat and breast pale gray, belly and undertail coverts pale yellow. Underparts are generally paler than in Brown-crested and less contrasting than in Great Crested. Seen from below, dusky tail shows entirely reddish inner webs and brown tips. As in all *Myiarchus* flycatchers, brief juvenile plumage shows mostly reddish tail. Ash-throated is common in a wide variety of habitats, including deserts, chaparral, woodlands. Rare fall and winter visitor to east. Distinctive call, heard year-round, is a rough *prrrt*. Also gives a burry *ka-brick* or *ka-wheer*, accented on second syllable. Song is a series of these calls.

Dusky-capped Flycatcher *Myiarchus tuberculifer*

L 7¹/₄" (18 cm) Brownish-olive above, with darker bushy crest; bill proportionately large. Throat and breast gray, darker on sides of breast; belly and undertail coverts lemon yellow, usually brighter than in Ash-throated Flycatcher. Dark tail shows only slight reddish edgings around each feather. Secondaries have reddish edges, unlike other *Myiarchus* flycatchers. Fairly common in sycamores and live oaks of mountain canyons, dense streamside woodlands. Call is a mournful, descending *peeur;* also gives a rolling whistled *pree-pree-prrreeit*. Casual in western Texas during migration. Casual visitor during late fall and winter in southern and central California, Nevada, Colorado. Formerly called Olivaceous Flycatcher.

Great Crested

Brown-crested

Ash-throated

Dusky-capped

bill comparisons

Great Crested Flycatcher

Brown-crested Flycatcher

Ash-throated Flycatcher

Dusky-capped Flycatcher

juvenile

adult

Great Crested

Brown-crested

Ash-throated

Dusky-capped

Greater Pewee *Contopus pertinax* L 8″ (20 cm)

A large flycatcher; sometimes shows slender, pointed crest. Upper mandible is dark, lower entirely orange. Wing bars indistinct. In worn summer plumage, upperparts are grayish-olive; pale throat and yellowish-white belly and undertail coverts contrast only slightly with gray breast. Fresh fall birds are slightly greener above, yellower below, but underparts always show less contrast than in Olive-sided Flycatcher; note also longer tail. Fairly common in mountain pine-oak woodlands. Casual during winter in southern Arizona, southern California. Distinctive song, a whistled *ho-say ma-re-ah*. Call is a repeated *pip*. Formerly called Coues' Flycatcher.

Olive-sided Flycatcher *Contopus borealis* L 7½″ (19 cm)

Large and proportionately short-tailed. Brownish-olive above; white tufts on sides of rump distinctive but often not visible. Throat, center of breast, and belly dull white or pale yellow. Sides and flanks brownish-olive and streaked; streaking may extend across breast. Bill is mostly black; center and sometimes base of lower mandible dull orange. Juvenile is browner above, yellower below, with browner sides. Fairly common in coniferous forests, bogs. Distinctive song, a clear *quick-three-beers,* the second note higher. Typical call, a repeated *pip*. Casual in winter on coastal slope of southern California.

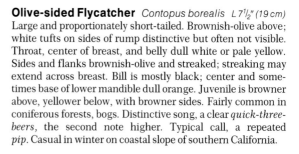

Eastern Wood-Pewee *Contopus virens* L 6¼″ (16 cm)

Generally indistinguishable from Western Wood-Pewee except by range and voice. Distinctive song is a clear, slow, plaintive *pee-a-wee,* the second note lower; this phrase often alternates with a downslurred *pee-yer*. Calls include a loud *chip* and clear, whistled, rising *pweee* notes. Plumage variable; generally dark grayish-olive above; throat dull white; breast and sides dark gray; belly, flanks, and undertail coverts whitish or pale yellow. Wing bars are whitish in adult, buffy or pale cinnamon in juvenile and fall immature. Bill of adult has black upper mandible, dull orange lower mandible. Juvenile and immature may have all-dark bill. Common and widespread in woodland habitats, from mature deciduous forests to urban shade trees. No winter records in U. S.

Western Wood-Pewee *Contopus sordidulus*

L 6¼″ (16 cm) Generally indistinguishable from Eastern Wood-Pewee except by range and voice. Calls include a harsh, slightly descending *peeer* and clear whistles that resemble *pee-yer* of Eastern Wood-Pewee. Song, heard chiefly on breeding grounds, consists of three-note *tswee-tee-teet* phrases mixed with the *peeer* note. Plumage variable. Base of lower mandible usually shows some yellow-orange. Common in open woodlands. Range of each species in area of overlap is uncertain; not known to interbreed. No winter records in U. S.

Greater Pewee

Olive-sided Flycatcher

fall

summer

immature

Eastern Wood-Pewee

juvenile

Western Wood-Pewee

Eastern Phoebe *Sayornis phoebe* L 7″ *(18 cm)*

Brownish-gray above, darkest on head, wings, tail. Underparts mostly white with pale olive wash on sides and breast; fresh fall birds are washed with yellow below. Molts before migration. Distinguished from pewees (preceding page) by all-black bill, lack of distinct wing bars, and habit of pumping and spreading its tail. Lacks the eye rings and wing bars of *Empidonax* flycatchers (following pages). Juvenile plumage, held only briefly, is browner above, with two buff wing bars, cinnamon rump. Common in woodlands, farmlands, suburbs, often nesting under bridges and in eaves and rafters. Distinctive song, a harsh, emphatic *fee-be*, accented on first syllable. Typical call note is a sharp *chip*. Rare fall migrant and winter visitor in the southwest and on the west coast.

Black Phoebe *Sayornis nigricans* L 6¾″ *(17 cm)*

Black head, upperparts, breast; white belly and undertail coverts. Juvenile plumage, held briefly, is browner, with two cinnamon wing bars, cinnamon rump. Common in woodlands, parks, suburbs; prefers to nest near water. Frequently pumps and spreads its tail. Four-syllable song, a rising *pee-wee* followed by a descending *pee-wee*. Calls include a loud *tseee* and a sharper *tsip*, similar to Eastern Phoebe's call.

Say's Phoebe *Sayornis saya* L 7½″ *(19 cm)*

Grayish-brown above, darkest on head, wings, and tail; breast and throat are pale grayish-brown; belly and undertail coverts tawny. Juvenile plumage, held briefly, is browner above; shows two cinnamon wing bars. Fairly common in dry, open areas, canyons, cliffs; perches on bushes, boulders, fences. Frequently pumps and spreads its tail. Song is a fast *pit-tse-ar,* often given in fluttering flight. Typical call is a thin, plaintive, whistled *pee-ee,* slightly downslurred. Highly migratory; casual vagrant in fall and winter on the east coast from Quebec and Nova Scotia south to Florida and the Gulf coast.

Vermilion Flycatcher *Pyrocephalus rubinus* L 6″ *(15 cm)*

Adult male strikingly red and brown. Adult female grayish-brown above, with blackish tail; throat and breast white, with dusky streaking; belly and undertail coverts are peach; note also whitish eyebrow and forehead. Juvenile resembles adult female but is spotted rather than streaked below; belly white, often with yellowish tinge. Immature male begins to resemble adult by mid-winter. Fairly common and approachable; found in streamside shrubs, bottomlands, and near small wooded ponds. Male in breeding season sings during fluttery display flight a soft, tinkling *pit-a-see pit-a-see;* also sings while perched. Typical call note is a sharp *tsik*. Frequently pumps and spreads its tail. Casual winter visitor to coastal southern California and the Gulf coast.

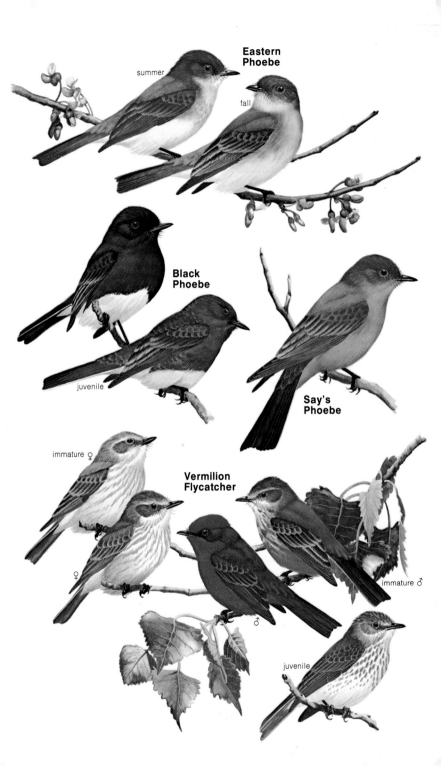

Eastern Phoebe

summer

fall

Black Phoebe

juvenile

Say's Phoebe

immature ♀

Vermilion Flycatcher

♀

immature ♂

♂

juvenile

Empidonax Flycatchers

The bane of birdwatchers, flycatchers of the genus *Empidonax* are extremely difficult to identify. All are drab, with pale eye rings and wing bars. As spring turns to summer, plumages grow duller from wear. Some species molt before their fall migration, acquiring bright fresh plumage in late summer. Identification depends on voice, habitat, behavior, and subtle differences in size, bill shape, tail length.

Gray Flycatcher *Empidonax wrightii* L 6" (15 cm)

Gray above, with a slight olive tinge in fresh fall plumage; whitish below, belly washed with pale yellow in fall. Head is proportionately small and rounded; white eye ring inconspicuous on pale gray face. Long bill; lower mandible pinkish-orange at base. Long tail, with thin whitish outer edge. Perched bird drops its tail down slowly, like a phoebe. Juvenile is brownish-gray above, with pale buffy wing bars; underparts tinged brownish-buff. Fairly common in dry habitat of Great Basin, especially in yellow pine or pinyon-juniper mixed with sagebrush, rabbitbrush. Regular migrant on California coast. Song is a vigorous *chi-wip* or *chi-bit* followed by a liquid *whilp* and trailing off in a gurgle. Call, a loud *wit*.

Dusky Flycatcher *Empidonax oberholseri* L 5¾" (15 cm)

Grayish-olive above; yellowish below, with whitish throat, pale olive wash on upper breast. Conspicuous white eye ring. Bill mostly dark, orange at base of lower mandible. Bill and tail slightly longer than Hammond's Flycatcher; outer tail feathers have whitish edges. Juvenile has grayer head, buffy wing bars, buffy tinge on breast and flanks. Worn late-summer and early-fall birds are variably gray and drab. Molt occurs after fall migration; fresh late-fall birds are quite yellow below. Breeds in open woodlands and brush of mountainsides. Calls include a *wit* note softer than Gray Flycatcher; mournful *deehic* call is heard on breeding grounds. Song has three or four phrases: a clear *sillit;* a lower *tsurrp;* another high *sillit,* often omitted; and a clear, high *seet*.

Hammond's Flycatcher *Empidonax hammondii*

L 5½" (14 cm) A small empid, fairly large-headed and short-tailed. White eye ring. Grayish head contrasts with grayish-olive back; throat grayish-white; gray or olive wash on breast and sides; belly tinged with pale yellow. Molt occurs before migration; fall birds are brighter olive above and yellower below. Short, slightly notched tail edged with gray. Bill is slightly shorter, thinner, and usually darker than in Dusky Flycatcher. Common; nests chiefly in coniferous forests. Most Hammond's Flycatchers migrate earlier in spring and later in fall than Dusky Flycatchers. Call note is a sharp *peek*. Song resembles Dusky's but is hoarser, more emphatic.

Gray Flycatcher

fall

summer

Dusky Flycatcher

summer

winter

Hammond's Flycatcher

summer

fall

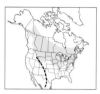

Least Flycatcher *Empidonax minimus* L 5¼" (13 cm)
Smallest eastern Empid. Proportionately large-headed. Gray or olive-gray above; bold white eye ring; two white wing bars. Throat whitish; breast washed with gray; belly and undertail coverts pale yellow. Underparts are usually paler than Hammond's Flycatcher (preceding page). Bill short, triangular, with lower mandible mostly pale. Molt occurs after fall migration. Juvenile is browner above, wing bars buffy. Common in the east, rare migrant through most of west. Inhabits open deciduous woods, orchards, parks. Song is a dry *che-bek,* accented on the second syllable. Call note is a sharp *whit,* often given in a rapid series.

Acadian Flycatcher *Empidonax virescens* L 5¾" (15 cm)
Olive above, with yellow eye ring, two buffy or whitish wing bars; very long primaries. Bill proportionately long and broad-based, with mostly yellowish lower mandible. Underparts vary; most birds show pale grayish throat, pale olive wash across upper breast, white lower breast, and yellow belly and undertail coverts. Worn late-summer birds show almost no yellow below. Molts before migration; fall birds have buffy wing bars. Juvenile is brownish-olive above, edged with buff; wing bars buffy; underparts whitish with olive wash on breast. Common in the deep shade of mature woodlands, swamps. The only Empid in the southeastern lowlands in summer; range is expanding in the northeast. Call is a soft *peet,* extended in song to an emphatic *peet-sa,* accented on first syllable. On breeding grounds, also gives a Flicker-like *ti ti ti ti ti.*

Willow Flycatcher *Empidonax traillii* L 5¾" (15 cm)
Lacks conspicuous eye ring. Upperparts brownish-olive; eastern birds slightly grayer. Whitish throat; pale olive breast; belly pale yellow. Distinguished from pewees (page 284) by smaller bill, shorter wings; also by habit of flicking tail slightly upwards. Molts after fall migration. Common in mountain meadows, along streams; dry, brushy upland pastures, especially in hawthorn. Where ranges overlap, generally found in drier habitat than Alder Flycatcher. Call is a liquid *wit;* song, a sneezy *fitz-bew;* often sings during spring migration. On breeding grounds, also gives a rising *brreet.* Formerly classified with Alder as one species, Traill's Flycatcher.

Alder Flycatcher *Empidonax alnorum* L 5¾" (15 cm)
Generally indistinguishable from Willow Flycatcher, but eye ring is usually bolder, upperparts slightly greener, bill slightly shorter. Best identified by range, habitat, and voice. Common in bogs, ponds, birch and alder thickets. Where ranges overlap, Alder is generally found in denser, wetter habitat. Call is a loud, piping *peep,* similar to Hammond's Flycatcher but louder. Distinctive song, a falling, buzzy *fee-beo;* also sings a *wee-bee* similar to Willow's song but not sneezy. On breeding grounds, also gives a hoarse descending *wheer.*

Least Flycatcher

juvenile

adult

adult

juvenile

Acadian Flycatcher

Willow Flycatcher

Alder Flycatcher

Yellow-bellied Flycatcher *Empidonax flaviventris*
L 5¹/₂" (14 cm) Proportionately short-tailed and big-headed. Olive above, yellowish below. Broad yellow eye ring. Lower mandible entirely pale orange. Tail is grayish-brown; wings blackish, with whitish or yellow wing bars. Underparts show a broad olive "vest," more extensive than in Acadian Flycatcher; lacks pale area between olive vest and yellow belly. Also, throat is yellow, rather than whitish; bill smaller. Molts after migration; worn late-summer birds and fall migrants are slightly grayer above, duller below. Common in bogs, swamps, damp coniferous woods. Song is a liquid *che-lek;* also a plaintive, rising *per-wee*. Distinctive call, a loud, emphatic, rising *chewee*.

Western Flycatcher *Empidonax difficilis* *L 5¹/₂" (14 cm)*
Brownish-green above, yellow below, with a brownish tinge on breast. Broad yellowish or whitish eye ring, usually broader behind eye. Lower mandible entirely bright orange. Tail longer than Yellow-bellied Flycatcher's; wings and back slightly browner, wing bars less conspicuous. Molts after migration; worn late-summer birds and fall migrants are paler below, duller above. Juveniles are browner above, with buffy wing bars; whiter below, almost entirely white in some coastal birds. Subspecies vary in size, brightness of plumage, and voice. Coastal birds sing a series of single, upslurred *suwheet* notes, often interspersed with high *seet* call. Song of interior birds is a loud *whee-seet,* the second note higher. Common in moist open woodlands, coniferous forests, shady canyons. Some authorities consider the coastal and interior forms to be separate species.

Buff-breasted Flycatcher *Empidonax fulvifrons*
L 5" (13 cm) Smallest *Empidonax* flycatcher. Brownish above; breast cinnamon buff, paler on worn summer birds. Whitish eye ring; pale wing bars; small bill, with lower mandible entirely pale orange. Buff-breasteds molt before migration. Rare and local; nest in small colonies in dry coniferous or mixed woodlands of canyon floors. Call note is a soft *pwit*. Typical song, a quick *chicky-whew* or *chee-lick*.

Northern Beardless-Tyrannulet
Camptostoma imberbe L 4¹/₂" (11 cm) Grayish-olive above and on breast; dull white or pale yellow below. Indistinct whitish eyebrow; small, slightly curved bill. Crown is darker than nape in many birds and is often raised slightly in a bushy crest. Distinguished from Ruby-crowned Kinglet (page 322) by buffy wing bars and lack of bold eye ring. Fairly common in southwestern range; rare in Texas. Often found near streams in sycamore, mesquite, and cottonwood groves. Difficult to spot; most easily located by voice. Song on breeding grounds is a descending series of loud, clear *peer* notes. Call is a loud, whistled *pee-yerp*.

Acadian Flycatcher
for comparison

**Yellow-bellied
Flycatcher**

**Western
Flycatcher**

juvenile

**Buff-breasted
Flycatcher**

**Northern
Beardless-Tyrannulet**

Rose-throated Becard *Pachyramphus aglaiae*

L 7¼" (18 cm) Rosy throat distinctive in male; Arizona adult males (shown here) have blackish cap, pale gray underparts. In females, note dark crown, browner back. Texas birds are darker overall. A stocky, large-headed, short-tailed bird; bushy crest sometimes raised. Winter immature male shows partially pink throat; full adult plumage is acquired after second summer. Becards are found in wooded canyons and bottomlands. Foot-long nest is generally suspended from limb of cottonwood or sycamore. Uncommon and local in southeastern Arizona; rare along lower Rio Grande in Texas. Call is a thin, mournful, descending *seeoo*, sometimes preceded by chatter.

Larks (Family Alaudidae)

Ground dwellers of open fields, larks are slender-billed seed and insect eaters. They seldom alight on trees or bushes. On the ground, they walk rather than hop.

Eurasian Skylark *Alauda arvensis* *L 7¼" (18 cm)*

Subspecies *A.a. arvensis*, introduced to Vancouver Island in the early 1900s, is resident there and on San Juan Islands on open slopes and fields. Plain brown bird with slender bill; slight crest is raised when bird is agitated. Upperparts heavily streaked; buffy-white underparts streaked on breast and throat. Dark eye prominent. The highly migratory Asian subspecies, *pekinensis,* rare on western Aleutians and Pribilofs, is darker and more heavily streaked above. All juveniles have a scaly brown mantle. In flight, Skylarks show a conspicuous white trailing edge on the inner wing and white edges on tail. Song is a continuous outpouring of trills and warblings, delivered in high, hovering or circling song flight. Call, a liquid *chirrup* with buzzy overtones.

Horned Lark *Eremophila alpestris* *L 7¼" (18 cm)*

Head pattern distinctive in all subspecies: black "horns," white or yellowish face and throat with broad black stripe under eye; black bib. Female duller overall than male, horns less prominent. Conspicuous in flight is the mostly black tail with white outer feathers, brown central feathers. In winter plumage, black areas on head and breast are partially obscured by pale edgings. Brief juvenile plumage is dark above with white spotting. Subspecies vary widely in overall color; extremes are shown here: pale *E.a. enthymia;* dark *alpestris;* yellowish *sierrae;* streaked *insularis;* and reddish *rubea.* Widespread and common, Horned Larks prefer dirt fields, gravel ridges, shores. Calls include a high *tsee-ee* or *tsee-titi.* Song is a weak twittering, delivered from the ground or in flight.

1st fall ♂

♂

♀

Rose-throated Becard

pekinensis

arvensis

Eurasian Skylark

enthymia ♂

alpestris ♂

♀

Horned Lark

sierrae ♂

juvenile

insularis ♂

rubea ♂

Swallows (Family Hirundinidae)

Slender bodies with long, pointed wings resemble swifts, but wrist angle is sharper and farther from the body; flight is more fluid. Adept aerialists, swallows dart to catch flying insects. Flocks perch in long rows on branches and wires.

Tree Swallow *Tachycineta bicolor* L 5³/₄″ (15 cm)
Dark, glossy greenish-blue above, greener in fall plumage; white below. White cheek patch does not extend above eye as in Violet-green Swallow. White of underparts may extend a little onto rump. Juvenile is gray-brown above, white below, usually with a grayish breast band, more diffuse than in Bank Swallow (next page). First-spring female shows varying amount of adult color on crown and back. Tree Swallows are common in any wooded habitat near water, especially where dead trees are abundant, providing nest holes. Also nests in fence posts, barn eaves, nest boxes. Generally migrates north earlier in the spring, lingers farther north in fall than other swallows. Flocks in migration may number in the thousands.

Violet-green Swallow *Tachycineta thalassina*
L 5¹/₄″ (13 cm) White on cheek extends above eye; white flank patches extend onto sides of rump. Compare with similar Tree Swallow. May also be confused with White-throated Swift (page 252). Female is duller above than male. Juvenile is gray-brown above; white areas other than rump patch may be mottled or grayish. Common in open woodlands, suburbs, and in coastal areas from central California north. Nests in hollow trees or rock crevices, often forming loose colonies.

Bahama Swallow *Tachycineta cyaneoviridis*
L 5³/₄″ (15 cm) Breeds in northern Bahamas; casual visitor to the Florida Keys, especially Big Pine Key, and mainland. Commonly found in pine trees. Deeply forked tail separates this species from the similar Tree Swallow.

Purple Martin *Progne subis* L 8″ (20 cm)
Male is dark, glossy purplish-blue. Female and juvenile are gray below. First-spring males have some purple feathering below. In flight, male especially resembles the European Starling (page 346); look for forked tail, longer wings, and typical swallow flight, short glides alternating with rapid flapping. Purple Martins are locally common where suitable nest sites are available. In the east and midwest, multiple-unit Martin houses encourage communal nesting; in the west, pairs more commonly nest in old woodpecker holes, usually in dead trees. Western population may be decreasing because of Starling competition. One subspecies nests in the saguaro desert of southern Arizona. Very early spring migrant in south; winters in South America.

Tree Swallow

juvenile

fall ♂

spring ♂

♀

1st spring ♀

juvenile

Violet-green Swallow

juvenile

♂

♂

♀

♂

Bahama Swallow

Purple Martin

♀

♂

1st spring ♂

♂

♀

Bank Swallow *Riparia riparia* L 5¹/₄" (13 cm)

Distinct brownish-gray breast band, often extending in a line down center of breast. Throat is white; note also that white curves around rear border of ear patch. Juvenile has thin buffy wing bars; compare with juvenile Northern Rough-winged Swallow and juvenile Tree Swallow (preceding page). Locally common throughout most of range. Nests in large colonies, excavating nest burrows in steep riverbank cliffs, gravel pits, and highway cuts. Winters chiefly in South America; often migrates in large flocks. Wingbeats are shallow and rapid, unlike Northern Rough-winged.

Northern Rough-winged Swallow

Stelgidopteryx serripennis L 5¹/₂" (14 cm) Brown above, whitish below, with gray-brown wash on chin, throat, and upper breast. Lacks Bank Swallow's distinct breast band; wings are longer, wingbeats deeper and slower. Juvenile has cinnamon wing bars. Nests in single pairs in riverbanks, cliffs, culverts, and under bridges. Migrates singly or in small flocks.

Cliff Swallow *Hirundo pyrrhonota* L 5¹/₂" (14 cm)

Squarish tail and buffy rump distinguish this swallow from all others except Cave Swallow. Most Cliff Swallows have dark chestnut and blackish throat, pale forehead. A southwestern form has cinnamon forehead like Cave Swallow, but throat is dark chestnut. All juveniles are much duller and grayer than adults; throat is paler, forehead darker. Locally common around bridges, rural settlements, in open country on cliffs. Range expanding southward in the east. Nests in colonies, building gourd-shaped mud nests.

Cave Swallow *Hirundo fulva* L 5¹/₂" (14 cm)

Squarish tail; buffy rump. Distinguished from most Cliff Swallows by buffy throat, cinnamon forehead, but compare with southwestern form of Cliff that also has a cinnamon forehead. A Central American and Caribbean species, apparently expanding U. S. range. Nests in colonies in limestone caves, sinkholes, culverts, and under bridges, sometimes with Barn and Cliff Swallows. West Indies form, casual spring migrant in south Florida, has more buff below and darker rump.

Barn Swallow *Hirundo rustica* L 6³/₄" (17 cm)

Long, deeply forked tail. Throat is reddish-brown; underparts usually cinnamon or buffy. Eurasian forms seen regularly off western Alaska are whitish below, with a complete dark breast band. In all juveniles, tail is shorter but still noticeably forked; underparts pale. Common; generally nests on or inside farm buildings, under bridges, and inside culverts, in pairs or small colonies. Range expanding in southeast.

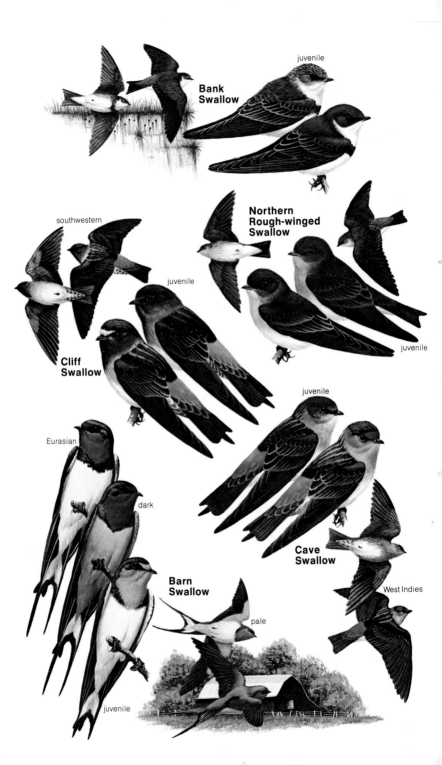

Bank Swallow

juvenile

Northern Rough-winged Swallow

southwestern

juvenile

juvenile

Cliff Swallow

juvenile

juvenile

Eurasian

dark

Cave Swallow

Barn Swallow

pale

West Indies

juvenile

Jays, Crows, Magpies (Family Corvidae)

Harsh voice and aggressive manner draw attention to these large, often gregarious birds. Crows and ravens are somber in hue, jays and magpies more colorful. In most species, bristles cover nostrils. Powerful all-purpose bill efficiently handles a varied diet.

Scrub Jay *Aphelocoma coerulescens* L 11¹/₂" (29 cm)
Blue head without crest; blue wings; long blue tail; whitish throat bordered by streaked blue-gray breast band. Back is bluish-gray, with a large gray-brown patch in the center. Birds of the interior are duller overall, with less contrast above, fainter breast band. All juveniles are grayish above, with blue on wings and tail. Isolated Florida subspecies has whitish forehead. Common inhabitant of scrub oak, chaparral, pinyon-juniper stands, suburbs. Winter visitors, usually the paler interior birds, are sometimes seen in desert areas. Flight is undulating. Varied calls include a raspy *shreeep*.

Gray-breasted Jay *Aphelocoma ultramarina*
L 11¹/₂" (29 cm) Blue above, with slight grayish cast on back, brownish patch on center of back. Lacks crest. Distinguished from Scrub Jay by absence of white throat and white eyebrow and by chunkier shape. Texas birds are generally darker above. Arizona juvenile has pale bill. Common in pine-oak canyons of the southwestern mountains, where it greatly outnumbers Scrub Jay. Calls include a loud, ringing *week*, given singly or in a series. Often nests in small, loose colonies; all birds share in the work of feeding nestlings. Flight is more direct than that of Scrub Jay. Formerly called Mexican Jay.

Pinyon Jay *Gymnorhinus cyanocephalus* L 10¹/₂" (27 cm)
Blue overall; blue throat streaked with white; lacks crest; bill long, spiky; tail short. Immature is paler, grayer overall. Generally seen in large flocks, often numbering in the hundreds; nests in loose colonies. Flight is direct, with rapid wingbeats, unlike Scrub Jay's undulating flight. Typical flight call is a high-pitched, piercing *mew*, audible over long distances. Also gives a rolling series of *queh* notes. Common in pinyon-juniper woodlands of interior mountains and high plateaus; in southern California, prefers yellow pine woodlands.

Scrub Jay

Florida

interior juvenile

west coast

interior

Gray-breasted Jay

Arizona juvenile

Pinyon Jay

immature

Blue Jay *Cyanocitta cristata* L 11" (28 cm)

Crested jay with black barring and white patches on blue wings and tail, black necklace on whitish underparts. Most common call of its varied repertoire is a piercing *jay jay jay;* also gives a musical *weedle-eedle* and mimics the call of Red-shouldered Hawk. Common in suburbs, parks, woodlands. Generally very noisy and bold. Often migrates in huge flocks. Breeding range is expanding steadily to northwest; casual fall and winter visitor to the west, especially the northwest.

Steller's Jay *Cyanocitta stelleri* L 11½" (29 cm)

Blue overall, with black crest, throat, and upper breast. Subspecies vary only slightly in overall coloring. Northwest coast form, *C.s. stelleri,* has blue-tipped feathers over eye; Rocky Mountain form, *macrolopha,* shows white flecking. The form (not shown) resident on the Queen Charlotte Islands off British Columbia is almost entirely black above. Juveniles are duller, with grayish underparts. Where ranges overlap in the eastern Rockies, Steller's Jay occasionally hybridizes with Blue Jay. Calls include a harsh *shaack shaack shaack.* Common in pine-oak woodlands and coniferous forests. Bold and aggressive; often scavenges at campgrounds and picnic areas. Casual winter visitor to lower elevations of the Great Basin, southern California, and southwestern deserts.

Gray Jay *Perisoreus canadensis* L 11½" (29 cm)

A fluffy, long-tailed jay with small bill, no crest. Representatives of the three subspecies groups are shown here. *P.c. canadensis,* one of several forms common in northern boreal forests, has a white collar and forehead, with brownish crown and nape; *capitalis,* common in the southern Rockies, has a paler crown, head appears mostly white; *obscurus,* resident along the northwest coast from Washington to northernmost California, has a larger, darker cap extending to the crown, with underparts paler than in other forms. Juveniles of all forms are sooty-gray overall, with a faint white moustachial streak. Gray Jays are familiar camp and cabin visitors, boldly snatching food scraps from around campfires or even from inside tents. Call notes include a whistled *wheeoo* and a low *chuck.* Formerly called Canada Jay.

Clark's Nutcracker *Nucifraga columbiana* L 12" (31 cm)

Chunky gray bird with black wings and black central tail feathers. White wing patches and white outer tail feathers are conspicuous in flight. Wingbeats are deep, slow, crowlike. Locally common in high coniferous forests at timberline. Like Gray Jay, a bold scavenger at campgrounds, farmhouses. Calls include a very nasal, grating, drawn-out *kra-a-a.* Every ten or fifteen years, Nutcrackers irrupt into desert and lowland areas of the west.

Blue Jay

Steller's Jay

stelleri

macrolopha

Gray Jay

juvenile

canadensis

capitalis

obscurus

Clark's Nutcracker

Brown Jay *Cyanocorax morio* L 16½" (42 cm)
Tropical species; range extends to southern tip of Texas, where it is resident but rare in woodlands and mesquite along the Rio Grande. Very large jay with long, broad tail. Dark, sooty-brown overall except for pale belly. Adult usually has black bill; juvenile bill is yellow. In transition to adult plumage, many Brown Jays have blotchy yellow-and-black bills. A noisy species; its harsh scream is similar to the call of a Red-shouldered Hawk. Another call sounds like a hiccup.

Green Jay *Cyanocorax yncas* L 10½" (27 cm)
Tropical species; range extends to southern tip of Texas. Resident and locally common in brushy areas and streamside growth of the lower Rio Grande Valley. Colorful plumage blends with dappled sun and shade in woodland habitat of this tropical jay. In winter it may visit ranches and towns, where it regularly comes to feeders. Gregarious and noisy; most common call is a series of raspy *cheh-cheh-cheh* notes. Somewhat inquisitive; often comes to investigate human intruders.

Black-billed Magpie *Pica pica* L 19" (48 cm)
Readily identified as a magpie by black and white markings and unusually long tail with iridescent green highlights. White wing patches flash in flight. Black bill distinguishes this species from look-alike Yellow-billed Magpie. Ranges almost overlap, and Blackbills casually stray south of normal range in winter. Common inhabitant of open woodlands and thickets in rangelands and foothills, especially along watercourses. Gregarious and noisy; typical calls include a whining *mag* and a series of loud, harsh *chuck* notes. Birds seen casually throughout the east may be escaped cage birds.

Yellow-billed Magpie *Pica nuttalli* L 16½" (42 cm)
Nearly identical to Black-billed Magpie, but almost never occurs in the Blackbill's normal range. Distinguished by its yellow bill and by a yellow patch of bare skin, variable in size, around the eye. Calls are similar to Blackbill; both species roost and feed in flocks, usually nest in loose colonies. Common resident of rangelands and foothills of northern and central Sacramento Valley and coastal valleys south to Santa Barbara County. Not prone to wandering, but casual north almost to Oregon. Prefers oak groves or streamside stands of trees. Also found in cultivated fields and residential areas.

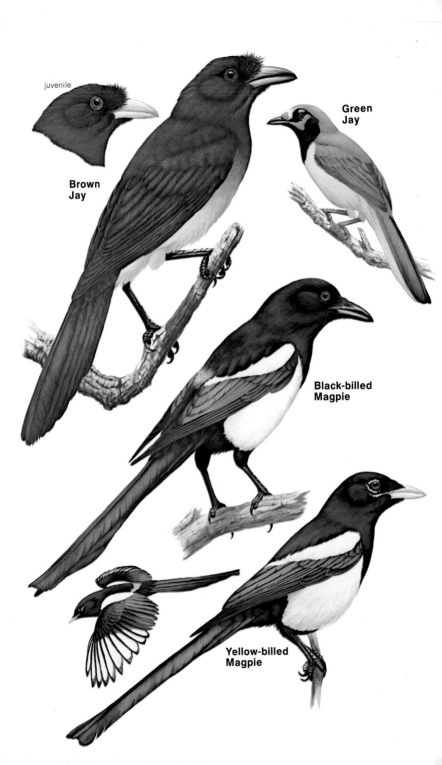

juvenile

Brown Jay

Green Jay

Black-billed Magpie

Yellow-billed Magpie

Eurasian Jackdaw *Corvus monedula* L 13" (33 cm)
Recent visitor to the northeast; has nested in Pennsylvania and perhaps elsewhere. A small crow, black overall, with gray nape and ear coverts, pale grayish eyes. Lively and inquisitive. Calls include a metallic *kow* and a softer *jack* note.

Mexican Crow *Corvus imparatus* L 14^1/$_2$" (37 cm)
Unknown in the U. S. until late 1960s; now winters along Rio Grande. Common at the municipal dump in Brownsville, Texas. Smaller and glossier than American Crow; ranges do not overlap. Distinctive call note, a low, froglike croak.

American Crow *Corvus brachyrhynchos* L 17^1/$_2$" (45 cm)
Our largest crow. Long, heavy bill is noticeably smaller than in ravens. Fan-shaped tail distinguishes all crows from ravens in flight. Adult American Crow is readily identified by familiar *caw* call but juvenile's higher pitched, nasal *cah* begging call resembles the call of the similar Fish Crow. Generally common throughout most of its range in a wide variety of habitats.

Northwestern Crow *Corvus caurinus* L 16" (41 cm)
(Not shown.) This species inhabits northwestern coastal areas and islands, where it is a common scavenger along the shore. Closely resembles American Crow; very difficult to distinguish in the field. Northwestern Crow is slightly smaller; call is hoarser, lower. Best clue is range. Considered by many authorities to be a subspecies of American Crow.

Fish Crow *Corvus ossifragus* L 15^1/$_2$" (39 cm)
Closely resembles the larger American Crow. Best identified by voice, a high, nasal, single- or double-note *cah*. Note, however, that juvenile American Crow's begging call is similar. Fish Crow favors tidewater marshes and low valleys along eastern river systems; less frequent inland, except along rivers. Sometimes seen in flocks with American Crows.

Chihuahuan Raven *Corvus cryptoleucus* L 19^1/$_2$" (50 cm)
Heavier bill and wedge-shaped tail distinguish both raven species from crows. Chihuahuan Raven's most common call, a low, drawn-out croak, is usually slightly higher pitched than call of Common Raven. Neck feathers are white rather than grayish at the base, but this distinguishing field mark is hard to see. Common in desert areas and scrubby grasslands. Formerly called White-necked Raven.

Common Raven *Corvus corax* L 24" (61 cm)
Large bird with long, heavy bill and long, wedge-shaped tail. Most common call is a low, drawn-out croak. Larger than Chihuahuan Raven; call is usually slightly lower pitched. At close range, note thicker, shaggier throat feathers. Found in a variety of habitats, including mountains, deserts, and rugged coastal areas. Numerous in western and northern part of range; uncommon and local, but spreading, in Appalachians.

Eurasian Jackdaw

Mexican Crow

American Crow

Fish Crow

Chihuahuan Raven

Common Raven

Wrentit (Family Muscicapidae)

Smaller and livelier than most other members of the thrush family (page 320), the Wrentit more closely resembles its namesakes, the wrens and titmice.

Wrentit *Chamaea fasciata* L 6½" (17 cm)

A perky little brown bird with a long, rounded tail, usually cocked. Plumage varies from reddish-brown in northern populations to grayish in southern birds. Note also distinct cream-colored eye and lightly streaked buffy breast. Common in chaparral and coniferous brushland, Wrentits are often heard before they are seen. Male's loud song, sung year-round, begins with a series of accelerating staccato notes and runs into a descending trill: *pit-pit-pit-tr-r-r-r*. Female's song lacks trill.

Titmice and Chickadees (Family Paridae)

Small, hardy birds with short bills, short wings, and drab plumage. Active and agile, they often hang upside down from twigs to feed, and flock together when not nesting.

Tufted Titmouse *Parus bicolor* L 6½" (17 cm)

Gray crest and blackish forehead identify this species over most of its range. In southern Texas, adult birds have whitish foreheads and blackish crests; were formerly considered a separate species, the "Black-crested Titmouse." In south-central Texas, zone of overlap between black-crested and gray-crested forms, birds show varied brown foreheads, dark gray crests. Common in deciduous woodlands, mesquite, parklands, suburban areas; a familiar visitor to feeders. Active and noisy; typical song is a loud whistled *peter peter peter*.

Plain Titmouse *Parus inornatus* L 5¾" (15 cm)

Plumage varies from gray-brown in coastal birds to very drab gray in interior populations. Small crest. Common and conspicuous resident of mixed woodlands; favors oak, juniper, pinyon, pine. Typical call, a harsh *tsick-a-der-der*, resembles that of the Mountain Chickadee (next page). Song, heard chiefly in spring, is a whistled *weety weety weety*.

Bridled Titmouse *Parus wollweberi* L 5¼" (13 cm)

Black-and-white facial pattern distinctive. Unlike other titmice, Bridled Titmouse has a small black bib. Crest distinguishes it from similar Mountain Chickadee (next page). Back and wings are gray; underparts whitish. Most common call is a rapid, high-pitched variation of *chick-a-dee-dee*. Less active and conspicuous than other family members. Common resident of woodland stands of oak, juniper, and sycamore in the mountains of southern Arizona and New Mexico.

northern

Wrentit

southern

Tufted Titmouse

"Black-crested Titmouse"

coastal

interior

Plain Titmouse

Bridled Titmouse

Black-capped Chickadee *Parus atricapillus*

L 5¹/₄" (13 cm) Black cap and bib and white cheeks readily identify this small bird over most of its widespread range. Usual range barely overlaps that of look-alike Carolina Chickadee; periodic fall and winter irruptions temporarily push Blackcap's range farther south. Note that Blackcap's wing coverts and secondaries are broadly edged in white; lower edge of black bib is a bit more ragged. These differences are obscured in worn late-summer birds. Best distinction is voice. Blackcap's call is a lower, slower *chick-a-dee-dee-dee* than Carolina's call; typical song, a clear, whistled *fee-bee* or *fee-bee-ee,* the first note higher in pitch. Where ranges overlap, the two species may hybridize. In the Appalachians, Blackcap generally inhabits higher elevations. Common in open woodlands, clearings, suburbs. Usually forages in thickets, low branches of trees.

Carolina Chickadee *Parus carolinensis* *L 4³/₄" (12 cm)*

Black cap and bib and white cheeks readily identify this small bird over most of its range. At northern edge, its range in some winters is invaded by the look-alike Black-capped Chickadee. Note that Carolina lacks broad white edgings on wing coverts; lower edge of black bib is usually neater. Best distinction is voice. Carolina's call is a higher, faster version of *chick-a-dee-dee-dee* than Blackcap's call; typical song is a four-note whistle, *fee-bee fee-bay.* Where ranges overlap, the two species may hybridize. In the Appalachians, Black-capped Chickadee generally inhabits higher elevations; the Carolina prefers valleys, foothills. Common in open deciduous forests, woodland clearings and edges, suburban areas. Feeds in trees and thickets; seldom descends to ground.

Mexican Chickadee *Parus sclateri* *L 5" (13 cm)*

The only breeding chickadee in its range. Extensive black bib is distinctive, along with dark gray flanks. Lacks white eyebrow of neighboring Mountain Chickadee. Song is a warbled whistle; call note, a husky buzz. A Mexican species, common resident in coniferous and pine-oak forests; found in U. S. only in Chiricahua Mountains of southeastern Arizona and Animas Mountains of southwestern New Mexico.

Mountain Chickadee *Parus gambeli* *L 5¹/₄" (13 cm)*

White eyebrow and pale gray sides distinguish this species from other chickadees; lack of crest separates it from the Bridled Titmouse (preceding page). Rocky Mountain forms are tinged with buff on back, sides, and flanks, and have broader white eyebrows. Call is a hoarse *chick-adee-adee-adee;* typical song, a three- or four-note descending whistle, *fee-bee-bay* or *fee-bee fee-bee.* Common resident in coniferous and mixed woodlands. Some descend to lower elevations in winter.

fall

Black-capped Chickadee

summer

Carolina Chickadee

Mountain Chickadee

Mexican Chickadee

Rockies

Chestnut-backed Chickadee *Parus rufescens*

L 4³/₄" (12 cm) Sooty-brown cap, white cheeks, black bib; back and rump chestnut. Over most of its range, this species has bright chestnut sides and flanks; birds on central California coast show almost no chestnut below. Common in coniferous forests; also found in deciduous woodlands. Call is a hoarse, rapid *tseek-a-dee-dee*. Generally feeds high in the trees.

Siberian Tit *Parus cinctus* *L 5¹/₂" (14 cm)*

Gray-brown above, whitish below, with white cheek patch, black bib, buffy sides and flanks. Distinguished from Boreal Chickadee by larger cheek patch, longer tail, paler flanks, and pale edges on wing coverts; also by call, a series of peevish *dee deer* notes. Rare; found in willows and spruces bordering tundra. Formerly called Gray-headed Chickadee.

Boreal Chickadee *Parus hudsonicus* *L 5¹/₂" (14 cm)*

Gray-brown above, whitish below, with white cheeks, black bib, brown sides and flanks. Distinguished from Siberian Tit by smaller cheek patch, shorter tail, all-gray wing coverts, darker flanks; also by call, a nasal *tseek-a-day-day*. Fairly common in coniferous forests. In some winters, small numbers wander hundreds of miles south of normal eastern range.

Verdins (Family Remizidae)

Small, spritely birds with finely pointed bills. They inhabit arid scrub country, where they feed in brush, chickadee-style, and build spherical nests.

Verdin *Auriparus flaviceps* *L 4¹/₂" (11 cm)*

Adult's dull gray plumage sets off chestnut shoulder patches, yellow head and throat. Juvenile is brown-gray overall; shorter tail helps distinguish it from Bushtit. Common in mesquite and other dense thorny shrubs of the southwestern desert. Song is a plaintive three-note whistle, the second note higher. Calls include a series of rapid *chip* notes.

Bushtits (Family Aegithalidae)

Longer tail distinguishes these tiny birds from other chickadee-like species. Usually feeds in large, busy, twittering flocks. Nest is an elaborate hanging structure.

Bushtit *Psaltriparus minimus* *L 4¹/₂" (11 cm)*

Gray above, paler below; fresh fall male may have pale pink flanks. Coastal birds have brown crown; interior birds show brown ear patch and gray cap. Juvenile male and occasional adult males in the southwest have black mask, were formerly considered a separate species, the "Black-eared Bushtit." Common in woodlands, chaparral, parks and gardens.

Chestnut-backed
Chickadee

coastal
central
California

Siberian
Tit

Boreal
Chickadee

Verdin

juvenile

"Black-eared Bushtit"
juvenile ♂

interior ♂

interior ♀

Bushtit

coastal ♂

Creepers (Family Certhiidae)

Little tree-climbers whose curved bills dig insects and larvae from bark. Stiff tail feathers serve as props.

Brown Creeper *Certhia americana* L 5¹/₄" (13 cm)
Camouflaged by streaked brown plumage, Creepers spiral upward from base to branches of a tree, then fly to a lower place on another tree. Call note is a soft, sibilant *see;* song, a high-pitched, variable *see see see titi see*. Fairly common but hard to spot. Nests in coniferous, mixed, or swampy forests. In winter, found in any woodland. Generally solitary, but sometimes seen in winter flocks of titmice and nuthatches.

Nuthatches (Family Sittidae)

These short-tailed acrobats climb up, down, and around tree trunks and branches, foraging for insects and larvae. Winter flocks roam with chickadees, kinglets.

White-breasted Nuthatch *Sitta carolinensis*
L 5³/₄" (15 cm) Black cap tops all-white face and breast; extent of rust below is variable. Females in the northeast have gray crowns. Great Basin birds have longer bills. Common; found in leafy trees in the east, oaks and conifers in the west. Typical song, a rapid series of nasal whistles on one pitch. Call is usually a low-pitched, repeated, nasal *yank;* higher pitched and given in a rapid series in Great Basin and Rockies birds.

Red-breasted Nuthatch *Sitta canadensis* L 4¹/₂" (11 cm)
Black cap and eye line, white eyebrow, rust underparts; female and juveniles have duller head, paler underparts. Resident in northern and subalpine conifers; gleans small branches, outer twigs. High-pitched, nasal call sounds like a toy tin horn. Irruptive migrant; numbers and winter range vary yearly. In the east, year-round range is expanding southward.

Pygmy Nuthatch *Sitta pygmaea* L 4¹/₄" (11 cm)
Gray-brown cap; creamy buff underparts. Pale nape spot visible at close range. Dark eye line bordering cap, most distinct in interior populations. Range closely parallels yellow-pine forest, except for birds in coastal California pines. Roams in loose flocks. Typical notes, a high, rapid *peep peep* and a piping *wee-bee*. Western counterpart of Brown-headed Nuthatch.

Brown-headed Nuthatch *Sitta pusilla* L 4¹/₂" (11 cm)
Brown cap; dull buff underparts. Pale nape spot visible at close range. Narrow dark eye line borders cap. Fairly common; found in pine woodlands. Call is a repeated double note like the squeak of a rubber duck. Feeding flocks also give twittering, chirping, and talky *bit bit bit* calls. Southeastern counterpart of the Pygmy Nuthatch.

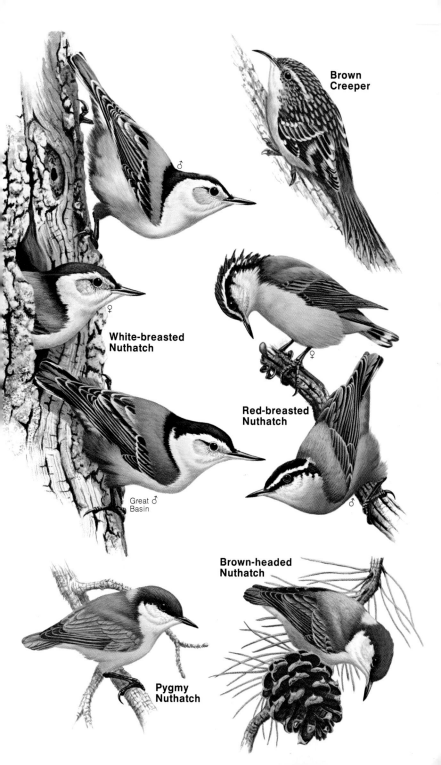

Brown Creeper

White-breasted Nuthatch

Red-breasted Nuthatch

Great ♂
Basin

♂

♀

Pygmy Nuthatch

Brown-headed Nuthatch

Wrens (Family Troglodytidae)

Found throughout most of North America, wrens are chunky birds with slender, slightly curved bills. Tails are often uptilted. Loud song and vigorous territorial defense belie the small size of most species. Highly inquisitive, wrens can often be lured into view by squeaky noises.

House Wren *Troglodytes aedon* L 4³/₄″ (12 cm)
Brown above with faint eyebrow. Distinguished from Winter Wren by longer tail, less prominent barring on belly, and larger overall size. Juvenile shows a bright rufous rump and darker buff on lower parts. Eastern birds are browner above, buffy below; western birds grayer above, paler below. Southern Arizona form, "Brown-throated Wren," has a slightly buffier throat and breast and a bolder eyebrow. Common in brush and shrubs, orchards and farmyards, urban gardens, parks. Exuberant song, a cascade of bubbling whistled notes. Winters casually north into summer range.

Winter Wren *Troglodytes troglodytes* L 4″ (10 cm)
Stubby tail; dark barring on belly. Eastern form has traces of mottling on breast; in western birds, breast is more uniformly buffy-brown. Birds on western Alaska islands are noticeably larger than continental birds. Uncommon and secretive, nests in dense brush, especially along stream banks, in moist coniferous woods; in winter may be found in any type of woodland. Very rare in south Florida. Song, a rapid series of melodious trills, much higher than song of House Wren; call, an explosive *chimp-chimp*. Winters casually into summer range.

Carolina Wren *Thryothorus ludovicianus* L 5¹/₂″ (14 cm)
Deep rusty-brown above, warm buff below; white throat and prominent white eye stripe. Common in the concealing underbrush of moist woodlands and swamps, wooded suburban areas. Vivacious, melodious song, a loud, clear *teakettle teakettle teakettle* or *cheery cheery cheery*. Sings any time of day or year. Nonmigratory, but after mild winters resident populations extend north of mapped range. After harsh winters, range limits retract.

Bewick's Wren *Thryomanes bewickii* L 5¹/₄″ (13 cm)
Long, sideways-flitting tail, edged with white spots; long white eyebrow. Eastern birds are reddish-brown above; distinguished from Carolina Wren by paler underparts and white on tail. Western birds much grayer. Found in brushland, hedgerows, stream edges, open woods. More common in the west than the House Wren. Sharply declining east of the Rockies, especially in areas east of the Mississippi. Song variable, a high, thin buzz and warble. Calls include a flat, hollow *chip*.

"Brown-throated Wren"

House Wren

western juvenile

eastern

western

Aleutians

Winter Wren

Carolina Wren

eastern

western

western

Bewick's Wren

eastern

Marsh Wren *Cistothorus palustris* L 5" (13 cm)

Plain brown crown; bold white eye line; black triangle on upper back, streaked with white. Underparts largely whitish; may have buffy belly and undertail coverts. Locally abundant in reedy marshes, cattail swamps, either freshwater or brackish. Large, football-shaped nest with side entrance is built a foot or more above water, anchored to reeds. Secretive, but may climb a cattail to sing or to investigate intruders. Sings day and night in breeding season, a series of loud, rapid, reedy notes and liquid rattles. Alarm call is a sharp *tsuk,* often doubled. Formerly known as Long-billed Marsh Wren.

Sedge Wren *Cistothorus platensis* L 4¹/₂" (11 cm)

Crown and back streaked; eyebrow whitish, indistinct; underparts largely buff. Found in wet, grassy meadows or shallow sedge marshes. Globular nest similar to that of Marsh Wren. Generally common but local; uncommon to rare in the east. More often heard than seen. Song begins with a few single notes followed by a weak staccato trill or chatter; call note, a rich *chip,* often doubled. Rare and local in winter to New Mexico. Formerly called Short-billed Marsh Wren.

Canyon Wren *Catherpes mexicanus* L 5³/₄" (15 cm)

An inconspicuous brown wren with white throat and breast, chestnut belly. Flattened crown and long bill aid in extracting insects from deep crevices. Common in steep, shady canyons and cliffs, near water; may also build its cup nest in stone buildings, chimneys. Loud silvery song, a decelerating, descending series of liquid *tee*'s and *tew*'s. Typical call is a sharp *jeet*. Nonmigratory, but may withdraw in winter from northernmost range, higher altitudes. Note separate population in the Black Hills of South Dakota and Wyoming.

Rock Wren *Salpinctes obsoletus* L 6" (15 cm)

Dull gray-brown above with contrasting cinnamon rump and buffy tail tips, broad blackish tail band. Breast finely streaked. Fairly common in arid and semiarid habitats, sunny talus slopes, scrublands, dry washes. Frequently bobs its head, especially when alarmed. Song is a variable mix of buzzes and trills; call, a buzzy *tick-ear*. Unique clue to this wren's presence, a path of pebbles or rock chips leading to a rock-sheltered nest. Casual in fall and winter to the east.

Cactus Wren *Campylorhynchus brunneicapillus*

L 8¹/₂" (22 cm) Dark crown, streaked back, heavily barred wings and tail, and broad white eyebrow distinguish this large wren from the similar Sage Thrasher (page 336). Breast is densely spotted. Common in cactus country and arid hillsides and valleys. Song is a low-pitched, harsh, rapid *cha cha cha cha cha,* a familiar voice of the desert, heard any time of year or day. Bulky nests, tucked into the protective spines of cholla cactus or thorny bushes, are built for roosting as well as nesting.

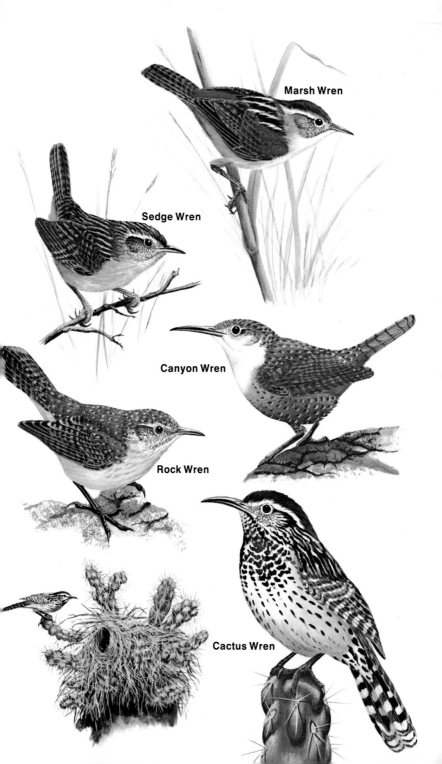

Marsh Wren

Sedge Wren

Canyon Wren

Rock Wren

Cactus Wren

Thrushes (Family Muscicapidae)

Eloquent songsters of open marshes and woodlands, the thrushes include many familiar species. With narrow notched bills they feed on insects and fruit.

Gray-spotted Flycatcher *Muscicapa griseisticta*
L 5¾" (15 cm) Asian flycatcher, rare late-spring migrant on western Aleutians. Gray-brown above, white below; breast streaked with gray-brown; faint white wing bar; white eye ring and lores. Tail is short and notched. Perches upright.

Red-breasted Flycatcher *Ficedula parva* *L 5" (13 cm)*
Eurasian species, casual in late spring on western Aleutians. Tail is black, with a large white oval on each side of base. Breeding male has a reddish-orange throat, bordered by a gray breast band; female has whitish throat, buffy breast.

Dusky Warbler *Phylloscopus fuscatus* *L 5½" (14 cm)*
Asian species, casual on western Alaska islands. Dusky-brown upperparts and lack of wing bar distinguish this species from Arctic Warbler; underparts dull whitish to buff; tail slightly rounded; bill shorter, thinner. Calls include a *tsack* similar to call of Arctic Warbler but softer. Frequently flicks wings.

Arctic Warbler *Phylloscopus borealis* *L 5" (13 cm)*
Yellowish-white eyebrow, often curving upward behind eye. Square tail, olive upperparts, and pale wing bar all unlike Dusky Warbler. Bill thicker, less downcurved than Orange-crowned Warbler (page 356); lacks streaking below. Wing bar may wear off by late summer. In the Alaskan form, *P.b. kennicotti,* immature and fall adult are yellower below than breeding adult. Extremes are shown here. Song is a loud, toneless series of reedy and buzzy notes. Calls include a harsh *zik* resembling the call of Dusky Warbler but sharper. Fairly common in western and central Alaska; nests on grassy tundra or in willow thickets. The Siberian form, *borealis,* is a rare migrant on the western Aleutians; note larger bill.

Middendorff's Grasshopper-Warbler
Locustella ochotensis *L 6" (15 cm)* Asian species, casual migrant mainly on westernmost Aleutians. Big, chunky warbler with whitish-tipped, wedge-shaped tail. Bill hefty and slightly downcurved. Fall bird is yellowish-brown below, with a faintly streaked breast. In breeding plumage, underparts are mostly whitish, lack streaking.

Lanceolated Warbler *Locustella lanceolata*
L 4½" (11 cm) (Not shown.) Eurasian species, casual in spring and summer on Aleutian island of Attu. Resembles Middendorff's Grasshopper-Warbler but smaller; strongly streaked above and on breast and sides; eyebrow less distinct. Highly secretive. Distinctive call, a metallic *rink-tink-tink*.

Red-breasted Flycatcher

♀

♂

Gray-spotted Flycatcher

Dusky Warbler

kennicotti fall

kennicotti breeding

borealis

Arctic Warbler

fall

Middendorff's Grasshopper-Warbler

breeding

Golden-crowned Kinglet *Regulus satrapa* L 4" (10 cm)

Tiny and plump. Orange crown patch of male is bordered in yellow and black; female's crown is yellow with black borders. Upperparts grayish-olive; underparts whitish; two white wing bars. Broad white eyebrow, striped crown, and paler underparts distinguish Golden-crowned from Ruby-crowned Kinglet. Common in coniferous woodlands. Call is a series of high, thin *tsee* notes, usually given in threes. Song, almost inaudibly high, is a series of *tsee* notes accelerating into a trill.

Ruby-crowned Kinglet *Regulus calendula* L 4¹/₄" (11 cm)

Tiny and plump. Grayish-olive above, with two white wing bars. Male's red crown patch seldom visible. Dusky underparts and lack of striped crown distinguish this species from Golden-crowned Kinglet. Compare also with Hutton's Vireo (page 350). Common in woodlands, thickets, brush. An active, nervous bird; flicks wings rapidly when calling. Calls include a scolding *je-dit je-dit*. Song begins with several high, thin *tsee* notes, followed by descending *tew* notes and concluding with a rich warbling of three-note phrases.

Blue-gray Gnatcatcher *Polioptila caerulea*

L 4¹/₂" (11 cm) Male is blue-gray above, female grayer; long tail is black above with white outer feathers. Male has black line on sides of crown in breeding plumage only. Female distinguished from female Black-capped Gnatcatcher by voice and by bolder eye ring. Call is a thin, querulous *pwee*. Song, a series of melodious but wheezy warbles. Active and conspicuous; common in woodlands, thickets, chaparral.

Black-capped Gnatcatcher *Polioptila nigriceps*

L 4¹/₄" (11 cm) Mexican species, very rare in spring and summer in southeastern Arizona; probably resident there. Distinguished from Black-tailed Gnatcatcher by white outer tail feathers and much longer bill. Note also that breeding male's black cap extends well below the eye. Female and winter male are best identified by tail pattern and voice. Distinctive call is a whining, descending *mew,* similar to call of coastal form of Black-tailed Gnatcatcher.

Black-tailed Gnatcatcher *Polioptila melanura*

L 4¹/₂" (11 cm) Blue-gray above, grayish-white below in interior form; darker and browner overall in coastal California form. Outer tail feathers are mostly black below. Male's black cap is absent in winter plumage but sides of crown often show a thin black line. Bill is shorter than in Black-capped Gnatcatcher; in interior forms, white eye ring is more distinct. Interior forms inhabit desert washes, arid brushlands; calls include a rapid series of *jee* notes on one pitch and a raspy *cheeeh*. California coast form is found on sagebrush mesas and dry coastal slopes; distinctive call is a rising and falling, kittenlike *mew* note. Many authorities regard the two types as separate species; note especially the difference in tail patterns.

322

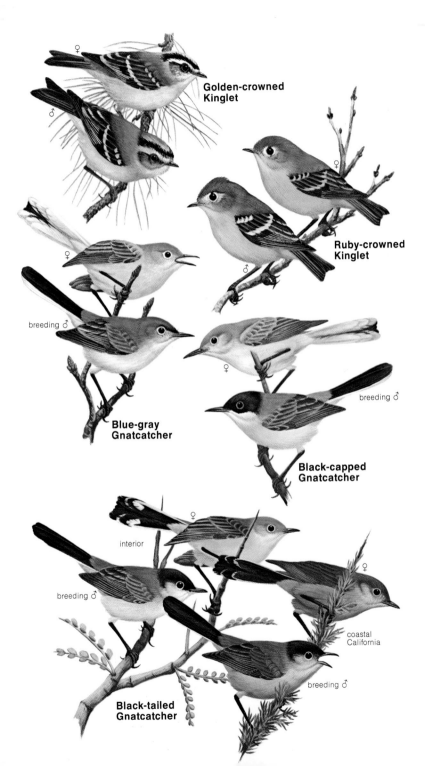

♀

♂

Golden-crowned Kinglet

♀

♂

Ruby-crowned Kinglet

♀

breeding ♂

Blue-gray Gnatcatcher

♀

breeding ♂

Black-capped Gnatcatcher

interior

♀

breeding ♂

♀

coastal California

breeding ♂

Black-tailed Gnatcatcher

Eastern Bluebird *Sialia sialis* *L 7" (18 cm)*

Chestnut throat, sides of neck, breast, sides and flanks; contrasting white belly, white undertail coverts. Male is uniformly deep blue above; female grayer. The subspecies resident in the mountains of southeastern Arizona is paler overall; compare with male Lazuli Bunting (page 384). All forms distinguished from Western Bluebird by chestnut on throat and sides of neck and by white, not grayish, belly and undertail. Found in open woodlands, farmlands, orchards. Nests in holes in trees and posts; also in nest boxes. Call note is a musical, rising *chur-lee*, extended in song to *chur chur-lee chur-lee*. Serious decline in recent decades was due largely to competition with Starling and House Sparrow for nesting sites. The provision of specially designed boxes by concerned birdwatchers has resulted in a promising comeback.

Western Bluebird *Sialia mexicana* *L 7" (18 cm)*

Male's upperparts and throat are deep purple-blue; breast, sides, and flanks chestnut; belly and undertail coverts grayish. Most birds show some chestnut on shoulders and upper back. Female duller, brownish-gray above; breast and flanks tinged with chestnut, throat pale gray. Common in open woodlands, farmlands, orchards; in desert areas during winter, found in mesquite-mistletoe groves. Nests in holes in trees, posts; also in nest boxes. Call note is a mellow *few*, extended in brief song to *few few fawee*.

Mountain Bluebird *Sialia currucoides* *L 7¹/₄" (18 cm)*

Male is sky blue above, paler below, with whitish belly and undertail coverts. Female is brownish-gray overall, with white belly and undertail coverts; white edges on coverts give folded wing a scalloped look. In fresh fall plumage, female's throat and breast are tinged with red-orange; grayish-brown flanks distinguish her from female Eastern Bluebird. Note also longer, thinner bill and longer wings of Mountain Bluebird. Inhabits open rangelands, meadows, generally at elevations above 5,000 feet; in winter, found primarily in open lowlands, desert. More often than other bluebirds, hovers above prey, chiefly insects, before dropping to catch them; also catches insects in flight. Nests in tree cavities, buildings. Call is a thin *few;* song, a low, warbled *tru-lee*. Highly migratory; casual in the east during migration and winter.

Townsend's Solitaire *Myadestes townsendi*

L 8¹/₂" (22 cm) Large and slender; gray overall, with bold white eye ring. Buff wing patches and white outer tail feathers are most conspicuous in flight. Fairly common in coniferous forests on high mountain slopes; in winter, also in wooded valleys, canyons, wherever juniper berries are available. Nests on the ground. Often seen on a high perch, from which it sometimes fly-catches. Call note is a high-pitched *eek;* song, a loud, complex, melodious warbling. Highly migratory; casual in fall and winter as far east as Newfoundland and New York.

juvenile

Eastern Bluebird

♀

♂

southwestern ♂

Western Bluebird

♀

♂

♀

♂

Mountain Bluebird

juvenile

Townsend's Solitaire

Wood Thrush *Hylocichla mustelina* L 7¾" (20 cm)
Reddish-brown above, brightest on crown and nape; rump and tail brownish-olive. Bold white eye ring conspicuous on streaked face. Whitish below, with large dark spots on throat, breast, and sides. A large, plump bird, common in swamps and moist deciduous or mixed woods. Loud, liquid song of three- to five-note phrases, most notes differing in pitch, each phrase usually ending with a complex trill. Calls include a rapid *pit pit pit*. Casual in the west. Range expanding in the northeast.

Veery *Catharus fuscescens* L 7" (18 cm)
Reddish-brown above, white below, with gray flanks, grayish face, incomplete and indistinct gray eye ring. Upperparts darker, breast more spotted in western *C.f. salicicolus* than in eastern *fuscescens*. Gray flanks, face pattern, and voice distinguish *salicicolus* from the *C.u. ustulatus* form of Swainson's Thrush. Common but shy; found in dense, moist woodlands, streamside thickets. Migrates east of dashed line on map. Range expanding in the southeast. Song is a descending series of *veer* notes; typical call, a low, whistled *phew*.

Swainson's Thrush *Catharus ustulatus* L 7" (18 cm)
Uniformly brownish above, with buffy lores and bold buffy eye ring; bright buffy breast with dark spots; brownish-gray sides and flanks. Pacific coast forms such as *C.u. ustulatus* are reddish-brown above, less distinctly spotted below; distinguished from *C.f. salicicolus* form of Veery by face pattern, buffy-brown sides and flanks, and voice. Fairly common but shy; found in moist woods, swamps, thickets. Song is an ascending spiral of varied whistles; common call, an abrupt *whit*.

Gray-cheeked Thrush *Catharus minimus* L 7¼" (18 cm)
Gray-brown above, with indistinct and incomplete eye ring. Underparts white, with bold dark spots on breast. Flanks brownish-gray. Breast usually less buffy than Swainson's; sometimes shows a pale yellow tinge. New England mountain form, *C.m. bicknelli*, is a warmer brown above; resembles *C.u. swainsoni* form of Swainson's Thrush, but lacks distinctly buffy lores and bold eye ring. Fairly common but shy; found in coniferous or mixed woodlands. Migrates east of dashed line on map. Thin, nasal song is somewhat like Veery's, but often rises sharply at end; call, a downslurred *wee-ah*.

Hermit Thrush *Catharus guttatus* L 6¾" (17 cm)
Complete whitish eye ring; reddish tail. Upperparts vary from brown-olive to gray-brown; breast buffy or whitish. Widespread eastern forms such as *C.g. faxoni* have buff-brown flanks. The larger, paler western mountain forms, such as *auduboni*, and the smaller Pacific coast forms, such as *guttatus*, have grayish flanks. Fairly common but shy; found in coniferous or mixed woodlands, thickets. Song is a serene series of clear, flutelike notes, the similar phrases repeated at different pitches. Calls include a low *chuck*, often doubled.

Wood Thrush

Veery

salicicolus

fuscescens

Swainson's Thrush

ustulatus

swainsoni

Gray-cheeked Thrush

minimus

bicknelli

auduboni

faxoni

guttatus

Hermit Thrush

Varied Thrush *Ixoreus naevius* L 9¹/₂" (24 cm)

Male has grayish-blue nape and back, orange eyebrow and wing bars; underparts orange with black breast band. Female distinguished from American Robin (next page) by orange eyebrow and wing bars, dusky breast band, and unmarked throat. Juvenile resembles female but has white belly, scalier looking throat and breast. In a rare variant phase, all orange color is replaced by white. Common in dense, moist woodlands, especially coniferous forests. Generally feeds in trees. Call is a soft *took;* song, a slow series of variously pitched notes, all rapidly trilled. Rare in winter as far east as New England and south to Virginia. Numbers vary from year to year in southern part of mapped winter range.

Eye-browed Thrush *Turdus obscurus* L 8¹/₂" (22 cm)

Asian species, regular spring migrant on the Aleutians, rare in fall; casual on the Pribilofs. Brownish-olive above, with distinct white eyebrow. Belly is white, sides pale buffy-orange. Male has dark gray throat and breast; female's throat is white and streaked. Wing linings pale gray. Call is a thin *zip-zip.*

Dusky Thrush *Turdus naumanni* L 9¹/₂" (24 cm)

Asian species, casual spring migrant on westernmost Aleutians; accidental on St. Lawrence Island and Point Barrow. White eyebrow conspicuous on blackish head. Upperparts strongly patterned; rump rust-colored; wings extensively rust. Below, white edgings give a scaly look to dark breast and sides. Note also distinctive white crescent across breast. Call is a raspy *shack shack* similar to Fieldfare.

Fieldfare *Turdus pilaris* L 10" (25 cm)

Breeds from Greenland to Siberia; winters to Mediterranean and China. Casual vagrant in Alaska, eastern Canada, and the northeastern U.S. Gray head and rump contrast with purplish-brown upper back, blackish tail. Below, dark arrowhead-shaped spots pattern the buffy breast and extend along sides. White wing linings flash in flight. Song is a noisy twittering; call note is a raspy *shack shack,* like Dusky Thrush.

Varied Thrush

juvenile

♀

♂

Eye-browed Thrush

♀

♂

Dusky Thrush

Fieldfare

American Robin *Turdus migratorius* L 10" (25 cm)
Gray-brown above, with darker head and tail; bill yellow; underparts brick red; lower belly white. Most western birds are paler and duller overall than eastern and northwestern forms. In most eastern birds (shown here), the tail has white corners, conspicuous in flight. Juvenile's underparts are tinged with cinnamon and heavily spotted with brown. Compare with spotted thrushes (page 326). Common and widespread, the American Robin brightens both forest and suburb with its loud, liquid song, a variable *cheerily cheer-up cheerio*. Varied calls include a rapid *tut tut tut*. Often seen on lawns, head cocked as it searches for earthworms; also eats insects, berries. Nests in shrubs and trees and on sheltered windowsills, eaves. In winter, found in moist woodlands, swamps, suburbs, parks. Numbers vary greatly from winter to winter in the southwest, California, and the northeast.

Rufous-backed Robin *Turdus rufopalliatus* L 9¹/₄" (24 cm)
Mexican species, casual visitor in winter to southern Arizona, accidental from southern and southwestern Texas to southern California. Distinguished from American Robin by reddish-brown back and wing coverts, uniformly gray head, and more extensively streaked throat. Somewhat secretive; found in treetops and dense shrubbery.

Clay-colored Robin *Turdus grayi* L 9" (23 cm)
Mexican species, rare visitor and very rare breeder in southernmost Texas. Brownish-olive above; tawny-buff below; pale buffy throat is lightly streaked with olive. Lacks white around eye conspicuous in American Robin. Very secretive; forages in dense thickets, streamside brush, woodlands. Calls include a nasal *meeoo;* song resembles American Robin's but is slower, clearer, much less varied.

Aztec Thrush *Ridgwayia pinicola* L 9¹/₄" (24 cm)
Mexican species, casual visitor to southeastern Arizona, southwestern Texas. Male is sooty-brown above, with white patches on wings, white uppertail coverts; tail broadly tipped with white; breast is dark; belly and undertail coverts white. Female is paler and browner. Juvenile is heavily streaked above with creamy-white; underparts are whitish and heavily edged with brown.

juvenile

American Robin

♀

♂

Rufous-backed Robin

Clay-colored Robin

juvenile

♂

♀

Aztec Thrush

Northern Wheatear *Oenanthe oenanthe* L 5¾" (15 cm)

Tail pattern distinctive: white rump, white tail with dark central feathers and dark terminal band. Eastern birds are cinnamon buff below; western birds are whitish with a buff tinge. Males in fall and winter resemble females. Compare immature to Siberian Accentor. Wheatears are active, perky little birds, bobbing their tails and flitting from rock to rock in search of seeds and insects. Prefer open, stony habitats. Nests are built in rocky crevices or other cavities. Fairly common on breeding grounds; casual along Atlantic coast during migration; accidental inland and on west coast.

Bluethroat *Luscinia svecica* L 5½" (14 cm)

Colorful throat pattern distinguishes breeding male from all other birds. In all plumages, rusty patches at base of tail are conspicuous in flight. In female and immature, note dark breast band. Uncommon; nests on the tundra in thickets near water. Generally furtive and shy, staying hidden in brush. In courtship, however, males sing from high perches. Loud, melodious song, often beginning with a crisp, metallic *ting ting ting*. Regular migrant on St. Lawrence Island; accidental on the Aleutians.

Siberian Rubythroat *Luscinia calliope* L 6" (15 cm)

Asian bird, rare spring and fall migrant off western Alaska, particularly on the western Aleutians. Adult male has a bright red throat. Female and immature have white throats, sometimes tinged with red; compare with smaller Bluethroat, which has rusty tail patches and paler underparts.

Accentors (Family Prunellidae)

Small Eurasian family, found chiefly in mountainous country. Sparrowlike, with thin bills. One species visits North America.

Siberian Accentor *Prunella montanella* L 5½" (14 cm)

Casual fall visitor in Alaska. Somewhat resembles female and immature Northern Wheatear, but lacks white on rump and tail; eyebrow and underparts are a uniform bright tawny-buff, with a diffuse dark breast band and a patch of gray on sides of neck. Also note the dark crown and streaked upperparts. The two whitish wing bars are only faintly visible.

western ♀

eastern breeding ♂

Northern Wheatear

eastern immature

western breeding ♂

juvenile

eastern immature

breeding ♂

immature ♀

Bluethroat

♀

♀

Siberian Rubythroat

♂

immature

Siberian Accentor

Shrikes (Family Laniidae)

These masked hunters scan the countryside from lookout perches, then swoop down on insects, rodents, snakes, small birds. Lacking talons, "butcher-birds" impale their prey on thorns or barbed wire or wedge it into a tree fork to eat it or store it for later.

Loggerhead Shrike *Lanius ludovicianus* L 9" (23 cm)
Slightly smaller and darker than Northern Shrike. Head and back bluish-gray; underparts white, very faintly barred. Broad black mask extends above eye and thinly across top of bill. All-dark bill, shorter than in Northern Shrike, with smaller hook. Rump varies from gray to whitish. Juvenile is paler and barred overall, with brownish-gray upperparts; acquires adult plumage by first fall. Loggerheads hunt in open or brushy areas, diving from a low perch, then rising swiftly to the next lookout. Seen in flight, wings and tail are darker and the white wing patches smaller than in Northern Mockingbird. Song is a medley of low warbles and harsh, squeaky notes; calls include a harsh *shack-shack*. Fairly common over much of range; rare and declining in the midwest and northeast. A few winter in northern part of range.

Northern Shrike *Lanius excubitor* L 10" (25 cm)
Slightly larger than Loggerhead Shrike, with paler head and back, lightly barred underparts; rump whitish. Mask is narrower than in Loggerhead Shrike, does not extend above eye; feathering above bill is white. Bill longer, with a more distinct hook. Juvenile is brownish above and more heavily barred below than adult. Immature is grayer; retains barring on underparts until first spring. Uncommon; often perches high in tall trees. Song and calls are similar to Loggerhead. Southern range limit and numbers on wintering grounds vary unpredictably from year to year.

Mimic Thrushes (Family Mimidae)

Notable singers, unequaled in North America for the rich variety and volume of their song. Some mimic the songs of other species. All have rather drab plumage and long tails. They feed on insects, seeds, berries.

Gray Catbird *Dumetella carolinensis* L 8½" (22 cm)
Plain dark gray with a black cap and a long, black tail, often cocked; undertail coverts chestnut. Generally common but tends to stay hidden in low, dense thickets in deciduous woodlands and residential areas. Song is a variable mixture of melodious, nasal, and squeaky notes interspersed with catlike *mew* notes; some individuals are good mimics. Most readily identified by its call, a downslurred *mew*.

Northern Mockingbird
for comparison

**Loggerhead
Shrike**

juvenile

**Northern
Shrike**

immature

juvenile

**Gray
Catbird**

Northern Mockingbird *Mimus polyglottos* L 10" (25 cm)
Dull gray above; paler below. White outer tail feathers and white wing patches flash conspicuously in flight and in territorial and courtship displays. Readily distinguished from shrikes (preceding page) by slimmer bill and lack of mask. Mockingbirds inhabit rural thickets, woodland edges, suburbs, towns. Song is a mixture of original and imitative phrases, each repeated several times. Imitates other species' songs and calls, squeaky gates, pianos, barking dogs, etc. Spring song, sung only by males, may continue for hours, day and night. Both sexes sing in fall, claiming feeding territories. Call is a loud, sharp *check*. Aggressive territorial defense; may attack any intruder. Range is expanding northward.

Bahama Mockingbird *Mimus gundlachii* L 11" (28 cm)
Caribbean species, casual on Dry Tortugas, Florida Keys, and southern Florida mainland. Larger and browner than Northern Mockingbird, with streaking on neck and flanks; tail has white tip. Lacks white patches on wings. Song is richly varied but not known to include imitations.

Sage Thrasher *Oreoscoptes montanus* L 8¹/₂" (22 cm)
Yellow eye, white wing bars, white-cornered tail. Grayish above, boldly streaked below. Worn late-summer birds show much less streaking, resemble Bendire's Thrasher (next page). Juvenile has streaked head and back; compare with Cactus Wren (page 318). Song is a long series of warbled phrases. Calls include a *chuck* and a high *churr*. Found in sagebrush plains. Casual vagrant to eastern U. S.

Brown Thrasher *Toxostoma rufum* L 11¹/₂" (29 cm)
Reddish-brown above, heavily streaked below. Distinguished from Long-billed Thrasher by shorter bill, redder head, and yellow eye. Immature's eye may be gray or brown. Compare also with Wood Thrush (page 326). Common in hedgerows, brush, and woodland edges, often close to human habitation. Sings a long series of varied melodious phrases, each phrase usually given only two or three times. Seldom imitates other birds. Calls include a sharp *chuck* and a low *churr*. Rare in fall and winter in the west; casual in spring.

Long-billed Thrasher *Toxostoma longirostre*
L 11¹/₂" (29 cm) Closely resembles Brown Thrasher but has gray head and neck, orange eye, and longer, more strongly curved bill. Song is very much like Brown Thrasher's. Inhabits dense bottomland thickets, woodland edges, and chaparral, searching the ground for insects. In spring and early summer, sings from a high, open perch.

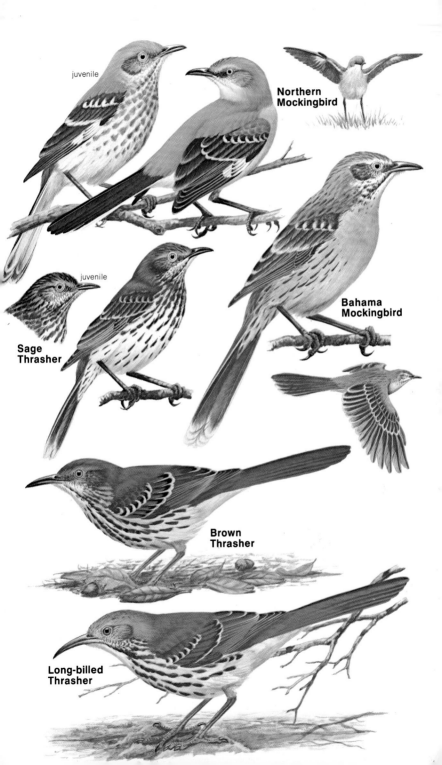

juvenile

Northern Mockingbird

juvenile

Sage Thrasher

Bahama Mockingbird

Brown Thrasher

Long-billed Thrasher

Curve-billed Thrasher *Toxostoma curvirostre*

L 11" (28 cm) Breast mottled; bill all-dark, longer, heavier, and usually more strongly curved than in Bendire's Thrasher. Breast spots are indistinct in the westernmost form, *T. c. palmeri*. Curve-billeds from extreme southeastern Arizona to Texas, such as *curvirostre*, are heavily mottled below and have pale wing bars and conspicuous white tips on tail. All immatures and early-winter adults have darker spotting. Distinctive call, a sharp *whit-wheet*, sometimes three-noted. Song is elaborate, melodic, includes low trills and warbles. Common; found in streamside brush, canyons, semiarid brushlands. Casual (*palmeri*) in southeastern California, the Great Plains, and upper midwest.

Bendire's Thrasher *Toxostoma bendirei* *L 9¾" (25 cm)*

Breast mottled; bill shorter and usually less curved than in Curve-billed Thrasher; base of lower mandible pale. White tail tips are similar to *curvirostre* form of Curve-billed. Distinctive arrowhead-shaped spots on breast are not present in worn summer plumage. Fairly common; found in open farmlands, grasslands, brushy desert. Song is a sustained, melodic warbling, each phrase repeated one to three times. Low *chuck* call is seldom heard. Casual to southern California coast in late summer, fall, and winter.

Crissal Thrasher *Toxostoma crissale* *L 11½" (29 cm)*

Large and slender, with a distinctive chestnut undertail patch and a dark whisker streak. Very secretive, hiding in underbrush. Song is varied and musical, its cadence more leisurely than in Curve-billed Thrasher. Calls include a repeated *chideery* and a whistled *toit-toit-toit*. Found mainly in dense mesquite and willows along streams and washes.

Le Conte's Thrasher *Toxostoma lecontei* *L 11" (28 cm)*

Palest of the thrashers, with pale grayish-brown upperparts, darker tail; undertail coverts tawny. Bill and eye are dark. Prefers arid, sparsely vegetated habitats. Runs with surprising speed, tail straight up, across open desert or along sandy washes. Song, heard chiefly at dawn and dusk, is loud, melodious, and sometimes repetitious. Calls include an ascending, whistled *tweeep*. Uncommon over most of range.

California Thrasher *Toxostoma redivivum* *L 12" (31 cm)*

Dark above, with pale eyebrow, dark eye, dark cheeks. Pale throat contrasts with dark breast; belly and undertail coverts tawny-buff. Darker overall than the Crissal Thrasher. Most common call is a low, flat *chuck*. Song loud and sustained, with some clear but mostly guttural phrases, often repeated once or twice. Imitates other species and sounds. Common in chaparral-covered foothills and brushy parkland where there is open ground under low, thick-woven branches.

curvirostre

palmeri

Bendire's
Thrasher

Curve-billed
Thrasher

Crissal
Thrasher

Le Conte's
Thrasher

California
Thrasher

Pipits and Wagtails (Family Motacillidae)

Sparrow-size ground dwellers with slender bills. Most species pump their tails up and down as they walk in open fields in search of insects and spiders.

American Pipit *Anthus rubescens* L 6¹/₂" (17 cm)
Brownish-gray above; faintly streaked, except on hindneck and rump. Breeding birds have grayer tinge above, less streaking below. Underparts usually uniformly rich buff in fresh fall plumage, often becoming whitish in late winter; moderately streaked below. Eyebrow matches color of underparts. Bill mostly dark; legs dark or tinged with pink. Tail has white outer feathers. An Asian subspecies, *A.r. japonicus*, rare in western Alaska, is more boldly streaked below; legs pink. Common and widespread, the American Pipit nests on tundra in the north, mountaintops farther south. Winter flocks are found in fields and on beaches. Call, given in flight, is a sharp *pip-pit* or *jee-eet*. Song is a rapid series of *chee* or *cheedle* notes.

Sprague's Pipit *Anthus spragueii* L 6¹/₂" (17 cm)
Dark eye prominent in pale buff face. Pale edges on rounded back feathers give a scaly look; rump is streaked. Underparts whitish, with a buffy wash and short, dark streaks on the breast. Legs pinkish. Outer tail feathers are more extensively white than in American Pipit. Uncommon, secretive, and somewhat solitary. Nests in grassy fields. Does not pump tail. Call is a loud, squeaky *squeet*, usually given two or more times. Song, given incessantly in high flight, is a descending series of musical *tzee* and *tzee-a* notes.

Olive Tree-Pipit *Anthus hodgsoni* L 6¹/₂" (17 cm)
Asian species, casual migrant on St. Lawrence Island and Pribilofs, rare on western Aleutians. Grayish-olive back, faintly streaked. Eyebrow orange-buff in front of eye, white behind eye. Broken white stripe extends around dark ear patch. Throat and breast rich buff, with large spots on breast. Belly pure white. Bill is mostly dark; legs pink. Call is a buzzy *tsee*.

Pechora Pipit *Anthus gustavi* L 6¹/₄" (16 cm)
Asian species, casual in spring off western Alaska. Resembles immature Red-throated Pipit, but note richly contrasting mantle stripes, black with bright rufous edges; stripes extend continuously from crown. Call is a hard *pwit* or *pit*.

Red-throated Pipit *Anthus cervinus* L 5¹/₂" (14 cm)
Pinkish-red head and breast are distinctive in breeding male, less extensive in breeding female and fall adults. Immatures and some breeding females show no red; compare with Pechora Pipit. Fairly common on breeding grounds; regular on western Aleutians; rare but regular fall migrant along California coast. Call, given in flight, is a high *seeep*.

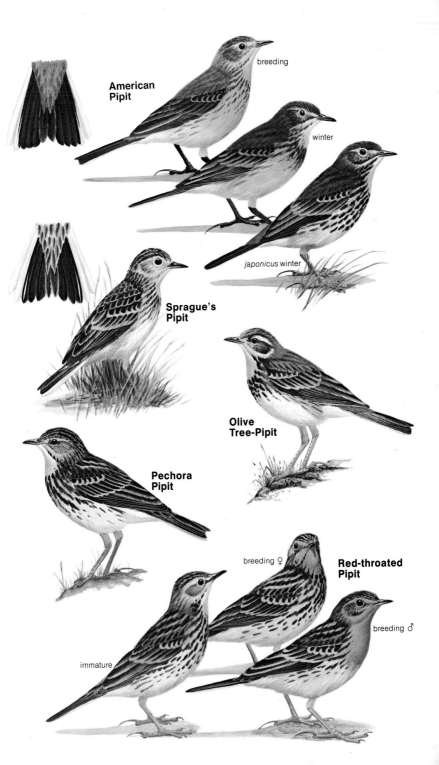

American Pipit

breeding

winter

japonicus winter

Sprague's Pipit

Olive Tree-Pipit

Pechora Pipit

breeding ♀

Red-throated Pipit

breeding ♂

immature

White Wagtail *Motacilla alba* L 7¹⁄₄" (18 cm)

Breeding adult has black nape, gray back. Face and underparts white, with black eye line, black throat and bib, and usually a black chin. In flight, shows mostly dark wings. Juvenile
and immature are almost identical to young Black-backed
Wagtail. Uncommon to rare in Alaska. Bobs its head as it
walks; frequently wags its tail. Like all wagtails, flight is
strongly undulating. Calls include a two-note *tschizzik*.

Black-backed Wagtail *Motacilla lugens* L 7¹⁄₄" (18 cm)

Asian coastal species, regular migrant on western Aleutians,
rare on Bering Sea islands; casual on west coast. Similar to
White Wagtail in all plumages. Breeding adult has blacker
back, usually a white chin. In flight, shows mostly white
wings. Juveniles of the two species are brownish above, with
two faint wing bars. Immature more closely resembles winter
adult but retains juvenile flight feathers. Immature Black-
backed has fainter wing bars and whiter base to flight feathers
than White Wagtail. Calls are similar to White Wagtail. Formerly classified as a subspecies of White Wagtail.

Yellow Wagtail *Motacilla flava* L 6¹⁄₂" (17 cm)

Grayish-olive above, yellow below; tail shorter than in other
wagtails. In breeding plumage, the Alaska form, *M.f. tschutschensis,* has a speckled breast band. Asian form, *simillima,*
seen regularly on Aleutians and Pribilofs, is greener above, yellower below. Females are duller overall. Fall and winter birds
vary from whitish to yellow below. In juveniles the breast band
tends to be blacker. Common to uncommon on Alaska breeding grounds; casual fall migrant on California coast. Call is a
loud *tsweep,* similar to call of Eastern Kingbird.

Gray Wagtail *Motacilla cinerea* L 7³⁄₄" (20 cm)

Eurasian species, rare spring migrant off western Alaska; accidental in fall. Gray above, with yellowish rump; yellow below; one white wing bar. Breeding male has black throat.
Female and winter birds have whitish throat, paler underparts. In flight, yellowish rump and white wing stripe distinguish Gray from Yellow Wagtail. Call is a metallic *chink-chink.*

Dippers (Family Cinclidae)

Stocky, robust birds that
lead an aquatic life, wading
and even swimming in
mountain streams to feed.

American Dipper *Cinclus mexicanus* L 7¹⁄₂" (19 cm)

Adult is sooty-gray overall, with dark bill; tail and wings are
short. Juvenile has paler, mottled underparts, pale bill. Fairly
common but solitary, Dippers are found along clear, rushing
mountain streams, as high as timberline. Generally nonmigratory, but may descend to lower elevations in winter. Song is
loud, musical, wrenlike.

White Wagtail

breeding

breeding ♂

breeding ♀

winter ♂

immature

Black-backed Wagtail

tschutschensis breeding ♀

immature

Yellow Wagtail

tschutschensis breeding ♂

juvenile

simillima breeding ♂

♀

Gray Wagtail

breeding ♂

juvenile

American Dipper

Waxwings (Family Bombycillidae)

Red, waxy tips on secondary wing feathers are often indistinct and sometimes absent altogether. All waxwings have sleek crests, silky plumage, and yellow-tipped tails. Where berries are ripening, waxwings come to feast in amiable, noisy flocks. Gorged birds may loll on branches or lawns, barely able to fly.

Bohemian Waxwing *Bombycilla garrulus* L 8¹/₄" (21 cm)
Larger and grayer than Cedar Waxwing; underparts gray; undertail coverts cinnamon. White and yellow spots on wings. In flight, whitish wing patch is conspicuous. Juvenile browner above, streaked below, with pale throat. Nests in open coniferous or mixed woodlands. Winter range varies widely and unpredictably; large flocks visit scattered locations, feeding on berries, small fruits. Also eat insects, flower petals, sap. Irregular winter wanderer to the northeast, usually in small numbers; annual in Maine. Individuals are sometimes seen in flocks of Cedar Waxwings. Distinctive call, a buzzy twittering, lower and harsher than call of Cedar Waxwing.

Cedar Waxwing *Bombycilla cedrorum* L 7¹/₄" (18 cm)
Smaller and browner than Bohemian Waxwing; belly pale yellow; undertail coverts white. Lacks yellow spots on wings. Juvenile is streaked; lacks white wing patches of juvenile Bohemian. Since this species usually nests late in summer, juvenile plumage is seen well into fall. Found in open habitats where berries are available; also eats insects, flower petals, sap. Highly gregarious in migration and winter. Call is a soft, high-pitched, trilled whistle.

Silky Flycatchers (Family Ptilogonatidae)

This New World tropical family of slender, crested birds is closely related to the waxwings. Family's common name describes their soft, sleek plumage and agility in catching insects on the wing.

Phainopepla *Phainopepla nitens* L 7³/₄" (20 cm)
Male is shiny black; white wing patch conspicuous in flight. In both sexes, note distinct crest, long tail, red eyes. Juvenile resembles adult female; both have gray wing patches. Phainopeplas nest in early spring in mesquite brushlands, feeding chiefly on insects, mistletoe berries. In late spring they move into cooler, wetter habitat and raise a second brood. Distinctive call note is a querulous, low-pitched, whistled *wurp?* Song is a brief warble, seldom heard. Distinctive flight, fluttery but direct, and often very high. Rare postbreeding wanderer north and east of mapped range.

Bohemian Waxwing

juvenile

Cedar Waxwing

juvenile

♂

♀

Phainopepla

Bulbuls (Family Pycnonotidae)

A large Old World family of the tropics of Asia and Africa. Dull colors camouflage these noisy, active birds. One species now inhabits North America.

Red-whiskered Bulbul *Pycnonotus jocosus* L 7" (18 cm)
Asian species, popular as a cage bird. A few birds that escaped from captivity in 1960 in Miami, Florida, are now established as a small population, found in suburbs and parklands south of Miami. Also local in Los Angeles area. Red ear patch and red undertail coverts are distinctive. Crest not apparent in flight. Juvenile lacks ear patch; undertail coverts are paler.

Starlings (Family Sturnidae)

Chunky, dark, and glossy birds, generally gregarious and bold. Three species of this large, widespread Old World family are now found in North America.

Crested Myna *Acridotheres cristatellus* L 9¾" (25 cm)
Asian species, introduced in Vancouver, British Columbia, in the 1890s. Fairly common in Vancouver, casual in surrounding area, but apparently not spreading. Identified by bushy crest on forehead, yellow bill and legs, white wing patch.

Hill Myna *Gracula religiosa* L 10½" (27 cm)
Asian species, excellent mimic, popular as a cage bird. A small population of escaped or released birds is resident in southeastern Florida. Glossy black body; bill red to orange; yellow wattles, yellow legs, white wing patch.

European Starling *Sturnus vulgaris* L 8½" (22 cm)
Adult in breeding plumage is iridescent black with a yellow bill. In fresh fall plumage, feathers are tipped with white and buff, giving an overall speckled appearance; bill becomes brownish. Black spring plumage appears as the feather tips wear off. Distinguished in flight from other black birds by short, square tail, stocky body, and short, broad-based pointed wings that appear pale gray from below. Juvenile is gray-brown above, paler below, with brown bill. A Eurasian species, the Starling was introduced in New York a hundred years ago and quickly spread across the continent. Now abundant in a variety of habitats. Bold and aggressive, often competes successfully with native species for nest holes. Varied call notes include squeaks, warbles, chirps, and twittering; also imitates the songs of other species. Outside of nesting season, Starlings are usually seen in large flocks, sometimes in company with grackles and blackbirds.

Red-whiskered Bulbul

juvenile

Crested Myna

Hill Myna

Common Grackle
for comparison

Brown-headed Cowbird
for comparison

European Starling

fall

winter

breeding

juvenile

Vireos (Family Vireonidae)

Short and sturdy bills slightly hooked at the tip characterize these small songbirds. Some have eye rings linked by loral stripes to form "spectacles"; these vireos always have wing bars. Other species have eyebrow stripes and no wing bars. Vireos are generally chunkier and less active than warblers. Intricate cup nest is suspended from the fork of a branch.

Black-capped Vireo *Vireo atricapillus* L 4¹/₂" (11 cm)
Olive above, white below, with yellow flanks, yellowish wing bars. Male's glossy black cap contrasts with white spectacles. Female's slate gray head and smaller size distinguish her from Solitary Vireo (next page). Immature birds are browner above, buffy below. Fairly common but somewhat hard to find, the Black-capped Vireo stays hidden in oak scrub, thickets. An active feeder, sometimes even hanging upside down to search for insects. Best located by song, a persistent string of hurried, twittering, varied two- or three-note phrases.

White-eyed Vireo *Vireo griseus* L 5" (13 cm)
Grayish-olive above; white below, with pale yellow sides and flanks; two whitish wing bars; yellow spectacles. Distinctive white eyes visible at close range. Juvenile is duller, with gray or brown eyes. Populations on the Florida Keys are grayer above, with less yellow below; bill larger. Common in dense, moist thickets and tangles. Typical song is a loud, scolding, variable five- to seven-note phrase usually beginning and ending with a sharp *chick*. Casual vagrant to California.

Yellow-throated Vireo *Vireo flavifrons* L 5¹/₂" (14 cm)
Bright yellow spectacles, throat, and breast; white belly; two white wing bars. Upperparts olive, with contrasting gray rump. Compare with the Pine Warbler's greenish-yellow rump, streaked sides, thinner bill, and less complete and distinct spectacles. The Yellow-throated Vireo is fairly common in most of its breeding range. Rare in winter along entire Gulf coast and in northern Florida; most birds winter from eastern Mexico south. Song is a slow repetition of harsh two- or three-note phrases separated by long pauses: *de-ar-ie come-here;* often concludes with a rising *three-eight*. Calls include a rapid, hoarse *heh heh heh*. Casual vagrant in the west.

Thick-billed Vireo *Vireo crassirostris* L 5¹/₂" (14 cm)
Caribbean species, accidental visitor to Florida Keys and Dry Tortugas. Gray head with yellow spectacles; two yellowish-white wing bars; underparts entirely yellow. Some reported sightings may actually have been young White-eyed Vireos.

Black-capped Vireo

♀

♂

immature

White-eyed Vireo

Florida Keys

Yellow-throated Vireo

Thick-billed Vireo

Pine Warbler
for comparison

Bell's Vireo   *Vireo bellii*   *L 4³/₄" (12 cm)*

Plumage highly variable. West coast form is grayish above, whitish below, with indistinct white spectacles; two faint white or whitish wing bars, the lower bar more prominent. Easternmost form is greenish above, yellowish below. Southwestern forms are intermediate. Short wings make tail look long. An active, nervous vireo; feeds in dense brush. Song is a series of fast, harsh, scolding notes. Generally common in moist woodlands, bottomlands, mesquite. Seriously declining in southern California, due largely to brood parasitism by cowbirds. Range is expanding slightly to the northeast.

Hutton's Vireo   *Vireo huttoni*   *L 5" (13 cm)*

Grayish-olive above, with large white spot on lores; white eye ring broken above eye; two broad white wing bars. Drab olive below. Subspecies vary from the grayer southwestern birds to the greener coastal forms. Distinguished from Ruby-crowned Kinglet by larger size, thicker bill, and lack of dark area below lower wing bar; also by voice: Song is a repeated rising or descending *ch-weet ch-weet;* calls include a low *chit*. Fairly common in moist woodlands, especially in live oaks.

Gray Vireo   *Vireo vicinior*   *L 5¹/₂" (14 cm)*

Gray above, white below; white eye ring; dull white lores; wings brownish, with two faint wing bars, the lower bar more prominent. Short wings make tail look long; compare especially with the smaller west coast form of Bell's Vireo. Fairly common in dry, brushy mesas and foothills; found in chaparral, mesquite, and pinyon-juniper stands. Flits restlessly through the undergrowth, flicking its tail as it forages. Song is a series of varied, musical *chu-wee chu-weet* notes, faster and sweeter than song of western races of Solitary Vireo.

Solitary Vireo   *Vireo solitarius*   *L 5¹/₂" (14 cm)*

Bold white spectacles; two bold white or yellowish wing bars. In eastern birds, bluish-gray head contrasts with greenish back; underparts are white with greenish-yellow sides and flanks. West coast breeding form is paler overall and smaller; compare with west coast form of Hutton's Vireo. A third form, *V. s. plumbeus*, breeding in the Rockies and mountains of the Great Basin, is dark gray above, with at most only a tinge of yellow on flanks; compare with Gray Vireo. Some authorities consider *plumbeus* a separate species. The Solitary Vireo is fairly common throughout its range in mixed woodlands. Feeds slowly, deliberately, generally staying fairly high in shrubs and trees. Song is a variable series of rich, two- to six-note phrases: *chu-wee cheerio*. Song of western forms is burrier, lower, less melodious than eastern forms.

Ruby-crowned Kinglet for comparison

interior

Bell's Vireo

west coast

west coast

Hutton's Vireo

southwest

Gray Vireo

Rockies and Great Basin

west coast

Solitary Vireo

eastern

Red-eyed Vireo *Vireo olivaceus* L 6″ *(15 cm)*

Blue-gray crown; white eyebrow bordered above and below with black. Dark olive back, darker wings and tail; white underparts. Lacks wing bars. Ruby red eye visible at close range. First-fall bird has brown iris. Immatures and some fall adults have pale yellow on flanks and undertail coverts. Distinctive subspecies, *V.o. flavoviridis,* casual in fall along California coast and in summer in extreme south Texas, is yellower above, bright yellow on sides, flanks, and undertail coverts; black lines on head are less distinct; formerly considered a separate species, "Yellow-green Vireo." The Red-eyed Vireo is abundant in eastern woodlands; rare migrant west of dashed line on map. Persistent song, sung all day, a variable series of deliberate, short phrases. Calls include a short scolding *mew*.

Black-whiskered Vireo *Vireo altiloquus* L 6¼″ *(16 cm)*

Variable black whisker stripe, often hard to see. Bill larger and longer than in Red-eyed Vireo. Gray crown; white eyebrow bordered above and below with black. Dull green above; whitish below, with variable pale yellowish wash on sides and flanks. Common in summer in the mangrove swamps of Florida Keys and along Florida coasts. Casual along rest of Gulf coast and in Florida interior. Song consists of deliberate one- to four-note phrases, somewhat hoarser and more emphatic than song of Red-eyed Vireo.

Warbling Vireo *Vireo gilvus* L 5½″ *(14 cm)*

Gray or olive-gray above; western birds tend to be slightly greener; extremes are shown here. Underparts white. Dusky eye line; white eyebrow, without dark upper border; brown eye. Lacks wing bars. Smaller and paler than Red-eyed Vireo. Whiter below than Philadelphia Vireo; lacks dark lores; crown does not contrast strongly with back. Distinguished from Tennessee Warbler by larger size, thicker bill. Many birds in fresh fall plumage are greener above with pale yellow sides, flanks, and undertail coverts. Warbling Vireos are common across most of North America in summer; found in open deciduous woods. Song is delivered in long, melodious, warbling phrases. Casual in winter in southern California.

Philadelphia Vireo *Vireo philadelphicus* L 5¼″ *(13 cm)*

Breeding adult variably yellow below, with whitish belly. Greenish above, with contrasting gray cap, dull grayish-olive wing bar, dull white eyebrow, and dark eye line. First-fall birds and most fall adults are entirely yellow below, palest on belly. Distinguished from Warbling Vireo by dark eye line extending through lores, darker cap, dark primary coverts, and yellow at center of throat and breast. Similar Tennessee Warbler has a thinner bill, whiter underparts. Philadelphia Vireo is uncommon throughout its range; found in open woodlands, burned-over areas, streamside willows and alders. Song resembles that of Red-eyed Vireo but is generally slower, thinner, and higher pitched.

"Yellow-green Vireo"

breeding

Red-eyed Vireo

1st fall

Black-whiskered Vireo

Philadelphia Vireo

Warbling Vireo

western 1st fall

eastern breeding

1st fall

breeding

Tennessee Warbler breeding ♂ for comparison

Warblers, Sparrows (Family Emberizidae)

A large family related by genetic characteristics but outwardly diverse.

Includes such distinct groups as the sparrows, orioles, and wood warblers.

Prothonotary Warbler *Protonotaria citrea*

L 5¹/₂" (14 cm) Large, plump, short-tailed, and very long-billed. Eyes are large, dark, and prominent. Male's head and underparts golden yellow, fading to white undertail coverts; wings blue-gray, without wing bars; blue-gray tail has large white patches. Female duller, head less golden. Fairly common. The only eastern warbler that nests in tree cavities or other crannies; usually selects a low site along streams or surrounded by sluggish or stagnant water. Casual or rare vagrant across most of the continent during migration, especially in fall. Song is a series of loud, ringing *zweet* notes.

Blue-winged Warbler *Vermivora pinus* *L 4³/₄" (12 cm)*

Male has bright yellow crown and underparts, white or yellowish-white undertail coverts, black eye line, blue-gray wings with two white wing bars. Female duller overall. In both sexes, bill is long and slender; bold white tail spots are visible from below. Locally common; inhabits brushy meadows, second-growth woodlands; nests on the ground. Typical song is a wheezy *beee-bzzz*, the second note lower. Range is expanding at northeastern and western edges; gradually replacing Golden-winged Warblers. Hybridizes with Golden-winged Warbler where ranges overlap. Hybrids may vary considerably from parent species in amount of black on head and throat, amount of yellow below, and size and color of wing bars. Some variations are shown here of the two main types, the more frequent "Brewster's Warbler" and the rare "Lawrence's."

Golden-winged Warbler *Vermivora chrysoptera*

L 4³/₄" (12 cm) Male has black throat; black ear patch bordered in white; yellow crown and wing patch. Female similar but duller. In both sexes, white tail spots are conspicuous from below; underparts are grayish-white; bill long and slender. Fairly common in parts of range but declining. Found in overgrown pastures, briery woodland borders; nests on the ground. Song is a soft *bee-bz-bz-bz*, longer than similar song of Blue-winged Warbler. Hybrids of these two species (see above) sing the song of either or both parents or variations all their own.

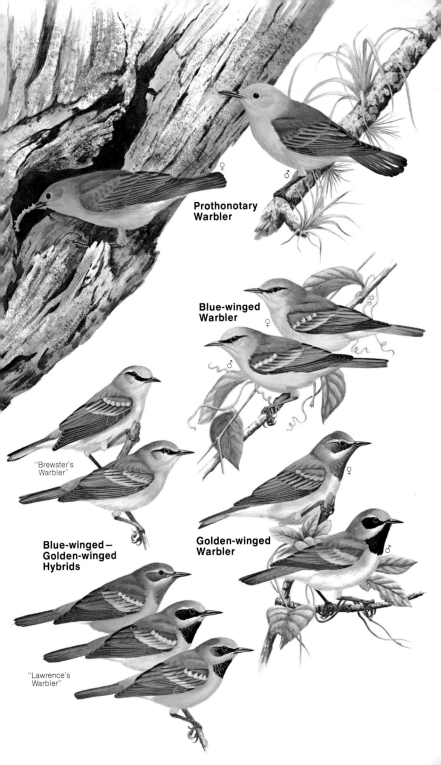

Prothonotary Warbler

♀

♂

Blue-winged Warbler

♀

♂

"Brewster's Warbler"

Blue-winged — Golden-winged Hybrids

Golden-winged Warbler

♀

♂

"Lawrence's Warbler"

Tennessee Warbler *Vermivora peregrina* L 4³/₄" (12 cm)
Plump, short-tailed, with long, straight bill. Male in spring is
green above with gray crown, bold white eyebrow; white below. Female is tinged with yellow or olive overall, especially in
fresh fall plumage. Adult male in fall resembles spring adult female but shows more yellow below. Immature also yellowish
below; resembles young Orange-crowneds, but is greener
above and has a shorter tail and white undertail coverts. Spring
male may be confused with Warbling and Red-eyed Vireos
(page 352); note especially Tennessee Warbler's slimmer bill,
greener back. Distinctive three-part song: several rapid two-
syllable notes followed by a few higher single notes, ending
with a staccato trill. Fairly common. Found in coniferous and
mixed woodlands in summer, mixed open woodlands and
brushy areas during migration. Nests on the ground; generally feeds high in trees. Rare winter vagrant to coastal California.
Most migration is east of the Rockies.

Orange-crowned Warbler *Vermivora celata*

L 5" (13 cm) Olive above, paler below. Yellow undertail coverts
and faint, blurred streaks on sides of breast distinguish this
species from the similar Tennessee Warbler. Note also that
Orange-crowned's bill is thinner and slightly downcurved; tail
is longer. Plumage varies from the brighter, yellower birds of
western U. S., such as *V.c. lutescens,* to the grayer *celata*
which breeds across Alaska and Canada and winters primarily
in southeastern U. S. Tawny-orange crown, absent in some females and immatures, is seldom discernible in the field. Immature *celata* can be particularly drab. Young birds are similar
to immature Tennessees but show yellow undertail coverts
and grayer upperparts. Common in the west; rarer in the east.
Inhabits open, brushy woodlands, forest edges, thickets.
Nests on the ground; generally feeds in low branches. Song is
a high-pitched staccato trill; call note, a sharp *chip.*

Bachman's Warbler *Vermivora bachmanii* L 4³/₄" (12 cm)
Our rarest warbler; on the verge of extinction. The few recent
sightings were in South Carolina's I'On Swamp. Bill is very
thin, long, somewhat downcurved; undertail coverts white in
both sexes. Male has yellow forehead, chin, and shoulders;
black crown and bib. Some males, probably younger adults,
have less black on crown and throat, less yellow on shoulders,
and more white on lower belly. Female generally drabber,
crown gray, throat and breast gray or yellow. Inhabits swamps,
low woodlands. Distinctive song, typically a rapid series of
buzzes on one pitch; sounds like Northern Parula. Bachman's
Warbler is often confused with Hooded Warbler (page 372).
Bachman's once bred in canebrakes and wet woodlands
throughout the southeastern U. S. but was probably never numerous. Winters in Cuba and on Isle of Pines.

fall ♀

breeding ♀

fall ♂

breeding ♂

Tennessee Warbler

♀

celata

♂

Orange-crowned Warbler

lutescens ♂

♀

♂

♂

Bachman's Warbler

Nashville Warbler *Vermivora ruficapilla* *L 4³/₄" (12 cm)*

Bold white eye ring, gray head, olive upperparts. Throat and underparts yellow; white area between yellow belly and yellow undertail is most conspicuous in western birds. Reddish crown patch seldom discernible in the field. Female is slightly duller than male. Some fall immatures are even duller; head may be brownish-gray or grayish-olive. Common; found in second-growth woodlands, spruce bogs; nests on the ground. Often wags its tail. Typical song is a series of high *see-weet* notes followed by a lower short trill. Call is a sharp *chink*.

Virginia's Warbler *Vermivora virginiae* *L 4³/₄" (12 cm)*

Bold white eye ring; gray head and back, greenish-yellow rump. Whitish below, with yellow patch on breast, yellow undertail coverts. Reddish crown patch seldom discernible in the field. Female is duller overall. Fall immature is brownish-gray above, with little or no yellow on breast. Common in brushlands and pinyon-juniper woods, usually at altitudes between 6,000 and 9,000 feet; nests on the ground. Often wags its tail. Song is a rapid, accelerating series of thin notes, often ending with several lower notes. Call is a sharp *chink*.

Colima Warbler *Vermivora crissalis* *L 5³/₄" (15 cm)*

Mexican species; range extends to the Chisos Mountains of Big Bend National Park, Texas. Larger and browner than Virginia's Warbler; sides brownish; rufous crown patch usually visible. Song is a brief trill ending with one or two lower notes.

Lucy's Warbler *Vermivora luciae* *L 4¹/₄" (11 cm)*

Pale gray above, whitish below. Male's reddish crown patch and rump distinctive. Female and immatures duller; immature female may lack red on crown. Fairly common in mesquite and cottonwoods along watercourses; nests in tree cavities. Lively song, a short trill followed by lower, whistled notes: *weeta weeta weeta che che che*. Call is a sharp *chink*.

Northern Parula *Parula americana* *L 4¹/₂" (11 cm)*

A tiny, short-tailed warbler, gray-blue above with yellowish-green upper back, two bold white wing bars. White eye ring broken by black eye line. Throat and breast bright yellow, belly white. In male, reddish and black bands cross breast. In female, bands are fainter or absent. Common in coniferous or mixed woods, especially near water. Rare vagrant throughout the west during migration. Song is a rising buzzy trill ending with an abrupt lower *zip*.

Tropical Parula *Parula pitiayumi* *L 4¹/₂" (11 cm)*

Resident but rare in the Rio Grande Valley of Texas. Black mask and lack of white eye ring distinguish Tropical from Northern Parula. Note also that yellow of throat extends farther onto sides of face. Male has only one breast band, generally indistinct. Song similar to that of Northern Parula. Formerly called Olive-backed Warbler.

Nashville Warbler

immature ♀

♂

Virginia's Warbler

immature ♀

♂

Colima Warbler

immature ♀

Lucy's Warbler

♂

Northern Parula

immature ♀

♂

Tropical Parula

♀

♂

Black-and-white Warbler *Mniotilta varia* L 5¹/₄" (13 cm)

The only warbler that regularly creeps along branches and up and down tree trunks like a nuthatch. Boldly striped on head, most of body, and undertail coverts. Male's throat and cheeks are black in breeding plumage; in winter, chin is white. Female and immatures have gray cheeks, white throat. Immature female has buffy sides and undertail coverts. Compare with Blackpoll Warbler (page 368). Common in mixed woodlands. Song is a slow series of high, thin *wee-see* notes. Calls include an emphatic *chimp* and a high *seep-seep*.

Black-throated Blue Warbler *Dendroica caerulescens*

L 5¹/₄" (13 cm) Male's black throat, cheeks, and sides separate blue upperparts, white underparts. Bold white patch at base of primaries. Appalachian males are darker above, almost black in southern Appalachians. Female's pale eyebrow is distinct on dark face; upperparts brownish-olive; underparts buffy; wing patch smaller, sometimes almost absent. Inhabits deciduous forests; usually seen in lower or mid-level branches. Typical song is a slow series of four or five wheezy notes, the last note higher: *I am so la-zee*. Call is a single sharp *dit,* like the call of a Dark-eyed Junco. Rare fall vagrant in the west. A few birds winter in Florida; most migrate to the Caribbean.

Cerulean Warbler *Dendroica cerulea* L 4³/₄" (12 cm)

Small and short-tailed; two wide white wing bars. Adult male is bluish above with dark streaks; white below, with black breast band and dark blue-gray streaking on sides. Female has greenish mantle, blue-green or bluish crown; pale eyebrow broadens behind the eye; breast and throat are pale yellowish. Immatures generally resemble the respective adults. Fairly common but local; found in tall trees in swamps, bottomlands, mixed woodlands near water. Song is a short, fast, accelerating series of buzzy notes on one pitch, usually ending with a single buzz note. Fall migration begins as early as late July. Range is expanding in northeast and south.

Blackburnian Warbler *Dendroica fusca* L 5" (13 cm)

Fiery orange throat and broad white wing patch conspicuous in adult male. Female and immatures have paler throat, two white wing bars; note also streaked back and bold yellow or buffy eyebrow, broader behind eye. Orange or yellow crown stripe and white in outer tail feathers are distinct in all males, less so in all females. Fairly common in coniferous or mixed forests of northern breeding range, pine-oak woodlands in the Appalachians. Generally stays in the upper branches. Variable song, commonly a short series of high *seet-say* notes followed by a very high trill. Vagrants are seen rarely in coastal California primarily during fall migration; very rare elsewhere west of dashed line on map.

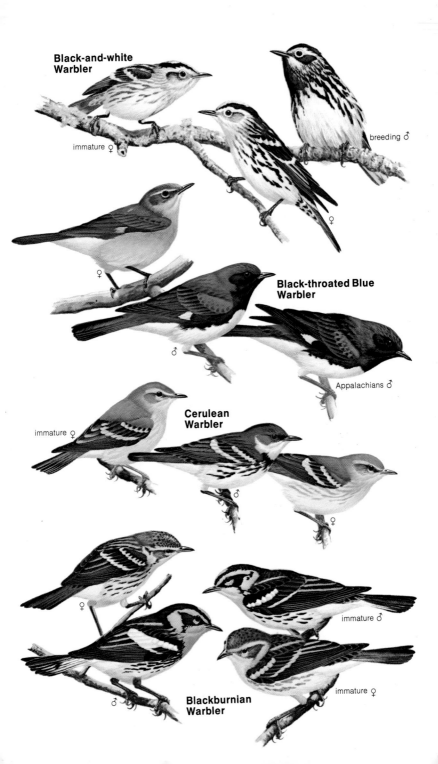

Black-and-white Warbler

immature ♀

breeding ♂

♀

♀

Black-throated Blue Warbler

♂

Appalachians ♂

Cerulean Warbler

immature ♀

♂

♀

♀

immature ♂

♂

immature ♀

Blackburnian Warbler

Chestnut-sided Warbler *Dendroica pensylvanica*

L 5" (13 cm) Adults in spring have yellow crown, black eye line, black whisker stripe; chestnut on sides. Note also boldly streaked back; two pale yellow wing bars. Fall adults and immatures are lime green above, with white eye ring, little or no streaking; underparts whitish; usually lack chestnut on sides. Immature's wing bars are bright yellow. Fairly common in second-growth deciduous woodlands. A small population breeds along the Front Range in Colorado. Rare migrant in the west; casual in winter. Song is a whistled *please please pleased to meetcha*. Frequently cocks its tail.

Cape May Warbler *Dendroica tigrina* *L 5" (13 cm)*

Most plumages have yellow on face, the color usually extending to sides of neck. Note also short tail; yellow rump; thin bill, slightly downcurved. Breeding male's chestnut ear patch and tiger-striped underparts distinctive; wing patch white. Female drabber, grayer, with two narrow white wing bars. Immature male's ear patch is less distinct. Immature female can be extremely drab, with gray face and only a tinge of yellow below and on rump; always has greenish edges on flight feathers. Fairly common in black spruce forests. Song is a high, thin *seet seet seet seet*. Call, a very high, thin *sip*. Rare in Texas in migration; casual throughout the west. Winters chiefly in the West Indies; a few birds winter in southernmost Florida.

Magnolia Warbler *Dendroica magnolia* *L 5" (13 cm)*

Male is blackish above, with white eyebrow, white wing patch, yellow rump; broad white tail patches. Underparts yellow, streaked on breast and sides; undertail coverts white; undertail white except for black band at tip. Female has two wing bars; eyebrow is grayer. Fall adults and immatures are drabber, with grayish-olive upperparts; white eyebrow fainter; faint gray band across breast. Compare immature Prairie Warbler (page 366). Fairly common in moist coniferous forests. Winters in southern Mexico, Central America, West Indies; casual in southern Florida. Rare throughout the west in migration. Song is a whistled *weety-weety-weeteo*.

Yellow-rumped Warbler *Dendroica coronata*

L 5½" (14 cm) Yellow rump, yellow patch on side, yellow crown patch, white tail patches. In northern and eastern birds ("Myrtle Warbler"), note white eyebrow, white throat and sides of neck, contrasting cheek patch. Western birds ("Audubon's Warbler") have yellow throat. The "Audubon's" that breeds in the interior is blacker above and below. All females and fall males are duller than breeding males but show same basic pattern. Abundant in coniferous or mixed woodlands. Variable song, a slow warble, usually rising or falling at the end in "Audubon's," a musical trill in "Myrtle." "Myrtle" is fairly common in winter in the west; "Audubon's" is casual in the east.

Chestnut-sided Warbler

breeding ♀

breeding ♂

fall

Magnolia Warbler

breeding ♀

breeding ♂

breeding ♀

breeding ♂

fall ♀

fall ♂

Cape May Warbler

immature ♀

immature ♂

interior breeding ♂

breeding ♀

breeding ♂

fall ♀

fall ♀

breeding ♂

Yellow-rumped Warbler

"Audubon's Warbler"

"Myrtle Warbler"

Black-throated Gray Warbler *Dendroica nigrescens*

L 5" (13 cm) Adult plumage is basically the same year-round: black-and-white head; gray back streaked with black; white underparts, sides streaked with black; small yellow spot between eye and bill. Lacks central crown stripe of the Black-and-white Warbler (page 360); undertail coverts are white. Immature male resembles adult male; immature female is brownish-gray above, streaking indistinct. Inhabits woodlands, brushlands, chaparral. Varied songs include a buzzy *weezy weezy weezy weezy-weet*. Rare during migration and in winter along the Gulf coast; casual on Atlantic.

Townsend's Warbler *Dendroica townsendi L 5" (13 cm)*

Dark crown, dark ear patch bordered in yellow. Olive above, streaked with black; yellow breast, white belly, yellowish black-streaked sides. Adult male's throat and upper breast are black; female and immature male have streaked lower throat. Immature female is duller, lacks streaking on back; streaking on underparts is diffuse. Fairly common in coniferous forests. Variable song, a series of hoarse *zee* notes. Townsend's-Hermit hybrids are occasionally seen; usually have the yellowish, streaked underparts of Townsend's, yellow head of Hermit.

Hermit Warbler *Dendroica occidentalis L 5½" (14 cm)*

Yellow head, with dark markings extending from nape onto crown. Male has black chin and throat; in female and immatures, chin is yellowish, throat shows less or no dark color. Immature female is more olive above. Fairly common in mountain forests; nests in tall conifers. During migration, also seen in lowlands. Song is a high *seezle seezle seezle seezle zeet-zeet*. Sometimes hybridizes with Townsend's Warbler.

Black-throated Green Warbler *Dendroica virens*

L 5" (13 cm) Bright olive green upperparts; yellow face with greenish ear patch. Underparts are white, tinged with yellow on sides of vent and often on breast. Male has black throat and upper breast and black-streaked sides. Female and immatures show much less black below; immature female generally has dark streaking only on sides. Fairly common in coniferous or mixed forests in summer. Typical song is a slightly hoarse *zeee zeee zee-zo-zee*.

Golden-cheeked Warbler *Dendroica chrysoparia*

L 5½" (14 cm) Dark eye line, lack of clearly outlined ear patch, and lack of any yellow on underparts distinguish this species from similar Black-throated Green Warbler. Male black above, with black crown, black bib, black-streaked sides. Female and immature male duller, upperparts olive with dark streaks; chin yellowish or white; sides of throat streaked. Immature female shows less black on underparts. Locally fairly common on the Edwards Plateau in central Texas; winters in Central America. Song, *bzzzz layzee dayzee,* ends on a high note.

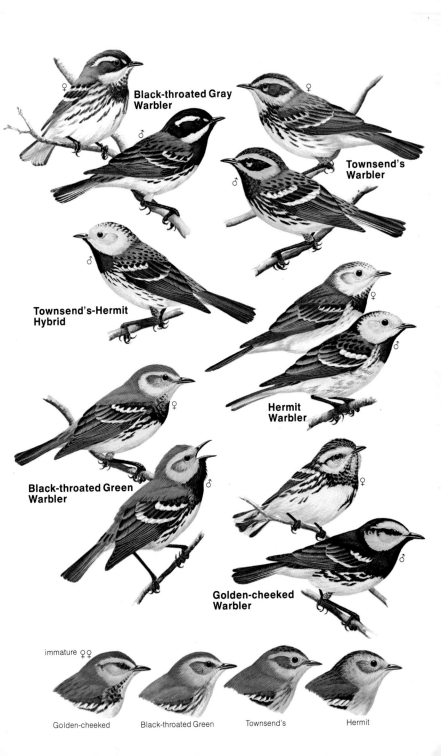

Black-throated Gray
Warbler

♀

♂

Townsend's
Warbler

♀

♂

Townsend's-Hermit
Hybrid

♂

Hermit
Warbler

♀

♂

Black-throated Green
Warbler

♀

♂

Golden-cheeked
Warbler

♀

♂

immature ♀♀

Golden-cheeked   Black-throated Green   Townsend's   Hermit

Yellow-throated Warbler *Dendroica dominica*

L 5½" (14 cm) Plain gray back, longer bill, and large white patch on each side of head distinguish Yellow-throated from Grace's Warbler. Male has black crown and face; in female, black is less extensive. Throat and upper breast bright yellow; rest of underparts white, with black streaks on sides; bold white eyebrow sometimes tinged with yellow. Southeastern birds have dark yellow lores. Fairly common in live oak and pine woodlands, cypress, sycamores. Usually forages high in the trees, creeping methodically along the branches. Song is a series of clear, downslurred whistles ending with a rising note. Casual in west during migration. Casual northward to southern Ontario and the Maritimes, chiefly in spring.

Grace's Warbler *Dendroica graciae* L 5" (13 cm)

Black-streaked gray back and absence of white neck patches distinguish Grace's from Yellow-throated Warbler. Throat and upper breast bright yellow; rest of underparts white, with black streaks on sides; yellow eyebrow, becomes white behind eye. Female slightly duller and browner above. Grace's Warbler inhabits coniferous or mixed forests of southwestern mountains, especially yellow pines. Song is a rapid, accelerating trill. Usually forages high in the trees, creeping along branches or darting out to catch flying insects. Casual vagrant to southern California during migration, chiefly in fall; casual in winter on southern California coast.

Kirtland's Warbler *Dendroica kirtlandii* L 5¾" (15 cm)

Blue-gray above, strongly black-streaked on back; yellow below, streaked on sides; white eye ring, broken by dark lores and eye line; two whitish wing bars, thin and indistinct. Adult female slightly duller; immature female is brownish above. Song is loud and lively, a variable series of low, sharp notes followed by slurred whistles. Frequently wags its tail. Kirtland's Warbler is an endangered species; present population estimated at fewer than 500. Known to nest only in a protected area in north-central Michigan, where controlled plantings and fires produce the required habitat, thickets of young jack pines. Also very rare and irregular in summer in Wisconsin and southern Ontario. Rarely seen in migration; only known wintering grounds are in the Bahamas.

Prairie Warbler *Dendroica discolor* L 4¾" (12 cm)

Olive above, with faint chestnut streaks on back; bright yellow eyebrow, yellow patch below eye; bright yellow below, streaked with black on sides of neck and body. Two pale, thin wing bars. Female and immature male are slightly duller. Immature female is duller still, grayish-olive above; tail pattern and lack of complete eye ring or gray breast band distinguish her from fall Magnolia Warbler (page 362). Common in open woodlands, scrublands, overgrown fields, mangrove swamps. Generally forages in lower branches and brush, twitching its tail. Distinctive song, a rising series of buzzy *zee* notes.

Yellow-throated Warbler

yellow-lored ♂

white-lored ♂

♀

Grace's Warbler

♂

immature ♀

Kirtland's Warbler

♀

♂

♀

♂

Prairie Warbler

immature ♀

Bay-breasted Warbler *Dendroica castanea*

L 5¹/₂" (14 cm) Breeding male has chestnut crown, throat, and sides; black face; creamy patch at each side of neck; two white wing bars. Female is duller. Fall adults and immatures resemble Blackpoll Warbler and Pine Warbler. Bay-breasted is brighter green above; underparts show little or no streaking and little yellow; flanks usually show some buff or bay color; legs entirely dark; undertail coverts are buffy or whitish. Long undertail coverts give both Bay-breasted and Blackpoll a short-tailed look. Common to abundant; nests in open coniferous forests. Migrates earlier in fall than Blackpoll; most migration is east of dashed line on map. Regular vagrant in the west. Song consists of high-pitched double notes.

Blackpoll Warbler *Dendroica striata* *L 5¹/₂" (14 cm)*

Solid black cap, white cheeks, and white underparts identify breeding male; back and sides boldly streaked with black. Compare with Black-and-white Warbler (page 360). Female is duller overall, slightly greenish above; crown is streaked; breast or entire underparts are sometimes washed with yellow. Fall adults and immatures resemble Bay-breasted and Pine Warblers. Blackpoll is mostly pale greenish-yellow below, with dusky streaking on sides; legs pale on front and back, dark on sides; undertail coverts long and usually white. Common; nests in coniferous forests. Migrates later in fall than Bay-breasted Warbler. Most migration is east of dashed line on map, overland in spring, along and off coast in fall. Regular vagrant in the west. Song is a series of high *tseet* notes.

Pine Warbler *Dendroica pinus* *L 5¹/₂" (14 cm)*

Relatively large bill; short undertail coverts make tail look long; throat color extends onto sides of neck, setting off dark cheek patch. Male is greenish-olive above, without streaking; throat and breast yellow, with dark streaks on sides of breast; belly and undertail coverts white. Female is usually duller. Immature is brownish or brownish-olive above, with whitish wing bars and brownish tertial edges; male is dull yellow below, female largely white; both have brown wash on flanks. Common in pine forests and groves in summer; also in mixed woodlands in winter. Song is a twittering musical trill.

Palm Warbler *Dendroica palmarum* *L 5¹/₂" (14 cm)*

Breeding adult has chestnut cap, yellow eyebrow and throat, yellow undertail coverts, and streaked breast and sides. Eastern birds are yellow below, western birds mostly whitish. Fall adults and immatures are drab; underparts grayish except for yellow undertail coverts; eyebrow is whitish, dark eye line distinct; chestnut on crown largely obscured. Fairly common; nests in brush at edge of spruce bogs. During migration and winter, found in woodland borders, open brushy areas, marshes. Habitually wags its tail as it forages. Migrates chiefly east of dashed line on map, but regular on west coast in fall and winter. Song is a rapid buzzy trill.

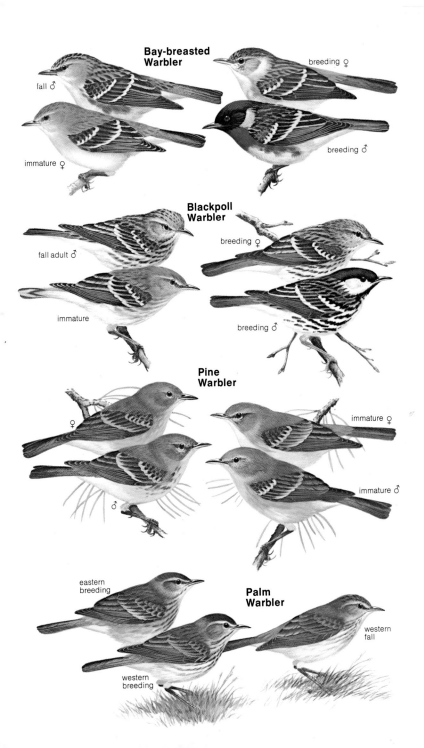

Bay-breasted Warbler

fall ♂

breeding ♀

immature ♀

breeding ♂

Blackpoll Warbler

fall adult ♂

breeding ♀

immature

breeding ♂

Pine Warbler

♀

immature ♀

♂

immature ♂

eastern breeding

Palm Warbler

western fall

western breeding

Yellow Warbler *Dendroica petechia* L 5" *(13 cm)*
Yellow overall; dark eye prominent in uniformly yellow face; reddish streaks below are distinct in male, faint or absent in female. Back, wings, and tail yellowish-olive, with yellow wing markings and tail spots. Northwestern birds are greener above. Immature male resembles adult female; immature female is much duller, almost gray in some subspecies. A plump, short-tailed warbler, common in wet habitats, especially in willows and alders; open woodlands, gardens, orchards. Frequently bobs its tail. Song is a clear, rapid, variable *sweet sweet sweet I'm so sweet*.

Mourning Warbler *Oporornis philadelphia* L 5¼" *(13 cm)*
Lack of bold white eye ring distinguishes adult male from Connecticut and MacGillivray's Warblers. Adult female and especially immatures may show a thin, nearly complete eye ring; compare with Connecticut. Immatures, especially females, generally have more yellow on throat than MacGillivray's; compare also with female Yellowthroat (page 376). Immature males usually show a little black on breast. Mourning Warbler's call is a flat, hollow *chip*. Song has two parts: a series of slurred two-note phrases followed by two or more lower phrases. Fairly common in dense undergrowth, thickets, moist woods; nests on the ground. Mourning Warblers hop; Connecticuts walk. Spring migration generally follows the Appalachians and the Mississippi River.

MacGillivray's Warbler *Oporornis tolmiei* L 5¼" *(13 cm)*
Bold white crescents above and below eye distinguish all plumages from male Mourning and all Connecticut Warblers. Crescents may be very hard to distinguish from the thin, nearly complete eye ring on female and immature Mourning Warblers. Immature MacGillivray's Warblers generally have grayer throat than immature Mournings and a fairly distinct breast band above yellow belly. Field identification is often difficult. Call is a sharp, harsh *tsik*. Song has two parts: a buzzy trill ending in a downslur. Fairly common; found in dense undergrowth; nests on the ground. MacGillivray's Warblers hop; Connecticuts walk.

Connecticut Warbler *Oporornis agilis* L 5¾" *(15 cm)*
Large eye with bold white eye ring conspicuous on male's gray hood and female's brown or gray-brown hood. Eye ring is sometimes slightly broken on one side only. Immature has a brownish hood and brownish breast band. A large, stocky warbler, noticeably larger than Mourning and MacGillivray's Warblers. Like Mourning, long undertail coverts give Connecticut a short-tailed, plump appearance. Uncommon; found in spruce bogs, moist woodlands; nests on the ground; generally feeds on the ground or on low limbs. Walks rather than hops. Loud, accelerating song repeats a brief series of explosive *beech-er* or *whip-ity* notes. Spring migration is chiefly west of the Appalachians.

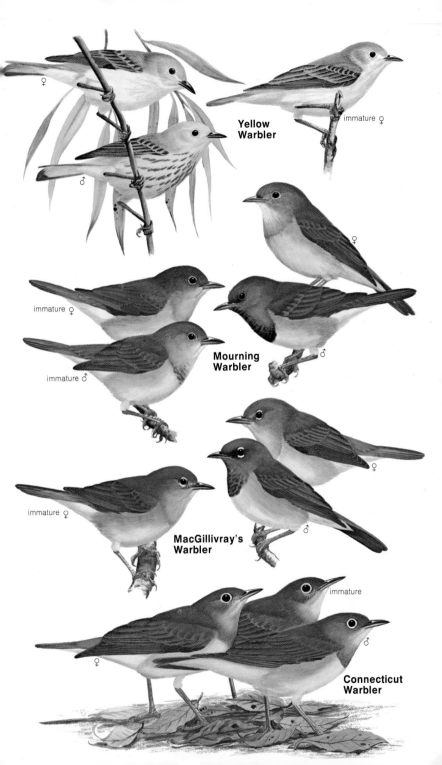

**Yellow
Warbler**

♀

immature ♀

♂

♀

immature ♀

immature ♂

**Mourning
Warbler**

♂

immature ♀

**MacGillivray's
Warbler**

♀

♂

immature

♀

♂

**Connecticut
Warbler**

Kentucky Warbler *Oporornis formosus* L 5¹/₄" (13 cm)
Bold yellow spectacles separate black crown from black on face and sides of neck; underparts are entirely yellow, upperparts bright olive. Black areas are duller on females. A short-tailed, long-legged warbler, common in rich, moist woodlands; nests and feeds on the ground in dense undergrowth. Song is a series of rolling musical notes, *churry churry churry,* much like the song of the Carolina Wren. Call is a low, sharp *chuck.* Winters from central Mexico to Venezuela; casual vagrant to California and the southwest.

Canada Warbler *Wilsonia canadensis* L 5¹/₄" (13 cm)
Black necklace on bright yellow breast identifies male; note also bold yellow spectacles. In female, necklace is dusky and indistinct. Male is blue-gray above, females duller. All birds have white undertail coverts. Common in dense woodlands and brush. Usually forages in undergrowth or low branches, but also seen fly-catching. Song begins with one or more short, sharp *chip* notes and continues as a rich and highly variable warble. Winters in South America. Casual fall migrant in the west; rare but regular along California coast.

Wilson's Warbler *Wilsonia pusilla* L 4³/₄" (12 cm)
Olive above; yellow below. Long tail is all-dark above and below, and often cocked. Male has yellow face, small black cap. In adult and immature female, cap is blackish or absent, forehead yellowish. Lack of white in tail helps distinguish female from female Hooded Warbler. Color of underparts varies geographically from bright yellow in the Pacific states (shown) to greenish-yellow in the east. Song is a rapid series of *chee* notes; common call, a sharp *chimp.* Fairly common, much more numerous in the west than in the east; nests in dense, moist woodlands, bogs, willow thickets, streamside tangles.

Hooded Warbler *Wilsonia citrina* L 5¹/₄" (13 cm)
Extensive black hood identifies male. Female shows blackish or olive crown and sides of neck; sometimes has black throat or black spots on breast. Note in both sexes that tail is white below; seen from above, white outer tail feathers are conspicuous as the bird flicks its tail open. Fairly common in swamps, moist woodlands; generally stays hidden in dense undergrowth and low branches. Sings loud, musical, whistled variations of *ta-wit ta-wit ta-wit tee-yo.* Calls include a flat, metallic *chink.* Rare migrant in the southwest and California; casual in other western states.

Kentucky Warbler

Canada Warbler

Hooded Warbler

Wilson's Warbler

Worm-eating Warbler *Helmitheros vermivorus*
L 5¹/₄" (13 cm) Bold, dark stripes on buffy-orange head; upperparts brownish-olive; underparts mostly buffy-orange; long, spike-like bill. Found chiefly in dense undergrowth on wooded slopes. Often feeds on branches in clusters of dead leaves. Song is a series of sharp, dry *chip* notes, like Chipping Sparrow's song but faster. Common call: *zeep-zeep*. Casual vagrant in California and the southwest.

Swainson's Warbler *Limnothlypis swainsonii*
L 5¹/₂" (14 cm) Pale eyebrow, conspicuous between brown crown and dark eye line. Brown-olive above, grayish below. Bill very long and spiky. Uncommon and secretive. Song is a series of thin, slurred whistles like song of Louisiana Waterthrush; often ends with a rising *tee-oh*. Calls include a loud, dry *chip*. Found in undergrowth in swamps, canebrakes; rare and local in mountain rhododendron.

Ovenbird *Seiurus aurocapillus* *L 6" (15 cm)*
Russet crown bordered by dark stripes; bold white eye ring. Olive above; white below, with bold streaks of dark spots; pinkish legs. A plump warbler, common in mature forests. Generally seen on the ground; walks, with tail cocked, rather than hops. Typical song is a loud *teacher teacher teacher,* rising in volume. Northern birds often sing a single-noted *teach teach teach*. Rare vagrant in the west. Casual in winter along Gulf and Atlantic coasts to North Carolina. Note small population along the Colorado Front Range.

Louisiana Waterthrush *Seiurus motacilla* *L 6" (15 cm)*
Distinguished from Northern Waterthrush by contrast between white underparts and salmon buff flanks; bicolored eyebrow, pale buff in front of eye, white and much broader behind eye; larger bill; bubblegum pink legs. Uncommon; found along mountain brooks and streams in dense woodlands, less often near ponds and in swamps. A ground dweller; walks, rather than hops, bobbing its tail constantly but usually slowly. Call note, a sharp *chink,* is slightly flatter than that of Northern Waterthrush. Song begins with three or four shrill, slurred notes followed by a brief, rapid jumble.

Northern Waterthrush *Seiurus noveboracensis*
L 5³/₄" (15 cm) Distinguished from Louisiana Waterthrush by lack of contrast in color between flanks and rest of underparts; buffy eyebrow, of even width throughout or slightly narrowing behind eye; smaller bill; drabber leg color. Some birds are whiter below, with whiter eyebrow. Found chiefly in woodland bogs, swamps, and thickets. A ground dweller; walks, rather than hops, bobbing its tail constantly and usually rapidly. Call note, a metallic *chink,* is slightly sharper than that of Louisiana Waterthrush. Song begins with loud, emphatic notes and ends in lower notes, with all notes evenly spaced.

Worm-eating Warbler

Swainson's Warbler

Ovenbird

Louisiana Waterthrush

Northern Waterthrush

Common Yellowthroat *Geothlypis trichas* L 5" (13 cm)

Adult male's broad black mask is bordered above by white, below by bright yellow throat and breast; undertail coverts yellow; upperparts dark olive. Female lacks black mask; face is olive, like crown, back, and wings, with whitish eye ring. Adults vary geographically in extent of yellow below, eastern birds generally showing less. Southwestern birds are brightest below and show the most yellow. Immatures are duller and browner overall. Young male's mask is less distinct than adult's. Abundant; stays low in grassy fields, shrubs, marshes; often holds tail cocked like a wren. Nests on the ground. Distinctive song is a loud, rolling *wichity wichity wichity wich.* Calls include a raspy *chuck,* similar to call of Marsh Wren.

Rufous-capped Warbler *Basileuterus rufifrons*

L 5¹⁄₄" (13 cm) Casual visitor from Mexico to the Big Bend area of Texas; accidental in southeastern Arizona. Dark olive above; reddish-brown crown and sides of head are crossed by a conspicuous white eyebrow. Throat and breast bright yellow; remainder of underparts whitish. Long tail, often held cocked like a wren. Inhabits dense brush and woodlands of foothills or low mountains, generally staying low in the undergrowth. Song begins with musical *chip* notes and accelerates into a series of dry, whistled warbles.

Golden-crowned Warbler *Basileuterus culicivorus*

L 5" (13 cm) Mexican species, casual in woodlands along the lower Rio Grande in south Texas, chiefly in winter. Resembles Orange-crowned Warbler (page 356) but crown shows a distinct yellow or buffy-orange central stripe, bordered in black; note also yellowish-green eyebrow, yellowish eye ring broken by dark eye line. Call is a rapidly repeated *tuck.*

Yellow-breasted Chat *Icteria virens* L 7¹⁄₂" (19 cm)

Our largest warbler. Long-tailed and thick-billed. White spectacles; white whisker stripe bordering bright yellow throat and breast. Belly and undertail coverts are white. Lores black in males, gray in females. For a short time during the breeding season, breast may become bright orange. Inhabits dense thickets and brush. Fairly common, but solitary and shy. Unmusical song, a jumble of harsh, chattering clucks, rattles, clear whistles, and squawks. Male sings from a conspicuous perch and also flutters up in brief, hovering display flight, legs dangling, wings beating slowly. Often sings at night. Regular straggler in fall in the Maritimes; casual in winter on the east coast.

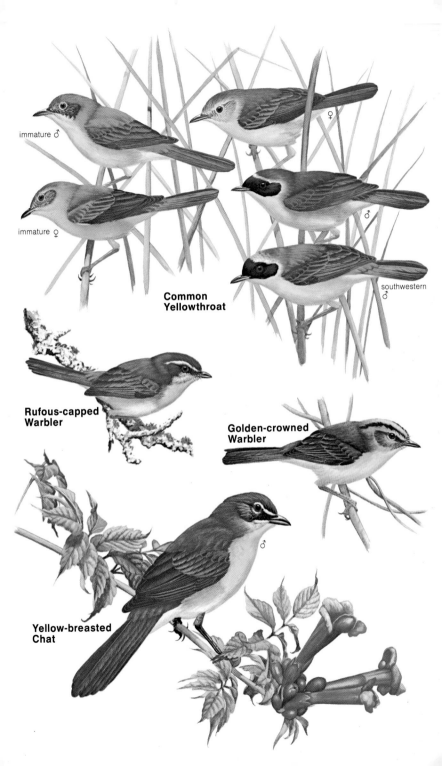

immature ♂

immature ♀

♀

♂

southwestern
♂

**Common
Yellowthroat**

**Rufous-capped
Warbler**

**Golden-crowned
Warbler**

**Yellow-breasted
Chat**

♂

American Redstart *Setophaga ruticilla* L 5¹/₄" (13 cm)

Male glossy black, with bright orange patches on sides, wings, tail; belly and undertail coverts white. Female is gray-olive above, white below with yellow patches. Immature resembles female. By first fall, young male's patches show some salmon; by first spring, breast has some black spotting; full adult male plumage is acquired by second fall. A common warbler in second-growth woodlands, small groves. Like other redstarts, actively pursues flying insects; often fans its tail and spreads its wings when perched, making the colorful patches conspicuous. Variable song, a series of high, thin notes usually followed by a wheezy, downslurred note. Rare to uncommon migrant in California and the southwest.

Slate-throated Redstart *Myioborus miniatus*

L 6" (15 cm) Middle and South American species, accidental in southeastern Arizona and southwestern New Mexico. Head, throat, and back are slate black, breast dark red. Chestnut crown patch visible only at close range. Lacks white wing patch of similar Painted Redstart; white on outer tail feathers less extensive. Found in pine-oak canyons, forests.

Painted Redstart *Myioborus pictus* L 5³/₄" (15 cm)

Bright red lower breast and belly; black head and upperparts; bold white wing patch. White outer tail feathers conspicuous as the bird fans its tail. Juvenile acquires full adult plumage by end of summer. Fairly common in pine-oak canyons, pinyon-juniper forests. Song is a series of rich liquid warbles; call, a clear, whistled *chee*. Very rare visitor in southern California.

Red-faced Warbler *Cardellina rubrifrons* L 5¹/₂" (14 cm)

Adult's red-black-and-white head pattern distinctive; back and tail gray, rump and underparts white. Juvenile is duller, face pinkish. A warbler of high mountains, generally found above 6,000 feet. Fairly common, especially in fir and spruce mixed with oaks. Nests on the ground. Song is a series of varied, ringing *zweet* notes. Casual to southern California.

Olive Warbler *Peucedramus taeniatus* L 5¹/₄" (13 cm)

Dark patch from bill to ear broadens behind eye. Long, thin bill, slightly downcurved. Two broad white wing bars; outer tail feathers extensively white. Adult male's head, throat, and nape tawny-brown. Female has olive crown, yellow face; pale yellow throat and breast. Juveniles and first-fall birds resemble female but are paler or whitish below; crown is gray. Young male's head shows some tawny color by first spring; full adult plumage is acquired by second fall. A Middle American species; range extends into high mountains of southwestern U. S.; generally found in the open coniferous forests of elevations above 7,000 feet. Nests and forages high in the trees. Typical song is a loud *peeta peeta peeta*, similar to call of Tufted Titmouse. Call is a soft, whistled *phew*.

378

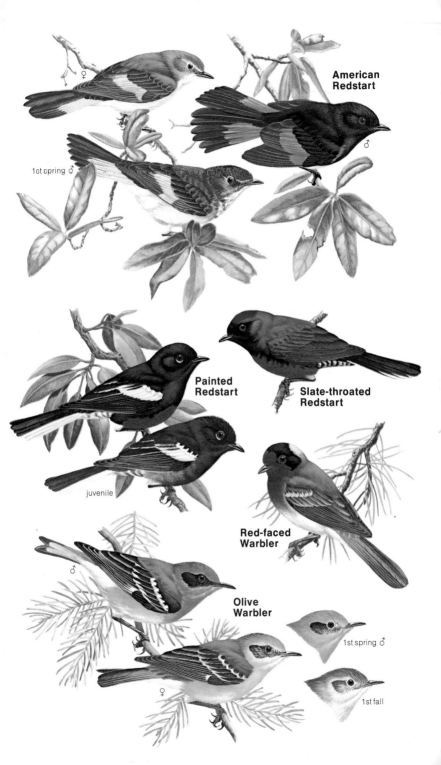

American Redstart

♀

1st spring ♂

♂

Painted Redstart

juvenile

Slate-throated Redstart

Red-faced Warbler

Olive Warbler

♂

♀

1st spring ♂

1st fall

Grosbeaks, Buntings, Sparrows

Widespread birds, all with conical bills. Some, such as cardinals, are conspicuous and bold. But many sparrows stay hidden except in spring, when males sing from more open perches.

Rose-breasted Grosbeak *Pheucticus ludovicianus*
L 8″ (20 cm) Large finch with a very large, triangular bill. Male has black head and back, rose red breast, white underparts, white wing bars, white rump. Rose red wing linings show in flight. Brown-tipped winter plumage is acquired before migration. Female's streaked plumage and yellow wing linings resemble female Black-headed Grosbeak, but underparts are more heavily and extensively streaked. Similar first-fall male is buffier above, with buffy wash across breast; often has a few red feathers on breast; red wing linings are also distinctive. The melodious, robin-like songs of the two species are similar. Rose-breasted Grosbeak's call, a sharp *eek*, is higher pitched and squeakier than the Black-headed's call. Common in open, second-growth woodlands and dense trees along water courses. Regular but rare throughout the west in migration. Annual in winter on southern California coast.

Black-headed Grosbeak *Pheucticus melanocephalus*
L 8¹⁄₄″ (21 cm) Large finch with a very large, triangular bill. Male has cinnamon underparts, all-black head. In flight, both sexes show yellow wing linings. Female plumage is generally buffier above and below than female Rose-breasted Grosbeak, with less streaking below; yellow wing linings distinguish her from similar first-fall male Rose-breasted. The first-fall male Black-headed is rich buff below, with little or no streaking. The melodious, robin-like songs of the two species are similar. Black-headed Grosbeak's call, a sharp *eek*, is lower pitched and less squeaky than Rose-breasted's call. Common in open woodlands, forest edges. Casual during migration and winter to the midwest and east. Hybridizes uncommonly with Rose-breasted in range of overlap in the Great Plains.

Yellow Grosbeak *Pheucticus chrysopeplus* L 9¹⁄₄″ (24 cm)
Mexican species, casual early-summer vagrant to southeastern Arizona, chiefly in open woodlands and river courses of foothills and mountains. Male distinguished by large size, massive bill, bright yellow plumage; black wings and tail with white patches. Female and immatures similar to male but duller; crown streaked. Compare with Evening Grosbeak (page 442).

Rose-breasted Grosbeak

breeding ♂

winter ♂

♂

1st fall ♂

1st spring ♂

♀

Black-headed Grosbeak

♀

♂

1st fall ♂

Yellow Grosbeak

♂

♀

Northern Cardinal *Cardinalis cardinalis* L 8³/₄" (22 cm)

Conspicuous crest; cone-shaped reddish bill. Male is red overall, with black face. Female is buffy-brown or buffy-olive, tinged with red on wings, crest, tail. Juvenile browner overall, bill dull brown; juvenile female lacks red tones. Bill shape helps distinguish female and juveniles from the similar Pyrrhuloxia. Abundant throughout the east, Cardinals inhabit woodland edges, swamps, streamside thickets, suburban gardens. Song is a loud, liquid whistling with many variations, including *cue cue cue* and *cheer cheer cheer* and *purty purty purty*. Both sexes sing almost year-round. Common call is a sharp *chink*. Nonmigratory, but this species has expanded its range northward during the 20th century; apparently also expanding southwest range slightly.

Pyrrhuloxia *Cardinalis sinuatus* L 8³/₄" (22 cm)

Thick, strongly curved bill helps distinguish this species from female and juvenile Northern Cardinal. Male is gray overall, with red on face, crest, wings, tail, underparts; bill orange-yellow. Female shows little or no red; bill is dull yellow. Fairly common in thorny brush and mesquite thickets of dry creek beds, desert, woodland edges, ranchlands. Song is a liquid whistle, thinner and shorter than song of Northern Cardinal. Call is a sharp *chink*. Casual to southeastern California.

Blue Grosbeak *Guiraca caerulea* L 6³/₄" (17 cm)

Wide chestnut wing bars, large heavy bill, and larger overall size distinguish male from male Indigo Bunting (next page). Females of these two species also similar; compare bill shape, wing bars, and overall size. Juvenile resembles female; in first fall, some immatures are richer brown than female. First-spring male shows some blue above and below; resembles adult male by second winter. In poor light, Blue Grosbeak resembles Brown-headed Cowbird (page 422); note bill shape and wing bars; also note Blue Grosbeak's habit of twitching and spreading its tail. Fairly common; found in low, overgrown fields, streamsides, woodland edges, brushy roadsides. Range expanding along Atlantic coast. Uncommon to rare in fall north to New England and the Maritime Provinces. Somewhat secretive; listen for distinctive call, a loud, explosive *chink*. Song is a series of rich rising and falling warbles.

Blue Bunting *Cyanocompsa parellina* L 5¹/₂" (14 cm)

Mexican species, rare in southern Texas, primarily in winter. Smaller than Blue Grosbeak; lacks wing bars. Male is dark blue overall, paler on crown, cheeks, shoulder, and rump. Contrasting colors and thick, strongly curved bill distinguish male from male Indigo Bunting (next page). Female distinguished by bill shape, overall richer color, and lack of streaking below. Found in brushy fields, woodland edges.

Northern Cardinal

juvenile ♂

♀

♂

Pyrrhuloxia

♀

♂

Blue Grosbeak

♂

♀

1st fall

Blue Bunting

♀

♂

1st spring ♂

Indigo Bunting *Passerina cyanea* L 5¹/₂" (14 cm)

Adult male deep blue. Smaller than Blue Grosbeak (preceding page); bill much smaller; lacks wing bars. In winter plumage, blue is obscured by brown and buff edges. Female is dull brown above, without obvious streaking; buffy below, breast diffusely streaked; wing bars may be indistinct. Closely resembles female Varied Bunting. Young birds resemble female. In late fall, young males molt to a plumage like winter adult male's; become mostly blue by first spring. Common in woodland clearings and borders, brushy pastures. Male sings well into August, later than most other singers. Song is a series of varied high-pitched phrases, usually paired. Range expanding in west and southwest.

Lazuli Bunting *Passerina amoena* L 5¹/₂" (14 cm)

Adult male bright turquoise above and on throat; breast and sides cinnamon; belly white. Two white wing bars, the upper bar wider. Compare with bluebirds (page 324). Female is grayish-brown above, rump grayish-blue; underparts white, with buffy wash on throat and breast. Juvenile resembles female but has distinct fine streaks across breast; immature male is mostly blue by first spring. Winter male's blue color is obscured by brown and buff edges. Found in open deciduous or mixed woodlands, chaparral, especially in brushy areas near water. Song is a series of varied phrases, sometimes paired; faster and less strident than Indigo Bunting's song. Hybrids of these two species occur in area of range overlap.

Painted Bunting *Passerina ciris* L 5¹/₂" (14 cm)

Adult male's gaudy colors are retained year-round. Female is bright green above, paler yellow-green below. Juvenile is much drabber; look for telltale hints of green above, yellow below. Molt to first-winter plumage begins during migration. First-winter male resembles adult female but colors are brighter; by spring, may show tinge of blue on head, red on breast. Locally common in low thickets, weedy tangles, streamside brush, woodland borders. Casual vagrant north on Atlantic coast to New York; west to California. Some of these sightings may be escaped cage birds. Song is a rapid series of varied phrases, thinner and sweeter than song of Lazuli Bunting. Distinctive call is a loud, rich *chip*.

Varied Bunting *Passerina versicolor* L 5¹/₂" (14 cm)

Spring adult male's plumage is colorful in good light; otherwise appears black. In winter, colors are edged with brown. Female is plain gray-brown or buffy-brown above, slightly paler below; closely resembles female Indigo Bunting. In close view, note that Varied Bunting's culmen is slightly curved; in Lazuli and Indigo Buntings, culmen is straighter. Positive field identification is, however, extremely difficult. First-spring male Varied Bunting resembles female. Locally common in thorny thickets in washes, canyons, often near water. Song is similar to song of Painted Bunting.

breeding ♀

late 1st fall ♂

winter adult ♂

**Indigo
Bunting**

1st spring ♂

breeding ♂

**Lazuli
Bunting**

♂

juvenile

♀

**Painted
Bunting**

1st spring ♂

♀

♂

**Varied
Bunting**

1st spring ♂

breeding ♂

winter ♂

♀

Olive Sparrow *Arremonops rufivirgatus* L 6¹/₄" (16 cm)

Mexican species, common in southernmost Texas in dense undergrowth, brushy areas, live oak. Dull olive above, with brown stripe on each side of crown. Lacks reddish cap of similar Green-tailed Towhee. Calls include a dry *chip* and a buzzy *speeee*. Song is an accelerating series of the *chip* notes.

Green-tailed Towhee *Pipilo chlorurus* L 7¹/₄" (18 cm)

Olive above with reddish crown, distinct white throat bordered by dark stripe and white stripe. Juvenile has two faint olive wing bars; plumage is streaked overall; upperparts tinged with olive; lacks reddish crown. Clear, whistled song begins with *weet-chur*, ends in raspy trill. Calls include a catlike *mew*. Fairly common in dense brush, chaparral, on mountainsides and high plateaus. Rare breeder in Guadalupe Mountains of west Texas. Casual in winter throughout the east.

Rufous-sided Towhee *Pipilo erythrophthalmus*
L 8¹/₂" (22 cm) Male's black upperparts and black hood contrast with chestnut sides, white underparts. White wing patches and white-cornered tail conspicuous in flight. Eastern females are brown above. In western forms, formerly known as Spotted Towhee, both sexes are spotted with white above, have two white wing bars. In southeastern birds, eye color varies from red-orange to, in Florida, white. All juveniles have dark streaks and spots but show adult wing pattern. Eastern birds' distinctive song sounds like *drink-your-tea-ee-ee-ee-ee*; call note, a rising *tow-whee* or *chee-wink*. Songs of western forms vary; call notes include a whining *chee-ee*. Common throughout breeding range in dense undergrowth, streamside thickets, forest edges, open woodlands. Nests on the ground. Like all species on this page, forages on the ground, scratching with both feet together.

Brown Towhee *Pipilo fuscus* L 8¹/₂" (22 cm)

Brown or gray-brown above, paler below; buffy throat bordered with dark streaks; undertail coverts rust. Pacific coast birds are dark with a brown crown. Interior populations are paler, with rust crown, dark spot on center of breast. Brown Towhees are common on brushy hillsides and wooded canyons; coastal birds are found in chaparral, suburban gardens. Song of interior birds is a mellow chipping trill; calls include a sharp *chiup*. Pacific birds' call is quite different, a metallic *chink;* song, an accelerating series of *chink* notes.

Abert's Towhee *Pipilo aberti* L 9¹/₂" (24 cm)

Black face; upperparts cinnamon brown, underparts paler, with cinnamon undertail coverts. Call is a sharp *peek;* song, a series of *peek* notes. Common within its range, but generally shy and secretive. Inhabits desert woodlands, streamside thickets, at lower altitudes than similar Brown Towhee. Also found in suburban yards, orchards.

Green-tailed Towhee

Olive Sparrow

immature

juvenile

western ♀

western ♂

eastern ♂

eastern juvenile

eastern ♀

Rufous-sided Towhee

interior

interior juvenile

Pacific coast

Abert's Towhee

Brown Towhee

Grasshopper Sparrow *Ammodramus savannarum*

L 5" (13 cm) Buffy breast and sides, usually without obvious streaking. A small, chunky bird with short tail, flat head. Dark crown has a pale central stripe; note also the white eye ring and, on most birds, the yellow-orange spot in front of eye. Lacks broad buffy-orange eyebrow and blue-gray ear patch of Le Conte's Sparrow (next page). Compare also with Savannah Sparrows, shown here and on page 392. Juvenile's breast and sides are streaked with brown. Immatures and winter adults are buffier below but never as bright as Le Conte's Sparrow. Subspecies vary in overall color from the dark Florida form, *A.s. floridanus,* to the pale, reddish *ammolegus* of southeastern Arizona. Eastern *pratensis* is somewhat darker, brighter, and bigger billed than the widespread *perpallidus,* found over most of the U.S. Fairly common in pastures, grasslands, palmetto scrub, old fields. Somewhat secretive; feeds and nests on the ground. Typical song is one or two high *chip* notes followed by a brief, grasshopper-like buzz; also sings a series of varied squeaky and buzzy notes.

Baird's Sparrow *Ammodramus bairdii* *L 5¹/₂" (14 cm)*

Head and nape rich buff with fine black streaks on nape and sides of crown and a plain, rich buff central crown stripe. Two dark stripes border each side of throat. Widely spaced dark streaks on breast form a distinct necklace. Note also chestnut on scapulars. Juvenile's head is paler, creamier; central crown stripe finely streaked; white fringes give a scaly appearance to upperparts; underparts more extensively streaked. Uncommon, local, and declining. Found in prairies, weedy fields. Secretive and hard to spot; when a bird is flushed, look for paler overall color and more white in tail than in Savannah Sparrow. Song consists of two or three high, thin notes, followed by a single warbled note and a low trill.

Henslow's Sparrow *Ammodramus henslowii*

L 5" (13 cm) Large flat head; large gray bill. Resembles Baird's Sparrow but head, nape, and most of central crown stripe are greenish; wings extensively dark chestnut. Juvenile is paler, yellower, with less streaking below; compare with adult Grasshopper Sparrow. Uncommon, local, and declining; found in wet shrubby fields, weedy meadows. In winter, found also in the understory of pine woods. Secretive, but after being flushed several times may perch in the open for a few minutes before dropping back into cover. Distinctive song, a short, quiet *se-lick,* accented on second syllable.

Grasshopper Sparrow

perpallidus

floridanus

pratensis juvenile

Savannah Sparrow
P. s. nevadensis
for comparison

pratensis

ammolegus

Baird's Sparrow

juvenile

juvenile

Henslow's Sparrow

Le Conte's Sparrow *Ammodramus leconteii* *L 5" (13 cm)*

White central crown stripe, becoming buffy at rear of crown, and chestnut streaks on nape distinguish Le Conte's from Sharp-tailed Sparrow. Bright, broad, buffy-orange eyebrow, blue-gray ear patch, thinner bill, and orange-buff breast and sides separate it from Grasshopper Sparrow (preceding page). Sides of breast and flanks have dark streaks. Juvenile plumage, seen only on breeding grounds, is tinged with buff overall; crown stripe is tawny, breast heavily streaked. A bird of wet grassy fields, marsh edges. Fairly common but secretive; scurries through matted grasses like a mouse. Song is a short, high, insectlike buzz. Casual migrant in the northeast and in California.

Sharp-tailed Sparrow *Ammodramus caudacutus*

L 5¹/₄" (13 cm) Gray central crown stripe and gray unstreaked nape distinguish all subspecies from Le Conte's Sparrow. Breast and sides buffy, with at least some streaking; belly white. Juveniles are buffy overall, streaked below; lack gray crown stripe. Adult plumages vary in overall coloration. In east coast forms such as *A.c. caudacutus,* face shows a bright orange triangle around a dark ear patch; breast is distinctly streaked. Northeast coast *subvirgatus* is duller, grayer. Inland forms such as the widespread *nelsoni* have a bright buff eyebrow, a more diffuse ear patch, and diffuse streaking below; most closely resemble Le Conte's Sparrow. Common but somewhat secretive. Found in salt marshes, lakeshores, often in spartina grass. Song is a short, raspy trill ending in one lower, clearer note. Rare in winter (*nelsoni*) to California; a few birds are present every winter in coastal estuaries.

Seaside Sparrow *Ammodramus maritimus* *L 6" (15 cm)*

Long, spike-like bill, thick-based and thin-tipped. Tail is short, pointed. Yellow lore patch; in some birds the color extends slightly above the eye. Dark whisker stripe separates whitish throat and broad, pale stripe along cheek. Breast is white or buffy, with at least some streaking. Juveniles are duller, browner, than adults. Seaside Sparrows vary widely in overall color. Most forms, like the widespread *A.m. maritimus,* are grayish-olive above. The greener *mirabilis,* formerly called Cape Sable Sparrow, inhabits a small area in southwest Florida. Gulf coast forms such as *fisheri* have buffier breasts. The darkest form, *nigrescens,* is blackish above, heavily streaked below; formerly called Dusky Seaside Sparrow, this subspecies was found only near Titusville, Florida, and is now apparently extinct in the wild. In general, Seaside Sparrows are fairly common in grassy tidal marshes; accidental inland. Song resembles that of Red-winged Blackbird but is buzzier.

Le Conte's Sparrow

juvenile

Sharp-tailed Sparrow

nelsoni

caudacutus juvenile

subvirgatus

caudacutus

maritimus

fisheri

nigrescens

maritimus juvenile

Seaside Sparrow

mirabilis

Vesper Sparrow *Pooecetes gramineus* L 6¼" (16 cm)

White eye ring; dark ear patch bordered in white along lower and rear edges; short, notched tail with white outer feathers. Lacks bold eyebrow of Savannah Sparrow. Distinctive chestnut shoulder patch not easily seen. Streaking across breast sometimes forms a central spot. Eastern birds are slightly darker overall than the most widespread subspecies, shown here. Fairly common in dry, open grasslands, farmlands, forest clearings, sagebrush. Song is rich and melodious, two long, slurred notes followed by two higher notes, then a series of varied, short, descending trills.

Savannah Sparrow *Passerculus sandwichensis*

L 5½" (14 cm) Highly variable. Most have yellow or whitish lores and eyebrow; pale crown stripe; dark whisker stripe. Upperparts streaked; tail short and notched. Sides and breast streaked, sometimes with a central spot; legs and feet pink. Savannah Sparrows are common in a variety of open habitats, marshes, grasslands. Song begins with two or three *chip* notes, followed by two buzzy trills, the second trill lower and briefer. Distinctive flight call, a thin *seep*. The numerous subspecies vary geographically in size, color, bill size, and extent of streaking. Extremes are shown here. Dark, heavily streaked *P. s. beldingi* inhabits southern California coastal marshes. Paler, small-billed *nevadensis* is typical of western interior forms. Eastern forms are intermediate. Largest form, *rostratus,* breeds on Colorado River delta, now rarely seen in U. S., chiefly at the Salton Sea; lacks streaking above; bill very large; breast streaking indistinct. Large, pale *princeps,* formerly called Ipswich Sparrow, breeds on Sable Island, Nova Scotia, winters along the east coast.

Song Sparrow *Melospiza melodia* L 6¼" (16 cm)

Highly variable. All subspecies have long, rounded tail, pumped in flight. All show broad grayish eyebrow and broad, dark stripe bordering whitish throat. Upperparts are usually streaked. Underparts whitish, with streaking on sides and breast that often converges in a central spot. Legs and feet are pinkish. Juvenile is buffier overall, with finer streaking; tail faintly barred. Generally common, Song Sparrows are found in brushy areas, especially dense streamside thickets. Typical song: three or four short clear notes followed by a buzzy *towwee,* then a trill. Distinctive call note, a nasal, hollow *chimp.* The numerous subspecies vary geographically in size, bill shape, overall coloration, and streaking. *M. m. melodia* typifies eastern forms; large Aleutian forms reach an extreme in the gray-brown *maxima;* paler forms such as *saltonis* inhabit southwestern deserts; *morphna* typifies the darker, redder forms of the Pacific northwest; *heermanni* is one of the dark California forms.

Vesper Sparrow

Savannah Sparrow

beldingi

rostratus

nevadensis

princeps

melodia juvenile

melodia

maxima

heermanni

Song Sparrow

morphna

saltonis

Lark Sparrow *Chondestes grammacus* L 6¹/₂" (17 cm)

Head pattern distinctive in adults; whitish underparts are marked only with dark central breast spot. Juvenile's colors are duller; breast, sides, and crown streaked. In all ages, white-cornered tail is conspicuous in flight. A large, plump sparrow, fairly common west of the Mississippi on prairies, roadsides, farmlands, open woodlands, mesas; nests on the ground. Often seen in flocks, especially in winter. Song begins with two loud, clear notes, followed by a series of rich, melodious notes and trills and unmusical buzzes. Call is a sharp *tsip,* often repeated as a rapid series. Formerly bred as far east as New York and Maryland; now local and irregular east of the Mississippi. Very rare on the east coast in fall and winter.

Black-throated Sparrow *Amphispiza bilineata*

L 5¹/₂" (14 cm) Black lores and triangular black patch on throat and breast contrast with white eyebrow, white whisker stripe, white underparts. Upperparts plain brownish-gray, without streaks or wing bars. Juvenile plumage, often held well into fall, lacks black on throat, but white eyebrow is conspicuous; breast and back finely streaked; wings show two indistinct buffy bars. In all ages, note that extent of white on tail is greater than in Sage Sparrow. Song is rapid, high-pitched, opening with two clear notes followed by a trill; calls are faint, tinkling notes. Fairly common in desert, especially on rocky slopes; casual to eastern U. S. in fall and winter.

Five-striped Sparrow *Amphispiza quinquestriata*

L 6" (15 cm) Mexican species; range barely reaches southeastern Arizona. Rare in breeding season; few winter records. Dark brown above; breast and sides gray; white throat bordered by black and white stripes. Dark central spot at base of breast. Juvenile lacks the streaks found on juveniles of other sparrows. Highly specialized habitat: tall, dense shrubs on rocky, semidesert hillsides, canyon slopes.

Sage Sparrow *Amphispiza belli* L 6¹/₄" (16 cm)

Gray-brown head sets off white eye ring, white lore spot or eyebrow, broad white moustachial stripe bordered by dark whisker stripe. Two pale wing bars; back buffy-brown with dusky streaks. White underparts, marked with dark central breast spot, dusky streaking on sides. Juvenile is duller overall and more heavily streaked; lore spot sometimes indistinct. Birds of the California coast are much darker overall. Fairly common on alkaline flats in sagebrush and saltbush; open arid desert in winter. Coastal form found in chaparral of slopes and foothills. The Sage Sparrow often runs from intruders, tail cocked up, rather than flying. Frequently twitches and waves its tail. From a low perch, male sings a jumbled, finch-like series of rising-and-falling phrases. Twittering call consists of thin, junco-like notes.

Lark Sparrow

juvenile

Five-striped Sparrow

Black-throated Sparrow

juvenile

coastal

Sage Sparrow

interior

interior juvenile

Bachman's Sparrow *Aimophila aestivalis* L 6" (15 cm)

A large sparrow with large bill, fairly flat forehead, and long, rounded, dark tail. Adults gray above, heavily streaked with chestnut or dark brown; sides of head buffy-gray; a thin dark line extends back from eye. Breast and sides buff or gray; belly whitish. Subspecies range in overall brightness from the reddish *A.a. illinoensis* of the western part of range to the grayer and darker *aestivalis* of the south. Birds from northeastern part of range are intermediate. Juvenile has a distinct eye ring; throat, breast, and sides are streaked. First-winter plumage usually retains some streaking. Inhabits dry open woods, especially pines; scrub palmetto. Secretive; best located and identified by song: one clear, whistled introductory note, followed by a variable trill or warble on a different pitch. Male sings from open perch; often heard in late summer when most other songbirds have stopped singing for the season. Northeastern range is steadily shrinking, for unknown reasons.

Botteri's Sparrow *Aimophila botterii* L 6" (15 cm)

A large, plain sparrow with large bill, fairly flat forehead; tail long, rounded, dusky-brown, lacking white tips and central barring of the very similar Cassin's Sparrow. Best located and identified by song: several high sharp *tsip* or *che-lik* notes, often followed by a short, accelerating, rattly trill. Upperparts streaked with dull black, rust or brown, and gray; underparts unstreaked; throat and belly whitish, breast and sides grayish-buff. Subspecies *A.b. arizonae* of southeastern Arizona is redder above; *texana* of extreme southern Texas is grayer above. Juvenile's belly is buffy; breast broadly streaked, sides narrowly streaked. Generally secretive; inhabits grasslands dotted with mesquite, cactus, brush. The *texana* form is declining because of habitat loss; now uncommon and local.

Cassin's Sparrow *Aimophila cassinii* L 6" (15 cm)

A large, drab sparrow, with large bill, fairly flat forehead. Long, rounded tail is dark gray-brown; distinctive white tips on outer feathers are most conspicuous in flight. In close view, look for dark bars on central tail feathers. Otherwise closely resembles Botteri's Sparrow. Best located and identified by song, often given in brief, fluttery song flight: typically a soft double whistle, a loud, sweet trill, a low whistle, and a final, slightly higher note. Also gives a trill of *pit* notes. Gray upperparts are streaked with dull black, brown, and variable amount of rust; underparts are grayish-white, usually with a few short streaks on the flanks. Juvenile is streaked below; paler overall than juvenile Botteri's. Secretive; inhabits arid grasslands with scattered shrubs, cactus, mesquite. Casual vagrant to the east and California.

aestivalis

illinoensis

illinoensis
juvenile

**Bachman's
Sparrow**

**Botteri's
Sparrow**

arizonae

arizonae
juvenile

texana

juvenile

**Cassin's
Sparrow**

Rufous-winged Sparrow *Aimophila carpalis*

L 5¾" (15 cm) Pale gray head marked with reddish eye line and two black whisker stripes on each side of face; sides of crown streaked with reddish-brown. Back is gray-brown, streaked with black; two whitish wing bars. Reddish lesser wing coverts distinctive but difficult to see in the field. Underparts grayish-white, without streaking. Tail long, rounded. Juvenile's facial stripes are less distinct; wing bars buffier; bill dark; breast and sides lightly streaked. Juvenile plumage may be held as late as November. Fairly common but local; found in flat areas of tall desert grass mixed with brush, cactus. Distinctive call note, a sharp, high *seep*. Variable song, several *chip* notes followed by an accelerating trill of *chip* or *sweet* notes.

Rufous-crowned Sparrow *Aimophila ruficeps*

L 6" (15 cm) Gray head with dark reddish crown, distinct whitish eye ring, rufous line extending back from eye, single black whisker stripe on each side of face. Gray-brown above, with reddish streaks; gray below; tail long, rounded. Lacks white wing bars of Chipping Sparrow (next page). Subspecies range in overall color from the paler, grayer interior form to the dark, reddish Pacific coast forms and pale, reddish Arizona forms. Juvenile buffier overall, dark brown above; breast and crown streaked; may show two pale wing bars. Locally common on rocky hillsides and steep brushy or grassy slopes. Distinctive call, a sharp *dear,* usually given in a series; song, a rapid, bubbling series of *chip* notes.

American Tree Sparrow *Spizella arborea* *L 6¼" (16 cm)*

Gray head and nape crowned with rufous; rufous stripe behind eye; diffuse rufous whisker stripe. Gray throat and breast, with dark central spot, rufous patches at sides of breast. Back and scapulars streaked with black and rufous. Two bold white wing bars. Tail notched; outer feathers thinly edged in white. Underparts grayish-white with buffy sides. Juvenile and winter birds are buffier. In winter adult, rufous crown obscured by gray and buff edges, sometimes forming a central stripe. Juvenile is streaked above and below. Western populations are paler overall. Fairly common. Breeds along edge of tundra, in open areas with scattered trees, brush. Winters in weedy fields, marshes, groves of small trees. Distinguished in mixed flocks by musical *teedle-eet* call. Song usually begins with several clear *seet* notes followed by a variable rapid warble.

Field Sparrow *Spizella pusilla* *L 5¾" (15 cm)*

Gray face with reddish crown, distinct whitish eye ring, bright pink bill. Back streaked except on gray-brown rump. Two white wing bars. Breast and sides buffy-red; belly grayish-white; legs pink. Notched brown tail, edged with gray. Juvenile is streaked below; wing bars buffy. Birds in westernmost part of range are paler and grayer; extremes are shown here. Fairly common in open, brushy woodlands, fields. Song is a series of clear, plaintive whistles accelerating into a trill.

398

Rufous-winged Sparrow

juvenile

Rufous-crowned Sparrow

coastal

interior

coastal juvenile

American Tree Sparrow

juvenile

breeding

winter

Field Sparrow

eastern juvenile

eastern

western

Chipping Sparrow *Spizella passerina* L 5¹/₂" (14 cm)

Breeding adult identified by bright chestnut crown, distinct white eyebrow, and black line extending from bill through eye to ear; note also the gray nape and ear patch; gray unstreaked rump; and two white wing bars. Tail is fairly long and notched. Winter adult has brown ear patch, dark lores, and streaked crown showing some rufous color. First-winter bird is similar but averages less rufous on the crown; breast and sides are tinged with buff. In juvenile plumage, often held into October, the underparts are prominently streaked; crown usually lacks rufous; rump may show slight streaking. Widespread and common, Chipping Sparrows are found on lawns and in grassy fields, woodland edges, and ponderosa forests. Song is a rapid trill of dry *chip* notes, all on one pitch. Common call is a high, hard *seep*.

Clay-colored Sparrow *Spizella pallida* L 5¹/₂" (14 cm)

Brown crown with black streaks and a distinct buffy-white or whitish central stripe. Broad, whitish eyebrow; brown ear patch sharply outlined in blackish-brown; pale lores; conspicuous pale stripe between ear patch and dark whisker stripe. Nape gray; back and scapulars are buffy-brown, with dark streaks; rump is not streaked but color does not contrast with back as in Chipping Sparrow. Tail fairly long, sharply notched. Adult in fall and winter is buffier overall. Juvenile and immature birds are much buffier; gray nape and pale stripe on sides of throat are more conspicuous; in juvenile, breast and sides are streaked. Fairly common in brushy fields, groves, streamside thickets. Winters primarily from Mexico south, uncommonly in southern and western Texas. Rare in fall, casual in winter and spring on both coasts and in Arizona. Song is a brief series of insectlike buzzes. Call is a thin *seep*.

Brewer's Sparrow *Spizella breweri* L 5¹/₂" (14 cm)

Brown crown with fine black streaks; lacks pale central stripe of Clay-colored Sparrow. Distinct white eye ring; grayish-white eyebrow; ear patch pale brown with darker borders; pale lores; dark whisker stripe. Head pattern lacks the strong contrast of Clay-colored Sparrow. Upperparts buffy-brown and streaked; rump buffy-brown, may be lightly streaked. Tail fairly long and notched. Juvenile is buffier overall, lightly streaked on breast and sides. Immature and fall and winter adult are somewhat buffy below. Common; breeds in mountain meadows, sagebrush flats. Song is a series of varied bubbling notes and buzzy trills at different pitches. Call is a thin *seep*, like call of Clay-colored Sparrow.

Chipping Sparrow

breeding

winter

juvenile

1st winter

Clay-colored Sparrow

immature

juvenile

breeding

Brewer's Sparrow

breeding

juvenile

Black-chinned Sparrow *Spizella atrogularis*

L 5¾" (15 cm) Medium gray overall; back and scapulars rusty, with black streaks; bill bright pink. Male has black lores and chin; lower belly is whitish-gray; tail all-dark. Female lacks black in lores; black on chin is less extensive, duller, or absent. Juvenile and winter adults lack any black on face. Juvenile resembles adult female but underparts are paler and lightly streaked. Inhabits brushy arid slopes in foothills and mountains. Plaintive song begins with slow *sweet sweet sweet* and continues in a rapid trill. Call is a high, thin *seep*.

Dark-eyed Junco *Junco hyemalis* L 6¼" (16 cm)

Variable; most forms have a gray or brown head and breast sharply set off from white belly. White outer tail feathers are conspicuous in flight. Formerly separated into four species. Male of the widespread "Slate-colored" form has a dark gray hood; upperparts are entirely gray or have varying amount of brown at center of back. Female is brownish-gray overall. Winters mostly in eastern U. S.; uncommon in the west. Male "Oregon Junco" of the west has blackish hood, reddish-brown back, buffy-orange sides; females generally drabber, browner. Pink-sided form of "Oregon Junco" breeding in the central Rockies has bright pinkish-cinnamon sides, blue-gray hood and black lores. "Oregon" types winter mainly in the west; casual during winter in the east. The "White-winged" form breeding in the Black Hills area is blue-gray above, usually with two white wing bars. In the "Gray-headed Junco" of the southern Rockies, pale gray hood is barely darker than underparts; back is bright rufous. In Arizona and much of New Mexico, breeding "Gray-headed" form has an even paler throat and a large, bicolored bill, black above, bluish below. Intergrades of some forms are common. Dark-eyed Juncos breed in coniferous or mixed woodlands. In migration and winter, found in a wide variety of habitats. Song is a musical trill on one pitch, often heard in winter. Varied calls include a sharp *dit* and, in flight, a rapid twittering.

Yellow-eyed Junco *Junco phaeonotus* L 6¼" (16 cm)

Bright yellow eyes, set off by black lores. Pale gray above, with a bright rufous back and rufous-edged greater wing coverts and tertials; underparts paler gray. Juvenile Yellow-eyed is similar to gray-headed forms of Dark-eyed Junco; eye is brown, becoming pale before changing to yellow of adult; look for rufous on wings. Yellow-eyed Junco is found on coniferous and pine-oak slopes, generally above 6,000 feet. Song is a variable series of clear, thin whistles and trills. Calls include a high, thin *tseet*, similar to call of Chipping Sparrow.

Black-chinned Sparrow

♀

♂

juvenile

Dark-eyed Junco

♀ "Slate-colored"

♂

juvenile

"Oregon"

♀

♂

♂

"White-winged"

"Oregon" pink-sided

"Gray-headed"

♂

♂

Yellow-eyed Junco

juvenile

♂

Harris' Sparrow *Zonotrichia querula* L 7¹/₂" (19 cm)

A large sparrow with black crown, face, and bib; pink bill. Winter adult's crown is blackish; cheeks buffy; throat may be all-black or show white flecks or partial white band. Immature resembles winter adult but shows less black; white throat is bordered by dark whisker stripe. Fairly common; nests in stunted boreal forest; winters in open woodlands, brushlands. Rare in winter in rest of U. S. outside mapped range. Song is a series of long, clear, quavering whistles, often beginning with two notes on one pitch followed by two notes on another pitch. Calls include a loud *wink* and a drawn-out *tseep*.

White-throated Sparrow *Zonotrichia albicollis*

L 6³/₄" (17 cm) Conspicuous and strongly outlined white throat; mostly dark bill; dark crown stripes and eye line. Broad eyebrow is yellow in front of eye; remainder is either white or tan. Upperparts rusty-brown; underparts grayish, sometimes with diffuse streaking. Juvenile's eyebrow and throat are grayish, breast and sides heavily streaked. Common in woodland undergrowth, brush, gardens. Hunched, short-necked posture is unlike the erect stance of White-crowned Sparrow. Song is a thin whistle, generally two single notes followed by three triple notes: *pure sweet Canada Canada Canada,* often heard in winter. Calls include a sharp *pink* and a lisping *tseet*.

White-crowned Sparrow *Zonotrichia leucophrys*

L 7" (18 cm) Black-and-white striped crown; pink, orange, or yellowish bill; whitish throat; underparts mostly gray. Juvenile's head is brown and buff, underparts streaked. Immature has pale eyebrow; compare with immature Golden-crowned Sparrow. Forms of the High Sierra, Rockies, and the Canadian tundra, such as *Z.l. leucophrys,* have black lores, large pink bill; *gambelii,* ranging from Alaska to Hudson Bay, has whitish lores and a smaller, orange-yellow bill; in coastal forms such as *nuttalli,* breast and back are browner, bill duller, lores whitish. Common in open woodlands, brushy grasslands, roadsides, parks. Song variable; usually one or more thin whistled notes followed by a twittering trill. Calls include a loud *pink* and sharp *tseep*.

Golden-crowned Sparrow *Zonotrichia atricapilla*

L 7" (18 cm) Yellow patch tops black crown; back brownish, streaked with dark brown; breast, sides and flanks grayish-brown. Bill is dusky above, pale below. Yellow is less distinct on immature's brown crown. Briefly held juvenile plumage has dark streaks on breast and sides. Winter adults are duller overall; amount of black on crown varies. Fairly common in stunted boreal bogs and in open areas near tree line, especially in willows. Winters in dense woodlands, tangles, and brush. Casual in winter in the east. Song is a series of three or more plaintive, whistled notes: *oh dear me*. Calls include a soft *tseep* and a flat *tsick*.

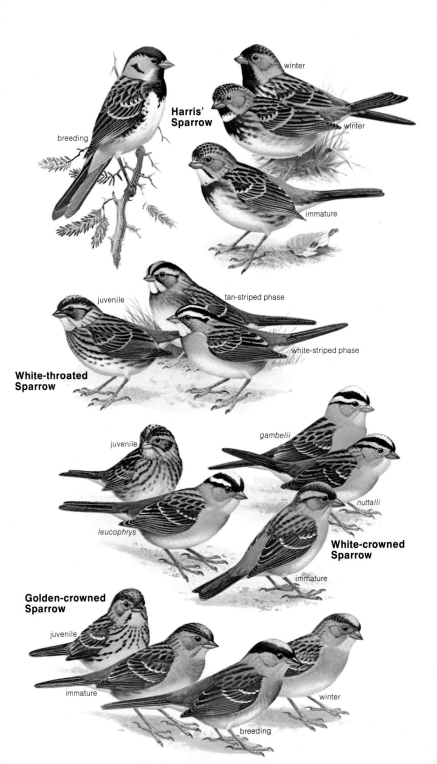

Harris' Sparrow

breeding

winter

winter

immature

White-throated Sparrow

juvenile

tan-striped phase

white-striped phase

juvenile

gambelii

leucophrys

nuttalli

White-crowned Sparrow

immature

Golden-crowned Sparrow

juvenile

immature

breeding

winter

Fox Sparrow *Passerella iliaca* L 7" (18 cm)
Highly variable. Most subspecies have reddish rump and tail; reddish in wings; and underparts heavily marked with triangular spots merging into a larger spot on central breast. Compare with Hermit Thrush (page 326); note especially bill shapes. Common; found in dense undergrowth in coniferous or mixed woodlands, chaparral. Loud, rich song, usually a few clear whistles followed by varied short buzzy trills. Reddish (fox-colored) subspecies breed across northern Canada and Alaska. The brightest, *P.i. iliaca,* breeds and winters chiefly in the east. The drabbest, *altivagans,* breeds in western Canada on eastern flank of Rockies, winters in the west. Birds of the western mountains have gray head and back, vary from small-billed Rockies forms such as *schistacea* to large-billed California forms such as *stephensi.* Dark coastal forms range from the sooty *fuliginosa* of the Pacific northwest to the paler *unalaschcensis* of southwest Alaska.

Lincoln's Sparrow *Melospiza lincolnii* L 5³/₄" (15 cm)
Buffy wash and fine streaks on breast and sides, contrasting with whitish, unstreaked belly. Gray central crown stripe, bordered by reddish-brown stripes; broad gray eyebrow; distinct buffy eye ring. Streaks on breast sometimes merge into a central spot. Briefly held juvenile plumage is paler overall than juvenile Swamp Sparrow. Distinguished from juvenile Song Sparrow (page 392) by slimmer bill and thinner whisker streak, often broken. A short-tailed sparrow, found in brushy bogs and mountain meadows; in winter prefers thickets, hedgerows, brambles. Somewhat shy; often raises slight crest when disturbed. Two call notes: a flat *tschup,* repeated in a series as an alarm call; and a sharp, buzzy *zeee.* Lincoln's and Swamp are the only sparrows that give a *zeee* call. Rich, loud song, a rapid bubbling trill.

Swamp Sparrow *Melospiza georgiana* L 5³/₄" (15 cm)
Gray face; rich rufous upperparts and wings; variable black streaks on back; white throat. Breeding adult has reddish crown, gray breast, whitish belly. Winter adult is buffier overall; crown is streaked, shows gray central stripe; sides are rich buff. Briefly held juvenile plumage is usually even buffier; darker overall than juvenile Lincoln's or Song Sparrow; wings and tail redder. First-summer plumage resembles winter adult. Fairly common but somewhat shy. Pumps tail in flight, as do other *Melospiza* sparrows. Nests in dense, tall vegetation in fresh and brackish marshes, swamps, streams. Winters in marshes, brushy fields, woodland edges. Typical song is a slow, musical trill, all on one pitch. Two call notes: a prolonged *zeee,* softer than call of Lincoln's Sparrow; and a metallic *chip,* like the call of an Eastern Phoebe.

unalaschcensis

Fox Sparrow

fuliginosa

schistacea

stephensi

altivagans

iliaca

Lincoln's Sparrow

juvenile

breeding

Swamp Sparrow

winter

juvenile

immature

Chestnut-collared Longspur *Calcarius ornatus*

L 6" (15 cm) White tail marked with blackish triangle. Wings short, rounded; in perched bird, wing tips barely extend to base of tail. Breeding adult male's black-and-white head, buffy face, and black underparts are distinctive; a few have chestnut on underparts. Lower belly and undertail coverts whitish. Upperparts black, buff, and brown, with chestnut collar, whitish wing bars. Winter males are paler; feathers edged in buff and brown, obscuring black underparts. Male has small white patch on shoulder; compare with Smith's Longspur (next page). Breeding adult female resembles winter female but is somewhat paler, usually shows some chestnut on nape. Juvenile's pale feather edgings give upperparts a scaled look; tail pattern and bill shape distinguish juvenile from juvenile McCown's Longspur. Fall and winter birds have grayish, not pinkish, bills. Fairly common; nests in moist upland prairies. Somewhat shy; generally found in dense grass, singly or in small flocks. Song, heard only on breeding grounds, is a pleasant rapid warble, given in song flight or from a low perch. Distinctive call, a two-syllable *kittle,* repeated two to five times. Also gives a soft, high-pitched rattle and a short *buzz* call. Casual during migration and winter on the east coast; more common on the west coast.

McCown's Longspur *Calcarius mccownii* *L 6" (15 cm)*

White tail marked by dark inverted T-shape. Note also that bill is stouter and thicker based than bills of other longspurs. Wings are pointed and longer than in Chestnut-collared Longspur; in perched bird, wings extend almost to tip of short tail. Breeding adult male has black crown, black whisker stripe, black crescent on breast; gray sides. Upperparts streaked with buff and brown, with gray nape, gray rump, bright chestnut wing patch. Breeding adult female has streaked crown; may lack black on breast and show less chestnut on wing. In winter adults, bill is pinkish with dark tip; feathers are edged with buff and brown. Winter adult female is paler than female Chestnut-collared, with fewer streaks on underparts and a broader buffy eyebrow. Winter male's gray rump is conspicuous; breast may show little or no black. Juvenile resembles adult female but is buffier below, with streaked breast; shows two buffy-white wing bars; pale edgings on feathers give upperparts a scaled look. Tail pattern and bill shape distinguish juvenile from juvenile Chestnut-collared Longspur. Fairly common but has declined; nests in dry shortgrass plains; in winter, also found in plowed fields, dry lake beds, often amid large flocks of Horned Larks. Look for McCown's chunkier, shorter tailed shape, slightly darker plumage, mostly white tail, thicker bill, and undulating flight. Song, heard only on breeding grounds, is a series of exuberant warbles and twitters, generally given in song flight. Calls include a dry rattle similar to calls of Smith's and Lapland Longspurs. Casual in fall and winter on the west coast, accidental on the east coast.

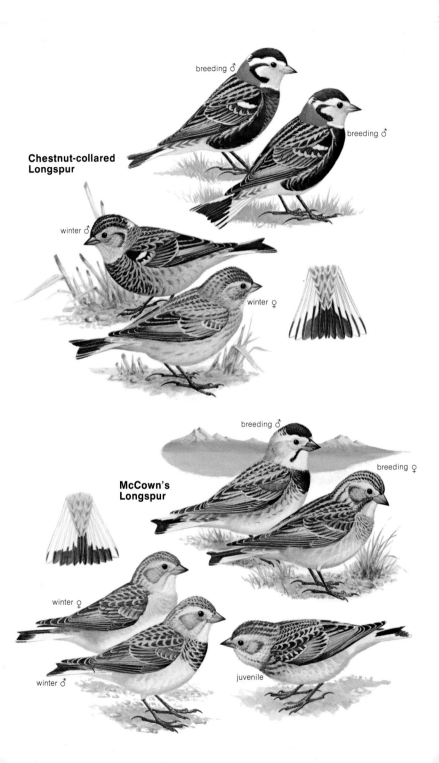

Chestnut-collared Longspur

breeding ♂

breeding ♂

winter ♂

winter ♀

McCown's Longspur

breeding ♂

breeding ♀

winter ♀

winter ♂

juvenile

Smith's Longspur *Calcarius pictus* *L 6¹/₄" (16 cm)*

Outer two feathers on each side of tail are almost entirely white. Bill is thinner than in other longspurs. Breeding adult male has black-and-white head, rich buff nape and under-parts; white patch on shoulder, often obscured. Breeding adult female and all winter plumages are duller; crown streaked; chin paler; dusky ear patch is bordered by pale buff eyebrow; underparts pale buff with thin reddish-brown streaks on breast and sides. Generally uncommon, solitary, and highly secretive, especially in migration and winter. Nests on open tundra and damp, tussocky meadows. Winters in open, grassy areas; sometimes seen with Lapland Longspurs. Regular spring migrant in the midwest, east to Illinois. Casual vagrant on east coast from Massachusetts to South Carolina. Typical call is a dry, ticking rattle, harder and sharper than call of Lapland and McCown's Longspurs. Song, heard only on the breeding grounds, combines ticking notes and rapid, melodious warbles, ending with a vigorous *wee-chew*.

Lapland Longspur *Calcarius lapponicus* *L 6¹/₄" (16 cm)*

Outer two feathers on each side of tail are partly white, partly dark. Note also, especially in winter plumages, the reddish edges on tertials and greater coverts. Breeding adult male's head and breast are black; broad white or buffy stripe extends back from eye and down to sides of breast; nape reddish-brown. Breeding adult female and all winter plumages are duller; note dark triangle outlining buffy ear patch, dark streaks or patch on upper breast, dark streaks on side. On all winter birds, note broad buffy eyebrow and buffier underparts; belly and undertail are white, unlike Smith's Longspur; also compare head and wing patterns. Juvenile is yellowish and heavily streaked above and on breast and sides. Fairly common, Lapland Longspurs breed on arctic tundra, winter in grassy fields, grain stubble, and on shores. Often found amid flocks of Horned Larks and Snow Buntings; look for Lapland's darker overall coloring and smaller size. Song, heard only on the breeding grounds, is a rapid warbling, given chiefly in short flights. Calls include a musical *tee-lee-oo* and, in flight, a dry rattle distinctively mixed with *tew* notes.

Smith's Longspur

breeding ♂

breeding ♀

winter ♂

Lapland Longspur

breeding ♂

breeding ♀

winter ♂

winter ♀

juvenile

immature ♀

Snow Bunting *Plectrophenax nivalis* *L 6¾" (17 cm)*

Rust and pale edgings of adult winter plumage wear off by spring, producing black-and-white breeding plumage. Bill is black in summer, orange-yellow in winter. In all seasons, note long black-and-white wings. Males usually show more white overall than females, especially in the wings. Juvenile is grayish and streaked, with buffy eye ring; very similar to juvenile McKay's Bunting. First-winter plumage, acquired before migration, is darker overall than adult; rust and brown edges wear away by spring to full adult plumage. Fairly common; breeds on tundra, rocky shores, talus slopes. During migration and winter, found on shores, especially sand dunes and beaches, and in weedy fields, grain stubble, along roadsides, often in large flocks that may include Lapland Longspurs and Horned Larks. Calls include a sharp, whistled *tew*, a short buzz, and a musical rattle or twitter. Song, heard only on the breeding grounds, is a loud, high-pitched musical warbling.

McKay's Bunting *Plectrophenax hyperboreus*

L 6¾" (17 cm) Adult breeding plumage mostly white, with less black on wings and tail than on Snow Bunting. Winter plumage edged with rust or tawny-brown, but still whiter overall than Snow Bunting. Juvenile is buffy-gray and streaked, with gray head, prominent buffy eye ring; very similar to juvenile Snow Bunting. McKay's is known to breed only on islands in the Bering Sea. Rare to uncommon in winter along west coast of Alaska; casual in winter southward and on Aleutians. Calls and song similar to Snow Bunting. Some authorities consider McKay's to be a subspecies of Snow Bunting.

Rustic Bunting *Emberiza rustica* *L 5¾" (15 cm)*

Eurasian species; winters in China and Japan; uncommon spring migrant on western and central Aleutians, rare in fall; casual spring visitor on St. Lawrence Island; accidental elsewhere along west coast. Both sexes have a slight crest, a whitish nape spot, and a whitish line extending back from eye. Male has black head; upperparts bright chestnut, streaked on back with buff and blackish; outer tail feathers white; underparts white, with chestnut breast band, streaks on sides. Female and fall and winter males have brownish head pattern. Female may be confused with Little Bunting (next page); note Rustic Bunting's larger size, heavier bill with pink lower mandible, diffuse rusty streaking below, and lack of eye ring. Call note is a hard, sharp *jit* or *tsip*. Song, a soft, bubbling warble.

breeding ♂

breeding ♂

winter ♀

breeding ♀

winter ♂

Snow Bunting

juvenile

winter ♀

winter ♂

breeding ♀

McKay's Bunting

breeding ♂

breeding ♂

winter ♂

Rustic Bunting

♀

breeding ♂

Common Reed-Bunting *Emberiza schoeniclus*

L 6" (15 cm) Eurasian species, casual vagrant on westernmost Aleutians in late spring. Solid chestnut lesser wing coverts distinctive in all plumages. Note also heavy bill, with curved culmen. Male in breeding plumage has black head and throat, a broad white moustachial stripe, and white nape; upperparts streaked black and rust, rump gray. Underparts white with thin reddish streaks along sides and flanks. Female has pale brownish rump, broad buffy-white eyebrow; dark lower border on ear patch extends forward to lower mandible; compare with female Pallas' Reed-Bunting. Fall male resembles female, but shows black on throat and a more distinct collar. Active and conspicuous, the Common Reed-Bunting often flicks and fans its tail, showing white outer tail feathers. Song is a series of squeaky notes, *tweak tweak tweak tititick*. Distinctive call, a clear, plaintive, upslurred *tseep*.

Pallas' Reed-Bunting *Emberiza pallasi* *L 5¹/₂" (14 cm)*

Asian species, casual spring vagrant in northwestern Alaska. Distinguished from the Common Reed-Bunting by smaller bill with straighter culmen, grayish lesser wing coverts. Breeding male has black and pearl gray streaks on back, two whitish wing bars. Female's buffy-brown ear patch usually has dark border only on lower rear corner. Like the Common Reed-Bunting, Pallas' often flicks and fans its tail, showing white outer feathers; note that tail is shorter than in Common Reed-Bunting. Song is a series of double notes, *tsi-tsi tsi-tsi tsi-tsi*. Distinctive call, a three-note *pee-see-oo*.

Little Bunting *Emberiza pusilla* *L 4³/₄" (12 cm)*

Eurasian species, accidental fall vagrant on the Aleutians and off northwestern Alaska. A small, short-legged, short-tailed bunting with a small triangular bill, bold creamy-white eye ring, chestnut ear patch, and two thin pale wing bars. Underparts whitish and heavily streaked. Outer tail feathers are white, but this species does not usually fan its tail. In breeding plumage, shows chestnut crown stripe bordered by black stripes. Many males show chestnut on chin. Immatures and winter adults have chestnut crown, tipped and streaked with buff and black; compare especially with female Rustic Bunting (preceding page) and female Common Reed-Bunting. Call note is a sharp *tsick*.

Gray Bunting *Emberiza variabilis* *L 6³/₄" (17 cm)*

Asian species, accidental spring vagrant on western Aleutians. A large, heavy-billed bunting; shows no white in tail. Breeding male is gray overall, prominently streaked with blackish above. Winter males are a bit browner above, paler below. Adult female is brown; chestnut rump is conspicuous in flight. Immature male resembles adult female above but is mostly gray below with some gray on the head; immature plumage is largely held through first spring.

**Common
Reed-Bunting**

fall ♂

♀

breeding ♂

♀

breeding ♂

**Pallas'
Reed-Bunting**

**Little
Bunting**

immature

breeding ♂

**Gray
Bunting**

immature ♂

breeding ♂

♀

Black-faced Grassquit *Tiaris bicolor* L 4¹/₂″ (11 cm)

West Indian species; accidental stray to south Florida. Adult male mostly black below, dark olive above; head is black. Female and immatures pale gray below, gray-olive above. Song is a buzzing *tik-zeee;* call, a lisping *tst.* Look for this species in winter flocks of Indigo Buntings.

White-collared Seedeater *Sporophila torqueola*

L 4¹/₂″ (11 cm) Mexican species, rare winter visitor to lower Rio Grande Valley, chiefly in San Ygnacio area. Tiny finch with thick, short, strongly curved bill; rounded tail. Adult male has black cap; white crescent below eye; incomplete buffy collar, often indistinct; may show some black on sides of neck; two white wing bars; white patch at base of primaries; underparts bright buff. Female and immatures are paler, lack cap and collar; wing bars are buffy or whitish. Compare with female Lazuli Bunting (page 384). Found in open grassy areas, brushlands. Song is pitched high, then low, a variable *sweet sweet sweet sweet cheer cheer cheer*. Calls include a distinct, high *wink*. Brighter subspecies seen in Texas and California are probably escaped cage birds.

Dickcissel *Spiza americana* L 6¹/₄″ (16 cm)

Yellowish eyebrow, thick bill, and chestnut wing coverts identify this finch in all plumages. Breeding male has black bib under white chin, bright yellow breast. Female lacks black bib, but has some yellow on breast; chestnut wing patch muted. Winter adult male's bib is less distinct. Immatures are duller overall than adults, flanks lightly streaked; female may show almost no yellow or chestnut. The Dickcissel breeds in open weedy meadows, grainfields, prairies. Abundant and gregarious, especially in migration, but numbers vary locally from year to year. Occurrence east of the Appalachians is spotty; population there is shrinking, although occasional breeding is reported north and south of area on map. Rare migrant and winter visitor to both coasts; more common in the east. Common call, often given in flight, is a distinctive electric-buzzer *bzrrrrt*. Song, a variable *dick dick dickcissel*.

Lark Bunting *Calamospiza melanocorys* L 7″ (18 cm)

A stocky, short-tailed bird. Breeding male is mostly black, with contrasting white patch on inner wings and under tip of tail; bill is heavy, bluish-gray. Female is streaked grayish-brown above; white below, with brown streaks, buffy sides. Immatures resemble adult female. Winter adult male looks similar, but grayer overall; retains black on chin. By late winter, underparts show some black; most males are patchy looking until late spring. Common; nests in dry plains and prairies, especially in sagebrush. Highly gregarious in migration and winter; often seen in mixed sparrow flocks. Distinctive call is a soft *hoo-ee*. Song, a varied series of rich whistles and trills, given from a perch or in hovering song flight. Rare in fall and winter on the west coast; casual in the east.

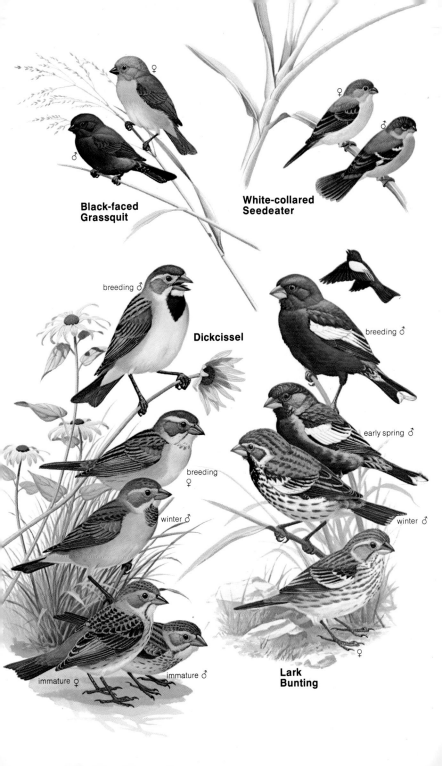

Black-faced Grassquit

♀
♂

White-collared Seedeater

♀
♂

breeding ♂

Dickcissel

breeding ♂

breeding ♀

early spring ♂

winter ♂

winter ♂

immature ♀

immature ♂

♀

Lark Bunting

Blackbirds and Orioles

Strong, direct flight and pointed bills mark this diverse and familiar group. Species vary in plumage from iridescent black to yellow to brilliant orange. They frequent a wide variety of habitats.

Bobolink *Dolichonyx oryzivorus* L 7" (18 cm)

Breeding male entirely black below; hindneck is buff, fading to whitish by midsummer; scapulars and rump white. Male in spring migration shows pale edgings, remnants of late-winter molt. Breeding female is buffy overall, with dark streaks on back, rump, and sides; head is striped with dark brown. Juvenile resembles female but lacks streaking below. Fall adults and immatures resemble breeding female but are darker above, richer buff below. In all plumages, note sharply pointed tail feathers. Bobolinks nest primarily in hayfields, weedy meadows, where male's loud, bubbling *bob-o-link* song, often given in flight, is heard in spring and summer. Flight call heard year-round is a repeated, whistled *ink*. Most birds migrate east of the Great Plains. Winter in South America.

Eastern Meadowlark *Sturnella magna* L 9¹/₂" (24 cm)

Black V-shaped breast band on yellow underparts; upperparts dark, with dusky edges. In fresh fall plumage, dusky edges are broader, obscuring black back and breast band. Generally darker above than Western Meadowlark, with blackish crown stripes and eye lines. Subspecies vary from the bright *S.m. argutula* of the southeast to the paler, grayer birds of the southwest, such as *lilianae,* which most closely resemble Western Meadowlark. In *lilianae* tail shows more white than in Western; eye line and crown stripes are darker; face is paler. Best distinguished by voice: Eastern's song is a clear, whistled *see-you see-yeeer;* distinctive call is a high, buzzy *drzzt;* also gives a rattling flight call. Common in fields, meadows; generally prefer slightly moister habitats than Western Meadowlark. Winter range of both species in the south and midwest is poorly known because of identification difficulty.

Western Meadowlark *Sturnella neglecta* L 9¹/₂" (24 cm)

Black V-shaped breast band on yellow underparts; upperparts dark, with dusky edges. Plumages parallel those of Eastern Meadowlark; best distinguished by voice. Western's distinctive call note is a low, throaty, explosive *chuck;* also gives a rattling flight call. Song is a variable series of bubbling, flutelike notes, accelerating toward the end. Western is paler and grayer than Easterns in the east; yellow of throat extends farther onto face; eye line and crown stripes are browner, less contrasting. Western Meadowlarks are common in fields and meadows, generally preferring drier habitat than Easterns. Hybrids occur in zone of range overlap. Range is expanding in the northeast.

early spring ♂

Bobolink

breeding ♂

breeding ♀

fall

juvenile

argutula fall

Eastern Meadowlark

argutula breeding

argutula juvenile

lilianae breeding

Western Meadowlark

argutula

lilianae

breeding

Yellow-headed Blackbird

Xanthocephalus xanthocephalus L 9¹/₂" (24 cm) Adult male's yellow head and breast and white wing patch contrast sharply with black body. Adult female is dusky-brown, lacks wing patch; eyebrow, lower cheek, and throat are yellow or buffy-yellow; belly streaked with white. Juvenile is dark brown with buffy edgings on back and wing; head mostly tawny. First-winter male resembles female but yellows are deeper, wing coverts tipped with white. Locally common throughout most of range, Yellowheads prefer freshwater marshes or reedy lakes; often seen foraging in open farmlands, grainfields. Song begins with a harsh, rasping note, ends with a long, descending buzz. Call note is a hoarse *croak*. Regular fall and winter visitor to the east coast. Casual in spring and fall as far north as southern Alaska.

Red-winged Blackbird *Agelaius phoeniceus*

L 8³/₄" (22 cm) Glossy black male has red shoulder patches broadly tipped with buffy-yellow. In perched birds, red patch may not be visible; only the yellow or whitish border shows. Females are dark brown above, heavily streaked below; sometimes show a red tinge on wing coverts or pinkish wash on chin and throat. First-year male plumage is distinguished from female Tricolored Blackbird by reddish shoulder patch. Males of the central California form, called "Bicolored Blackbird," have pure red shoulder patches with no border; females are darker, more like Tricolored Blackbird. Redwing's song is a liquid, gurgling *konk-la-reee,* ending in a trill. Most common call is a *chack* note. This abundant, aggressive species is often found in immense flocks in winter. Generally nests in thick vegetation of freshwater marshes, sloughs, dry fields; forages in surrounding fields, orchards, woodlands. Casual in summer as far north as northern Alaska and Mackenzie.

Tricolored Blackbird *Agelaius tricolor* L 8³/₄" (22 cm)

Glossy black male has dark red shoulder patches, often hidden, broadly tipped with white; tips are buffy-white in fresh fall plumage. Females usually lack any red on shoulder; plumage is sooty-brown and streaked overall; streaking on underparts is usually more diffuse than in female Red-winged Blackbird and bill is more sharply pointed, but identification can be extremely difficult. Tricolored Blackbird gives a variety of calls much like Redwing calls; harsh, braying *on-ke-kaaangh* song lacks Redwing's liquid tones. Highly gregarious; found year-round in large flocks foraging in wet meadows, rice fields, rangelands; nests in large colonies in marshes.

Yellow-headed Blackbird

juvenile

♀

♂

1st winter ♂

Red-winged Blackbird

♀

immature ♀

1st year ♂

♀

"Bicolored Blackbird"

♂

♂

Tricolored Blackbird

♂

♀

Rusty Blackbird   *Euphagus carolinus*   L 9" (23 cm)

All adults and fall immatures have yellow eyes. Fall adults and immatures are broadly tipped with rust; tertials and wing coverts edged with rust. Fall female has broad, buffy eyebrow, buffy underparts. Fall male is darker; eyebrow usually fainter. The rusty feather tips wear off by spring, producing the dark breeding plumage. Male has a faint greenish gloss. Juveniles resemble winter adults but have dark eyes. Fairly common in wet woodlands, swamps; nests in shrubs or conifers near water. In fall and winter, forms large flocks with other blackbirds but not seen in open fields. Call is a harsh *tschak;* song, a high, squeaky *koo-a-lee*. Very rare in fall and winter west of mapped range and in southern Florida.

Brewer's Blackbird   *Euphagus cyanocephalus*

L 9" (23 cm)   Male has yellow eyes; female's are usually brown. Male is black year-round, with purplish gloss on head and neck, greenish gloss on body and wings. A few fall males show rusty feather edgings, but never as rusty as in Rusty Blackbird and never on tertials or wing coverts. Note also the shorter, thicker bill. Female and juveniles are gray-brown. Common in open habitats; forages in large flocks with other blackbirds. Typical call is a harsh *check;* song, a wheezy *que-ee* or *k-seee*. Scattered populations breed throughout the central Great Plains. Casual in winter northeast of mapped range.

Brown-headed Cowbird   *Molothrus ater*   L 7½" (19 cm)

Male's brown head contrasts with metallic green-black body. Female is gray-brown above, paler below. Juvenile is paler above, more heavily streaked below; pale edgings give a scaled look to its back. Young males molting to adult plumage in late summer are a patchwork of buff, brown, and black. Increasingly common; found in open woodlands, farmlands, suburbs. Habit of feeding with tail cocked up distinguishes both cowbird species in mixed blackbird flocks, except from Tricolored Blackbird. Eggs are laid in the nests of other species. Male's song is a squeaky gurgling. Calls include a harsh rattle and squeaky whistles. Southwestern birds are distinctly smaller than eastern; Rockies and Great Basin birds are larger.

Bronzed Cowbird   *Molothrus aeneus*   L 8¾" (22 cm)

Red eyes distinctive at close range. Bill larger than in Brown-headed Cowbird. Adult male is black overall, with bronze gloss; wings and tail blue-black. Thick ruff on nape and back gives male a hunchbacked look. Adult female of the Texas form, *M.a. aeneus*, is duller than male; juveniles are dark brown. In southwestern form, *milleri*, female and juveniles are gray. Locally common in open country, farmlands, brushy areas, wooded mountain canyons; forages in flocks. Typical call is a harsh, guttural *chuck*. Song is a wheezier, shorter version of Brown-headed Cowbird's gurgling song.

Rusty Blackbird

fall ♀

fall ♂

breeding ♀

breeding ♂

Brewer's Blackbird

fall variant ♂

♂

♀

♀

molting juvenile ♂

juvenile

Brown-headed Cowbird

♂

milleri ♀

aeneus juvenile

aeneus ♀

♂

Bronzed Cowbird

Common Grackle *Quiscalus quiscula* L 12¹/₂" (32 cm)

Long, keel-shaped tail; pale yellow eyes. Plumage appears all-black at a distance. In good light, males show glossy purplish head, neck, and breast. Birds in New England and west of the Appalachians generally have a bronze sheen on rest of body; east of the Appalachians they show more purple overall. Tail is longer and bill larger than in Brewer's Blackbird (preceding page). Females are smaller and duller than males. Juveniles are sooty-brown, with brown eyes. Common Grackles are abundant and gregarious, roaming in mixed flocks in open fields, marshes, parks, suburban areas. Song is a short, creaky *koguba-leek;* call note, a loud *chuck.* Casual in Pacific states and Alaska, primarily in late spring.

Boat-tailed Grackle *Quiscalus major*

♂ L 16¹/₂" (42 cm) ♀ L 14¹/₂" (37 cm) Large grackle with a very long, keel-shaped tail. Adult male is iridescent blue-black. Adult female is tawny-brown with darker wings and tail. Eye color varies from yellow in Atlantic coast birds to brown in Florida birds. Gulf coast birds are intermediate, with brown or dull yellow eyes. Juvenile males are black but lack iridescence; young females show a hint of spotting or streaking on breast. Juveniles resemble respective adults by mid-fall. In the narrow zone of range overlap, Boat-taileds are distinguished from Great-tailed Grackles by their duller yellow or brown eyes, smaller overall size, and more rounded crown. Calls include a quiet *chuck* and a variety of rough squeaks, rattles, and other chatter. Most common song is a series of harsh *jeeb* notes. This common, noisy grackle seldom strays beyond coastal saltwater marshes, except in Florida where it also inhabits inland lakes and streams. Nests in small colonies. Range is expanding northward on the Atlantic coast.

Great-tailed Grackle *Quiscalus mexicanus*

♂ L 18" (46 cm) ♀ L 15" (38 cm) A large grackle with very long, keel-shaped tail, golden yellow eyes. Adult male is iridescent black with purple sheen on head, back, and underparts. Adult female's upperparts are brown; underparts cinnamon buff on breast to grayish-brown on belly; shows less iridescence than male. Juveniles resemble adult female but are even less glossy and show some streaking on underparts. Juvenile males are like adult males by mid-fall. Females west of central Arizona are smaller overall and paler below than eastern birds. In narrow zone of range overlap, Great-tailed Grackles are distinguished from Boat-tailed by bright yellow eyes, larger size, and flatter crown. Varied calls include clear whistles and loud *clack* notes. Common, especially in open flatlands with scattered groves of trees and in marshes, wetlands. Casual far north of breeding range; rapidly expanding north and west.

Common Grackle

purple ♂   bronze ♂   juvenile

juvenile ♀

Boat-tailed Grackle

juvenile ♂

♀

♂

Great-tailed Grackle

juvenile ♀

♀

♂

western ♀

Scott's Oriole *Icterus parisorum* L 9" (23 cm)

Adult male's black hood extends to back and breast; rump, wing patch, and remainder of underparts lemon yellow. Adult female is yellowish-olive and streaked above, dull greenish-yellow below; throat shows variable amount of black. Immature male's head is mostly black by first spring. Females and immatures average more streaking above and are grayer and larger overall than female Hooded Oriole (next page). Common in arid and semiarid habitats. Common call note is a harsh *shack;* song, a mixture of rich, whistled phrases, suggestive of Western Meadowlark. A few Scott's Orioles winter in southern California, mainly in desert canyons.

Orchard Oriole *Icterus spurius* L 7¼" (18 cm)

Adult male is chestnut overall, with black hood. Adult female is olive above, greenish-yellow below. Immatures resemble adult female; immature male acquires black bib and, sometimes, traces of chestnut by first spring. Smaller size and lack of orange tones or whitish belly distinguish female and immatures from Northern Oriole. Compare also with Hooded Oriole (next page). Locally common in suburban shade trees, orchards, streamside groves. Calls include a sharp *chuck.* Song is a loud, rapid burst of varied whistled notes, downslurred at the end. Casual migrant in Arizona; rare in California.

Audubon's Oriole *Icterus graduacauda* L 9½" (24 cm)

Tropical species, resident but uncommon in southern Texas. Male distinguished from Scott's Oriole by greenish-yellow back. Female is slightly duller. Secretive; often seen foraging on the ground. Song is a series of soft, three-note warbles. Formerly called Black-headed Oriole.

Northern Oriole *Icterus galbula* L 8¾" (22 cm)

Formerly considered two species: the "Baltimore Oriole" in the east and "Bullock's Oriole" in the west. Adult male "Baltimore" form has black hood and upper back, bright orange rump and underparts; black tail has large orange patches. Adult male "Bullock's" differs by having large white wing patch, orange face with black eye line. Adult female "Bullock's" is gray-olive above; head and breast pale yellow; belly whitish. Adult female "Baltimore" is brownish-olive above, with blackish markings on head; underparts dull orange, palest on belly. Immature male "Baltimore" resembles adult female but is brighter. First-fall female is duller, grayer above, lacks black on head but note distinctive (from "Bullock's") dusky markings on face. Young male "Bullock's" shows some black on center of throat by first fall. The two subspecies interbreed in zone of range overlap in the Great Plains. Northern Orioles are common in open woodlands, river groves, suburban shade trees. Typical call of eastern form is a rich *hew-li;* song is a musical, irregular series of *hew-li* and other notes. Western form's common call is an emphatic *skip;* song is like eastern but less varied and somewhat harsher.

1st fall

Scott's Oriole

♀

1st spring ♂

♂

♀

1st spring ♂

♂

Orchard Oriole

Audubon's Oriole

1st fall ♀

Northern Oriole

"Baltimore Oriole"

♂

♂

"Bullock's Oriole"

♀

"Baltimore"-"Bullock's" Intergrade ♂

Hooded Oriole *Icterus cucullatus* L 8" (20 cm)

Bill long and slightly curved. Breeding male is orange or orange-yellow with black upper back, wings, and tail; black patch extending from lores to throat; two whitish wing bars, the upper bar broader. Males in western Texas (shown here) are brightest orange; Arizona and California birds are yellower. Texas birds show black on forehead. All winter birds have buffy-brown tips on back, forming a barred pattern; compare with Streak-backed Oriole. Adult female Hooded lacks pale belly of female and immature "Bullock's" form of Northern Oriole (preceding page); bill is longer and more curved. Compare also with female Orchard Oriole. Immatures resemble adult female. Immature male shows black lores and throat by first spring. Common in varied habitats but especially around palms. Breeding range is expanding northward on west coast. Calls include a loud, whistled, rising *wheet*. Song is a rapid series of throaty whistles, trills, and rattles.

Streak-backed Oriole *Icterus pustulatus* L 8¹/₄" (21 cm)

Mexican species, casual in fall and winter in southeastern Arizona, southern California. Distinguished from winter Hooded Oriole by streaked, not barred, upper back; deeper orange head; and thicker based, straighter bill. Female is duller than male. Immatures resemble adult female, but immature female lacks black on throat. *Wheet* call is softer than Hooded Oriole's call and does not rise in pitch. Other calls resemble those of the Northern Oriole (preceding page). Formerly known as Scarlet-headed Oriole.

Altamira Oriole *Icterus gularis* L 10" (25 cm)

Distinguished from the Hooded Oriole by larger size, much thicker based bill, and, in adult, a distinct orange shoulder patch. Lower wing bar whitish. Immatures are yellower than adults; shoulder patch is yellowish; resemble adult by second fall. Locally fairly common in southernmost Texas in groves of tall trees, willows, mesquite. Calls include a low, raspy *ike ike ike*. Song is a series of clear, varied whistles. Formerly known as Lichtenstein's Oriole.

Spot-breasted Oriole *Icterus pectoralis* L 9¹/₂" (24 cm)

Mexican and Central American species, introduced and now established in southern Florida. Adults have an orange or yellow-orange patch on shoulders; black lores and throat; dark spots on upper breast; extensive white on wings. Young birds are yellower overall; immatures may lack breast spots. Found in gardens, open woodlands. Florida population is apparently not expanding. Song is a long, loud series of melodic whistles.

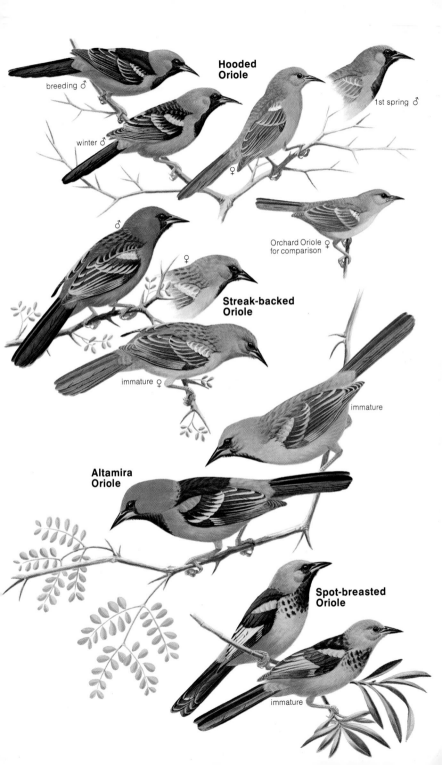

Hooded Oriole

breeding ♂

winter ♂

1st spring ♂

♀

Orchard Oriole ♀ for comparison

♂

♀

Streak-backed Oriole

immature ♀

immature

Altamira Oriole

Spot-breasted Oriole

immature

Scarlet Tanager *Piranga olivacea* *L 7″ (18 cm)*

Breeding male bright red with black wings and tail. In late summer, becomes splotchy green-and-red as he molts to yellow-green winter plumage. Female is distinguished from other female tanagers by uniformly olive head, back, and rump; whitish wing linings; bill smaller than in Summer Tanager. Immature male Scarlet resembles female but is brighter below, with brownish primaries retained through first summer; wing coverts are black. Some immatures show faint wing bars, much less distinct than in Western Tanager. Robin-like song of raspy notes, *querit queer query querit queer*, is heard in deciduous forests, where Scarlet Tanager is common in summer. Call is a hoarse *chip-burr*. Winters in South America; casual vagrant in the west.

Western Tanager *Piranga ludoviciana* *L 7¹/₄″ (18 cm)*

Conspicuous wing bars: upper bar yellow in male, often paler and thinner in female; lower bar pale yellow or whitish. Male's red head becomes yellowish and finely streaked in winter. Note female's saddleback pattern: grayish back contrasting with greenish-yellow nape and rump. Some females are duller below, grayer above. Thicker bill and chunkier shape helps distinguish female tanagers from female orioles (pages 426, 428). Common, especially in coniferous forests. Winters primarily from central Mexico south; casual to uncommon as far north as southern Oregon, chiefly on or near coast. Rare or casual along Gulf and Atlantic coasts, especially in winter.

Summer Tanager *Piranga rubra* *L 7³/₄″ (20 cm)*

Adult male is rosy red year-round. First-spring males are patchy green-and-red; full adult plumage is acquired by second fall. Some eastern females show an overall reddish wash. In most females, plumage varies from mustard to gold below, with darker tinge above; lacks olive tones of female Scarlet Tanager; bill is larger. Western birds are larger and paler; females generally grayer above than eastern females. Song is robin-like; call, a staccato *ki-ti-tuck*. Common in pine-oak woods in the east, cottonwood groves in the west. Range is slowly shrinking in the east; rare vagrant north of summer range. Regular in winter in southern California.

Hepatic Tanager *Piranga flava* *L 8″ (20 cm)*

Large grayish cheek patch and gray wash on flanks set off brighter throat, breast, and cap in both sexes. Male retains dull red plumage year-round. Juvenile resembles yellow-and-gray female but is heavily streaked overall; immature male attains adult male plumage by second fall. Song is robin-like. Call note, a single low *chuck,* is easily mistaken for Hermit Thrush's call. Inhabits mountain forests, usually conifers mixed with oaks. Similar western form of Summer Tanager is usually found in lower valleys.

Scarlet Tanager

♀

breeding ♂

winter ♂

molting ♂

Western Tanager

♀

♀

winter ♂

breeding ♂

Summer Tanager

eastern ♀

western ♀

eastern ♀

western ♂

Hepatic Tanager

♀

♂

juvenile

Stripe-headed Tanager *Spindalis zena L 6³/₄″ (17 cm)*
West Indian species, casual visitor from Bahamas to southern
Florida. Brightly patterned male has two white stripes on black
head; chestnut collar and rump; thick bill. Female is greenish
above, with a small square white patch at base of primaries.

Bananaquit *Coereba flaveola L 4¹/₂″ (11 cm)*
Tropical species; casual visitor from the Bahamas to southern
Florida. Note thin, downcurved bill. Adult has conspicuous
white eyebrow, yellow rump; underparts white, with yellow
breast; small white wing patch. Immature is duller; eyebrow
and yellowish rump less conspicuous.

Weaver Finches (Family Estrildidae)

Generally small seedeaters known for their untidy nests. Plumages range from red to green to dull brown. One species introduced into our region from southeast Asia.

Java Sparrow *Padda oryzivora L 6″ (15 cm)*
Resident of Java. Introduced and breeding locally around Miami, Florida. Note massive pink bill; large white cheek patch; red eye ring; wine red wash on flanks, belly. Immature is brownish, with buffy-white throat and belly.

Weavers (Family Passeridae)

A large Old World family. Two species have been successfully introduced in North America. Resemble native sparrows but have shorter legs, thicker bills.

Eurasian Tree Sparrow *Passer montanus L 6″ (15 cm)*
Old World species, introduced and now locally common in
parks, suburbs, and farmlands around St. Louis, Missouri, and
in nearby Illinois. Brown crown, black ear patch, and black
throat distinguish adult. Compare with House Sparrow's gray
crown and more extensively black throat. Juvenile has dark
mottling on crown, dark gray throat and ear patch.

House Sparrow *Passer domesticus L 6¹/₄″ (16 cm)*
Male in breeding plumage has gray crown, chestnut nape,
black bib, black bill. Fresh fall plumage is edged with gray, obscuring these markings; bill becomes brownish. Female is
best identified by the combination of streaked back, buffy eye
stripe, and unstreaked breast. Juveniles resemble adult female. Abundant and aggressive, House Sparrows are omnipresent in populated areas. Also known as English Sparrow.

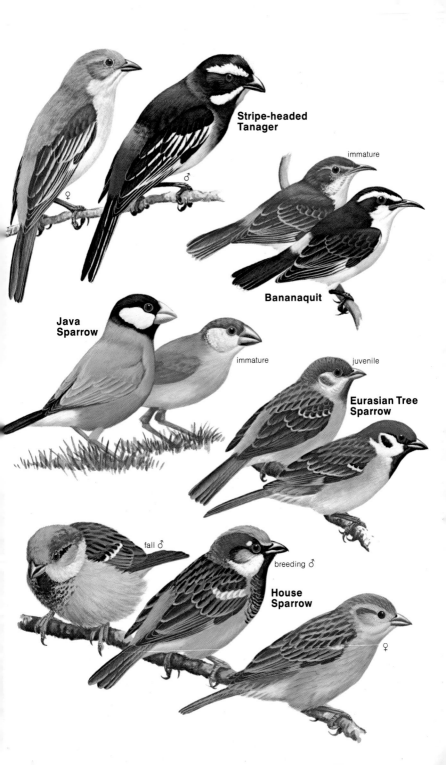

Stripe-headed Tanager

♀

♂

immature

Bananaquit

Java Sparrow

immature

juvenile

Eurasian Tree Sparrow

fall ♂

breeding ♂

House Sparrow

♀

Finches (Family Fringillidae)

Seedeaters with an undulating flight. Many nest in the far north; in fall, flocks of "winter finches" may roam south, appearing here one year, there the next.

Pine Siskin *Carduelis pinus* L 5" (13 cm)
Prominent streaking; yellow at base of tail and flight feathers conspicuous in flight; bill thinner than in other finches. Juvenile's overall yellow tint is lost by late summer. Gregarious; may flock with goldfinches in winter. Calls include a rising *tee-ee* and, in flight, a harsh, descending *chee*. Song is similar to that of American Goldfinch but much huskier. Found in coniferous and mixed woods in summer; forests, shrubs, and fields in winter. Winter range is erratic.

American Goldfinch *Carduelis tristis* L 5" (13 cm)
Breeding adult male is bright yellow with black cap; black wings show white bars, yellow shoulder patch; uppertail and undertail coverts white; tail black-and-white. Female is duller overall, olive above; lacks black cap and yellow shoulder patch. White undertail coverts distinguish female from most Lesser Goldfinches. Winter adults and immatures are either brownish or grayish above; male may show some black on forehead. Juvenile plumage, held into November, has cinnamon buff wing markings and rump. Common and gregarious; found in weedy fields, open second-growth woodlands, roadsides, especially in thistles, sunflowers. Song is a lively series of trills, twitters, and *swee* notes. Distinctive flight call, *per-chik-o-ree*. Widely known as "wild canary."

Lesser Goldfinch *Carduelis psaltria* L 4½" (11 cm)
Entire crown black on adult male; back varies from black in eastern part of range to greenish in western birds. Most adult females are dull yellow below; except for a few extremely pale birds, they lack the white undertail coverts typical of American Goldfinch. Immature male lacks full black cap. Juveniles resemble adult female. All birds have a white wing patch at base of primaries. Common in dry, brushy fields, woodland borders, gardens. Call, a plaintive, kittenlike *tee-yee*. Song is somewhat similar to that of American Goldfinch. Casual in Great Plains; accidental east to Louisiana and southern Ontario.

Lawrence's Goldfinch *Carduelis lawrencei*
L 4¾" (12 cm) Wings extensively yellow; upperparts grayish in breeding plumage; underparts largely yellow. Male has black face and yellowish tinge on back. Winter birds are browner above, duller below. Juvenile is faintly streaked, unlike other goldfinches. Fairly common in spring and early summer; may flock with other goldfinches, but generally prefers drier grassy slopes, chaparral. Erratic but usually uncommon at other seasons. Call is a bell-like *tink-ul*. Mixes *tink* notes into jumbled, melodious song.

Pine Siskin

juvenile

American Goldfinch

breeding ♀

breeding ♂

winter ♂

winter ♀

juvenile

♀

Lesser Goldfinch

black-backed ♂

green-backed ♂

pale ♀

immature ♂

Lawrence's Goldfinch

winter ♀

winter ♂

juvenile

breeding ♂

Red Crossbill *Loxia curvirostra* *L 6¼" (16 cm)*

Bill with crossed tips identifies both crossbill species. Red Crossbill's dark brown wings lack the bold white bars of White-winged Crossbill. Plumage highly variable. Most males are reddish overall, brightest on crown and rump; but may be pale rose or scarlet or largely yellow. Males always have red or yellow on throat. Most females are yellowish-olive; may show patches of red. Throat of female is always gray except in small Alaska form where yellow extends to center, but not sides, of throat. Juveniles are boldly streaked; a few juveniles and a very few adult males show white wing bars, the upper bar thinner than the lower. Immatures are like the respective adult but juvenile wing is retained. All birds except adult males have olive edges on wings. Subspecies vary widely in size; extremes are shown here. All have large heads and short, notched tails. Fairly common, Red Crossbills inhabit coniferous woods. May nest at any time of year, especially in southern range. Highly irregular in their wanderings, dependent upon cone crops. Any subspecies may turn up almost anywhere. Irruptive migrant. Has bred as far south as Georgia. Distinctive call, given chiefly in flight, is a series of *jip* notes. Song begins with several two-note phrases followed by a warbled trill.

White-winged Crossbill *Loxia leucoptera* *L 6½" (17 cm)*

Bill with crossed tips identifies both crossbill species. All White-winged Crossbills have black wings with white tips on the tertials, two bold, broad white wing bars. Upper wing bar is often hidden by scapulars. Adult male is bright pink overall, paler in winter. Immature male is largely yellow, with patches of red or pink. Adult female is mottled with yellowish-olive or grayish; rump pale yellow; underparts grayish-olive, with yellow wash on breast and sides. Juvenile is heavily streaked; wing bars thinner than in adults. Fairly common, White-winged Crossbills inhabit coniferous woods. Highly irregular in their wanderings, dependent upon cone crops. Irruptive migrant. Distinctive flight call, a rapid series of harsh *chet* notes. Variable song combines harsh rattles and musical warbles.

Pine Grosbeak *Pinicola enucleator* *L 9" (23 cm)*

Large, plump, and long-tailed. Bill is dark, stubby, strongly curved. Two white wing bars, sometimes tinged with pink in adult male. Male's gray plumage is tipped with red on head, back, and underparts, pinker in fresh fall plumage. Female and immature are grayer overall; head, rump, and underparts variably yellow or reddish; some females and immature males are russet. Fairly common; inhabits open coniferous woods. In winter, found also in deciduous woods, orchards, suburban shade trees. Usually unwary and approachable. Typical flight call is a whistled *pui pui pui;* alarm call, a musical *chee-vli.* Irruptive winter migrant in the east.

Red
Crossbill

♂
juvenile

Alaska ♀

typical ♀

typical ♂

♂

White-winged
Crossbill

immature ♂

juvenile

♀

winter ♂

♀

♂

russet

Pine
Grosbeak

Common Redpoll *Carduelis flammea* L 5¼" (13 cm)

Red or orange-red cap or "poll," black chin. Closely resembles Hoary Redpoll; often difficult to distinguish. Common Redpoll usually has distinct streaks on flanks, rump, and undertail coverts; bill is slightly larger. Male usually has rosy breast and sides, brighter than in Hoary. Both sexes are paler, buffier overall in winter. Juveniles lack red cap until late-summer molt; males acquire pinkish breast by the end of the following summer. Fairly common; breeds in subarctic forests and tundra scrub. Interbreeds with Hoary where ranges overlap. Some authorities consider the two to be a single species. In winter, redpolls frequent brushy, weedy areas, also catkin-bearing trees like alder and birch. Unwary and social, forming large winter flocks. Flight is undulating. When perched, gives a *swee-ee-eet* call. Song combines trills and twittering. Flight call, a dry rattling.

Hoary Redpoll *Carduelis hornemanni* L 5½" (14 cm)

Red or orange-red cap or "poll"; black chin. Closely resembles Common Redpoll but is usually frostier and paler overall and has a slightly smaller bill. Streaking on rump, flanks, and undertail coverts minimal or absent. Male's breast is usually paler and pinker than on Common Redpoll; color does not extend to cheeks or sides. Fairly common; nests on or near the ground above arctic tree line; interbreeds with Common Redpoll where ranges overlap. Calls and song are like those of Common. *C.h. hornemanni*, which breeds on Canadian arctic islands and Greenland, is larger and paler than the more widespread *exilipes*. Rare sightings of *exilipes* occur south of Canada in winter, usually with Common Redpolls.

Rosy Finch *Leucosticte arctoa* L 6¼" (16 cm)

Plumage variable among the many subspecies. "Black" and "Brown-capped" forms were once considered separate species. All forms show pinkish-brown in wings and lower body. Back of head often gray, forehead black. Underwings largely silver. Juveniles lack pink tones and gray crown. Females are duller and grayer, especially in "Brown-capped" and "Black" forms. Winter birds are also duller, with a yellowish black-tipped bill. "Gray-crowned" coastal forms, such as "Hepburn's" and the birds found on the Aleutians and Pribilofs, show larger amounts of gray on face and vary in size as shown. Interior forms have narrower gray area on head. "Gray-crowneds" nest in rocks and cliffs high in western mountains or on Alaskan tundra. "Brown-capped" is the rosiest form; common year-round in Colorado Rockies and neighboring ranges. The uncommon "Black" form is distinctly darker; breeds on mountaintops and high slopes in the Great Basin, central and northwestern Rockies. Rosy Finches winter at lower altitudes; sometimes seen in towns. Casual in winter in the midwest. Unwary and easily approached. Calls include a series of *cheew* notes at varying high pitches. Winter flocks often include more than one subspecies.

Common Redpoll

juvenile

breeding ♀

breeding ♂

winter ♀

winter ♂

Hoary Redpoll

exilipes winter ♀

exilipes winter ♂

hornemanni winter ♂

Rosy Finch

juvenile

interior

"Hepburn's" winter ♂

"Gray-crowned"

Pribilofs winter ♂

breeding ♂

breeding ♀

"Black"

breeding ♂

breeding ♀

breeding ♂

"Brown-capped"

Purple Finch *Carpodacus purpureus* L 6" (15 cm)

Not purple, but rose red over most of adult male body, brightest on head and rump. Rose color, acquired in second fall, is most intense in worn plumage of summer. Back is streaked; tail strongly notched. Pacific coast form, *C.p. californicus*, is buffier below and more diffusely streaked than the widespread *purpureus*, especially in females. Adult female and immatures are heavily streaked below; closely resemble Cassin's Finch. Ear patch and whitish eyebrow and cheek stripe are slightly more distinct in Purple Finch; bill slightly stubbier and more curved; undertail coverts are usually not streaked. Compare also with female House Finch. Fairly common; found in coniferous or mixed woodland borders, suburbs, parks, orchards; on the Pacific coast, inhabits coniferous forests, oak canyons, lower mountain slopes. Calls include a musical *chur-lee* and, in flight, a sharp *pit*. Song is a rich warbling, shorter than Cassin's song, lower and less strident than House Finch song.

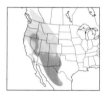

Cassin's Finch *Carpodacus cassinii* L 6¼" (16 cm)

Crimson of adult male's cap ends sharply at brown-streaked nape. Throat and breast paler than Purple Finch; streaks on sides more distinct. Red hues begin to appear late in second summer. Tail strongly notched. Undertail coverts always distinctly streaked, unlike most Purples. Adult female and immatures otherwise closely resemble Purple Finch. Cassin's facial pattern is slightly less distinct; bill is slightly straighter and longer. In flight, Cassin's gives a dry *kee-up* or *tee-dee-yip* call. Lively song, a variable warbling, longer and more complex than song of Purple Finch. Fairly common in upper mountain forests and open evergreen woodlands. Casual winter vagrant east of range and west in California.

House Finch *Carpodacus mexicanus* L 6" (15 cm)

Male has brown cap; front of head, bib, and rump are typically red but can vary to orange or occasionally yellow. Bib is clearly set off from streaked underparts. Tail is squarish. Adult female and juveniles are brown-streaked overall; lack distinct ear patch and eyebrow of Purple and Cassin's Finches. Young males acquire adult coloring by first fall. Abundant; found in semiarid lowlands and slopes up to about 6,000 feet. Introduced in the east in the 1940s, where its range is rapidly expanding, especially in urban areas. Lively, high-pitched song consists chiefly of varied three-note phrases; includes strident notes, unlike Purple Finch's song; usually ends with a nasal *wheer*. Calls include a whistled *wheat*.

Common Rosefinch *Carpodacus erythrinus*

L 5¾" (15 cm) Eurasian species; rare migrant, chiefly in spring, on the western Aleutians and other western Alaska islands. Strongly curved culmen. Lacks distinct eyebrow. Adult male's head, breast, and rump are red. Female and immatures are diffusely streaked above and below, except on pale throat.

californicus ♀

Purple Finch

purpureus ♀

californicus ♂

purpureus ♂

Cassin's Finch

♀

♂

House Finch

typical ♂

variant ♂

♀

♀

♂

Common Rosefinch

Evening Grosbeak *Coccothraustes vespertinus*

L 8" (20 cm) Large, stocky, noisy finch with big bill. Black tail and wings, with prominent white patch on inner wing. Wing linings yellow. Bill pale yellow or greenish by spring, whitish by fall. Yellow forehead and eyebrow on adult male; dark brown and yellow body. Grayish-tan female has thin, dark whisker stripe, white-tipped tail; white patch on inner wing smaller than male's; second patch, on primaries, conspicuous in flight. Juveniles have brown bills; female resembles adult female; male is yellower overall, with wing and tail similar to adult male. Loud, strident call: *clee-ip* or *peeer*. Breeds in mixed woods; in the west, mainly in mountains. In winter frequents woodlots, shade trees, feeders. Winter numbers vary greatly from year to year. Range is expanding in the east.

Hawfinch *Coccothraustes coccothraustes* *L 7" (18 cm)*

Eurasian species. Rare spring stray on western Aleutians; casual off other islands of western Alaska. Big, stocky, like Evening Grosbeak, but has black throat and lores. Yellowish-brown above; pinkish-brown below. Big bill is blue-black in spring, yellowish in fall. Female resembles male, but is paler, grayer. Conspicuous white band shows on extended wing. Flight is high, fast, and undulating. Walks with parrotlike waddle. Call is a loud, explosive *ptik.*

Eurasian Bullfinch *Pyrrhula pyrrhula* *L 6¹/₂" (17 cm)*

Eurasian species. Casual migrant on Aleutians; casual in winter on Alaskan mainland. Cheeks, breast, and belly rosy red in adult male, brown in female. Black cap and face, gray back, prominent whitish bar on wing, distinct white rump. In profile, top of head and bill form unbroken curve. Juvenile resembles female, but with brown cap. Call is a soft, piping *pheew.*

Oriental Greenfinch *Carduelis sinica* *L 6" (15 cm)*

Eurasian species. Casual migrant, mainly in spring, on outer Aleutians. Adult male has greenish face and rump, dark gray nape and crown, bright yellow wing patch and undertail coverts. Adult female is paler, with a brownish head. Juvenile has same yellow markings as adults but is streaked overall.

Brambling *Fringilla montifringilla* *L 6¹/₄" (16 cm)*

Eurasian species; fairly common but irregular migrant on the Aleutians; casual in fall and winter in southern Alaska, Canada, and central and western states. White rump is conspicuous in flight. Adult male has tawny-orange shoulders, spotted flanks, white belly. Head and back are fringed with buff in fresh fall plumage; these fringes wear down to black by spring. Female and juvenile have mottled crown, plain gray face, and striped nape. Bramblings may twitch their tails while perched. Flight call, a nasal *check-check-check.*

Evening Grosbeak

breeding ♂

juvenile ♂

breeding ♀

Hawfinch

breeding ♂

Eurasian Bullfinch

♂

♀

Oriental Greenfinch

♂

♀

juvenile

Brambling

breeding ♂

fall ♂

♀

Index

The main entry for each species is listed in **boldface** type and refers to the text page opposite the illustration.

A check-off box is provided next to each common-name entry so that you can use this index as a checklist of the species you have identified.

Type composition by National
Geographic's Photographic
Services. Color separations by
The Lanman-Progressive
Companies, Washington,
D. C. Printed and bound by
R. R. Donnelley & Sons,
Willard, Ohio.

Library of Congress CIP Data

Field guide to the birds of
North America.
　Includes index.
　1. Birds—North America—
Identification. I. National
Geographic Society (U. S.) II.
Title: Birds of North America.
QL681.F53　1987
598.297　86-33249
ISBN 0-87044-692-4

The Artists

Cover by *Patricia A. Topper*

Marc R. Hanson,
pages 25-37, 97-101

Cynthia J. House,
pages 61-95

H. Jon Janosik,
pages 19-23, 39-47, 103,
107-111, 121

Donald L. Malick,
pages 183-187, 191, 195-205,
229, 239-247, 263-275

John P. O'Neill,
pages 10-11, 233, 295, 309-313,
419, 427, 429

Kent Pendleton,
pages 189, 193, 206-223

Diane Pierce,
pages 49-59, 123, 125, 129, 135,
381-417, 435-443

John C. Pitcher,
pages 105, 115-119, 127,
131, 133

H. Douglas Pratt,
pages 2-3, 225, 227, 231, 235,
237, 255-261, 277-293,
297-307, 315-379, 421-425,
431, 433

Chuck Ripper,
pages 173-181, 249-253

Thomas R. Schultz,
pages 141-171

Daniel S. Smith,
pages 113, 136-139

Additional artwork by
Veronica Freeman
Betsy Reeder
Lee Marc Steadman
Patricia A. Topper

Acknowledgments

Many people generously contributed their time and knowledge to the production of this guide. In particular we express our gratitude to Claudia P. Wilds, who played a substantial role in the initial planning for the book and continued to assist us throughout its progress, especially with the sections on shorebirds, rails, mimic thrushes, and doves.

Our thanks go also to Thomas A. Allen, J. Phillip Angle, Stephen Bailey, Lawrence G. Balch, Dr. Richard C. Banks, John Barber, Louis Bevier, Daniel Boone, Danny Bystrak, Charles T. Clark, William S. Clark, Robert Dixon, Peter Dunne, Victor Emanuel, Kimball Garrett, Freida Gentry, Daniel D. Gibson, Peter Grant, John A. Gregoire, Dr. James L. Gulledge, Dr. George A. Hall, Rebecca Hyman, Lars Jonsson, Kenn Kaufman, Wayne Klockner, Lasse J. Laine, Greg W. Lasley, Paul Lehman, Guy McCaskie, Joseph Morlan, Killian Mullarney, Gerald Oreel, Dennis Paulson, Betsy Reeder, Dr. J. V. Remsen, Robert F. Ringler, Philip D. Round, John Rowlett, Rose Ann Rowlett, Will Russell, Robert T. Scholes, James Stasz, Thede Tobish, Dr. John Trochet, Laurel Tucker, Nigel Tucker, Arnoud van den Berg, Terence R. Wahl, Tony White, Hal Wierenga, Alan Wormington, and Kevin Zimmer. We also thank the staff of the U. S. Fish and Wildlife Service's Patuxent Wildlife Research Center in Laurel, Maryland.